Period Style
for the
Theatre

Period Style for the Theatre

Second Edition

DOUGLAS A. RUSSELL

Stanford University

Allyn and Bacon, Inc.
Boston London Sydney Toronto

The cover photograph is from an engraving based on
the painting by G. Harlow showing a scene from an
1819 production of *Henry VIII.* Photo courtesy of the
Norman Philbrick Library, photograph by Fred English.

Library of Congress Cataloging in Publication Data

Russell, Douglas A.
    Period style for the theatre.

    Bibliography: p. 365
    Includes index.
    1. Acting—History.   2. Costume—History.   3. Theater—
Production and direction—History.   4. Theaters—Stage-
setting and scenery—History.   5. Arts and society—
History.   6. Civilization, Occidental—History.
I. Title.
PN2061.R75   1987   792'.02   87-1482
ISBN 0-205-10488-6

Printed in the United States of America

10 9 8 7 6 5 4 3   92 91 90

*To the memory of Norman Philbrick,
teacher and friend*

Acknowledgments

The author and publisher wish to thank the following for permission to quote material:

Alternative Theatre—for permission to quote from "Wroclaw, the Paratheatrical Experience" by Steven Weinstein, which appeared in the March/April 1976 issue.

American Heritage Publishing Company, Inc.—for selections from the Daily Life in Five Great Ages of History series. The individual books include *Daily Life in Ancient Rome:* quotations from Pliny and *Daily Life in the Middle Ages:* quotations from the city records of Paris.

George Braziller, Inc.—for selections from the Culture of Mankind series. The individual books include *Medieval Culture:* quotations from "Sir Gawain and the Green Knight" by Tour de Landry; *Renaissance Culture:* quotations from *The Prince* by Machiavelli; *The Age of Reason:* quotations from *Honnête Homme* by Nicolas Faret and from the *Diary of Samuel Pepys; The Enlightenment:* quotations from "On Commerce" by Voltaire; and *Romanticism:* quotations from the Preface to *Cromwell* by Victor Hugo and from *The Decay of Living* by Oscar Wilde.

The Clarendon Press; Oxford University; Oxford, England—for permission to quote from *The Recluse* by William Wordsworth and edited by Selincourt and Dardishire.

David Higham Associates Limited and David Poynter, Publisher, London—for selections from books of etiquette and courtesy taken from *The Polite World* by Joan Wildeblood.

Doubleday-Anchor Books—for permission to quote from *The Book of the Courtier* by Castiglione. Copyright © 1959 by Charles Singleton and Edgar N. Mayhew. Reprinted by permission of Doubleday & Company, Inc.

Harcourt Brace Jovanovich, Inc.—for permission to quote from *The Waste Land* by T. S. Eliot, which appears in *Collected Poems 1909–1962.*

The New Graphic Society; Greenwich, Connecticut—for a selection from "A Theory of Style," an essay by James S. Ackerman, which appears in *The Arts on Campus,* edited by Margaret Mahoney and assisted by Isabel Moore, 1970.

Plays and Players magazine—for permission to quote from an interview with Peter Brook, copyright March 1976 by John Lahr and for permission to quote from "More Things in Heaven and Earth," an article about Roger Planchon and the Théâtre National Populaire, copyright April 1976 by Michael Kustow.

Random House, Inc., Alfred Knopf, Inc.—for permission to quote from *The Counterfeiters, with Journal of the Counterfeiters* by André Gide and translated by Justin O'Brien and Dorothy Bussey, 1962.

Time Inc.—for permission to quote from a *Time* magazine essay on January 20, 1978 by Frank Tippet.

Time-Life Books, Inc.—for selections from The Great Ages of Man series: quotations from Aelfric the Grammarian on life in the Middle Ages and from Jean Bodin, the French jurist, on witchcraft.

Estate of Mr. Arnold Toynbee—for permission to quote from "The Genesis of Pollution," an article by Arnold Toynbee, which appeared in *Horizon* magazine, Summer 1973.

University of California Press—for permission to quote from "Cantique de Saint Jean" from *Hériodiade* by Mallarmé, which appears in *Selected Poems of Mallarmé,* translated by C. F. MacIntyre. Copyright © 1957 by the Regents of the University of California.

University of Michigan Press—for permission to quote from *The Life of Charlemagne* by Einhard and translated by S. E. Turner.

The Viking Press—for permission to quote from a letter written by Madame Sévigné to her daughter, which appears in *The Portable Age of Reason Reader,* edited and translated by Crane Brinton, and from *Finnegans Wake* by James Joyce.

W. W. Norton & Co—for permission to quote page 208 from *Darwin,* a Norton Critical Edition 1979.

Contents

Preface

For many years, in conjunction with my work in costume design, I taught a course on the relationship of the visual arts to theatrical production from the time of the ancient Greeks to the present. At first, this course was just a survey on how the visual arts can be used as sources for the design of theatrical productions, but gradually it began to focus on how the visual style of a production relates to the structure of the play and to the arts of the period in which the play is written. Both my previous books, *Stage Costume Design* (Prentice-Hall, Inc., 1973) and *Theatrical Style: A Visual Approach to the Theatre* (Mayfield Press, 1976), and my later book, *Costume History and Style* (Prentice-Hall, Inc., 1983), are indebted to this approach. Also about twelve years ago I was asked to teach a course on period style for the first-year students in the training program of the American Conservatory Theatre in San Francisco; it was at that time that much of the material for this text was first developed. The students were primarily interested in acting, though some were potential directors and a few potential designers. The course was taught once a week over a year's time and depended greatly on the ability of students with a minimum of historical background to analyze why two works of art, two theatrical productions, or two figures of fashion from different periods represent different cultural and theatrical styles. Over the years, I have found that students like to argue about how theatrical style relates to cultural style. Because talented students of acting, directing, and design frequently have the sensitivity and instinct to get beyond facts and dates to the essence of what makes up the artistic and cultural mood of a period (an ability students of political, intellectual, and cultural history sometimes lack), this text probes the inner life and feelings of a particular period style. In doing so, it makes intuitive and sometimes rather personal statements of analysis and comparison and thus may be criticized for being subjective and arbitrary. Just as a director seldom tries to balance all the cultural and theatrical forces at work in a particular period play but concentrates on the inner qualities of the period found in the play, so this text stresses the essential character of a period at the expense of minor trends, balance, and complexity.

This text involves a method of teaching as much as it does a survey on the facts of period style. (It liberates students from historical facts and leads them into a creative journey to the inner life of a character or play.) Although the teacher should cover the key facts affecting the style in each period, he or she should make much more use of the Socratic method—questioning students about what they see in a painting, how it relates to a play, and how they would feel in a particular room or in front of certain architecture. Students should be encouraged to place themselves inside the culture and style of a particular period.

Though the text derives from a course taught for actors, it is equally useful for directors and designers and all other students of the theatre. It provides an overview of period style by drawing together the creative, artistic, and intellectual threads that create that style. In no way is this text intended as a "how to do it" manual for performance. It is aimed at college-level students who have some basic historical background and at young professional trainees working in a professional training program prior to taking a position in the professional theatre. At the college level, this text could be used either in survey courses or at the intermediate levels in acting, directing, and design.

The text covers the major periods of Western culture from primitive man to the present, found in books on art and culture. Each chapter begins with a general discussion of art in relation to culture. Musical developments are then briefly mentioned followed by a section on life and cultural ideals, which includes quotations from writers or critics of the time. Discussions of interiors, furnishings, costume, movement, manners, and developments in the theatre and in playwriting then follow. Each chapter concludes with discussions of one or two plays that typify the style of the period and of the acting and design problems encountered within the particular period style. Following each chapter, students are given projects and problems that require them to ask questions about style, to place themselves inside the clothing and culture of the period, and to develop exercises that will enhance their knowledge of the period. Finally, there is an extensive annotated bibliography of books on art, theatre, and culture.

Many ideas in this book have evolved over a period of thirty years from my work as a designer, teacher, and playgoer. Other ideas have come from students and colleagues with whom I have been closely involved over the years. I would particularly like to thank the following: my teachers, Virginia Opsvig, Hubert Heffner, and Frank Bevan, particularly the latter who instilled in me a strong sense of the meaning of style in the theatre; Norman Philbrick for his friendship, advice, and encouragement during the writing of all my books and for the generous use of his extensive library; the American Conservatory Theatre and its two leaders, William Ball and Allen Fletcher, for their willingness to experiment in their first-year program with a course on period style for the theatre; and the supportive students in the first-year training program at the American Conservatory Theatre during the past twelve years. Finally, I wish to thank my wife, Marilyn, for her helpful advice and editorial assistance.

Introduction

The word *style* is frequently an obstacle when discussing period plays because to many theatre people it means a superficial composite of manners, movement, and customs to be incorporated into a production. Admittedly, the term is a treacherous one—vague and meaning different things to different people. Yet in contemporary language, we speak frequently of a person's "life-style" and have quite a confident sense of what we mean. A person's "life-style" is taken to mean the way a person lives, the things he or she likes and dislikes, and the tasks he or she performs in everyday life. If we merely enlarge this definition to include an entire culture during a certain period of time, then we are describing that period's "style."

A period's style is seldom defined by the daily choices of the common people, however, but by the work of its artists, writers, and intellectuals—those sensitive observers and questioners of the life of the times who through their work give leadership to the period and define its character. One must also distinguish between the style of the individual artist and the style of the period in which he or she lives. The style of a period reflects the social and political history of the times, and the changes that occur in a society are then reflected in the patterns and shifting artistic trends that develop within the period. Artists, writers, and intellectuals contribute to the pattern directly and indirectly; some even work in opposing directions. Neither one nor all the work of a single artist fully reveals the style of a period. Period style is never fully operative in a single poem, play, painting, musical composition, or theatrical production. Each work generates its own style. One must analyze the entire life's work of an artist to understand his or her overall style, and one must look at all the major artistic works of a period to gain a complete sense of that period's style.

James S. Ackerman in an essay entitled "A Theory of Style" gives an excellent definition of period style:

> We might visualize a style as a great canvas on which generations of artists have painted. The

earliest ones sketch a composition, later ones keep some of it, rub some out and add some of their own, the next do the same and so on. At any moment in the process there is a complete picture, but no indication of what it will look like after the succeeding artist has done his share. At the close of the process, when some artists have started on another picture, this one is abandoned. But the final image, although composed of contributions from every artist, cannot be said to represent the aims of the earlier ones, nor to represent a solution to the problem posed by the first of them.

In any attempt to abstract the major trends and developments found in this large canvas that we call the style of a particular period of culture, generalizations and even half truths must be stressed in order to give the student an understanding of the period—an intuitive as well as a rational view of those elements that are the most distinctive characteristics of the times. Summarizing factual information or recounting the highpoints in the political, cultural, intellectual, and social history of the times is not enough. As students of the theatre, who deal with the inner psychology of characters in relation to the periods in which they lived, we must gain entry to the inner life of a period.

How is this best done? The arts have always shown the inner life of man in a particular period better than political, intellectual, or social history. For the theatre, the visual arts, in particular, are the key to the inner life of a particular period style. Most importantly, we want to know how the people dress, how they move, how they like to see themselves and others, what they sit in, what kind of rooms they move in, and what kind of architecture provides an appropriate background for their formal and informal ceremonies. Secondarily, we want to know about the music that may have supported their ceremonies or theatre performances and to have some idea from a study of the literature of the people's values and cultural ideals. Finally, since we are in the theatre and feel that it is one of the great art forms that draws all these disparate artistic and intellectual threads to-

gether, we want to refresh our knowledge about the presentation of plays or theatrical performances in terms of staging, costuming, directing, and acting. A sharp picture of the staging of a particular scene in a particular play in a particular period must emerge since it is what we need to have with us even when we present the most modern and abstract versions of period plays. No truly brilliant contemporary production of a classic or a lesser known period play is achieved without a thorough understanding of the play and the period in which it was written.

There are a number of other problems related to the study of period style. One is the relationship between style and reality. The invention of the box camera made people think that it gave a new definitive statement of visual truth, whereas it is merely a tool or invention for projecting realism (or other styles if the camera is used poetically, or impressionistically). In many people's minds, realism is not a style but represents the truest way of presenting productions and viewing past periods. Realism in this innocent way of thinking means the absence of style and a close fidelity to the facts of life; style means an artificial and rather unreal view of life that characterizes the plays and outlook of certain periods. This concept of realism as outside of, or superior to, other styles still remains in many students' minds. Realism is actually a style that is just as calculated, self-conscious, and artificial as any other style, though it doesn't seem that way; it *seems* more lifelike and real. Anyone who has read Flaubert's comments on *Madame Bovary* or Ibsen's comments about his plays knows that the literary and dramatic techniques that they used were complex, calculated, manipulative, and to a certain extent, artificial. They were intended to make the reader or the audience believe they were seeing or imagining scenes from real life. In summation, in some periods of style, artists do work to derive their art from nature, and in others, they strive to demonstrate a triumph over nature by transforming their work through exaggeration and abstraction.

Another problem in the history of Western culture has been the seeming alternation of styles between those that reflect the rational and procedural aspects of human beings versus those that reflect their intuitions and senses. In recent years, much study has been done on the two sides of the brain—the left side, which processes analytical data, and the right side, which is the seat of creativity, intuition, and imagination. The ideal is a perfect balance between the two, but in most human beings there is a tendency toward either the intuitive or the analytical; the history of art as well as human history has seen a continuous attempt to reconcile these opposites. In great personalities this balance is sometimes achieved, but it seldom can be continued beyond the life of a single person, or beyond a very limited time in the history of culture.

Even in primitive culture, we can see the gradual shift from the intuitive, sensational, magic approach to nature and art in the paintings of the Old Stone Age to the abstact, rational, organized approach found in the art of New Stone Age man in which structure, layout, form, and storytelling values take precedence over nature. Later in periods of higher cultural development, such as the fifth century in Greece and the High Renaissance in Italy, art reflects a balance between these opposing rational and intuitive forces. We get a momentary "golden age" in the development of art and culture. In recent history, these two aspects of human cerebral activity as expressed in the overall cultural emphases of a period have been given the labels romantic and classic. Unfortunately the term *classic* has also been used to label those "golden ages," or moments of balance between the rational and the intuitive, and thus we have two meanings of the term—one designating a period that is interested in structure, organization, and form often at the expense of the intuitive and sensational aspects of human existence, and the other signifying a perfect balance between these two forces.

Western cultural development seems to have followed certain cycles reminiscent of human development. First, there is a period of formal learning and development—the adolescence of the culture—followed by a brief period of balance and maturity—a kind of golden age—and then a long period of excess, decadence, and decline before, as Ackerman says, a new canvas is begun. This pattern holds true as we move through the Archaic, classic, and Hellenistic Greek periods, for the Romanesque, high Gothic, and late Gothic medieval periods, and for the Early, High, and later mannerist Renaissance. It also can be seen in the adolescence of the romantic style in the late eighteenth century, in its climactic development around 1830, and then in its slow decline into various paths of repressed romanticism, realism, and symbolism at the end of the nineteenth and the beginning of the twentieth centuries.

The dividing line between the analytical and the sensational view of life and nature is never simple and clear, any more than is the political line that divides liberal and conservative, but critics often try to explain a particular period in art by using this method of comparison. One widely known attempt to do this is Heinrich Wölfflin's *Principles of Art History* (a comparison of the Renaissance with the Baroque), which sets up five opposing forms of representation. We can also use these polarities to explain and organize the art of other periods, and, by extension, to understand a literary art like drama in relation to a visual art like theatre. It may therefore be very useful to the student of theatrical design and directing, who must always be making a translation from a literary script to a visual production.

Wölfflin's first polarity is between the linear and the painterly. A linear style emphasizes clarity of contour and the decorative isolation of ornamental details; a painterly style blurs the edges, merges objects, and gives illusory and shifting appearances to objects (Compare Figures 5–5 and 7–3). Michelangelo's *David* is linear, Rodin's *Balzac* is painterly. Apply this concept to the theatre, and Racine's works are linear, Shakespeare's painterly.

Wölfflin's second polarity is the distinction between depth in plane and depth in recession in the organizing of compositional space. On depth in plane, space is organized as a series of receding planes; in recessional depth, the sense of plane is broken and visual space goes back in depth on a diagonal and sharply foreshortened lines. For example, *The School of Athens* by Raphael is planear, while that of Tintoretto is recessional (compare Figures 5–9 and 6–4). In the theatre, depth in plane and depth in recession can be seen by comparing *Romeo and Juliet* and *Hamlet*. The former seems to project a series of horizontal actions on a series of shallow planes against a flat, balanced background of city architecture and interiors. The latter involves Hamlet in action that moves from forward soliloquy directly back into full-scale court scenes, while the space and background around him create a labyrinthine illusion of great depth.

A third polarity involves open versus closed composition. In a closed composition, objects are rigidly framed and enclosed, while in an open composition, they are merged with outside space. Closed composition suggests a stable, limited, unchanging world; open composition, a world that flows into infinity or into a realm beyond the work. Again Raphael's *The School of Athens* is closed while Tintoretto's is open (compare Figures 5–9 and 6–4). In the theatre one can contrast the pictorial illusion framed by the theatre proscenium with a production that moves out into the audience. This polarity is reflected in the tight classical comedies of the Renaissance as opposed to the operatic productions of the Baroque, where members of the corps de ballet moved down the steps at the front of the stage onto the floor of the auditorium.

Another polarity, which is as vividly apparent in theatre as in art, is that between multiplicity and unity. In the former, individual details retain their identity while fitting harmoniously together, while in the latter the details disappear and the individual elements cannot be distinguished. Look at the interior in *The School of Athens* from the high Renaissance in comparison with the ceiling of the Barbarini Palace painted by Pietro Cortona in the early Baroque period (compare Figures 5–9 and 8–4). In the work by Raphael all parts remain clear, separate and are added together by the eye; in the Cortona ceiling all undulates and blends into a single crescendo of movement. In the theatre, "classical" costumes and sets should be designed so that each part is clearly set off from the other parts, while "romantic" sets and costumes blend into an overall effect.

Wölfflin's last polarity is between relative and absolute clarity, a contrast similar to painterly versus linear, but stressing light rather than composition. The light and color of a painting, statue, or building may be used to clarify and illuminate or to blur and distort so that objects become subjective symbols that create mystery and stir the imagination. A painting by the realist Gérôme might be compared to one by Monet (compare Figures 13–4 and 14–1). The Tissot gives facts and information through its clarity; the Monet creates a mysterious inner impression. In the theatre the lighting designer can manipulate this polarity, as can costume and scenic designers, by using surfaces and textures to reflect light in differing ways.

Other polarities were developed by Wylie Sypher in his book, *Four Stages of Renaissance Style*. He makes a case for a distinction between art that is in phase with culture and art that is out of phase through seeing how some paintings have a cyclical unified look, while others have a distorted broken look. Raphael's *School of Athens* is a good example of the former while El Greco's *View of Toledo* exemplifies the latter. He also makes a point of comparing art that is at rest, such as the art of Poussin, versus art that is constantly in motion, as in the paintings of Rubens. In the theatre the slow stately pace of Racine might be compared with the full movement of Shakespeare. Or there is the simple contrast between representational and presentational, in which one artist tries to represent the way life and nature really are, while another will present distortions and abstracts to bring us inside the artist's own vision of reality. Or again there is the contrast of art that appeals to the eye versus that which appeals to the touch. One can also contrast the geometric organization of a work with free organization—Mondrian versus Miró, or the balanced symmetry of *Romeo and Juliet* versus the freer organization of *Measure for Measure*. There is also the contrast between dark and light in art—between Botticelli and Rembrandt, or between *Macbeth* and *The Two Gentlemen of Verona*. In composition or in stage blocking there is the contrast between the balance and equilibrium of horizontal and vertical energies, as in a painting by Botticelli, versus the oblique angles and spiralling effects in the mannerist art of Tintoretto. Or again, there is relaxed seeing as in the sculpture of Maillol versus intensified seeing as in the sculpture of Rodin, just as a costume designer can create relaxed seeing for an audience through certain shapes and textures versus intensified seeing through the use of rough textures, distressed fabric, and heavily painted garments.

An understanding of all of these contrasts, although they may not fully explain changes of style, certainly assists the designer and director in discussing and pinpointing the particular style of the production on which they are to collaborate.

Finally, it is important for all students of the theatre to have a solid grasp of how the structure of a play (that is, how it is conceived and put together) relates to the period within which it was written. Some plays are very closely tied to specific cultural mores, and it is difficult for a director to change the period in production. Other plays that have a human or philosophic universality may be shifted from one period to another to gain exciting visual and histrionic effects, provided the acting, design, and directing are still related to the way the play was written. If mere novelty, however, is the reason for changing the period, then a superficial envelope of costumes,

settings, manners, and movement will be grafted onto the play without these things developing from the play itself. For example, placing a production of Molière's *The Miser* in the 1840s just because the director thinks that the audience will better relate to a central character reminiscent of Scrooge in Dickens's *A Christmas Carol*, will cause the play to suffer unless the cluttered romanticism of Dickens's day is reorganized and developed within the classical framework of Molière's play structure. A cluttered, asymmetrical room filled with excessively romantic costumes will not bring forth the directness, balance, and simplicity in Molière's script.

To be true to a period script, directors need not do the play in the period of its writing, but they should understand how the play's fundamental structure expresses the ideals of that period before shifting the production to another time. This may seem a rigid or overly simplified concept, but an honest theatre artist must understand the play and the period that produced it before plunging into an original production. Only critics and an audience can decide if the "new" play is better than the old, a distortion of the original, or a totally new interpretation that merely uses the old play as a kind of libretto. The more students of the theatre study how different playwrights gain different effects from the same story, how stories change when set in different cultures, and how poorly organized and poorly written plays still project the world outlook of their time, the more they will understand about period style. Only when students of theatre have a secure feeling about period style in relation to plays and playwrights are they ready to act, design, and direct with a conscious and mature understanding of what can be accomplished in a particular kind of production.

1

The Ancient World

Though acting as an art form is usually associated with the beginnings of Greek drama, the importance of earlier ceremonial rituals in the development of the histrionic instinct should not be overlooked. Early primitive man, at least in his art, demonstrated a naturalism and fidelity to visual reality not found in the later storytelling and symbolic art usually labeled Neolithic or New Stone Age development. How could the extraordinary cave paintings of northern Spain and southern France have preceded the pictographic stick figures and geometric art that followed? The answer is that these cave paintings were a form of sympathetic magic, part of a ritual in which images were incised on the walls of caves deep within the earth in order to ensure a successful hunt. Instinct, rather than thought, predominated at this stage in man's development; no clear distinction was made between images and reality. The picture became a magic "trap" for a particular animal as evidenced by the use of darts, spears, and diagrams of traps in these cave paintings. The animal so set down had symbolically come within the power of Old Stone Age man. A "dead" animal image, one on which the ritual of the kill had been performed, was then no longer important and could be forgotten. The pictorial image, depicting the anticipation of a desired result, was so imprinted in the mind of the artist that he reproduced it exactly onto the cave wall. The picture was as real to him as the animal itself and emotionally and psychologically reinforced his courage and conviction that the animal was already his (Figure 1–1). Even today, very primitive people confuse a photo with reality and drawn images with actual natural forms; for example, if they see bison drawings in a book, they assume that the animals have been removed from the real world.

At this stage in man's development, what is remarkable is that this sympathetic magic, uncomplicated by mental conceptualization and division of the world into parts, did produce an art in the famous cave paintings that

1

Figure 1–1 Polychrome bison, from the caves of Altamira in northern Spain, c. 20,000–10,000 B.C. An example of the strong naturalism in this art of sympathetic magic. Photo courtesy of the Spanish Tourist Office.

man and animals, attest to the early development of the idea that a "created" or "made" image or thing could be as real as the original. With man's use of this creation in a magic ritual and his imitation of animals and creation of them on cave walls came the earliest stirrings of the acting instinct. Look at the drawing of a man disguised as a deer on a wall of the Cave of the Three Brothers in southern France. (Figure 1–2). He was probably an early medicine man participating in

Figure 1–2 Medicine man wearing antlers and skin of a deer, from a cave in the southern Pyrenees of France, c. 25,000–15,000 B.C. From George Altman, Ralph Freud, William Melnitz, and Kenneth Macgowan, *Theatre Pictorial* (Berkeley: University of California Press, 1953). Photo courtesy of William Melnitz.

is so brilliantly subtle in its direct response to nature. The rendering of motion, the subtleties of shading, the color distinctions, and the use of line were all lost by the New Stone Age when directness of sensation was replaced by the inflexibility of concepts and categories. Man in the Old Stone Age was a true child of nature at one with the universe—a "sensationalist," certainly not a rationalist. Metaphorically, he was Adam in the Garden of Eden before he had gained the knowledge and realization of what it was to be human. Thus it is not even correct to speak of the "art" of this age, since the images and artifacts are not so much aesthetic forms but practical magic—tools for aiding man in sustaining his place in nature.

The key elements in the cave drawings that relate to the development of the histrionic instinct in primitive man are "similarity" and "imitation." The hand prints or silhouettes on the walls of the caves, which undoubtedly preceded the actual drawings of

some kind of imitative animal pantomime intended to increase food supply. He is the first recorded actor, marking the beginning of that great, long process of development that culminated in the Greek Golden Age drama and in the establishment of acting as a profession.

The New Stone Age

The metaphorical expulsion from the Garden of Eden came with the Neolithic Revolution, or New Stone Age, characterized by man's transition from hunting to agriculture. This transition began in the Near East sometime about 8000 B.C., when man made the first successful attempt to domesticate animals and raise grains. In contrast to the Old Stone Age man, who led an unsettled life always at the mercy of the forces of nature, the New Stone Age man settled down in communities, had greater control over the food supply, and began to develop a disciplined order for group living. Long before the use of metals in the Iron and Bronze ages, new crafts, such as pottery and weaving, as well as the beginnings of planned architecture in huts and houses, were introduced during the New Stone Age. The stone tools and weapons were more beautiful and subtle in shape than those of the Old Stone Age, and the pottery and weaving projected a complex abstract ornamental design totally lacking the direct naturalism of the Old Stone Age.

Why this change to the abstract and geometric? With the transition from food gathering and hunting to cattle breeding and planting, the entire rhythm of life changed. Man now felt separate from the animal and plant world though very dependent on it; he gradually developed a dualistic view of a world divided into the real and the super real, the visible and the spiritual. Man saw himself as having a mortal body with a spirit inside and each thing in nature as having an outer reality and inner spirit. This animistic view produced all kinds of new complex rituals, modes of worship, use of idols, and "ceremonial architecture," such as the ritual monuments at Carnac and Stonehenge. The older magic view regarded the world as *one* in a simple texture of uninterrupted forward movement, while the new animism divided everything into inner and outer parts. Whereas the older outlook was based on the senses and the concrete facts of daily existence, the newer outlook stressed spiritual, invisible forces and used abstract symbols to express them. It signified the beginning of intellectualization in art; concrete images gave way to signs, symbols, and abbreviations. The literal picture gradually changed into a pictographic sign language or narrative shorthand (Figure 1–3). This use of signs and symbols in geometric form also evidenced a more tightly organized, disciplined, social organization with a dualist religious outlook.

With this great social revolution came the priest or medicine man to turn the whole realm

Figure 1–3 Figures on the skin of a Lapp drum, from northern Sweden, c. A.D. 1800. Illustrates the abstract, geometric, storytelling qualities in Neolithic art. Photo courtesy of the Museum fur Völkerkunde, Munich.

of sympathetic magic into a complex profession combining aesthetic, histrionic, and religious instincts. An entire class of unproductive specialists developed who spent time developing, augmenting, and polishing the myths and rituals that had been created to explain and influence the complex spirit world behind all natural things. The animal mask and disguise now turned into the wonderfully imaginative faces and forms of deities, and the simple imitation of animal movements matured into complex dance rituals that told stories about the gods. These stories about the many deities controlling and manipulating all natural forces and influencing all human destiny became the myths on which written drama eventually was founded. Since primitive man made little distinction between religion and life, there was a close relationship between the way these myths developed rhythmically, sequentially, verbally, and the way the tribe actually lived.

In the ceremonial rituals presided over by priests and medicine men, the mask was the key accessory for doing business with the spirit world through a rhythmic dance in which "man in action" was projected before the gods (Figure 1–4). Though these New Stone Age rituals, still practiced today by some primitive peoples, were not drama, the performers and priestly leaders exploited all the dramatic instincts. Each performer played his role in the most expressive, striking, and accomplished manner, making normal speech and movement abnormal, mysterious, and excitingly theatrical. By using these attributes to command attention, the actor gained a sense of power and belief that he was a self-contained unit who could perform alone or with a group anywhere or at any time as long as there was someone to watch him. With the aid of mask and costume, the actor stepped outside himself into the larger world of the ritual and its story.

The complex masks and headdresses that supported this dramatic expression give evidence, even among primitive peoples today, of a fantastic creative imagination in man's attempts to tell stories about the gods and to

Figure 1–4 Mask of the Basonge tribe of the Belgian Congo. From the Ralph Altman Collection. Photo courtesy of the Stanford University Art Department slide file.

influence them on his own behalf. The ceremonial rituals primarily concerned ancestor worship, fertility, initiation into the tribe, medical cures, and power in warfare. The masks ranged from birds emerging from the head to suggest the flight of the inner soul, to fantastic decorations emphasizing the eye as the window of the soul, to the frightening and even monstrous faces of evil spirits. Even in our sophisticated world today, masks are still a potent theatrical device. In all masked figures, the stress is on the face and torso rather than on the limbs of the human figure; the total visual effect is usually awe-inspiring and frightening (Figure 1–4).

In some more developed areas of New

Stone Age culture, massive monumental stone constructs were built as religious sites. Look at the famous site at Stonehenge for a moment and attempt to reconstruct the excitement of the ritual performance that must have taken place there during the summer solstice each year (Figure 1–5). Even today, the site is awe-inspiring and mysterious because of the size of the stones, some of which are seventy feet high and weigh several tons. Though the questions of why and for what purpose Stonehenge was originally built have never been completely answered, its development appears to have been tied to a knowledge of astronomy and the movement of the sun and moon. The entire structure is oriented toward the position at which the sun rises on the day of the summer solstice. With the first rays of the rising sun, a slab of stone to the east of the central stone, or altar, casts a shadow directly on that altar. One can imagine the worshipers gathered in excited and fearful anticipation of the dawn, each prepared to participate in a ritual involving them individ-ually and collectively in the powers of the universe. As the sky lightened to the east, there would have been a deathly silence, with the communal breath withheld as the sun ascended over the horizon to catch the tip of the heelstone, spreading a shadow, like the finger of a god, directly across the altar.

The ensuing ceremonial would have involved each participant directly in the greatest seen power in the universe, the power of the sun itself. Such a natural phenomenon coupled with the histrionic instinct tapped in each performer-participant constitutes one of the most theatrical events of all time. Even sophisticated and blasé modern man in a visit to Stonehenge can be struck by the same sense of awe that must have gripped the original primitive participants at sunrise on the morning of the summer solstice. By coupling this stupendous natural event with the elements of primitive rituals (dance, masks, costumes, and vocal chanting or storytelling), we have some idea of the dramatic power and religious importance of early ritual theatre.

Figure 1–5 Stonehenge, Salisbury Plain, Wiltshire, England, c. 1800–1400 B.C. A circle of stones 97′ in diameter and 13½′ high used as a religious ceremonial site and as an astronomical calendar. Photo courtesy of the British Tourist Authority, New York.

Long before the erection of Stonehenge, in the fertile areas around the eastern end of the Mediterranean basin, historic cultures replaced the prehistoric ones of the New Stone Age. With the development of written records some 6,000 years ago, man's condition again changed. With the possibility of recording history, man seems to have wanted to make more history so that he could record it. In the fertile river valleys of Egypt and Mesopotamia, dynamic societies developed that were challenged less by nature than by human forces within and outside their own societies. One of the first social changes was the development of urban living with its concentration of population and subsequent social and intellectual stimulation resulting from the close contact of different levels of society.

From a modern perspective, it is difficult to view Egypt as representing an increase in cultural change. It seems the most rigidly conservative civilization that ever existed; yet, close study reveals that Egypt had more shifts, changes, and developments than any primitive, prehistoric culture. Certainly there are strong and enduring patterns in Egyptian art and institutions that continued from the early years around 3000 B.C. until the period of

Greek dominance about 400 B.C.; still, if the culture had been as inflexible as sometimes portrayed, it would not have survived those 2,500 years.

Recording their history in terms of the various dynasties of their rulers, the Egyptians signified their strong sense of continuity and the overwhelming importance given to the pharaoh or king. He was not merely a ruler but also a god. The Egyptian belief in the absolute divinity of the ruler gave their art and storytelling ritual its formal hierarchical character. Also, their religious beliefs about life after death led to complex burial rites and massive tomb building. Though domestic dwellings were built of impermanent materials, the tombs, temples, statues of the gods, and images of the pharaohs were made from imperishable stone. In the seemingly timeless, cyclical seasonal world in the valley of the Nile, a civilization developed that was devoted to permanence, religion, and an unchanging and ageless order.

This sense of permanence can be quickly seen in an early painted frieze called *Geese of Medum* done in dry fresco about 2600 B.C. (Figure 1–6). A comparison of the clarity and formality of this work with the subtle

Figure 1–6 *Geese of Medum,* dry fresco, approximately 18″ high, c. 2600 B.C. Demonstrates the Egyptian love of exact, subtle, frozen form as a symbol of continuity and control. Egyptian Museum, Cairo. Photo courtesy of the Hirmer Fotoarchiv, Munich.

spontaneous naturalism of the cave paintings (Figure 1–1) underscores the totally different cultural outlooks of their artists. The Egyptian artist had a consuming interest in precise measurement, relationship to ground line, and placement and proportion. The artist who painted the bison was conscious of the bison's actual appearance. He felt the animal's size, shape, movement, bulk, and color. The Egyptian artist endeavored to create a timeless, exacting, perfectly executed image that would freeze his subject into a pattern for all time. This was not the art of sympathetic magic created to control the animal and then discarded. Instead, it was the beginning art of a people who believed that every act and artistic product were distinctive punctuation marks in the great unrolling pattern of their unchanging culture.

Many of us will recall the image of the Great Sphinx framed against the Pyramid of Khafre in the background. No matter how many times we see them in photos or movies, they never fail to convey the power of the Old Kingdom pharaohs. But the total static power of these breathtaking monuments should not be allowed to obviate their other qualities. One should also feel the living forces of experimentation, individualism, and expansion of traditional forms. The dynamic forces in Egyptian civilization were probably greater than the static ones at a time when the urban outlook replaced Neolithic static culture. Today, however, we are more interested in the Egyptian drive for religious continuity and autocratic political power as evidenced by the sheer size, formality, and grandeur of these works. For example, look at the seated figure of Pharaoh Chefren in a statue from Giza, dated about 2530 B.C. (Figure 1–7). Here the four-square quality of the Sphinx is even more accentuated. The statue stresses angularity by retaining the squared feeling of the block of stone and also exhibits the same sense of precision and measure as the *Geese of Medum* (Figure 1–6). The emphasis on symmetry, formality, and a certain geometric order underlying all natural form removes the seated figure from the natural world to a timeless world beyond nature. Yet in spite of this for-

Figure 1–7 *Pharaoh Chefren,* from Giza, c. 2530 B.C. Illustrates the angular, closed, cubic view of an Egyptian god king symbolizing the religious and political concept of continuity and total power. Egyptian Museum, Cairo. Photo courtesy of the Hirmer Fotoarchiv, Munich.

malistic emphasis, the figure seems to live inside its image because of the treatment of the muscles, the resilience of the body, and the expression around the eyes and mouth. This statue is a living embodiment of both the immutable, eternal laws that control the uni-verse and human life and of the intellectual, haughty and yet gracious human monarch. An actor able to communicate this feeling could dominate a performance just by sitting regally on stage.

Egyptian Costume and Movement

When we look at Egyptian art for information about Egyptian costume, the clothing appears to have been distorted by the formal angularity and stiffness emphasized by the artist. This distortion is not due to an artistic inability to achieve a more rounded figure and softer clothing but is the deliberate choice of the artist, who is presenting the artistic, cultural ideal of the Egyptian upper classes. The people of a culture always try to look as much as possible like the stylistic elements emphasized in their art.

Thus the loin cloth and headdress worn by Pharaoh Chefren were stiffened in real life to embody the rigidity and angularity they have in stone. (Figure 1–7). The flat angularity of the figure in dress and in placement makes one conclude that the loin cloth and headdress were deliberately distorted. In truth, however, the clothing did have an angularity because it was made from linen that was starched and pleated. One cannot but marvel at the effort the human spirit will make to look like the culture's artistic ideals. The same is true for the transparent look of tunics, particularly those worn by women. The linen was actually woven into such a thin, transparent texture that the body appeared as through a veil. The thin, transparent linens were pleated so that the dress, made heavier and more fluid by the pleating, clung lightly to the contours of the body and fell into a pattern of fine lines following the shape of the drapery. Thus, in the Egyptian culture (and in all others), life reflects art more than art reflects life.

Over the many centuries, Egyptian dynastic culture became more complex, and clothing changed from less to more. The Old Kingdom emphasized the loin cloth, collar, and headdress for men and the long, close-fitting skirt for women. By the time of the Middle Kingdom, there was more variation in loin cloths, and a type of shirt had been added. With the coming of outside influences in the New Kingdom, clothing was even more varied. There were long-sleeved tunics, robes for ceremonial occasions, girdles and collars over tunics, and often one tunic over another. The heavy use of makeup, wigs, and false beards for the pharaoh's ceremonial occasions witness Egypt's sophisticated sense of abstraction and triumph over the shifting changes and imperfections in nature. All the famous sacred symbols—for example, scarabs (beetles), uraeuses (cobra heads), sun discs, vultures, and lotus and papyrus blossoms—used extensively in decoration and symbolic headdresses are so abstracted from nature and so beautifully reformed into pure symbolic ornament that they add the perfect accent to the quiet, stiff, timeless, angular poses of all Egyptian figures.

Egyptian Theatre

Whether drama—or even theatre, as we define it—existed in ancient Egypt has long been debated. Certainly, there were many ritual ceremonies, and we have numerous hieroglyphic texts and visual scenes depicting the tribulations through which a human spirit had to pass before being accepted into the afterlife. In fact, there are more than fifty surviving "Pyramid Texts" that some scholars argue were religious dramas enacted by priests; other scholars think that they were merely plans for a particular ceremony that included spoken passages. There is no concrete evidence that the Pyramid Texts were actually performed.

The most important of all Egyptian ritual ceremonies was the Abydos Passion Play dealing with the death and resurrection of the god Osiris. He was son of the earth and sky who married his sister Isis, was killed by his brother Seth, and whose body was buried in various parts of Egypt. Osiris was finally brought back to life by his sister and Anubis, the god of embalming. Unable to remain on earth, he went to dwell in the underworld as the judge of souls. This play is one of the great mythic tales, similar to certain aspects of the Greek stories of Dionysus and to the life of Christ.

A ritual based on the myth of Osiris was performed at Abydos from about 2500 to 550 B.C. What little we know about it comes from a hieroglyphic tablet account dated 1868 B.C. by Ikhernofret, who evidently was a producer of, and a participant in, this ritual. The action seems to have moved from place to place, culminating at the Temple of Osiris. It is very difficult to tell if actual roles were assumed and if dialogue and conflict took place. As students of the theatre, however, we can certainly imagine what the movement, rhythm, dress, and makeup must have been like. The choruses would have moved with a controlled beauty and stiff angularity; no movement, action, or vocal utterance would have been left to chance. Costumes would have been white and heavily starched or tightly transparent against shiny brown bodies; girdles, collars, and headdresses would have been accented with the Egyptian colors of red, gold, and blue. Makeup would have been heavily artificial, and there would have been many symbolic properties and headdresses.

Though modern plays placed in an Egyptian setting, like *Caesar and Cleopatra*, may demand a realism in characterization and movement, they also need to preserve Egyptian formality and removal from the world of nature. These can be portrayed by the use of Egyptian dress. Ceremonial costumes, in particular, will make the actor feel that he is a decorative symbol in the ritual patterns of life rather than an individual, since it is very difficult to move and act in a casual human manner while wearing such clothing. Even for a basically realistic play like *Caesar and Cleopatra*, the student of theatre should study Egyptian art and culture in order to integrate costume with the background and movement of the production. This artistic integration will create a believable world for the audience that is not unnatural or distracting.

Mesopotamian Culture

In the Tigris Euphrates valley, the Sumerian civilization, another historic, urban culture, developed at the same time as the Egyptian civilization. It was quite different in geography and societal outlook from Egypt. Because stone was very difficult to obtain in the delta area of the Tigris Euphrates, the early Sumerians built and sculpted from brick and clay. Since life after death and continuity of life in death were less important here, the Sumerians did not preserve every aspect of their culture in tomb furniture and decoration. Consequently, because of this deemphasis on an afterlife and the perishability of the building materials, fewer artifacts from succeeding cultures in this area have been preserved. In addition, because the major occupation in this area changed from sheepherding to finance and business rather than to farming, hieroglyphic tablets and written materials were used to record financial transactions rather than rituals or ceremonial events as in Egypt. Also, this area was more vulnerable to outside invasion than Egypt. The complications of military and political history brought about a long sequence of changing political and cultural control.

Because of the geography and the materials available for art in this area, the Sumerians also developed a very different set of self-images and artistic interests. Most of these held constant through all the shifts and changes of Mesopotamian civilization. An early Sumerian statue has the same rounded lines and interest in fleece textures that a very developed Assyrian figure has (Figure 1–8). Though stone was later substituted for clay, the cylindrical forms reflecting the work of a potter remain and contrast sharply with the

Figure 1–8 *King Ashurbanipal II,* from Nimrud, c. 883–859 B.C. This rounded warlike figure with curled hair and fringe represents the art of the Assyrians during the period of their control of Mesopotamia. Reproduced by courtesy of the Trustees of the British Museum.

angular, block form used in Egyptian art. Sheepherding gave the culture a strong identification with fleece as a symbol of virility and fertility. In various abstracted forms, fleece became one of the most admired forms of decoration, particularly as fringe and as a stylistic model for creating curled beards and hair. Even though the Sumerians were gentle and the Assyrians, who swept down from the highlands of the North, were fierce, the similarity in their concentration on beards, hair, and fringe is striking. To use such effects on stage is to create an image of brutal strength and physical power.

The last civilization to dominate Mesopotamia before Alexander the Great's sweep through the area brought Hellenistic culture was the great Persian Empire dealt with in Aeschylus' play *The Persians.* The most important source of our knowledge about this great empire and its culture is the Palace of Darius at Persepolis, built about 500 B.C., on a high plateau to the east of the Tigris Euphrates valley. A few years ago, this great monument to the emperors Darius and Xerxes was the site for the twenty-five hundredth anniversary celebration of the Persian Empire. The ruins show a mixture of earlier Mesopotamian stylistic effects and columns and fluting that can only be attributed to Grecian influence. Certainly, the processional figures carved along the sides of the great stairway have a greater naturalness than in earlier Mesopotamian carving, and the royal robe of the emperor shows an interest in draping characteristic of the Greeks.

Among the king's subjects, we note some clothing effects never seen before. Many of the cupbearers and soldiers wear very tight-fitting tunics or coats and long trousers (Figure 1–9). This clothing was derived from the early nomadic Persians in the highlands about the Caspian Sea who wore wraparound skins, since woven tunics were not available. The clothing that developed thus looked more like a skin for the body than a rectangle to be cut and hung from the figure. These jacket and trouser effects are closer to our own idea of

Figure 1–9 Detail of a royal procession from the stairway to the Royal Audience Hall at Persepolis, c. 500 B.C. Illustrates the Persian use of Greek-influenced draping in tunics worn with close-fitting oriental trousers and jackets. Photo courtesy of the Oriental Institute, University of Chicago.

clothing than either Egyptian or Mesopotamian costume are. Note the contrast between this skinlike clothing and the draped gown of the emperor. It would be interesting to stage one of the battles in which the Greeks defeated the Persians in order to place the ideals of Greek dress against the basically Oriental-Mesopotamian ideals. Probably the most striking realization would be how little the Mesopotamian ideal resembles the Greek interest in the body's natural lines and movements.

Mesopotamian dress emphasized the spiral draping of great shawls, the tight cylindrical shape of long tunics, and the heavy use of fringe; the most striking personal accent was undoubtedly the tightly curled hair and beards. In every way, the human figure seemed heavier and coarser in surface texture than the Egyptian, primarily because of the materials available and admired. Whereas the Egyptians relied on linen, the Mesopotamians used the wool available in the Tigris Euphrates valley for tunics and shawls. Because of the early emphasis on fleece and fur as a texture, this rich tactile accent continued through all the cultures that inhabited this area. Gradually, the Persians put aside the rich tactile effects, except for hair and beards, in favor of the draping accents taken from the Greeks.

Mesopotamian Costume and Movement

The movement engendered by such clothing, though stressing some of the formality of the Egyptians, must have been much heavier in step and pose. In every way the costumes were heavier and thicker than those of the Egyptians and gave added weight to gestures and body movement. There were no transparent garments. Wrapped up in a great fringed shawl spiraling several times around the body, one certainly must have felt encumbered by the thick and rather matted textures that allowed no natural or easy movement. Whereas Egyptian movement must have been elegantly stiff in its formality, this must have been ponderously heavy. Even the furniture was heavy and consisted of a high stool-chair with animal feet. The sitter then rested his sandaled or slippered feet on a padded footstool rather than placing them on the floor.

Mesopotamian Theatre

Like many early peoples, the Mesopotamians left tablet records of ceremonies presented in connection with birth, death, maturation, and the seasons of the year, but nothing indicates the existence of any dramatic performances similar to those of the Greeks. From studying sculptured processions and layouts of temples and palaces, we can imagine what these theatrical rituals must have been like, although we have no scripts or even scenarios to aid us. What we do have are some interesting plays and operas from the nineteenth and twentieth centuries with Mesopotamia as a historical setting. The Romantics, in particular, liked this area for its exotic overtones. We have Verdi's opera *Nabucco*, based on the fall of Nebuchadnezzar, the great Babylonian emperor from the Bible; Byron's play *Sardanapalus*, on which Delacroix based a famous painting; the famous *Samson and Delilah* by Delibes; and Rossini's minor and little-known opera *Semiramide*, whose overture is well known.

But undoubtedly the most interesting dramatic piece for the student of theatre is *The Persians* by Aeschylus. In this play's presentation, great dramatic effects can be gained by contrasting through clothing and art the mysterious and closed society of the Persians with the far more open society of the Greeks. Particularly effective would be a production that has the chorus wearing masks with fringed hair and beards and heavy fringed robes and shawls and that incorporates the massive architecture of the Palace of Darius (Figure 1–10).

Figure 1–10 Scene from *The Persians* by Aeschylus, produced by De Niewe Komedie of The Hague; Holland Festival, Amsterdam, 1962. Directed by Erik Vos. Photo courtesy of Erik Vos, photograph by Henk Jonker, Amsterdam.

PROJECTS AND PROBLEMS

1. Devise a scenario for a primitive dramatic ritual.

2. Plan a ceremonial dance with the performers wearing animal heads and skins, as in the drawing of the medicine man (Figure 1–2).

3. Elaborate on this primitive drama by developing rituals on fertility, rain, initiation into the tribe, and ancestor worship.

4. Demonstrate a ritual dance to other members of your class.

5. Design some primitive, ritualistic dance costumes.

6. Draw or model in clay some primitive ritualistic dance masks for members of a fertility ritual, a rain dance, an initiation rite, and ceremony for the worship of tribal ancestors.

7. Design a performance site for ceremonial rituals; include an altar, dance area, and spectator arrangement in relation to a particular natural setting.

8. Develop a ritual that might have taken place at Stonehenge (Figure 1–5) during the predawn hours of the summer solstice.

9. Design the lighting for a primitive ritual using fire, torches, or natural sources.

10. Why are religion and primitive theatre so closely connected?

11. Why are man's instincts for imitation and storytelling so strong?

12. Make two drawings, one exemplifying the art of the Old Stone Age (Paleolithic man), the other of the New Stone Age (Neolithic man).

13. How did the supernatural magic of Paleolithic man differ from the supernatural religious worship of Neolithic man?

14. Why do the geese in the *Geese of Medum* (Figure 1–6) seem both real and abstract?

15. Make a simple headdress of papier maché or cardboard that approximates the size and shape of Chefren's headdress (Figure 1–7). Then put it on and describe how it feels.

16. Approximate the stiff, pleated linen loin cloth worn by Egyptian men (Figure 1–7). Wear it and then describe how it feels.

17. Develop an Egyptian dramatic ritual for the dead.

18. For a production of Shakespeare's *Antony and Cleopatra* to be done in authentic Egyptian clothing, plan Cleopatra's death scene and design or describe the qualities of her dress.

19. How do Shaw's *Caesar and Cleopatra* and Shakespeare's *Antony and Cleopatra* differ in respect to their treatment of the same period and characters?

20. After looking at many visual images of Egypt, explain in writing or orally your impression of the Egyptians and their view of themselves.

21. How do the statue of King Ashurbanipal II (Figure 1–8) and the statue of Pharaoh Chefren (Figure 1–7) compare in mood, sculptural method, and cultural outlook?

22. Place a large fringed shawl diagonally about your body to approximate the draping on King Ashurbanipal II (Figure 1–8). Describe what happens to your movement when wearing it.

23. Wear sweat pants and a loose coat to the knees like those worn by the Persian retainers on the stairway to the Royal Audience Hall at Persepolis (Figure 1–9). Describe how different this dress feels from the stiff loin cloths of the Egyptians and the heavy, fringed shawl of the Assyrians.

24. Design costumes and masks for the characters in Aeschylus' play *The Persians*.

25. Find production pictures of Verdi's opera *Nabucco* to bring to class for discussion.

BIBLIOGRAPHY

Boas, Franz. *Primitive Art*. New ed. New York: Dover Press, 1955. An excellent and easy-to-follow survey on how art developed as a magical tool for ancient man to use in hunting and later in primitive religion.

Burkitt, Miles C. *The Old Stone Age*. 3rd ed. New York: University Press, 1956. An excellent coverage of the development of ancient man during the early Paleolithic period.

Casson, Lionel. *Ancient Egypt*. The Great Ages of Man Series. New York: Time-Life Books, 1965. A beautifully illustrated book with extensive color photographs; it covers the major intellectual, artistic, and cultural developments in ancient Egypt.

————. *Daily Life in Ancient Egypt*. A Horizon Book. New York: American Heritage, 1975. A very fascinating and useful book, with excellent illustrations, on all aspects of living in ancient Egypt.

Fagg, W., *African Sculpture*. Loan Exhibition. Washington: International Exhibitions Foundation, 1970. Excellent for visual browsing.

Fakhry, Ahmed. *The Pyramids*. Chicago: University of Chicago Press, 1962. A fascinating study of the meaning of the pyramids and of how they were built.

Frankfort, Henri. *The Art and Architecture of the Ancient Orient*. Pelican History of Art Series. Baltimore: Penguin Books, 1955. A comprehensive survey on the development and growth of art in Mesopotamia and surrounding areas from the earliest primitive times to the advent of the Greek conquest.

Fraser, James G. *The Golden Bough*. New York: Macmillan, 1958. This one-volume edition of the theories of James Fraser, originally published in London in twelve volumes, provides invaluable material on the magic, religion, customs, and social relationships of primitive man.

Garbini, Giovanni. *The Ancient World*. Landmarks of the World's Art Series. New York: McGraw-Hill, 1966. An excellent and beautifully illustrated survey, with many color plates, on the development of art in ancient Egypt and Mesopotamia. The text is secondary to the plates.

Herskovits, M. J. *The Backgrounds of African Art*. Denver: Denver Art Museum, 1946. Gives the student an excellent introduction to the field.

Hunningher, Benjamin. *The Origin of the Theatre*. New York: Hill and Wang, 1961. A very helpful guide to the many theories about how drama and theatre developed before the advent of the Greeks.

Kramer, Samuel Noah. *Cradle of Civilization*. The Great Ages of Man Series. New York: Time-Life Books, 1967. Beautifully illustrated with extensive color photography, this concise and useful text covers the major intellectual, cultural, and artistic developments in the ancient Near East.

Lange, Kurt, and Hirmer, Max. *Egypt*. London: Phaidon, 1956. Another very useful look at the art and culture of ancient Egypt.

Levi-Strauss, Claude. *The Savage Mind*. Chicago: University of Chicago Press, 1966. A fascinating study of primitive man and the workings of his mind.

Lloyd, Seton. *The Art of the Ancient Near East*. New York: Praeger, 1961. A beautifully illustrated survey on the arts of the Tigris Euphrates Valley and surrounding areas from the earliest primitive times until the Greek conquest.

Lommel, Andreas. *Prehistoric and Primitive Man*. Landmarks of the World's Art Series. New York: McGraw-Hill, 1966. Covers all aspects of primitive art in all parts of the world.

Powell, T. G. *Prehistoric Art*. New York: Praeger, 1966. Another finely illustrated volume on the art of primitive man before the rise of Egypt and Mesopotamia.

Saggs, H. W. F. *The Greatness That Was Babylon*. New York: American Library, 1968. A fascinating study of what it was like to live in the rich and exotic city of Babylon before the Persian conquest.

Sandars, N. K. *Prehistoric Art in Europe*. Pelican History of Art Series. Baltimore: Penguin Books, 1968. Provides extensive information on the development of art in Europe before the advent of the written word.

Sieber, R. "Masks as Agents of Social Control." *African Studies Bulletin* 5 (May 1962):8–13. A wonderful introduction to the art of the mask.

Smith, William Stevenson. *The Art and Architecture of Ancient Egypt*. Pelican History of Art Series. Baltimore: Penguin Books, 1958. Provides an excellent overview of the entire field of ancient Egyptian art.

————. *Interconnections in the Ancient Near East*. New Haven: Yale University Press, 1965. Details the cross-currents and interconnections in Mesopotamian art before the rise of Hellenistic culture.

Strommenger, Eva, and Hirmir, Max. *5000 Years of the Art of Mesopotamia.* New York: Abrams, 1964. A beautifully illustrated book on the art of the ancient Near East from its beginnings to Roman times.

Ucko, P. J., and Rosenfeld, A. *Paleolithic Cave Art.* New York: McGraw-Hill, 1967. An excellent place to begin a survey of primitive man's art.

2

Greek Style

Though the art and culture of Crete during the high development of the Minoan Age are often linked with the oriental cultures of the Mesopotamian area, they were also related to developments on the Greek mainland. Historians are aware of how much the Mycenaean Greeks who appear in *The Iliad*, *The Oresteia*, and *The Trojan Women* borrowed from the Minoan civilization of Crete, and thus any discussion of Greek style must mention Cretan art and culture. From reading about the Cretans and looking at their art, one is immediately struck by the freedom and joyousness of their life compared to that of the Egyptians and Mesopotamians. Religion and worship were subordinate to city life and commerce. Surrounded by water, Crete had no need for weighty fortification; as a result, the Palace of Knossos, which often appears to have grown as needed, has a casual, luxurious quality, and its decoration has a playful Rococo air that is sophisticated and amusing rather than hierarchical. Evidently, the courtly and elegant way of life here furthered this sense of chance arrangement and free pictorial composition. The viewer often sees the Minoan style as more "European" than "Oriental" and seemingly more natural than the art of Egypt and Mesopotamia.

Examine, for example, the statue of one of the numerous snake goddesses found at the Palace of Knossos (Figure 2–1). Compared to sculpture in Egypt and Mesopotamia, the figure is diminutive, hardly more than a talisman or fetish figure of fertility, but charmingly open, with arms spread in a momentary and active pose. The clothing is unlike the draped and wrapped costume seen in the Near East, and the art of cutting and sewing here is highly developed. The silhouette is almost like a nineteenth-century lady with breasts exposed. An actress wearing such a costume would feel both dignified and playful, casual and formal, tightly constricted and very daring.

Although the exact circumstances responsible for this civilization's end are un-

Figure 2–1 *Snake Goddess,* fertility symbol, approximately 13½" high, made of faience, c. 1600 B.C. Archaeological Museum, Heraklion. Photo courtesy of the Hirmer Fotoarchiv, Munich.

It was the Mycenaeans on the mainland of Greece, however, who *were* actually immortalized by Homer in *The Iliad* and *The Odyssey;* their mythical and historical deeds combined were a major subject of Greek drama. The Mycenaeans became influential and powerful in Greece about 1500 B.C. and, after coming in contact with the Minoan civilization of Crete and possibly with Egyptian culture, reached a high point between 1400 and 1200 B.C. Though they borrowed much and appeared to have acquired much gold—incorporated prominently in their art—the Mycenaeans remained very primitive, warlike, and barbaric in comparison with the Minoans.

The famous Lion Gate of the Palace of Mycenae, through which Agamemnon presumably marched when he returned to his wife, Clytemnestra, after the defeat of Troy, has a massive cyclopean weight and roughness in sharp contrast to anything in Crete, even though the column between the two lions is directly borrowed from the Palace of Knossos. The lions themselves seem closely allied to similar images in Mesopotamia. The gateway conveys warlike strength and primitive power quite unlike any of the impressions one receives on first reading the sophisticated plays about these Greeks and their Trojan enemies written some 700 years later. Also note the vase from this period showing a group of warriors marching to battle, presumably the troops of Agamemnon and Menelaus embarking for Troy (Figure 2–2). Again the shock is great. They seem more like the soldiers from *Macbeth* or *The Ring of the Nibelung* than the Greek warriors in *The Iliad.* With their horned helmets with fur tails, leather tunics, leg guards, and studded metal decoration, they are anything but the classical warriors of the later Greek dramas. This is not unusual. The barbarians in early medieval legend who produced the Hamlet story on which Shakespeare built his play are also quite unrelated to the sophisticated Renaissance prince created by Shakespeare. In 700 years, one would expect Greek drama to reflect its own time rather than that of Mycenae.

The truly exciting experience for

known, sometime around 1450 B.C. the palaces were destroyed; the Mycenaeans from mainland Greece established themselves on the island and absorbed many aspects of the culture. Certain island people have a central position in the myths developed in the following Homeric Age; in particular, the Palace of Knossos is believed to be the labyrinth in the tale of the Minotaur, because of its complex basement layout. Certainly there are enough connections between the subject matter in the Greek dramas of the fifth century and Cretan culture for theatre directors to base Greek plays on this culture when they wish to portray the sophisticated yet primitive sexuality and sensuality in Minoan art.

Figure 2–2 *The Warrior Vase*, from Mycenae, approximately 14″ high, c. 1200 B.C. Our one image of what the Mycenaean soldiers who went to reclaim Helen from Troy may have looked like in their skins, furs, and studded helmets. National Museum, Athens. Photo courtesy of the Hirmer Fotoarchiv, Munich.

twentieth-century interpreters of Greek plays is discovering how much primitive ritual these polished classical dramas do contain; in fact, recent productions have emphasized this primitivism. The primitive, barbaric atmosphere found in the Lion Gate and *The Warrior Vase* has been incorporated more and more into productions of the great classical dramas of the fifth century. Imagine on stage the figures in *The Warrior Vase* as a chorus of soldiers wearing studded helmets, leather tunics, animal skin capes, and heavy beards; what a different effect they would create from the classical draped figures usually associated with Golden Age Greek tragedy.

The Homeric epics were recorded in the Dark Ages after the Dorians swept down from the Balkans and destroyed the Mycenaean civilization. In this dark period, art returned to a simple, rigid, and controlled geometric pattern, and the tribal organization gradually grew into a tight system of aristocratic feudalism. Not until after 700 B.C., when urban life began to supplant this feudal peasant society, did geometric formalism diminish slowly and lead gradually to the brilliant awakening of Greek culture in the humanistic

glories of classical naturalism. The primitive and rigid art of the sixth and seventh centuries gradually became more sophisticated as the culture moved from aristocratic control toward a limited democracy. This period is usually known as the Archaic and extended from about 776–490 B.C.

Look at a statue from the end of this long period, *Kouros from Tenea,* dated about 510 B.C. (Figure 2–3). The striking thing is the loosening of the form from its previous rectangular geometric shape. The figure strikes a much more relaxed, free-standing pose, balanced easily and naturally on the balls of the feet, though there is still the severe, structured formality characteristic of most Doric Greek art during the Archaic period. There is also much attention to the tightly curled decorative formality of the hair and only a foreshadowing of the movement toward a unified simplicity of structure. The artist was, however, beginning to experiment with certain complex natural phenomena, and the work was beginning to derive from experiment and observation rather than from rules and regulations. Gradually, the intimate relationship between art and religion declined, with increasing emphasis on secular subject matter. No longer a means to an end, art was slowly becoming an end in itself. Art that had always been a tool of religion and the state, a means for influencing gods and men, was on the brink of an era in which it was practiced for its own sake—as an interpreter and imitator of nature in terms of line, color, rhythm, and harmony. Of course, at this same moment, the theatre developed from a storytelling ritual presented by a chorus into a new dramatic reality of human beings in conflict before the gods and with one another.

The Golden Age of classical Greece seems to have arrived too rapidly and abruptly to be believable. Within a period of fifty years, there developed an entirely new view of man and nature that perfectly balanced the formal and the natural, the real and the ideal. Undoubtedly spurred by the great sense of patriotism and national pride released after the Greek defeat of the great Persian Empire, the Golden Age came at a time in Athenian social and

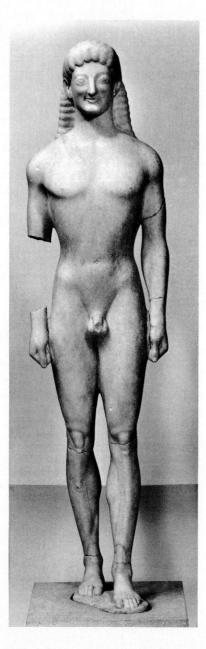

Figure 2–3 *Kouros from Tenea,* marble, approximately 5' high, c. 570 B.C. Illustrates the slowly awakening Greek Archaic interest in the natural proportions of the human body and retention of the Greek love of abstract structure and exactness of form. Staatliche Antikensammlungen, Munich. Photo courtesy of the Hirmer Fotoarchiv, Munich.

political development when there was a balance between the aristocratic structures of the past and the newer forces of democracy. For the first forty years of the fifth century, aristocratic conservatism still dominated and produced the so-called severe style in art and in the plays of Aeschylus.

One supreme example of this style is the famous *Poseidon (Zeus) of Cape Artemision,* dating from about 460 B.C. (Figure 2–4). Though alive, fully human, and strikingly natural in comparison to any late Archaic work, the statue still retains a severity, aloofness, and dignity that separates it from the more relaxed and graceful figures of the next sixty years. This is the austere image of a hero from a play by Aeschylus—a figure aloof from common society, larger than life in soul and personality and close to the gods in his thoughts and actions. The severe classic moment in Greek art encapsulates the style that is most appropriate for a production of the plays by Aeschylus. Compare this figure, for example, with *The Dying Niobid,* dated about 440 B.C., which depicts the moment before the death of Niobe's child from an arrow pierced in her

Figure 2–4 *Poseidon (Zeus) of Cape Artemision,* bronze, 6' 10" high, c. 460–450 B.C. Illustrates the transitional or severe classic style of the early fifth century and is one of the few images suggesting the character of classic Greek theatre masks. National Museum, Athens. Photo courtesy of the Hirmer Fotoarchiv, Munich.

back (Figure 2–5). The artist has broken from the restraints and aloofness of the severe style to create a perfect balance between motion and emotion, the individual and the ideal, the specific and the general. Here, for the first time, human suffering is eloquently expressed within a concept of noble restraint—the key to high classic art and to the dramatic method and style of the playwright Sophocles. There is a serenity and balance in the work of Sophocles, a humanity and lyric harmony, and a flexibility and relaxation that reflect the qualities found in high classic Greek art. *The Dying Niobid* could be a metaphor for the structure, mood, and emotions in *Antigone,* and represents the high classical style, which extended from about 460–410 B.C.

Since moments of full integration and balance in human nature and culture do not last, with the eruption of the Peloponnesian War came the doom of Periclean Athens. The serene idealism of the fifth century, with its balance of mind and matter, of man and the state, gave way to social and political unrest,

wars, skepticism, and cynicism. In art, theatricality and individuality replaced ideal beauty; by the time that Alexander the Great had spread Hellenic culture throughout the entire eastern Mediterranean and the Mideast, the ideals of moderation and balance were but memories. The period following the close of the Peloponnesian War is known as postclassical and extended from 410–146 B.C. The period following the death of Alexander the Great in 323 B.C. is known as Hellenistic.

Look at the statue of Mausolus, the king of a state in Asia Minor at the middle of the fourth century B.C. (Figure 2–6). It clearly

Figure 2–6 "Mausolus," from the mausoleum of Halicarnassus, marble, 9' 10" high, c. 359–351 B.C. A postclassical image of individualism, theatricality, and grandeur in which the clothing gives strength and weight but none of the beauty of draping found in fifth-century Greek sculpture. British Museum, London. Photo courtesy of the Hirmer Fotoarchiv, Munich.

Figure 2–5 *The Dying Niobid,* marble, 59" high, c. 450–440 B.C. Illustrates the high classical style of fifth-century Greece reflected in the plays of Sophocles. Museo delle Terme, Rome. Photo courtesy of Alinari, Florence.

projects a personal character rather than an abstract ideal. The treatment of the draperies is very realistic; they encase the body in robes of authority to create a theatrical effect and symbol of power rather than simply clothing the body in beautiful draperies.

The entire postclassical age to the time of Roman domination combined eclectic borrowings from the past, strong interest in individuality, and an emphasis on the emotional and theatrical. This was the age portrayed in the plays of Euripides, even though he died before it had really begun. By virtue of the number surviving, his plays were more easily understood and appreciated by the Hellenistic age than those of Aeschylus and Sophocles. They are realistic and often melodramatic, employing very individualized characters and exciting theatrical effects; they are the response of a skeptical and modern mind to the cynicism and materialism in a burgeoning mercantile world that had lost its national tradition and religious ideals. It is this culture that was then absorbed and reinterpreted by the Romans.

Life and Cultural Ideals

In some ways, life in Athens was as simple and disciplined as in Sparta; in other ways, it was zestful, exciting, fun-loving, and sometimes even frivolous. Athenians were accused by other Greeks of being unable to lead a quiet and restrained life, even though the record of banquets and parties emphasizes good talk and a leisurely evening of good company rather than roistering excess.

Greek children of the Golden Age were brought up at home in the charge of the mother and led a carefree life of play, amusement, and sport until their sixth year, when boys and girls were separated. The girls then remained at home, and the boys went off to school to become men. After the freedom of the nursery, the children were raised in a very strict manner. In daily classes, often held in the open air, the boys learned reading, writing, arithmetic, poetry, and music. Meanwhile, the girls were trained in the household arts by their mothers and their marriages arranged by the parents. They were expected to become dutiful wives; for example, when their husbands entertained, the women remained in their rooms on the second floor, anointing their bodies with sweet-smelling oils and staring distractedly out of the window until their husbands joined them for the night. Yet when the family was alone, there was great companionship and a true sense of family love and consideration.

During the day the center of activity was the marketplace with its mingled odors of animals, perfume, fish, produce, and humanity. It was crowded with little shops accented by a few large businesses in which a handful of slaves would be working side by side with the owner. No trade was frowned on as long as it did not demean the human spirit or interfere with participation in the great assembly of the city.

In the evening the Athenian came into his own at a banquet. The suppers like those Plato described at the house of Agathon, where lofty discourse was the major diversion, were characteristic of intellectuals; the dinner Xenophon described was much more the banquet of the ordinary Athenian gentleman. Reclining on couches, the guests gave full attention to the food until the drinking session that followed the meal began. The symposiarch, or leader of this session, was chosen by lot and took charge of the amount of water mixed with the wine. He also called in the entertainment of dancing girls and acrobats or musicians and selected individual guests to talk or perform. As the wine flowed more freely, a dancing girl might be chased about the room or auctioned off to a guest; someone might be challenged to give an oration; or riddles would be posed to challenge the befuddled wits of the guests. A wine-laden husband might not arrive home until the early hours of the morning, hammering on his door with the butt of his extinguished torch until his resigned wife let him in and put him to bed. These little insights into Greek life during the Golden Age of Athens are readily found in writings and vase paintings of the time.

Greek ornament had a simplicity and quiet formality not seen in other early cultures and a love of clear, bright-hued color. Many of the statues were polychromed; even the Parthenon had rich blue and gold color in the pediment, and clothing was richly colored with vegetable dyes.

In its early stages, Greek ornament was heavily dominated by oriental influences; the patterns were usually strongly geometric and sharply simplified. Gradually those motifs changed to purely geometric shapes and those representing natural or vegetable forms. The geometric forms used most frequently were the rosette, the key or fret motif, the *dentil*, the *guilloche*, and many arrangements of squares, diamonds, and stars. The natural forms that predominated were the egg and dart and the wave and meander. The vegetable or leaf forms included the acanthus, laurel, waterleaf, anthemion, ivy, and many medallions inspired by leaf forms. Sometimes birds and animals were used, but they were uncommon by classical times. Such ornament appeared in the entablatures in architecture, panel decoration in houses, and on the borders of clothing.

Unfortunately, there is little information about Greek interior decoration. More is

Ornament, Interiors, and Furniture

known about the interior of the Minoan Palace of Knossos than about the interior of classical Greek houses; but from vase painting, excavations, and later Hellenistic dwellings, one can guess about the general nature of interiors. Houses were built to look inward, receiving light from an inner courtyard open to the sky with rooms grouped around it. A peristyle of columns surrounded the court, and the chambers themselves were probably decorated like a vase painting with ornamental borders framing simple flat scenes of storytelling. Because of the importance given pottery, many functional and ornamental urns and vases would have been placed throughout the house. Reliefs of Greek furniture indicate that it had gracefully curved lines and beautiful proportions (Figure 2–8). Made of wood or bronze, chairs had curving backs and legs reminiscent of Empire furniture. Tables were small and low, beds were narrow with decorated headboards, and couches were low and richly equipped with mattresses and cushions. Like the Romans, the men reclined on these couches when dining. All Greek design had an exact balance, continuous rhythm, and striking simplicity; the union of the natural and relaxed with the structured and formal was complete.

Costume and Accessories

As we have already seen, the artificial silhouette, fitted lines, and exaggerated presentation of the female form in the *Snake Goddess* from the Minoan civilization (Figure 2–1) is completely unrelated to the costume of the Egyptians, Mesopotamians, Mycenaeans, or Archaic Greeks. Instead, the female dress reflects that playful artificiality associated with the term "Rococo," often used to characterize Minoan art. The male costume was evidently closer to the tunic forms of the Near East and to the loin cloths of the Egyptians but more artificial in silhouette, since the loin cloth pinched in the waist like a corset.

Minoan dress is so intriguing and so unlike the majority of the garments in the ancient world that directors and designers are frequently tempted to use Cretan costume in Greek tragedy. Its use here is usually ineffective, however, because the image projected is charming, whimsical artificiality, more appropriate in comedy than in serious drama. Minoan dress also represents an age and civilization so different from the later Greek that it usually distracts from the ideas projected in Greek drama.

Mycenaean dress, as seen from the soldiers on *The Warrior Vase* (Figure 2–2), was also quite different from Cretan dress or classical Greek costume. Though Mycenaeans borrowed from Minoan civilization, the clothing was harsh and barbaric in comparison. The leather, thongs, fringes, horns, and heavy metal in the clothing of the warriors clearly indicate an animalistic-physical emphasis. It is from this image that so many twentieth-century productions of the Greek tragedies, wishing to stress the primitive ritual beginnings of Greek drama, have taken their visual cue.

Because of the spread of Greek culture to Ionia during the centuries preceding the defeat of the Persians, Archaic Greek clothing resembled the tunic and shawl characteristics of Mesopotamian dress and its oriental-geometric border ornamentation. Like Greek art, however, it differed in its symmetrical, geometric, structured control of the costume line. The rectangular overfold on the Doric *chiton,* the narrow rectangular line to the body of the chiton, and the tight geometric border decoration emphasize the fact that the clothing was intended to frame and shape the movement of the body (Figure 2–7). Greek philosophy and culture had not yet developed to the point where the natural, relaxed grace of the body was allowed to balance this sense of structure and control.

By the beginning of the classical period, the change in clothing was striking—unlike the formalities in dress evident before. The most apparent change was the total emphasis on draping fabric softly over the body, thus eliminating control except at key spots where the fabric was pinned or caught in with a cord. This was accomplished by abandoning, at least during the high period of classical development, the sewing together of pieces of fabric. Sewing always tended to stiffen the fabric and to control its flow. Now the emphasis was on designing clothing so that the natural grace and controlled beauty of the body would project through the fabric and guide its line and

Figure 2–7 Section from the *Vase from Volci* by Exekias, sixth century B.C. Illustrates the rectangular, geometric form of Archaic Greek clothing before the stress on soft, supple draping began to dominate clothing at the beginning of the fifth century. The Etruscan-Gregorian Museum, Vatican City. Photo courtesy of the Vatican Museum, photograph by the Vatican Museums.

movement. In sculpture, this ideal developed to the point of the so-called wet draperies found on figures from the Parthenon. Regardless of whether the soft, almost transparent linen or woolen fabric of the chiton was actually wetted, it did achieve the ideal of showing the body as completely as possible through the garment without inhibiting or constricting it (Figure 2–8). Even the shorter chiton worn by the active younger man emphasized the beauty of the draped line and the perfect freedom of movement. The draped shawl or *himation,* worn by both men and women, afforded such easy and complete

Figure 2–8 *Grave Stele of Hegeso,* Dipylon Cemetery, Athens, marble, 59″ high, c. 410–400 B.C. Illustrates the liquid softness in the draping of the Greek chiton in the fifth century and the beauty of the furniture lines. Photo courtesy of the Hirmer Fotoarchiv, Munich.

control of fabric and movement that no one considered it a heavy encumbrance.

Compare for a moment the draped chiton on the seated woman in the *Grave Stele of Hegeso* with the draperies swathing the body of Mausolus (Figures 2–6 and 2–8). Besides the fact that one figure is a quiet female and the other a powerful male ruler, they differ in their portrayal of the chiton and himation. On the female, the fabric is draped delicately over the figure, creating a fluid effect that allows the grace and natural beauty of the body to show. In the statue of Mausolus, the draperies swathe the body, hiding its natural lines in the thick and twisted folds of fabric, and project an image of position and power. With the coming of the Hellenistic age, when strong contact was reestablished with the East, simplicity and beauty gave way to oriental embroidery, rich metallic decoration, and greater variety. Individuality and richness in dress were the rule; garments were once again cut and sewn into T-shaped tunic forms that were easier to wear, once again hiding the natural beauties of the human form. Greek classical dress emphasized every movement and gesture through constantly shifting fabric folds and strongly underlined the difference between movement and repose. It was simple, lucid, and beautiful. Hellenistic dress emphasized position, power, and individuality and complemented the mercantile capitalist culture of this later period.

Movement

Since there is no documentation, information about Greek body movement must be obtained from studying the human body in Greek art and the dress of the time. Thus one would assume that Minoan movement would have reflected the graceful serpentine lines of Cretan art, while the Mycenean interest in rough, harsh, and heavy artistic forms and animal textures would have led to a body movement projecting a powerful animal strength with little attempt at intellectual control. The movement in Archaic Greek times, on the other hand, must have stressed a great deal of formality and control, which was, of course, reinforced by the tight envelopment of the clothing.

As already mentioned, the movement ideal of classical Greece was beautiful and graceful and must have been the result of constant physical exercise, sports, and training in bodily control. From the vase paintings detailing the fierce competitive spirit of the Olympic Games, we can gain some idea of the strength, grace, suppleness, and vitality of the male body involved in all kinds of competitive feats of physical prowess. We can also see that the Greeks exercised nude since they were proud of their physically fit bodies. This is another reason why, during the fifth century B.C., Greek clothing was so easy to remove—unclasp a pin and the whole garment fell to the feet. Since the Greeks believed that the individual was always part of a larger whole or ideal of humanity, special characteristics in clothing and movement were always subordinate to the generalized ideal of the human form. All exercise and movement were undertaken to develop this sense of the ideal physical form. The static beauty of line and balance between individualism and a universal ideal found in sculpture and vase paintings was, in real life, turned into a smoothly graceful, nonexcessive series of actions and movements that gave a certain style and continuity to everything from moving a chair to eating a meal. This sense of style was not self-conscious because it developed from a way of life in which a beautiful body exhibiting beautiful movements was a cultural ideal. In the centuries following the Peloponnesian War, individualized movement, specialized dress, and a profusion of cultural ideals from the East mixed with the Greek ideals to produce the varied manners and customs prevalent in Hellenistic times.

The Theatre

The Hellenic theatre probably originated with the dances and songs performed in honor of the god Dionysus, though he may have been merely the presiding deity and not the inspiration. In his more primitive manifestations, Dionysus was a god of wine and procreation, the deity of orgiastic revels celebrating the good life. Later he became a more serious figure but lost his influence when choric storytelling developed toward more dramatic ends. Instead, the storytelling focused on legends about the heroes of the dark and misty beginnings of Greek culture when the gods spoke and interacted with man. Festival days were set aside each year for these dithyrambic or choric storytelling rituals; and in 534 B.C. the City Dionysia, or major play festival in the city of Athens, presented a tragedy contest. Supposedly, the dramatist–choral leader who won this first contest was an actor-dancer named Thespis. At this point in the development of the drama, a single actor took all the speaking parts, using a number of masks to make the changes clear. Later this expanded to three actors. The ritual chorus was the unifying factor in the action, since it was to it that the various characters, played by the single actor, spoke.

The theatres were originally circles for ritual dances usually located on a hill and surrounded on three-quarters of their circumferences by spectators. As the festivals became more a part of the official city government policy, the relationship of the orchestra, or central circular area, to the background and audience became more important; by the fifth century B.C., the official shape and arrangements of the Greek theatre were fully established. The orchestra remained the key area for the action dominated by the chorus; it was backed by a *skene* house that served three functions, namely, as a dressing room, as a background for entrances, and as the site of major climactic scenes; seating surrounded the orchestra on three sides and spread up the hillside to accommodate thousands of spectators.

Since the performances began at daybreak, members of the audience would come to their seats long before the first light of day. The citizens would often sit through three tragedies and a satyr play (a grotesque satire on a tragedy with the actors frequently disguised as animals); the entire proceedings were considered an essential part of a Greek education. The admission charge was refunded to playgoers who could not afford it, and they could even ask to be reimbursed for the day's wages lost due to watching a performance. During the drama festivals, all business was suspended in Athens; law courts were closed, prisoners were released from jail, and even women, barred from most public events, were allowed to watch the plays.

This relatively simple form of the Greek theatre did not continue into postclassical and

Hellenistic times. As the actors became more important than the playwrights and the chorus, the *skene* building became more prominent. It changed from one to two stories in height, acquired a raised upper platform for major scenes of conflict, and had a background accommodating more scenic effects. Moreover, the chorus and audience were almost completely separated from the actors. Originally, scenic changes were limited to those in the *skene* façade that transformed a palace into a temple or another dwelling. Gradually machinery, such as cranes and rolling platforms, was used to bring on gods, ghosts, and dead bodies. The three actors and the hired extras played in large padded robes or chitons with larger-than-life masks.

The wearing of masks instantly identified the character as old, young, happy, or sad; sometimes, the mask had different expressions on each side of the face so that an actor could establish a change of mood by merely shifting his head. In addition, the mouths of the masks were often shaped to aid voice projection. In the fifth century B.C., the masks were simple, idealized portrayals made of light-weight linen, cork, or wood; only in the later Hellenistic period did the exaggerated and melodramatic outsized masks so frequently recorded in stone become the standard wear in Greek tragedy. A comparison of the head of Zeus or Poseidon from the statue at Cape Artemision with a stone copy of a Hellenistic tragic mask illustrates the immense changes in mask design and performance that occurred between the fifth century and the Hellenistic age (Figures 2–4 and 2–9). We can only assume that the same development took place in the Greek actor's robe, or chiton. By Hellenistic times the theatrical robe was larger, covering much more of the actor's body than it did in the fifth century, though even then the theatrical robe was more expansive than the civilian chiton. Similarly, the famed raised shoes, or *cothurni*, worn by actors in tragedy were much more exaggerated in height and size than those worn in the fifth century.

Comedy demanded quite different ef-

Figure 2–9 Terracotta mask of old King Priam, third century B.C. Illustrates the melodramatic, excessively theatrical expressions used in masks for tragic actors in the Hellenistic period. Photo courtesy of the Staatliche Museum, Berlin.

fects. Developed later than tragedy, it was not granted a separate chorus or separate day for performance in the great City Dionysia of Athens until 487 B.C.; moreover, official state support did not come until about 442 B.C. The emphasis in comedy was on exaggerated and fantastic physical activity. Costumes were usually very tight, consisting of a short chiton and flesh-colored tights over padded legs and buttocks. This ludicrous effect was further emphasized by the phallus and fantastic masks, particularly those worn by the chorus that often depicted creatures like frogs, birds, or wasps. Always coupled with the exuberant fantasy and exaggerated action was a disciplined precision and grace like that in evidence in the vase painting on which the choral scene from Aristophanes' play *The Knights* is based (Figure 2–10).

Figure 2–10 Knights riding on men disguised as horses, from a black-figured vase, end of the sixth century, B.C. It is the basis for the chorus metaphor in Aristophanes' play *The Knights* and illustrates the imaginative physical humor found in the choruses in Old Comedy. Photo courtesy of the Staatliche Museum, Berlin.

Cithara and flutes accompanied comedy, along with clappers and tympana, and the typical dance was the licentious *kordax*. There are vase paintings showing this comic movement. In one, three men with grotesque faces, two of whom have bald heads, ass's ears, and protruding tongues, tilt forward on the tips of their toes while they kick their legs in a twirling dance and pull their clothes tightly over their padded bodies. Thus to understand the extant comedies of Aristophanes, one must keep in mind the rollicking and fantastic figures of the vase paintings, which symbolize the complex blend of sharp satire, uncouth character, indecency, and choric control found in the plays.

After Aristophanes' brilliance, Greek comedy gradually lost its fantastic exuberance and involvement with social, political, and philosophical problems. In the New Comedy that developed at the end of the fourth century B.C., the plays dealt with the domestic affairs of middle-class citizens. The chorus danced and sang at various intervals throughout the play but was not a central part of the action. The actors in New Comedy—whose leading playwright was Menander—retained masks with exaggerated character traits but lost the exuberant body padding and movement of Old Comedy. The comic slave, courtesan, pedant, boasting warrior, and miserly father were the stock characters in New Comedy, which became the basis for the Roman comic tradition that developed in the third century B.C.

The Plays

The classical Greek tragedy most frequently analyzed and used as a model against which to measure the other Greek tragedies is *Oedipus Rex*, since it was primarily on this play that Aristotle based his model for the perfect tragedy. The play represents Sophocles and Greek culture at that moment of transition between the severe and the high classic—between the *Poseidon (Zeus) of Cape Artemision* (Figure 2–4) and *The Dying Niobid* (Figure 2–5). One is struck by the complexity of the play and the utter simplicity of the plot. The events appear to be inevitable; the time on stage is actual time; and all the action takes place in a single location. Keeping the distilled rhythms in the myth on which the play is based, the playwright has merged them into a precise and very rational dramatic organization. The play is thus a perfect wedding of the Dionysian and Apollonian aspects of Greek culture. Its progress can be likened to a seasonal celebration of the hope and renewal of spring after the withering of winter. Yet the play can also be viewed as an exciting murder mystery in a simple and rationally perfected form; the playwright, like the visual artists of fifth-century Greece, leads his audience to a heightened sense of nature and its truths.

Sophocles is not interested in the character's looks, position, and background but in the psychological and ethical attributes that each carries in relation to the story. We know about them only what is absolutely essential to the forward movement of the plot, though they seem fully developed personalities. The play has a number of strong themes: that no man can escape the pain of life until he has come to its end; that man's vision is limited by fate or the will of the gods; and that to attempt to avoid this fate is to become deeply entangled with evil.

The language of the play is as spare, polished, and direct as its structure; the imagery, based on the central ideas in the drama, carries the action from reason to passion, from ritual symbol to natural fact, and from tragic poetry to simple prose with directness and ease. This variety offers the actor great histrionic possibilities. Also key to the play's power in performance are the choral passages, presented by the chorus to the accompaniment of music. The resulting rhythm is strong and insistent as it swings with the action from forward movement to backward-looking exposition. The choral interludes act as emotional punctuation deepening the mood and mysterious atmosphere that lies behind and beneath the surface of the play.

Greek music—under the protection of those imaginary daughters of Zeus, the muses—was considered an inseparable part of lyric poetry, tragic and comic drama, choral dancing, and song. Greek melodies and rhythms were developed by combining specific moods or modes—fixed tonal intervals on an octave created by adjusting the pitch of a tone (like the modern major and minor modes). These tonal modes or moods allowed poets and dramatists to underline and support a great variety of emotional effects for an audience. It is important to remember that the Athenian dramatists were responsible for the music, the training of the chorus, and the staging of the play as well as for the written script. It is also important to remember that the music in Euripides' plays differed considerably from that of Aeschylus and Sophocles. His "new" music was more ornate and complex and evidently demanded more highly skilled singers.

The visual demands in *Oedipus Rex* are sharply limited. The background is the palace; the costumes need project only the station of the individual and his nobility of character; the masks used need only indicate age and

personality and Oedipus' blindness. Visual variety should come primarily from the movement of the chorus in relation to the major characters in the drama and from the relationship of the audience to the play's action. The play was performed before thousands of spectators as a combination of performance and ritual; one should keep in mind that it was about sixty feet from the central acting area (the arena in front of the palace door) to the first row of seats. By relating this play to the visual arts of the time and to one's own experience of life as a mixture of the mysterious, irrational, and mythical with the rational, factual, and intellectual, the contemporary theatre person should be able to understand why *Oedipus Rex* and other Greek tragedies are still powerful works of theatrical art after twenty-five hundred years (Figure 2–11).

An excellent example of Old Comedy is Aristophanes' *The Birds*, a blend of fantasy, farce, and poetry. The plot revolves around the attempt of Euelpides and Pisthetaerus to establish a new way of life in the land of the birds—far removed from the pettiness of Athenian life. They urge the birds to claim sovereignty over the world and to build an enormous wall in mid-air so that none of man's foolish sacrifices can reach the sky. In the conclusion of this exuberant caricature of the schemes and ambitions of the City of Athens, even the gods are forced into submission.

Structurally, as in all Old Comedy, the play follows a pattern composed of a *prologue*, in which the happy idea is conceived; the *parados*, or entry of the chorus; the *agon*, or debate about the merit of the idea; the *parabasis*, a choral interlude directed at the audience with commentary on current events; a series of *episodes* in which the central comic idea is put into practice; and the *komos*, or conclusion of revelry and celebration. Compared to *Oedipus Rex*, the play is less unified; here the "happy idea" and the chorus, rather than a sequence of causally related ideas, give unity. Certainly the number of episodes demonstrating the results of the birds' establishing a new city could be increased or reduced without much effect

Figure 2–11 Scene from *Oedipus Rex* by Sophocles, produced by Tyrone Guthrie at the Stratford Shakespeare Festival, Stratford, Ontario, 1955. Production designed by Tanya Moiseiwitsch. Photo courtesy of the Stratford Festival, Canada.

on the play, but the built-in comic intensity is carefully planned, as is the balance between outrageous fantasy and detailed facts about contemporary affairs.

The characters are motivated primarily by selfishness and greed, and great emphasis is placed by the playwright on their physical attributes. Major characters are either well-to-do landowners or common men; Aristophanes goes to great lengths to make the audience feel superior to the characters, to make the audience believe they can make wiser and better choices than the characters do. By underlining the ludicrous decisions and fantastic actions of his characters, Aristophanes gives great weight to his moral belief in the conservative, traditional values in Athenian life, a theme prevalent in all his plays.

The language is a compound of personal invective, social satire, obscenity, and fantastic imagery. In translation, much of the savage wit and earthy exuberance is lost, and a modern audience cannot follow the topical allusions; but the physical action, extravagant costumes, and elaborate "sight gags" suggested by the script can make the comedy a great success in the contemporary theatre. Certainly the bird costumes offer a major opportunity for visual extravagance, and all kinds of marvelous comic effects can be achieved by the deft use of the chorus, lively music, and exuberant dancing. Like all the best of Aristophanes' works, the play celebrates the combination of instinctive with rational action (Figure 2–12). A contemporary production might substitute current political and social targets for Athenian ones and a modern visual metaphor for the chorus of birds (perhaps, a punk rock group?). It is essential that the play seem clever, witty, irreverent, and up-to-date.

Figure 2–12 Scene from *The Birds* by Aristophanes, produced by the San Francisco Actors' Workshop, 1964. Directed by Herbert Blau, designed by James Hart Stearns. Photo courtesy of Hank Kranzler.

Acting and Directing the Plays

In examining the problems faced by the actor, we should remember some of the original conventions in Greek tragedy and comedy. For example, in *Oedipus Rex*, all speaking roles were played by only three actors, with one probably portraying Oedipus; the second presenting Creon and the Messenger from Corinth; and the third (very busy changing masks and costumes) playing the Priest, Tiresias, Jocasta, the Herdsman, and the second Messenger. The first actor had to be the most powerful, while the third had to be the most versatile. In addition to these three, a number of supernumeraries were required for several scenes. Probably the two suppliants in the opening scene returned later as Ismene and Antigone, while others appeared later as servants and attendants. Finally, there was the chorus, which originally stood at fifteen, although obviously this number can be changed.

The physical actions specified in the play are few. These include kneeling, pouring sacrificial offerings, displaying outbursts of anger, and torturing the herdsman. All these rather impersonal and unindividualized actions—coupled with the use of masks and enlarged draped costumes—must have created an overall effect that was rather removed and abstract. One can assume that their impression was a majestic, flowing, and rhythmic one; gestures were simple, large, and based in the upper planes of the body; and the actors primarily faced the audience directly or stood in a three-quarter turn. In addition, they had limited physical contact with one another and almost never sat down. On the other hand, Greek classic tragedy when first performed was not the exaggerated, melodramatic, overly theatrical visual and physical presentation characteristic of Greek theatre after the close of the fifth century B.C. The acting of the Greek Golden Age must have been both real and abstract, emotional and yet reserved, exciting yet controlled—all attributes of the balance that was the Greek ideal of the time.

In looking back to fifth-century Greece to gain a personal visceral sense of what acting Greek tragedy must have been like, the student of theatre should keep several things in mind: first of all, there was the impact of size. When the actor stood in front of the *skene*, he was approximately sixty feet from the first row of seats. Despite the perfection of the theatre acoustics, the size of a performance was very important. Second, there was a vast amount of open space in front of the *skene*. The human body in action dominated this area in front of the *skene* and the orchestra; a close proximity and intimacy between characters must have been rare. Third, because of the outdoor setting of trees and hills for walls and the heavens for a roof, the actor would have always been an accent within the mysteries and grandeur of nature. Finally, there was the language—musical, formal, mysterious, dignified, and grand—that magnified and or-chestrated the action and emotions without losing touch with the truth of human feeling.

As far as Old Comedy is concerned, the acting emphasized—besides the physical and the ridiculous—many details from everyday life: eating, sleeping, taking a bath, snoring, lighting lamps, and making out account books. This is not to say the comedy was realistic; its required exaggerations made it, in many ways, as abstract as tragedy but in a different way. Comedy stressed acrobatic, physical actions, much bodily contact, a great sense of fantastic invention, rapid and shifting pace, and an expanding exuberance of rhythm. In many ways the acting requirements were the exact opposite of those required in Greek tragedy.

Designing the Plays

The first decision that a designer faces with the director in a production of *Oedipus Rex* is whether to emphasize the rational or irrational elements in the play. Given the choice today between the classical restraint and formality of the play's structure and the ritualistic, violent, primitive aspects of the myths on which the script is based, most modern directors would choose the latter. Rather than suggesting a completely formal palace of smooth textures and balanced forms, the contemporary English-speaking director and designer will more often choose rough textures, broken forms, muted colors, and exaggerated—even grotesque—effects in masks or makeup to stress the primitive, ritual background of the drama. In other words, the Lion Gate of Mycenae would become a better artistic image for the designer than would the classical temples of the fifth century. Occasionally in France and West Germany, where cool, intellectual, classical productions are admired, a designer might use modern visual effects equivalent to the mature classical style of mid-fifth-century Greek art.

A designer could achieve a balance between the rational and the irrational elements found in the script. By arranging symmetrically the space for the play's action, with the palace squarely placed behind the chorus, and by choreographing the choral movements in balanced patterns, the designer and director could lay the groundwork in rational values. Against this they could play the mysterious, primitive, ceremonial elements in the drama through the choice of masks, fabric textures, and floor and wall surfaces. If masks cannot be used because of the closeness of the actors to the audience, the makeup could be heightened to project the symbolic qualities of a mask. If masks are used, they should reflect that balance of form and underlying expression found in fifth-century Greek statuary (Figure 2–4). To use masks that are too melodramatic and theatrical (as were some of those in the famed Stratford, Ontario, production of 1955) is to lose some of the subtlety and depth found in Greek tragedy, particularly in the plays of Sophocles (Figure 2–11).

Since the robes worn by Greek actors and members of the chorus completely covered their bodies—to allow three actors to play all the roles and to give a symbolic, larger-than-life look to the human figure—there is merit in retaining this visual effect in contemporary production. By concentrating the attention of the audience on the mask and the movement of the body under the soft, heavy, draped lines of the robe, audience response will be less to the tactile, human, and natural, and more to the ethical, ideal, and ritualistic. In Greek art, color, although bright, was simple, direct, and usually subordinate to line, shape, and texture. Thus, the costume designs for a production of *Oedipus Rex* should probably be in a limited range of color, with a strong use of neutrals and metallic accents. In this way color will give unity and atmosphere, rather than the pictorial illustration of story and character, and will allow for the strong three-dimensional lighting of the masks and the stage movement.

In the use of ornament a balance should be struck between flat patterns that might appear in costume borders and the raised, three-dimensional patterns in pins, brooches, belts, and tiaras. Raised ornament gives strength, punctuation, and focus to the various parts of the costume.

The visual design for *Oedipus Rex* will, then, be both ritualistic and mysterious, formal and natural. The challenge is to create a production with an appropriate tension: the ritualistic and formal aspects of the legend with the natural and deeply human psychological reality of the character relationships. Simple, symmetrical, richly textured settings, severe masks, and heavy, draped costumes are the most direct means for achieving this balance.

PROJECTS AND PROBLEMS

1. Approximate a costume having the basic lines of that worn by the Minoan snake goddess (Figure 2–1) and then model it, imagining that you are standing within the loggia from the Palace of Knossos. Describe how you feel.

2. Why are Minoan art and costume so different from, and yet similar to, Egyptian and Mesopotamian art and costume?

3. Select a Greek tragedy that might employ a Cretan-Minoan costume and background and describe how you would use them in the play.

4. Using Mycenaean sources, devise a production scheme for *Agamemnon* that includes lighting effects.

5. What are the differences and similarities among the Archaic Greek Kouros (Figure 2–3), the Pharaoh Chefren (Figure 1–7), and the Assyrian King Ashurbanipal II (Figure 1–8)? Describe the feeling each gives.

6. Why do Golden Age drama and art represent a perfect balance between aristocratic organization and democratic individualism?

7. What happened to art and culture in Greece between the sculpting of the Archaic Kouros (Figure 2–3) and the famous *Poseidon (Zeus) of Cape Artemision* (Figure 2–4)?

8. After studying the *Poseidon (Zeus) of Cape Artemision* (Figure 2–4), what would you say were the great virtues of Golden Age Greek art? What were its drawbacks?

9. What is meant by the opposing Apollon-ian and Dionysian tendencies in Golden Age Greek drama?

10. What difference in outlook do the *Poseidon (Zeus) of Cape Artemision* (Figure 2–4) and *The Dying Niobid* (Figure 2–5) convey?

11. What change in human and cultural outlook occurred between the creation of the *Poseidon (Zeus) of Cape Artemision* (Figure 2–4) and the statue of Mausolus (Figure 2–6)?

12. Imagine yourself sitting on Greek furniture (Figure 2–8). How do you feel? What does it do to the body? How comfortable is it?

13. What amazing change in clothing has taken place between the development of the Archaic Greek chiton (Figure 2–7) and the classical chiton (Figure 2–8)?

14. Construct rough approximations of Archaic and classical chitons. Put each on and then describe the difference in feeling and body movement each conveys.

15. What is the difference in feeling and effect between classical draping (Figure 2–8) and Hellenistic draping (Figure 2–6)?

16. Briefly describe the layout of classical Greek theatre.

17. Draw a diagram of the area in front of the *skene*, including the orchestra, to gain some sense of the size and space relationships of classical Greek theatre.

18. Based on a comparison of the head of *Poseidon (Zeus) of Cape Artemision* (Figure 2–4) with

the Hellenistic tragic mask (Figure 2–9), what seems to have happened to Greek acting and to the tone of the performance?

19. In Aristophanes' play *The Knights,* how closely do the demands on the chorus approximate the portrayal of knights riding men as horses in the vase painting from the sixth century B.C. (Figure 2–10)? What other similar comic visual effects might be used for a play similar in concept to *The Knights?*

20. Summarize the use of the chorus in Greek tragedy and comedy.

21. Why does the playwright begin his story of Oedipus just before its resolution?

22. What is meant when a director takes a Dionysian approach to *Oedipus Rex?* An Apollonian approach?

23. Draw or sculpt in clay two masks for Oedipus to wear during the course of the tragedy. What factors should be considered in making these masks?

24. What factors must be considered in designing costumes for the tragedy? How large will they be? Will the actors wear cothurni?

25. What modern analogies and visual sources can be used for a contemporary production of *The Birds* that will retain the original tone of the play?

26. How do you think the original bird costumes for the chorus were designed? How would you design them today?

27. Recite Agamemnon's opening speech in *The Agamemnon,* imagining that you are in a Greek theatre. What vocal and physical problems are created by the theatre's size and shape?

28. Act a scene from a Greek play with another actor, first standing fairly close to the other person and then farther apart. Why is it more effective to stand farther apart?

29. First study a number of good colored photos of the ruins of Greek theatres and then do a speech from a Greek play trying to feel and visualize the full effect of performing in these theatres.

30. Play a scene from a Greek play in a mask. What is the effect? Try a scene with another actor also in a mask. How do the masks affect the way the two of you relate? How do they affect your vision, projection, and facial expression? How do they help you in acting?

BIBLIOGRAPHY

Arnott, Peter D. *An Introduction to the Greek Theatre.* London: Macmillan, 1959. A very good basic introductory work on all aspects of classical Greek and Hellenistic Greek theatre.

Berve, H.; Gruben, G.; and Hirmer, Max. *Greek Temples, Theatres, and Shrines.* New York: Abrams, 1962. A very thorough look at the religious and theatrical architecture of ancient Greece.

Bieber, Margarete. *The History of the Greek and Roman Theatre.* 2nd ed. Princeton, N.J.: Princeton University Press, 1961. The most comprehensively illustrated work in English on the nature of the classical theatre.

Bowra, C. M. *Classical Greece.* The Great Ages of Man Series. New York: Time-Life Books, 1965. A concise text covering the major artistic, cultural, and cultural developments from Archaic Greek through Hellenistic times. Explains classical Greece to the nonacademic reader; beautifully illustrated with extensive color photography.

Brooke, Iris. *Costume in Greek Classical Drama.* New York: Theatre Arts, 1961. A very useful book with clear line drawings of costume in the Greek theatre.

Carpenter, Rhys. *The Esthetic Basis of Greek Art of the Fifth and Fourth Centuries B.C.* Rev. ed. Bloomington: Indiana University Press, 1965. A very interesting and illuminating discussion of the aesthetic principles behind the development of art in classical and postclassical times.

Demargne, Pierre. *The Origins of Greek Art.* Translated by Stuart Gilbert and James Emmons. New York: Golden Press, 1964. A very useful book that explains how classical Greek art developed.

Hamilton, Edith. *The Greek Way.* New York: W. W. Norton, 1952. An excellent introduction to all aspects of Greek life and culture.

Harsh, Philip W. A. *A Handbook of Classical Greek Drama.* Stanford, Calif.: Stanford University Press, 1941. A very useful reference book on classical drama.

Higgins, Reynold. *Minoan and Mycenaean Art.* New

York: Praeger, 1967. A well-illustrated explanation of the nature and development of art in Crete and mainland Greece before 1000 B.C.

Hildebrand, Alice, ed. *Greek Culture.* The Cultures of Mankind Series. New York: Braziller, 1966. An excellent compilation of writings from original Greek sources on the nature of the Greek cultural outlook.

Houston, Mary G. *Ancient Greek, Roman, and Byzantine Costume and Decoration.* 2nd ed. London: A. & C. Black, 1959. An excellent technical explanation of the cut and drape of Greek clothing with a few color plates and over 250 line drawings.

Jaeger, Werner. *Paideia: The Ideals of Greek Culture.* 3 vols. Translated by Gilbert Highet. New York: Oxford University Press, 1939–1944. A comprehensive look at all aspects of Greek culture during the late Archaic, classical, and postclassical periods.

Lawrence, Arnold W. *Classical Sculpture.* London: Cape, 1929. One of the best studies of classical Greek sculpture.

———. *Greek Architecture.* Pelican History of Art Series. Baltimore: Penguin Books, 1957. A very comprehensive study on the nature of ancient Greek architecture.

Pfuhl, Ernst. *Masterpieces of Greek Drawing and Painting.* Translated by Sir John Beazley. New York: Macmillan, 1955. A very detailed look at the surviving paintings and drawings of the ancient Greeks with commentary on many masterpieces that did not survive.

Pollitt, J. J. *The Art of Greece.* Englewood Cliffs, N.J.: Prentice-Hall, 1965. A compendium of sources and documents from the past that give information and insight into Greek art.

Richter, Gisela. *A Handbook of Greek Art.* 2nd rev. ed. London: Phaidon, 1960. A very useful reference on all phases of Greek art.

Robertson, M., and Frantz, A. *The Parthenon Frieze.* New York: Oxford University Press, 1975. An excellent book from which to gain a sense of the visual and cultural ideals of high classic Greek art.

Strong, Donald. *The Classical World.* Landmarks of the World's Art Series. New York: McGraw-Hill, 1965. Deals with Greek art from the early Minoan period to the Roman conquest; beautifully illustrated with many color plates.

Taplin, O. P. *Greek Tragedy in Action.* Berkeley, Calif.: University of California Press, 1979. A recent book that is very useful for studying Greek tragedy for production.

Webster, T. B. L. *Greek Theatre Production.* 2nd ed. New York: Barnes and Noble, 1971. A readable, comprehensive overview of Greek theatre and its production methods by one of the finest classical scholars of recent times.

Roman Style

The melodramatic and overly theatrical qualities of Hellenistic art gradually merged into Roman art by the second century B.C. when the great city on the banks of the Tiber began to dominate the eastern Mediterranean world. After throwing off Etruscan dominance and establishing an oligarchic republic that stressed discipline and military valor, Rome expanded rapidly and eventually dominated the entire Mediterranean world. As Rome grew, the framework of the original city-state administration became inadequate for ruling a vast empire; after bitter warfare and several temporary dictatorships, Julius Caesar became "perpetual dictator," and his grandnephew Octavian later assumed absolute imperial powers as Augustus Caesar.

During the Augustan Age, Roman culture and art were still highly influenced by Greek art, particularly that of Hellenistic times. Gradually, however, during the reigns of the Flavian emperors, the specialized Roman characteristics in the culture gained the upper hand.

A comparison of the Greek Parthenon with the Roman Colosseum brilliantly illustrates the differences between Roman and Greek style (Figures 3–1 and 3–2). In the Parthenon, a great monument to the perfected balance of the high classic style of the fifth century B.C., the refinements made on earlier Archaic temples reach the peak of perfection. The many slight alterations in the proportions and in the horizontal and vertical forces create an even greater sense of beauty and perfection. The vertical and horizontal forces are in equal balance, creating a sense of majesty, simplicity, and complete unity. Everything about the Parthenon has an austere, balanced grace. The Roman Colosseum, completed in Rome over 500 years later in A.D. 80, creates a sharp and instructive contrast. This great amphitheater for gladiatorial games symbolizes Rome's interest in power, strength, and display. Unlike the Greeks, the imperial Romans placed more emphasis on entertainment and high living than on matters of

Figure 3–1 Model of the Parthenon in Athens, 447–432 B.C. The finest example of Greek classical architecture, which balances highly subtle and sophisticated proportions with very simple and natural forms. Photo courtesy of the Metropolitan Museum of Art, purchase, 1890, Levi Hale Willard Bequest.

Figure 3–2 The Colosseum, Rome, A.D. 72–80. Illustrates the great size of imperial Roman public architecture and the complex technical skill of Roman architects in their use of a round arch, barrel vault, and concrete construction faced in stone. Photo courtesy of Alinari, Florence.

religion and abstract beauty; and in every way, Roman public buildings exhibit this interest. The Roman Colosseum is also a tribute to Roman inventiveness in engineering; this great arena is as much an engineering feat as it is a piece of architecture. The Romans were above all pragmatic and practical. They perfected concrete, vaulted construction to the point that they could construct buildings, bridges, amphitheaters, and viaducts of tremendous size and utility. In the Colosseum, one can see the piled-up layers of arches and the marshaled ring of tunnels that give more spatial variety and flexibility than were ever conceived by the Greeks with their limited post and lintel system. What remains Greek are the architectural orders (Doric, Ionic, and Corinthian), which are applied here as mere decoration.

In many ways, the best statement of the Roman outlook and its development through the centuries can be found in Roman sculptural busts. Compare the famous bronze *Portrait of a Bearded Man* (commonly called Brutus) of the Republican period with the head of Trajan Decius, dated about A.D. 250 (Figures 3–3 and 3–4). In the "Brutus," the typical Roman interest in individual personality (as opposed to the idealizing of the Greeks) is coupled with all the Republican virtues— strength, discipline, formality, and toughness of character. Brutus is both a specific person and an embodiment of the ideal Republican Roman virtues. In contrast, the bust of Trajan Decius exhibits not only an individualized realism but also the tensions and worries of a ruler facing the decline of the empire. The stylistic point here is that throughout Roman artistic history the Roman artist was a master of illusionistic realism; in his depiction of Romans he did not hesitate to use ugliness and beauty to attain his effects.

With the decline of the Roman Empire

Figure 3–4 *The Emperor Trajan Decius,* marble, life size, C. A.D. 250. The perplexities of the emperor symbolize those of Rome during this period of gradual cultural and political decline. Photo courtesy of Alinari, Florence.

Figure 3–3 *Portrait of a Bearded Man* ("Brutus"), bronze, 12⅝" high, c. second century B.C. Illustrates the stoic, disciplined realism emphasized by portrait sculptors during the Roman Republican period. Conservatori Museum, Rome. Photo courtesy of Alinari, Florence.

and the acceptance of Christianity as the state religion also came the decline of illusionistic realism. In Trajan Decius (Figure 3–4) there is still an interest in the struggles and spiritual problems of the inner man, but in *Constantine the Great,* dating from about 324 to 330, illusionism has been abandoned (Figure 3–5). Constantine, who accepted Christianity as the Roman state religion, saw himself as an embodiment of both spiritual and temporal power. With the rise of Christianity, interest in nature gave way to an interest in the spiritual and the symbolic; the artist who created the head of Constantine was not interested in how Constantine actually looked but in presenting an awesome image of his godlike attributes and imperial power. An actor could easily identify with, and play, Brutus or Trajan Decius but not Constantine. From this point on, illusionism and naturalism declined as a style and were not fully revived until the Renaissance.

Figure 3–5 *Constantine the Great,* marble, 8' high, early fourth century A.D. Illustrates the abandonment of illusionism in favor of awesome size, grandeur, and mystical power in imperial portrait busts after the Roman conversion to Christianity in the early years of the fourth century. Photo courtesy of Alinari, Florence.

Life and Cultural Ideals

The life of a Roman gentleman during the Empire period was very similar to the aristocratic world of a Boston Brahmin at the beginning of the twentieth century. The Roman supported charities, managed a large household staff, involved himself in business affairs and politics, attended artistic and literary events, patronized the arts, and (in his grandly draped toga) gave important speeches before legal or political gatherings. In the summer he retired from the city to a country retreat. Pliny gives us a beautiful description of how a Roman gentleman spent his leisure time:

I wake when I please, generally at dawn, often earlier, rarely later, I don't open the shutters, in the stillness and darkness being wonderfully removed from distractions. . . . I concentrate on what work I have on hand . . . then call my secretary and, letting in the daylight, dictate what I have composed. . . .

About the fourth or fifth hours [8:30–10:30 A.M.] . . . I go to either the terrace or the covered portico, depending on the weather, think out and dictate the rest. Then into my carriage, to continue concentrating just as when lying abed or walking, . . . a short siesta, then a walk, and then I recite aloud a speech in Latin or Greek clearly and with emphasis, not so much for the sake of my voice as my digestion, though of course both are equally strengthened. Another walk, a rub-down with oil, exercise, and a bath. If I dine with my wife or a few people, we have a book read to us. After dinner, reading of a comedy or music. Then a walk about with my staff, some of whom are learned men. And so we pass the evening chattering on various topics. . . . Friends dropping in from nearby towns take up part of my day; at times, when I am feeling tired, the interruption is welcome and helps. Occasionally I go hunting—but with pen in hand, so that I come back with something even when I have bagged nothing!

The life of an ordinary citizen and his wife was somewhat different, however, from that of the cultural and intellectual elite. A variety of sources give us the following outline of a day's activities. The master of the house had a very simple morning toilette. Having slept in his underclothes—a sleeveless tunic and loin cloth—he dashed some cold water over his face, donned his sandals and outer tunic and also a toga if his morning were to include a visit to the Senate or law courts. His valet, who was a quick-witted slave, helped him with the complex folds of his toga and brought him a bite of breakfast. His wife's toilette was more complicated. Having slept in her own room, also in underclothes composed of loin cloth, brassiere, and shift, she needed to allow a good amount of time for her *ornatrix*, or slave, to do her hair. The slave girl also helped her with makeup—chalk or white lead on the brow, ashes or powdered antimony on the eyelids, and red lead or various plant dyes for the cheeks and lips. The lady then put on a *stola* draped with a *palla* before spending the early part of the morning giving instructions to the servants and the later part receiving formal callers. Housekeeping was not a problem as there were no rugs, relatively little furniture, and mosaic floors were easily washed.

By 9:00 A.M. in winter and 7:00 A.M. in summer, the master was pleading a case before the courts, making a speech in the Senate, dictating correspondence to a secretary, or consulting with an accountant about taxes and rents. By noon the day's work was done, and the master joined his wife for a light lunch, took a nap, possibly visited the barber's for a shave and gossip, and then headed for the great public baths. Here, he lifted weights, played a form of hand ball, or pushed a medicine ball around to develop strength. He also had an oil massage and what we now call a Turkish bath. Then the master went home to dress for dinner in a lighter and brighter tunic. His wife, who had been involved in correspondence, social calls, or a visit to the marketplace, also returned home to don a grander *stola* for evening. Dinner, served to them while they reclined on couches, was a leisurely affair lasting well into the evening. It was accompanied by reading or musical entertainment and followed by a stroll into the garden, during which the master and his wife and a guest or two talked while passing through the peristyle, a colonnaded court.

Workmen and shopkeepers put in a very different day with very long hours. Most shops opened at 7:00 A.M. and did not close until dusk. There was no official day of rest, though there were many official holidays. All the bureaucrats (secretaries, cashiers, bookkeepers, and those who handled the paperwork of government administration) were slaves. Even the bank managers who handled the finances of noble Roman citizens were usually slaves, and, of course, all menial labor was done by the large slave population.

Most of the Roman population lived in cramped apartments spread over five stories; since there was no public transport, all people had to walk to get from one part of the city to another. Rome did have, however, a good water supply, a relatively good sanitation system, a quite adequate method of food distribution, well-organized police and fire protection, and (in addition to the public baths already mentioned) a full range of recreation and entertainment from the theatres to the great circuses and amphitheatres.

Ornament, Interiors, and Furniture

The typical Roman house was the atrium type, flush on the street, with entry through a narrow doorway into a vestibule opening into an atrium. The atrium had an opening in the ceiling and a pool below to collect the water. Along the sides were small rooms and behind them was the *tablinum* in which the busts of the family were kept. The tablinum could be shut off from the atrium or left open into a peristyle, containing fountains and a garden, around which were arranged the family's private apartments. At the far back, there was sometimes a vegetable garden or small orchard; along the street sides of the house were the shops. The entire arrangement thus faced inward but was full of light and air from the open courts. With the atrium and tablinum fully opened, one gained a charming view of gardens, fountains, statues, mosaics, and brightly covered walls. Since the Romans placed great emphasis on the family, their houses had an almost religious character testifying to their sacred feeling for home and family.

As for ornament, the Roman interest was in rich decoration that relegated the more severe and restrained Greek ornament to lesser architectural functions. Although rich and showy, Roman ornament kept within organized boundaries.

Other pictorial ornamental schemes were often found on the walls of wealthy Roman houses. For example, look at a bedchamber from Villa Boscoreale near Pompeii that has been reconstructed at the New York Metropolitan Museum of Art (Figure 3–6). One can see the love of rich color, the combination of marble mosaic and painting, and how the wall paintings make the room seem larger by carrying the eye outside and beyond the wall in an elaborate perspective. Clarity and organization are achieved by the painted columns

Figure 3–6 Reconstructed *cubiculum,* or bedroom, from Villa Boscoreale near Pompeii, first century B.C. Contains a couch and footstool with bone carvings and glass inlay, part of a mosaic pavement, and reconstructed fresco wall panels. Photo courtesy of the Metropolitan Museum of Art.

or pilasters that frame the pictures, and the favorite column capital is the Corinthian one because of its decorative richness. The furniture is sparse, limited to a bed, table, washstand, and chamber pots. Here the bed is made of wood with glass inlays and legs of bone, and it would have been covered with wool or linen mattresses and a blanket or two. It certainly does not look very comfortable; in fact, all Roman furniture seems shaped and decorated for visual effect and not for comfort. On stage the overall effect of this chamber would be quite gaudy in its use of color and very busy in its use of decorative and pictorial ornamentation. The only sense of the classical comes from the strong vertical and horizontal structuring of the walls and floor. This fact serves to remind us that the Romans were anything but colorless, severe figures interested only in politics and power.

Costume and Accessories

At first glance, many Roman costumes look like those worn by the Greeks, and certainly Greek costume ideals did have a strong influence on Roman dress. As in their architecture and sculpture, however, the Romans were more interested in grandeur and power on the one hand and in variety and comfort on the other than they were in perfect grace and ideal beauty. The costume thus had the superficially classical draped lines of Greek dress but not its simplicity, subtlety, and beauty. The female dress was closest to the Greek: the *chiton* became the *tunica*, over which was worn a second tunic or *stola* and then a cloak, or *palla*, derived from the Greek *himation*. The head was covered by this cloak or by a veil. Unlike her Greek counterpart, who never wore more than two garments, the Roman lady would have worn three or four layers. Underneath her light tunica, the Roman woman wore a scarf or band to support her breasts; on her feet, a pair of sandals. She girdled her garments below the breasts with rich cording or jewelled bands. The material was either finely woven wool or a mixture of wool and silk, but silk was very costly since it had to be imported from China.

The variety and grandeur of the Roman matron's coiffure illustrate the real difference between Greek and Roman dress. Here we have decoration, grandeur, variety, individual taste, and a pure sense of personal display (Figures 3–7 and 3–8). Ovid commented, "I cannot keep track of fashion. Every day, so it seems, brings in a different style." Certainly, we know that Roman women were adept with curling irons, hairnets, dyes,

Figure 3–7 *Antonia, Wife of Drusus,* marble, life size, first to second century A.D. Illustrates the complex coiffures and simple, draped garments of the upper-class Roman lady. Museo Nazionale, Naples. Photo courtesy of Alinari, Florence.

circular in shape, was worn over the tunica, the Roman male version of the Greek chiton. It was folded in half before being placed on the left shoulder. In front, the material reached to the ankles, while in back, the material was passed around the back, under the right arm,

Figure 3–8 *Giulia, Wife of the Emperor Titus,* marble, life size, c. A.D. 90. Illustrates the rich complex coiffures that create a diadem of decorative effect above the face. Capitoline Museum, Rome. Photo courtesy of Alinari, Florence.

switches, and hairpins; occasionally, dark Latin ladies clipped the blonde tresses of captured German slave girls and made them into wigs. The Roman love of display has no better testimony than the various women's hairdos popular during the Roman Empire period.

Male fashion was, of course, dominated by the *toga,* that masterpiece of draped grandeur that became the symbol of Roman authority and power and remained such long after this power had disappeared. Neither before nor since Roman times has such a magnificently imposing and complicated garment been created from a single piece of material without cutting it or fastening it with pins or buckles. The material was usually white wool, though other colors were used for certain ceremonial occasions. The toga, basically semi-

Figure 3–9 *The Emperor Tiberius,* marble, life size, third century A.D. Illustrates the size, suppleness, and draping line of the Roman toga as it was worn over the simple tunic. The Louvre, Paris. Courtesy of the French Musées Nationaux, photograph by Chuzeville.

across the chest, and once more over the left shoulder or arm, from which the second loose end hung down. Sometimes the overfold across the back and under the right arm was pulled over the head for protection or for ceremonial wear, and the material hanging down the front left side could be pulled up and over the folds crossing the chest to form a pocket in which a purse or a hand could rest. In imperial times this toga became even larger and elliptical in shape—four to five yards long and about three yards wide—a truly monumental garment that demanded that the left arm always be extended above the waist and that a dignified stance be maintained at all times. The togas of senators (and later knights) were bordered in Tyrian purple. The emperor's toga eventually was made of silk with rich and ornamental patterns in purple and gold. It was worn over several layers of tunics, the most important of which was the decorated, wide-sleeved *tunica dalmatica* that remained the tunic for imperial coronations down to the sixteenth century.

The toga, a symbol to the Romans of their citizenship, was worn for all public occasions; but for travel, home wear, and private occasions, the tunica could be worn in conjunction with a variety of simple cloaks. The most important was the *pallium* derived from the Greek himation. It was this cloak that was worn by Christ and the apostles and that one sees on so many statues of saints in the Roman Catholic and Orthodox Greek churches.

As with architecture, the emphasis on dress changed from a restrained and simple Republican soberness and dignity, strongly influenced by the Greeks, to an almost oriental preoccupation with richness and luxury in the later Empire. In general, Roman costume was always heavier, more layered, and more complicated than the Greek and frequently had more fabric, like the voluminous toga. In addition, more decoration was involved, and the dominant draped line inherited from the Greeks was used and developed more for display than for grace and simple beauty (Figure 3–9).

Movement

Since most clothing was not constricting, body movement was easy, relaxed, and dignified but lacking the subtle grace and elegance found in the Greeks. Salutations were made by extending the right arm at full length at the shoulder level or by extending the arm above the head in what we now call a fascist salute. Close friends greeted by clasping each other's elbows rather than by the embracing of modern Italy. When they dined, both men and women draped themselves over a couch, similar in shape to a modern chaise longue, with their feet up, and supported themselves by pillows or by their elbows. Even when sitting, the Romans tended to recline into the curved back of the chair. A modern actor can learn most about Roman movement by studying reproductions of the furniture and by actually wearing facsimile garments.

The Theatre

Roman theatre was adapted in many respects from the Hellenistic Greek theatre. For example, much in the comedies of Plautus and Terence, who wrote at the same time as the playwrights of Greek New Comedy, is borrowed from Menander. The Romans were rather late, however, to develop a full-fledged architectural adaptation in solid masonry of the Hellenistic Greek theatres. The comedies of Plautus and Terence were performed on long, narrow, temporary, wooden platforms bounded by a makeshift stage house at the back and sides; three doors in the back wall served as entrances to the characters' houses. Although costumes varied with the type of play, those worn in the plays of Plautus and Terence were close to those worn in Greek New Comedy. The clothes were realistic but very padded and exaggerated. There is some evidence that colors and costumes were standardized with certain colors and lines used to signify specific characters or occupations. The standardization carried over to masks and wigs so that it was possible to double parts and to create identical twins as in *The Menaechmi*.

As in Greece, the grand and permanent theatre structures were built after the best Roman drama had already been written. The first permanent theatre at Pompeii was dedicated about 75 B.C., the first in Rome about 55 B.C. Unlike the Greek theatre usually built into a hillside, the Roman theatre was built up from level ground; and the stage and auditorium were a single architectural unit, uniform in height. The orchestra was a half circle, with the front of the stage set on its diameter. The stage was about five feet above this orchestra. The seating radiated out from the circumference and typically accommodated between 10,000 and 15,000 spectators. The central part of this seating area was frequently covered by an awning.

The acting area was about 120 feet in length and about 20 feet in depth and had a permanent architectural background that was lavishly ornamented and of great height. It was penetrated by three doors and usually by another door at each end of the stage. A curtain was often dropped into a slot at the front of the stage at the beginning of a performance and raised at the end, and the stage also had a partial roof that protected the elaborate *scaenae frons* at the rear of the stage (Figure 3–10).

Figure 3–10 Reconstruction of the theatre at Ostia, 30–12 B.C. Illustrates the size, grandeur, and height of a typical Roman theatre with its central door, raised stage, and semicircular orchestra. From d'Espouy, *Fragments d'Architecture Antique*, vol. I, 1901.

The costumes and masks for the serious plays and spectacles done in these later permanent theatres were very exaggerated in size and effect, and the *cothurni*, or raised shoes of the Greeks, became even higher and heavier in the hands of the Romans (Figure 3–11). Sensation and eroticism were emphasized in most performances under the Empire; and gradually interludes, such as gladiatorial contests and sea battles staged in a flooded orchestra, became more important than the dramatic action on stage.

Figure 3–11 Ivory statue of a tragic actor, late Hellenistic or Roman period. Illustrates the high headdress, distorted and exaggerated mask, thick-soled shoes, and heavy robe of a tragic actor. Petit Palais, Paris. Photo courtesy of the Archives Photographiques, Paris.

The Plays

In the comic plays of Plautus and Terence, there is no longer a chorus; music is scattered throughout the action as an accent or interlude; and the problems presented are neither ethical nor political ones but domestic matters based on mistaken identity, lost children, and parental obtuseness. For example, in *The Menaechmi* by Plautus, the most important character is now the comic slave, and the names— Peniculus (the Broom), Erotium (Sensuality), Cylindrus (the Rolling Pin)—are descriptive of personality or profession. The dialogue is direct and utilitarian, used to further the plot, make comic descriptions, and project bawdy jokes. Nothing of the fantasy, poetry, or subtle satire of Greek Old Comedy remains. Comic effects are achieved by matching an expression, a word, or a brief visual description to a physical action. There is little sense of theme or idea in the play, merely a good-humored cynicism about the weakness of human character and the ridiculous complications that can occur in life because of incomplete communication and accidental events. The rhythm of the play is fast paced

and furious, geared to strenuous physical action with no breathing time for analysis or thought. (The original version of *The Menaechmi* did contain a number of songs dispersed throughout the dialogue, but they have been lost.)

Roman tragedy played an important role in the theatre at the beginning of the Roman Empire period but later deteriorated into the melodramatic storytelling of mime and pantomime. Heavily indebted to Greek tragedy in general form, Roman tragedies can be classified into two types: those based on Greek themes and those concerning strictly Roman subject matter. Both types were even more melodramatic and violently theatrical than Hellenistic Greek tragedy, stressing horror, depravity, spectacle, and bombastic rhetoric. The only existing tragedies are those of the philosopher and satirist Lucius Annaeus Seneca, who wrote about the middle of the first century A.D., and was a principal adviser to the Emperor Nero. Five of his nine extant tragedies are direct rewrites of Euripides' plays; all seem to be closet dramas written more for his and his friends' amusement than for actual theatrical production.

Seneca's tragedies are divided into five sections of action that helped to develop the five-act play structure in the Renaissance. The choral interludes between them are entirely irrelevant and can easily be eliminated. The characters' speeches are elaborate and complex, filled with moral comment and short proverbial sayings. More like public rhetoric than dialogue, the speeches are set against violent and sensational action carried out by ruthless emotional personalities lacking all restraint. Unlike the Greek plays, the violence is shown on stage. For example, in Seneca's *Oedipus Rex*, Jocasta rips open her abdomen in a long and agonizing death; in *Thyestes*, the title character unknowingly banquets on the bodies of his children before being served their heads on a platter. Almost invariably the major character motivation is revenge.

In their use of the supernatural, the soliloquy, and the confidant (a character who listens and responds to the lead), Seneca's plays sometimes seem closer to the Renaissance ideal of tragedy than to the Greek, but they also reflect Rome in the first century A.D.

and its interest in sensationalism, violence, and spectacle.

By the second century A.D., both comedy and tragedy were superseded by short farces, mime, and pantomime. The farces, with their very exaggerated, ugly, deformed, and often depraved stock characters, were concerned with chicanery and buffoonery, usually in a rural setting. The mimes, initially improvised playlets, became more literary in the first century A.D. and were concerned with sex, love, and adultery, using much indecent language but without the rough and tumble byplay of the farces. The most popular form of dramatic entertainment in the later Roman Empire was the pantomime, which starred the talented performer in the role of storyteller. While the chorus narrated the story, the storyteller mimed it, playing all roles with the aid of mask changes. Music accompanied the entire action. This type of entertainment was popular with the upper classes because it could be performed in their homes; the arenas and theatres were left to the increasingly rowdy and bloodthirsty masses who were fed on gladiatorial fights, sea battles, water ballets, and animal fights.

Acting and Directing the Plays

Even before the second century B.C., acting was highly developed in Rome; the natives of the Italian peninsula had a special gift for mimicry, improvisation, lively gesture, and skillful manipulation of language. In the later Republic (first and second centuries B.C.) and early Empire (first and second centuries A.D.), an actor's training was very demanding. Cicero commented that the good actor needed as much physical training as an athlete or dancer did, while Quintilian said that all able public speakers should emulate the gestures of the actor. Unlike Greek acting, Roman theatrical art in its early development separated storytelling, consisting of recitation and song, from mimetic performance. Attitudes and gestures had, therefore, to correspond exactly to the spoken word or music, and exactness in the rhythmic timing of a performance must have been even more important than in Greek

drama. Also the mime performers, like the Greeks, did not always wear masks and thus were able to mimic facial expression along with movement and voice in the presentation of farcical situations.

The Roman comedies of Plautus and Terence do, however, very much reflect their Greek sources; the Roman terracotta figurines that have survived show comic actors who express an easier and more controlled sense of comic gesture and attitude than do those New Comedy actors depicted in Greek figurines. A study of these figures is essential for the modern actor playing Plautus or Terence if he is to achieve the same sense of easy assurance, exact timing, and balance between the ludicrous and serious that comes from the perfect union of stance and costume.

In contrast, the actor of Roman tragedy conveyed an exaggerated sense of size. The first thing that strikes us in looking at the famous ivory statuette of the tragic actor from the Petit Palais in Paris is its mannikinlike clumsiness (Figure 3–11). In a very large theatre, the combination of rich, heavy costumes, elaborate spectacle, and music must have made Roman tragedies seem somewhat false and overbearing. Moreover, all the Roman masks and accoutrements for tragedy had a frightening mannikinlike exaggeration that must have made movement rather slow and awkward.

The mime actor, on the other hand, who sometimes spoke but often acted to a script spoken by another, must have projected an appealing spirited naturalism with his lack of costumes and masks. We know that the mime actor was admired for his expressive face and eloquently supple movement and gestures. The pantomimist, in turn, who never spoke, exhibited even more refined gesture, and the development of his art was probably a reaction to the excesses found in the tragic performances of the public theatres. Usually a

highly refined and educated artist, the pantomimist gave a solo performance that was closer to the work of a trained dancer than to that of an actor.

Although Roman theatre gave the actor a variety of roles, the modern actor is most likely to play only those burlesque, physical roles found in the comedies of Plautus and Terence. In playing Roman characters in later plays written about Roman times, the actor and director must take the major direction from the play itself. It is pointless to learn many factual details about Roman life and society when one is performing in a version of *Julius Caesar* presented in an Elizabethan setting. Yet, many modern playwrights do study Rome at great length before writing a drama about characters placed in Roman times. The actor and director should do the same. The end product, however, should not be a series of gestures and costume manipulations testifying to the amount of historical research, but a sense of having been inside the cultural psychology of the times (Figure 3–12).

Figure 3–12 Scene from *Julius Caesar* by Shakespeare, produced by the American Conservatory Theatre, San Francisco, 1977. Directed by Edward Payson Call, costumes designed by John Conklin. Photo courtesy of the American Conservatory Theatre, photograph by William Ganslen.

The first thing that strikes the reader about *The Menaechmi* by Plautus is its similarity to a certain kind of modern musical like *The Boys from Syracuse* and *A Funny Thing Happened on the Way to the Forum,* and it is true that these are based on the work of Plautus. Similar in their songs, rude jokes, and superficial sentiment, these musicals and Roman comedy both benefit from a burlesque-vaudeville technique in design. Whatever period is chosen for a production of *The Menaechmi,* a designer will probably want to design both sets and costumes with flat, bright colors, sharp outlines, exaggerated forms, and crisp, flat textures that one associates with cartoons, comic strips, and early twentieth-century musical comedy. The play has frequently been produced with costumes, makeup, and settings based on a particular comic strip popular at the time, and the result was very successful. The fluted columns and heavily draped Roman togas would be out of place in a two-dimensional, comic production unless these were sharply simplified and exaggerated. The short-phrased, rapid-fire dialogue should be reflected visually in sets and costumes: all costumes and set lines should be short and broken; color should be as hard and loud as the boisterous action; ornamentation should be simple, large, and flat; and black outlines for set pieces and costume ornament could be used to accentuate and create a sense of flat illustration. Although the masks and wigs originally used in productions of Roman comedy would be effective in exaggerating character, they would have the disadvantage of hiding the comic expressions of the actors. Padding, which is very evident in Greek New Comedy and Roman comedy figurines, would not only contribute to the desired grotesqueness and caricature in a production but would also help to make the twins in *The Menaechmi* look more alike. The sculpted figurines of Greek New Comedy and of Roman comedy can serve as inspiration for costume effects.

If, by some rare chance, a designer is called upon to design a Roman tragedy such as Seneca's *Oedipus,* the mood and method should be similar to that of a modern horror film; strong exaggeration of texture, line, and color will support the sense of melodrama and horrific violence without achieving a comic or ludicrous result. Or, as in the famous Peter Brook production of Seneca's *Oedipus,* absolute bare-bones simplicity will support a highly stylized physical-vocal production in which all emphasis is on the actors.

PROJECTS AND PROBLEMS

1. Briefly describe the difference in artistic outlook between Roman and Greek sculpture.

2. Build a model or draw a detailed diagram of a Roman theatre; then explain the differences between Greek and Roman theatre in terms of performance and the audience's relationship to the actors.

3. Imagine yourself standing before the Parthenon in Athens (Figure 3–1) and then before the Colosseum in Rome (Figure 3–2). What is the difference in feeling?

4. What differences in feeling would an actor experience by switching from the role of Brutus (Figure 3–3) to the role of Trajan Decius (Figure 3–4)?

5. Look closely at the head of Constantine (Figure 3–5). Why is his personality, at least as it appears in the statue, so different from that of

Brutus and of Trajan Decius and so difficult to play? Describe how you would portray this emperor on stage.

6. How does the description of the daily life of an upper-class Roman citizen and his wife (see page 41) compare to that of a modern upper-class citizen?

7. Decribe what it would be like to sleep on the bed in the reconstructed room from the Villa Boscoreale (Figure 3–6).

8. Describe the room (Figure 3–6) as a whole. Is it warm, cold, cozy, open, closed, airy, or oppressive?

9. Decribe your impression of the clothing, hairdo, posture, and feminine quality in the statue of Antonia, wife of Drusus (Figure 3–7)?

10. How would you play the role of Antonia (Figure 3–7)? What kind of a person would you be? What kind of voice would you have? What kind of movement would you use?

11. Look at the bust of Giulia (Figure 3–8). What kind of woman is she? How would you play her? What does her hairdo tell about this woman?

12. Describe what it must be like to move in the Roman *palla* and *stola* (Figure 3–7).

13. How does the costume of Tiberius (Figure 3–9) affect his posture and movement?

14. Cut a piece of fabric roughly the size of a Roman toga and drape yourself in it until you get roughly the effect of the toga worn by Tiberius (Figure 3–9). Make different movements and gestures while wearing it and describe the result.

15. Describe briefly the requirements for presenting a play by Plautus or Terence.

16. What is the primary attribute of the reconstruction of the Roman theatre at Ostia (Figure 3–10)? What kinds of plays would best lend themselves to performance on this stage? What do you think was the audience's preference in plays and performance?

17. Imagine yourself as a tragic actor (Figure 3–11) on the stage of the theatre at Ostia (Figure 3–10). Describe your gestures, movement, and use of voice.

18. Wearing a mask, shoes with a lift, and a heavy draped costume like that of the tragic actor (Figure 3–11), perform a scene from a Seneca play in front of a mirror. Describe the effect.

19. Explain what is meant when it is stated that the characters in *The Menaechmi* operate on a very limited number of motivations.

20. Describe the basic rhythm in *The Menaechmi*.

21. Compare *The Menaechmi* to a modern musical comedy.

22. Would it be effective to design costumes and scenery for a production of *The Menaechmi* as if they were from a comic strip or cartoon? Why or why not?

23. Name some major visual sources of inspiration for a production of *The Menaechmi*.

24. What are the problems in doing *The Menaechmi* with masks? Without?

25. Do one of the orations from the forum scene in *Julius Caesar* as if it were from a Roman play rather than from a Renaissance play. Describe the layout of the scene, the costume you will wear, the voice qualities you will use. Put on the costume, play the scene, and describe the result.

BIBLIOGRAPHY

Beare, William. *The Roman Stage: A Short History of Latin Drama in the Time of the Republic.* 3rd ed. London: Methuen & Co., 1978. An excellent refresher survey on the essentials of Roman drama at the time of Plautus and Terence.

Bieber, Margarete. *The History of the Greek and Roman Theatre.* 2nd ed. Princeton, N.J.: Princeton University Press, 1961. The most comprehensive set of photographs relating to Roman theatre of any major work in print.

Brilliant, R., *Roman Art*. Oxford: Phaidon, 1969. A very fine summary of the major developments over the full range of Roman art.

Brown, Frank E. *Roman Architecture*. New York: Braziller, 1961. An excellent and very useful survey on the development of Roman architecture.

Carcopino, J. *Daily Life in Ancient Rome*. New Haven: Yale University Press, 1940. A less up-to-date and more academic treatment of Roman life than the Casson book.

Casson, Lionel. *Daily Life in Ancient Rome*. A Horizon Book. New York: American Heritage, 1975. Provides interesting insights into Roman life, along with excellent and infrequently published illustrations.

Duckworth, George E. *The Nature of Roman Comedy*. Princeton, N.J.: Princeton University Press, 1952. The standard work on the nature and character of Roman comedy.

Hadas, Moses. *Imperial Rome*. The Great Ages of Man Series. New York: Time-Life Books, 1965. Written for the average reader, this beautifully illustrated text with extensive color plates covers the major intellectual, cultural, and artistic developments in ancient Rome.

Hamilton, Edith. *The Roman Way*. New York: W. W. Norton, 1932. An excellent introduction to all aspects of Roman life and culture.

Hanfmann, George M. A. *Roman Art*. Greenwich, Conn.: New York Graphic Society, 1952. A well-illustrated excellent survey on all the major trends in Roman art.

Hanson, J. A. *Roman Theatre—Temples*. Princeton, N.J.: Princeton University Press, 1959. An interesting study of the relationship between theatres and temples in ancient Rome and in Roman religious rites.

Harsh, Philip W. A. *A Handbook of Classical Greek Drama*. Stanford, Calif.: Stanford University Press, 1941. A useful reference book on classical drama.

Houston, Mary G. *Ancient Greek, Roman, and Byzantine Costume and Decoration*. 2nd ed. London: A. & C. Black, 1959. An excellent technical explanation of the cut and drape of Roman dress with a few color plates and over 250 line drawings.

Kähler, Heinz. *The Art of Rome and Her Empire*. Translated by J. R. Foster. New York: Crown Publishers, 1963. A good survey on Roman art that covers the art of the far reaches of the Empire as well as of Rome itself.

Mau, August. *Pompeii: Its Life and Art*. Translated by F. W. Kelsey. New York: Macmillan, 1904. A useful and fascinating account of the people and culture of Pompeii before it was destroyed in A.D. 79.

Mauri, Amedeo. *Roman Painting*. New York: Skira, 1953. One of the first finely illustrated books on Roman painting, containing many tipped-in color plates that capture the true character of Roman painting.

Nash, Ernest. *Pictorial Dictionary of Ancient Rome*. 2nd ed. 2 vols. New York: Praeger, 1968. An excellent compendium of pictorial material on ancient Rome invaluable when preparing any dramatic presentation involving Rome.

Norwood, Gilbert. *Plautus and Terence*. New York: Longmans, Green & Co., 1932. A standard and very useful study of these two Roman comic playwrights.

Politt, J. J. *The Art of Rome and Late Antiquity*. Sources and Documents in the History of Art. Englewood Cliffs, N.J.: Prentice-Hall, 1966. Primarily useful to those interested in consulting original sources on the development of Roman art; of secondary interest to the student of the theatre.

Segal, Erich W. *Roman Laughter: The Comedy of Plautus*. Cambridge, Mass.: Harvard University Press, 1968. A very readable study by a man who is both a sound academic and a popular novelist; a good book from which to begin a study of Roman comedy.

Strong, Donald. *The Classical World*. Landmarks of the World's Art Series. New York: McGraw-Hill, 1965. Deals with art from early Minoan period to the Roman conquest. Beautifully illustrated.

————. *Roman Imperial Sculpture: An Introduction to the Commemorative and Decorative Sculpture of the Roman Empire Down to the Death of Constantine*. London: Tiranti, 1961. An exhaustive in-depth study of the changes in Roman sculpture from the time of the Emperor Augustus to Constantine the Great.

Toynbee, Jocelyn M. C. *The Art of the Romans*. New York: Praeger, 1961. Another standard, very useful book on Roman art.

Wheeler, Sir R. E. Mortimer. *Roman Art and Architecture*. New York: Praeger, 1964. A large-format volume, excellently illustrated, on the entire range of Roman art and architecture.

Wills, Garry, ed. *Roman Culture.* The Cultures of Mankind Series. New York: Braziller, 1966. An excellent and very useful compilation of writings from original Roman sources on the Roman view of life and the nature of Roman culture.

The Medieval World

Early Christian and Byzantine Style

Rome was a long time dying. Even in the fifth and sixth centuries A.D., many Roman organizational methods, institutions, and ideas still influenced the cultural life around the Mediterranean. By the beginning of the fourth century A.D.,however, the Roman classical outlook began to change to a medieval one. Emperor Constantine's acceptance of Christianity as the state religion and his move of the capital from Rome to Byzantium were two principal causes of this change. From this point on, western Christianity centered in Rome gradually separated from the culturally and philosophically different Christianity centered in Byzantium. Rome soon fell prey to invasions by Germanic tribes while the eastern, or Byzantine, part of the Empire continued to grow in strength until the development of Islam in the seventh century. By this time East and West were separate in religion and culture. The eastern version of Christianity was based on a complete union of church and state under the control of the Byzantine emperor, while the western version had an independent relationship between church and state and was headed by the Bishop of Rome, an independent figure of great power. With the migration of many peoples throughout Europe during the first 500 years of the Christian era, the West eventually developed in a new direction with new ideals, while the East stagnated under the rigid hierarchical framework of the Byzantine imperial court. Yet this Eastern Empire, continually reduced in size, maintained itself until 1453 when Constantinople finally fell to the Turks.

Christianity was responsible for many changes in late classical times. During the late Roman period, before Christianity was accepted by the state, the religious art adorning the walls of the catacombs, where many Christians were buried, was merely a variant of Roman artistic methods but with an otherworldly spiritual orientation that gradually made the Roman interest in naturalism and illusion unimportant. Like the Egyptians, the early Christians, whose faith was based on an afterlife, stressed the burial rite and the safeguarding of the tomb.

Look, for example, at the sarcophagus of Junius Bassus (Figure 4–1). Here the physical reality of the figures is sharply reduced in favor of a much greater emphasis on storytelling symbols. The colonnaded front of the sarcophagus is divided into ten square compartments showing a mixture of Old and New Testament scenes: in the top section, left to right—the sacrifice of Isaac, St. Peter taken prisoner, Christ enthroned between Peter and Paul, Christ before Pilate (two compart-

ments); in the lower section—the misery of Job, the fall of Man, Christ's entry into Jerusalem, Daniel in the lion's den, and St. Paul led to martyrdom. The story seems disjointed until one realizes that the theme is the divinity of Christ. The central scenes stress Christ as King of Heaven and entering Jerusalem as King, while Adam and Eve denote the burden of guilt to be redeemed by Christ, and the sacrifice of Isaac prefigures Christ's sacrificial death. Job and Daniel carry the same message as Jonah—they all support man's hope of salvation.

Figure 4–1 Sarcophagus of Junius Bassus, Vatican Grottos, Rome, marble, 3' 10½'' × 8', c. 359. Illustrates the loss of realism in its symbolic juxtaposition of Old and New Testament events and a medieval outlook in its tight compartmentalization and framing of each event. Photo courtesy of Alinari, Florence.

There is no visible dramatic action; any one scene staged in a theatre would present a restricted, static tableau. The doll-like bodies with enlarged heads do not act out the stories physically or emotionally but draw attention to a higher symbolic meaning—an unworldly religious calm. There are some hints of classicism in the portrayal of the draperies since Junius Bassus, though a recently converted Christian, probably had strong artistic ties to the Roman cultural and artistic past. The overall effect of the sarcophagus, however, is closer to medieval art of a millennium later—particularly in the tight, restrictive frame, or proscenium, that encloses each scene. There has been critical speculation by theatre historians that this tight framing, which developed so early in the medieval period, may have represented an artistic attempt to place great dramatic events inside a frame representing the central door of the Roman theatre. (The Early Christian mass mind would still remember that the great moments in a play always appeared against the central doorway of the theatre.) Whether or not this is the reason for the tight medieval framing of important religious scenes and characters, the practice continued without interruption until the development of the Renaissance in the early fifteenth century.

Once the Roman Empire was divided by Constantine's moving his capital to Byzantium, the West came under more and more pressure from the migrating Germanic tribes from north of the Alps. Early in the fifth century, when Alaric, king of the Visigoths, threatened to overrun Italy, the Emperor Honorius moved his capital to Ravenna, a city on the Adriatic surrounded by swamps, thus easier than Rome to protect. Then, in 476,

Ravenna fell to Odoacer, the king of the Ostrogoths; in 493 it was chosen capital of the Ostrogothic kingdom of Theodoric. In 539 the Byzantine general Belisarius conquered Ravenna for the famed Emperor Justinian of Constantinople, and the city remained under Byzantine control for the next 200 years. The reign of Justinian is usually considered the first Golden Age of Byzantine style, and the richest monuments of this period are found in this Italian outpost, Ravenna. In the Church of San Vitale, dedicated in 547, the two mosaic panels flanking the altar are the most arresting examples of early Byzantine art available for modern analysis.

In the Theodora panel, we see the empress portrayed as an absolute authority in spiritual as well as in temporal affairs (Figure 4–2). Though reminiscent of Graeco-Roman artistic ideals, the panel has a formal, mysterious, awesome, oriental splendor that removes it completely from the real world. The presentation has been translated into cold pageantry, and we can guess how court ritual in Constantinople must have blended imperceptibly into religious ceremony. The figures with their dangling feet float weightlessly against the gold background; the translucent irises of their eyes stare uncomprehendingly through us and our world of reality; and the ceremony of the Eucharist in which the empress and her retinue are involved seems an unchanging ritual for all time. For an actor or director attempting to probe this sociological symbol of Byzantine power, the removal of individual volition and action is striking. The ideal is for everyone to subjugate himself or herself to the combined divine and worldly power embodied in the emperor and his wife.

The clothing that developed primarily in the Eastern Empire between the time of Constantine and the reign of Justinian was like rich church vestments that clothed the entire body, leaving only the hands and face uncovered. This stemmed from the Christian idea that the

Byzantine Costume and Accessories

body was sinful and should not be exposed. The garments, which can be seen in the Theodora mosaic, also made use of embroidered squares and circles on cloaks and tunics. These embroidered patches gradually were absorbed into church vestments as the *orphreys* and *apparels* still seen on the alb, dalmatic, and chasuble today.

One other slight yet important change in clothing in early Christian and Byzantine times that strongly influenced the design of church vestments was the shift from a completely draped garment to a semifitted one. Draped garments call attention to the graceful physical movement of the body under clothing, while semidraped, semifitted garments give a flat and less changing silhouette, appropriate for a culture that did not wish to call attention to the body. One need only compare the tunics and mantles in the Theodora mosaic (Figure 4–2) with the draped effects of Roman costume (Figure 3–9) to see the difference.

In the secular garments that appear in the Theodora mosaic (Figure 4–2), the basic precepts of Byzantine costume are already established. The strongly oriental effect comes from the richly jeweled and embroidered decoration that began its development, making Byzantine rulers look more and more like walking mosaics. Folds completely disappeared, and

Figure 4–2 *The Empress Theodora and Her Retinue,* a mosaic from the Church of San Vitale, Ravenna, c. A.D. 547. The empress, carrying a golden chalice for the celebration of the Eucharist, and her attendants advance in a stately procession toward Christ represented in the apse. Note the large eyes, the dignity, and the awesomeness of this scene in which the empress's collar and headdress make her look like a walking mosaic. Photo courtesy of Alinari, Florence.

light now played over the stiff surfaces to create a kind of bejeweled armor. Thus Byzantine dress was a complex of glittering de-

tails and stiff silhouettes with great splendor but little sense of unity or plastic effect.

The theatre and its actors were a favorite target for the early Christians for three reasons. First, the theatre was associated with pagan festivals; second, it was considered licentious; and third, comic actors frequently ridiculed Christian sacraments and ceremonies. From about the time of Constantine, the church councils discouraged all Christians from attending the theatre. By the beginning of the fifth century, Christians could be excommunicated for attending the theatre on holy days. In addition, actors were forbidden to partake of the sacraments of the church unless they renounced their profession. The barbarian kings who ruled Italy in the fifth century also hastened the demise of the theatre by castigating it as an example of Roman decadence, even though they sometimes supported it for political reasons. The last definite record of a performance in Rome is found in a letter written in 533, shortly before Belisarius reconquered most of the Italian peninsula for the Emperor Justinian and established the city of Ravenna as the Byzantine outpost.

The Eastern Empire continued to support theatrical performances for a much longer time. Even though the Eastern Church was powerful enough to ban mime and other theatrical performances by the Trullan Council in 692, it was unlikely that the theatrical tradition in Constantinople completely died out. There is evidence that pagan mimes were still performed, that a few plays with Christian themes were written and presented, and that the great spectacles, including chariot races, animal fights, gladiatorial contests, and forms of ballet continued. Perhaps one reason for this continuance was that the famed Empress Theodora, wife of Justinian (Figure 4–2), was a mime player before she married the emperor.

Since no Early Christian or Byzantine plays have survived, the contemporary student of the theatre need not be concerned about performing them. The student, how-

Byzantine Theatre

ever, should have a knowledge of Byzantine style since occasionally a director will choose to present certain plays of Shakespeare and those adopted from biblical stories in a modified Byzantine period approach.

Probably the best-known presentation of a religious play in which the actors appear as Byzantine mosaics is the Everyman Players' production of *The Book of Job* (Figure 4–3). The purpose is threefold: to submerge the indi-

Figure 4–3 Scene from *The Book of Job,* produced by the Everyman Players at Georgetown College, 1957. Designed and directed by Irene and Orlin Corey. Illustrates the use of the Byzantine mosaic style in makeup and costumes. Photo courtesy of the Anchorage Press, Inc., photograph by Jerry Mitchell.

vidual actor in order to stress the faith and religious power in the Book of Job, to create figures larger than life to match the importance of the material, and to develop a production that is at home in church sanctuaries. The mosaic effect is created by gluing squares of satin to a black cotton background; by meticulously making up the actors' faces to look like the faces in the mosaic of Theodora (Figure 4–2); and by formalizing the movement so that the audience feels as if they are watching mosaics come to life. The production, seen over the United States, England, and South Africa, has been widely acclaimed for its evocative re-creation of early Byzantine style.

A number of directors and designers have also presented Shakespeare's *The Winter's Tale*

in a modified Byzantine approach. Certainly the atmosphere in the Court of Sicilia and the ritual reconciliation at the end of the play accommodate the dark and mysterious formality of the Byzantine period. By setting the Court of Sicilia against a more relaxed and natural court in Bohemia, the director and designer can emphasize the difference between these two worlds.

The student of theatre should understand that the actor gains power, mystery, and removal from reality when dressed in Byzantine costume and placed in a Byzantine atmosphere but also risks losing individuality and personality. A Byzantine period style works best when formality and pageantry are preferred to reality.

Early Medieval Style

During the decline and fall of the Roman Empire in the West and the rise of the Byzantine Empire in the East, the nomadic tribes of the so-called barbarians—who had gradually moved into the northern shores of the Mediterranean all the way from Greece to Spain—absorbed some artistic ideals of late Roman times. For the most part, however, they brought with them a unique art that, unlike the Mediterranean cultures' interest in "man" as a subject, was essentially tense and abstract and based on highly stylized animal and vegetable motifs. This art is reminiscent of Iron Age art that can be traced to Scythian and Sarmatic ornamental styles from the heart of Asia; in every way, it conflicts with the remaining classical ideals in the Mediterranean basin. With its entangled, plaited, and spiraling patterns, based primarily on geometrical and abstracted animal forms, it is a fascinating decorative style. Throughout the dark period from the reign of Justinian until the establishment of Charlemagne's empire, this fierce, almost nightmarish animal interlace style dominated the decorative arts in western Europe.

The *Animal Head from the Oseberg Ship Burial*, dating from the early ninth century, illustrates this style perfectly (Figure 4–4). Every area of the surface is webbed over with

a tense interlacing and geometric pattern; the overall atmosphere of the surface decoration and the fierce silhouettes suggest fiend-filled forests, violent fighting, and superstitious fear. It is the art of peasant tribes closely tied to a

Figure 4–4 *Animal Head from the Oseberg Ship Burial,* wood, approximately 5'' high, c. 825. An example of the fierce animal imagery in barbaric art and the love of geometric and interlace patterning that gives an abstract tension to the entire surface. Photo courtesy of the University Museum of Antiquities, Oslo.

completely rural life. The tension and vigor of its zoomorphic interlace patterns is characteristic of all art from the early medieval period in Europe.

During the development of this artistic expression, European society was in a dark period marked by the continuous shifting and warring of those large tribal entities that gradually became the basis of the major western European kingdoms. The old Roman urban-centered life died slowly and was replaced by a completely rural culture of small villages, provincial loyalties, and the first crude feudal castles. During the whole period from the death of Justinian in 565 until Charlemagne was crowned Holy Roman Emperor in 800, no important city developed in barbaric Europe, though the Arabs at the same time were founding great cities like Baghdad and Cordoba. Finally, in the closing years of the eighth century, the dynamic Frankish King Charlemagne did make a major effort to recapture some of the glory of Rome.

The Carolingian Renaissance was a deliberate attempt to return to classical tradition. After his grandfather had driven the invading Moslems back to Spain in 732 and had consolidated the area on both sides of the Rhine, Charlemagne ruled the Franks from 768 until about 814. By the end of the eighth century, he had succeeded in controlling most of what is now Italy, France, and Germany. Charlemagne had himself crowned by the Pope in Rome on Christmas Day 800 as Emperor of the Holy Roman Empire. He proceeded to gather at his court city, Aix la Chapelle, the best intellects and artists of the age in order to establish a new cultural tradition that would hopefully revive the ideals of imperial Rome.

The most significant piece of architecture remaining in his court city is the palace chapel (Figure 4–5). Dedicated in 805, it has a central plan similar to that of the Church of San Vitale in Ravenna, but there is little else reminiscent of early Byzantine style. The interior is strong, heavy, and rather stark, with a massiveness and simplicity quite unlike the mysterious and sophisticated decorative beauty of the Church of San Vitale. Particularly interesting are the

Figure 4–5 Interior of the Palatine Chapel of Charlemagne, Aachen, 792–805. Looks superficially like the interior of San Vitale, but on closer analysis presents a simpler, less sophisticated, more massive effect with striped arches that emphasize the barbaric background of the structure. Photo courtesy of Ann Münchow, Aachen.

alternating light and dark stone arches that echo the checkerboard effect found on the fierce head from the Oseberg Ship Burial (Figure 4–4). Viewed as a theatrical setting, this interior seems more related to the castle interiors in *Macbeth* than to Roman or Byzantine interiors. It has all the masculine strength one would expect in a chapel built to please a warrior king who was almost illiterate and yet had an intense desire to bring civilization to the North.

In a manuscript depicting Charlemagne's grandson, Charles the Bald, and his court (Figure 4–6), we can also see the tension and agitation of the earlier animal interlace line in clothing and overall feeling. Also, for theatrical purposes it is important to note that the piece is very tightly framed by an arch containing a piece of cloth draped within. This tight framing method goes back to the sarcophagus of Junius Bassus (Figure 4–1) and again probably represents a memory of the curtained central door of the Roman theatre—the position in which all great events in the classic theatre had taken place.

Charlemagne's empire survived him by less than thirty years; then incursions from the Vikings and the Huns brought a renewed period of desolation and despair—another dark age similar to that between the close of the sixth and the middle of the eighth centuries.

As the tenth century drew to a close, all across Christian Europe, groups of clerics and Christian laymen prepared for the Last Judgment that was to occur when the first millennium ended. When this did not occur, a feeling of relief and of renewed hope in life spread

Figure 4–6 *Bible of Charles the Bald,* Bibliothèque Nationale, Paris, ms. lat. 1, f. 423, ninth century. An active and agitated grouping with little formal organization, it uses the framing arch and symbolic curtain recalling the memory of great events that occurred in the central doorway of the classic Roman and Greek theatre. Photo courtesy of the Bibliothèque Nationale, Paris.

Figure 4–7 *The Prophet Isaiah,* from the trumeau of the south portal of the Church of St. Pierre, Moissac, c. 1115–35. Illustrates the fervent, mystical, distorted, cross-legged figures found in Romanesque sculpture, which resemble those in manuscript illuminations. Photo courtesy of Jean Roubier, Paris.

throughout Christendom. A great surge of artistic activity began that culminated in the great sculptural and architectural works of the Romanesque style. The sponsors of this development were the monasteries, particularly the reform movement within the Benedictine order that was centered at Cluny in Burgundy.

The Romanesque style owed its character to monks and their fears and fantasies; it thus frequently has an agitated, unnatural, expressionist quality. For example, look at the figure of the Prophet Isaiah on the side of the *trumeau*, or central door division, from the Church of St. Pierre in southern France, dating from the early twelfth century (Figure 4–

7). It is what we would term expressionistic in modern descriptive terms. This spidery, dancing Isaiah with pointed beard strands, crossed legs, and almost transparent drapery is pressed in by a family of monstrous creatures who retain their demoniacal vitality even though they seem more domesticated than their predecessors. Not merely decorative figures, they embody all the dark forces now invoked for the role of guardian figures of the church. Both Isaiah and the animal figures are otherworldly, suggesting a monkish imagination inspired by spiritual values and dark demonology.

Early Medieval Costume and Accessories

In the early Middle Ages following the fall of the Roman Empire, the most striking difference in clothing was that the barbaric invaders from the North wore trousers and close-fitting tunics while the southern people in the Mediterranean basin still wore draped garments. During the entire Graeco-Roman period, trousers were never a part of civilized dress, though they had been worn by the Persians and by most of the migrating tribes moving westward into Europe. Although trousers were introduced to the Romans by the Gauls and were adapted by the Roman army as short knee pants, they were always viewed as uncivilized garments. The most striking change in male wear after the fall of Rome was the covering of the entire leg with a form of trouser or *bracchae*, related to the more sophisticated Byzantine *hosa*, which were hip-length hose rather than trousers. In Germany and France in the period before Charlemagne, trousers were usually cross-laced with thongs and covered with knee-high leggings. At this time a short, coarsely woven tunic covered the body, and a cloak of animal skins or coarse wool was fastened over the shoulders with a huge metal brooch. The male's hair was worn long, the face was bearded, and metal helmets set with wings and horns covered the head. The female's hair was usually long and braided; and she wore long, semifitted tunics,

often woven in stripes or squares, with a mantle pinned over the shoulders.

By the time Charlemagne established his Holy Roman Empire, the standard dress was more sophisticated, but it was still a tunic and mantle combination for both men and women, displaying the semifitted lines of earlier medieval dress with some attempt at draping (Figure 4–6). The standard male dress was a linen undershirt and drawers, a long-sleeved, knee-length tunic bloused over a girdle, and close fitted trousers or *bracchae*. A half circular mantle was fastened with a large *fibula*, or brooch, on the left shoulder; a metal circlet held the hair; and soft leather shoes completed the outfit. The Byzantine dalmatic was reserved for ceremonial occasions, and the floor-length tunic was worn by the aged. A metal helmet with a nose guard was worn in battle, as was a shirt of mail formed either by sewing metal disks to a leather tunic or by interlinking metal circles into chain mail. Women of Charlemagne's time wore a chemise, or *camisa*, as an undergarment, then another undertunic, and then frequently a wide-sleeved overtunic like the male dalmatic. A semicircular mantle was also worn as an outer garment, and the female's hair was covered by a *couvrechef*, or large kerchief.

As the Romanesque period developed, the basic lines of dress changed very little.

The most stylish male tunics were now laced and lifted at the sides of the waist to create tense draped folds at the front of the figure; these remind one of the zigzag effects in the animal interlace patterning of the barbaric past. This laced and draped tunic was called a *bliaut;* the feminine version was similar, though floor length with a slight train. It was laced to the body at the sides and back to give a smooth fit to the hips without complex darting and cutting. The older, loose, floor-length tunic for both men and women was called the *cote,* and the loose, wide-sleeved overtunic was called the *surcote.* The woman's head was now completely muffled, first by the *gorget* draped under the chin and then by the kerchief, or *wimple,* draped over the head. Mantles for men and women were still cut in a half circle and fastened in the front or on the right shoulder. There was a new outer garment, the hooded cloak, which had originally been worn only by the common man. It was now adopted for both monks' habits and noblemen's wear. For court wear, the cloak had scalloped edges to the short shoulder cape and a long tail to the hood.

Early Medieval Theatre

From the fall of the Roman Empire in the fifth century until the close of the twelfth century, theatre is usually considered limited to the new liturgical drama that developed within the church in the tenth century. Numerous sources give evidence, however, that there were also strolling players, entertainers, jugglers, exhibitors of animals, and others whose profession was to provide some type of theatrical entertainment at fairs, feasts, and festivals. Aside from these itinerant professionals making a precarious living throughout early medieval Europe, there were spring fertility rites, midwinter festivities, and other basically pagan rituals practiced despite the expanding power of the Church. These rites made use of masks, dances, costumes, and primitive acting. In fact, some of the elements in these pagan rites were incorporated into religious ceremony to make it more theatrical.

Yet the Church was responsible for the revival of drama. By the tenth century, the mass was divided into two parts: the introduction that varied in its inclusion of sermons, prayers, and devotional readings; and the sacrament itself, which had changed very little. Toward the end of the century, the textual portion of the mass was injected with interpolations of choral dialogue; these *tropes,* or interpolations, signified the beginning of medieval drama.

The earliest written trope for an Easter service dates from about 925. It reads:

Angels: Whom seek ye in the tomb, O Christians?

The Three Marys: Jesus of Nazareth, the Crucified, O Heavenly Beings.

Angels: He is not here, He has risen as He foretold. Go and announce that He is risen from the tomb.

This little introduction to the Easter mass paved the way for including interpolations in the Christmas mass and other high holy day masses. The first support came primarily from the Benedictine monasteries, who found these dramatic moments an excellent way to retain the attention of parishioners who could not read and were easily bored by the regular pattern of the mass. By the eleventh century some rather complicated playlets were included in the mass, and more space and properties were required to tell the story.

The stage arrangement conformed to the space limitations around the altar. The action took place in front of the altar, along the sides of the nave, and even behind the congregation. Small scenic structures called *mansions* were used to symbolize the setting of the scene and to house any properties required; and the open space around the mansion, called the *platea,* was used for acting. These mansions were very tiny, often just big enough for an actor to enter or depart from, but this was not a problem for the storytelling symbolism of the medieval mind. As the sarcophagus of Junius Bassus illustrates (Figure 4–1), even fourth-century artists projecting biblical stories were not interested in pictorial reality but in framing their narrative moment in a tight, direct way to emphasize its religious symbolism. As we saw earlier, this technique may have come from the Roman theatrical practice of framing major dramatic moments in the great central door at the rear of the stage. Whatever the source, it is a very important medieval visual device for storytelling.

For the most part, costumes were church vestments to which realistic or symbolic accessories were often added. Sometimes the Three Kings were given elaborate nonclerical garments, and women were dressed in the enveloping *cote* or long-sleeved tunic. The actors were lower-level clergy and choir boys, while the directors were upper-level clergymen. In the detailed prescriptions from the

church manuals of the period, more attention is given to stage directions about movement, voice, and gesture than to the lines of the dialogue. Clearly, even this early phase of liturgical dramatic development emphasized theatre, not drama.

Unfortunately, there are only a few surviving manuscript illuminations and sculptured scenes from the Romanesque period to tell us what performances were like. One is *The Last Judgment* on the tympanum of the Cathedral of Conques in south-central France, dating from the early twelfth century (Figure 4–8). It is not an imagined scene but a practical design for presenting a playlet about the Last Judgment with a mansion containing the open jaws of the Hellmouth, a hinged door through which the mouth projects, and an area beyond where actors in devil costumes

Figure 4–8 *The Last Judgment,* from the tympanum of the central portal, Cathedral of Conques, Sainte Foy, France; twelfth century. A sculptural scene whose iconography is based on the Last Judgment plays presented in and outside the medieval church. The gate of hell, the Hellmouth, and the devils are particularly illuminating. Photo courtesy of Jean Roubier, Paris.

torture the damned. We know from later medieval times that these devil costumes were very realistic, and the few masks that remain are creatively varied in their ugly ferocity. Every aspect of this scene attests to the naïve but very theatrically creative medieval mind at work; it is no wonder that theatrical performances soon had to move outside the church.

Usually in acting medieval liturgical plays, we are performing in Gothic or later medieval scripts; but, if one were to present one of the playlets from the existing mystery cycles within an early medieval setting, the stress would be on simplicity in the use of hose, tunics, and mantles but with great attention lavished on special characters like angels, the deity, and devils. Movement would be simple, honest, natural, youthful, and uncomplicated with no attempt at self-consciousness. To gain insight into the early medieval mind, the student of theatre should carefully study the poses and the way clothing is worn in the art of the period.

Sometimes the play may be a modern adaptation of a biblical story within an early medieval setting. For example, the Everyman Players have performed in churches throughout the country a very interestingly designed adaptation of the Book of Romans by St. Paul, based on sculptured figures from late Romanesque art such as the Isaiah Figure from the Church of St. Pierre (Figure 4–9). The effect is again to lift the actor above reality to a biblical symbolism in which gestures and movements guided by the costume have a simple, heightened significance.

Figure 4–9 Scene from *Romans by St. Paul,* produced by the Everyman Players, First Baptist Church, Shreveport, Louisiana, 1963. Illustrates the use of Romanesque sculpture as a visual image for a production. Designed by Irene Corey. Photo courtesy of Anchorage Press, Inc., photograph by Jerry Mitchell.

The distinction between Romanesque and Gothic style is more a matter of mood and cultural outlook than a major shift in all artistic forms. Certainly, Henry Adams's distinction between Romanesque style as being primarily masculine in its imagery and Gothic style as being more feminine is still a very useful though simplified generalization. The primary shift during the late medieval Gothic period was from a static, mentally stagnant, rural outlook to a more dynamic participation in the life of the past and present. The pagan philosophers Plato and Aristotle were adapted to Christian doctrine; universities were founded; towns once again grew to a fair size because of renewed trade throughout all Europe; and scientific ideas and goods from the infidel world of Islam were accepted. After the experience of the Crusades, all western Europe came to life once again; the center of life shifted from the rural monasteries and feudal castles to the new urban centers, where a small but prosperous middle class emerged, establishing the foundations of capitalism. Money, not barter, became the universal means of exchange; banks developed; credit was given; and loans were made. This expansion also caused a gradual breakdown in the power of the individual feudal duke and lord and in the spiritual power of the Pope. In contrast, the power of the various royal families and their emerging nation states grew. For example, the royal domain of France at the end of the twelfth century extended only about a hundred miles from Paris; by the end of the fifteenth century, it included almost all of what is now modern France.

One of the first artistic changes marking this transition from Romanesque to Gothic style was the dedication in 1144 of the Church of St. Denis by Abbot Suger, chief adviser to Louis VII and founder of that alliance between Church and State that enabled succeeding French kings to give much more authority to the monarchy. This church had great significance because it was the shrine of the patron saint of France and the burial place of French kings. Abbot Suger was determined to give it spiritual significance by opening up the architecture with a great play of interior light. The ambulatory, which remains the same as when dedicated, no longer has walls but a network of columns, ribs, varying pointed arches, and quite large stained-glass windows. This design makes the church less heavy and more open to light than Romanesque churches.

In this first attempt at skeletal architecture, as opposed to solid wall construction, we have the basis for Gothic style. This emphasis on strict geometric planning in order to divide the weight of a structure and to open it to light was closely related to the religious thoughts of this time; namely, that light was the key to the mystic revelation of the spirit of God and that a unified, well-balanced structure was like the harmonious unity found in church history, theology, and teaching. The creation of a harmonious effect through the use of structure and light was the primary purpose of Gothic art until an emphasis on ornament and decoration finally diminished the importance of spiritual principles.

The view of man also began to change in the sculptural images carved on the jambs of church doors. Note the statues on the three front portals of Chartres Cathedral (Figure 4–10). (Though the cathedral was destroyed by fire in 1194, the west front containing these statues was saved and retained in the high Gothic church that arose between 1194 and 1226.) They combine the abstract unworldliness of the Romanesque style and the awakening humanism of early Gothic art. Their decorative draped lines still contain a great deal of tension and the bottom edges of the outer garments still demonstrate the zigzag line of Romanesque and barbaric statues. Yet, despite the complex checkerboard and interlace decoration on the bases of the statues and even though the figures are still abstract and arbitrarily elongated to fit the cylindrical columns to which they are attached, they have a new quietness, dignity, and refinement that seem almost to separate them from their background. Obviously, the artist was more in-

Figure 4–10 Jamb statues from the west portal of Chartres Cathedral, c. 1145–70. Though these solemn, columnar kings and queens still retain a tight, abstract otherworldliness, they also demonstrate a new quietness, dignity, and refinement and a suggested separation from their architectural background. Photo courtesy of Jean Roubier, Paris.

Figure 4–11 Jamb statues from the south transept portal of Chartres Cathedral, c. 1215–20. These figures, which are far more natural and human than those of the west front, seem to have awakened from a long sleep and are ready to converse and step away from the architecture. The figure of the Christian knight St. Theodore (left), who stands in a draped tabard with his weight shifted to one foot, suggests the statues of classical times. Photo courtesy of Jean Roubier, Paris.

terested in human personality and less in abstract symbolism. These peaceful images, lacking the fervor and the tension of earlier Romanesque ones (Figure 4–7), clearly predict the transition in religion from a total concentration on the world of the spirit to a more balanced emphasis on this world and the next.

To see how rapid and great was the shift, one need only look at the statues on the south transept portal of Chartres, completed between 1215 and 1220 (Figure 4–11). Sculpted barely sixty years after the statues on the front door, these figures seem to have come to life, to have awakened from the long sleep of the earlier Middle Ages. They are ready to step away from the column and the wall and to

converse. In particular, the figure of St. Theodore on the left, the epitome of the Christian knight, stands in a position reminiscent of classical contrapposto with sword, chain mail, and tunic carefully observed and naturally sculpted. An actor would have little difficulty understanding the clothing, pose, and philosophical outlook of these figures. Yet the final image is as idealistic as it is realistic—that balance between natural and spiritual values that was the hallmark of High Gothic or "classic" Gothic art during the first half of the thirteenth century.

Even more Gothic than Chartres is the

Cathedral of Notre Dame in Paris, begun in 1163 and completed about the middle of the thirteenth century (Figure 4–12). It includes major attributes from the entire period of high Gothic architecture. Compared to the separate, accumulated look of most Romanesque churches, Notre Dame is extraordinarily unified and compact. The walls seem to have disappeared in favor of skeletal ribbing and buttressing; the clerestory windows have greatly increased in size; the vertical has been stressed throughout; and all decoration and ornament both inside and out have been carefully planned and integrated into a very coherent whole in which all knowledge of heaven and earth is harmoniously ordered and

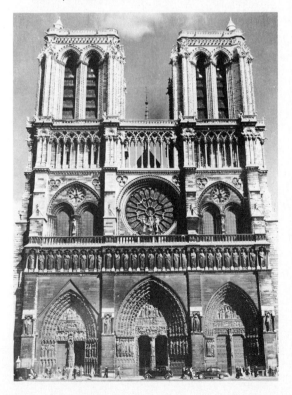

Figure 4–12 West façade of Notre Dame Cathedral, c. 1163–1250. Illustrates the new unity, organization, proportion, and balance found in Gothic cathedrals at the opening of the thirteenth century. Photo courtesy of the French Government Tourist Office.

compartmentalized. The front is a perfect balance between horizontal forces that represent the earth and the aspiring vertical forces that reach toward the heavens. This cathedral, rising in a city that was the home of the developing scholastic thought and method of the period, stands, as do all the great High Gothic churches, as a metaphor for that impossible balance between the worlds of nature and the spirit attempted by men like Dante and St. Thomas. This double vision can be felt in the aspiring leap of the vaults and the buttresses, in the airiness of the ornament, in the openness of the enclosed space, and in the translucence of the interior lighting. In contrast, the soaring towers and overreaching vaults denote a strain and instability, a feeling of danger and impracticality. The rapidity with which delicate, lacy ornamental effects began to erode the organized and disciplined unity of Gothic style testifies to the impossibility of maintaining this balance, just as it was impossible to maintain the balance in classical Greece between the real and the ideal. The stained-glass rose window in the south transept at Notre Dame, dating from the later part of the thirteenth century, portrays the growing tendency toward weightless openwork and arabesque effects. Eventually, this fairy-tale sense of decoration undermined and destroyed all sense of structure.

In the period from about 1300 to 1500, spiritual values throughout Europe were replaced with far more secular concerns, and all religious art reflected the richness and sophistication dominant in the courts of nobles and kings. The growing power of the middle class and the great increase in wealth and trade made materialism a dominant life goal and thus gradually eclipsed the concept of knighthood, feudal vows, and belief in the absolute power of the Church. Yet the nobility, supported by the wealthy upper-middle class, continued with more and more elegant fantasy and imagination the masquerade of knightly tournaments, courtly love, and religious ritual and ceremony. This was the age of fairy-tale kings, queens, princesses, and knights acting out an unreal existence. Most dramatizations of medieval legends and fairy tales are set in these times; the period style is very seductive for designers, directors, and actors.

The façade of the Church of St. Maclou in Rouen, begun about 1434, is a dramatic example of this late Gothic style in architecture (Figure 4–13). Gone is the heroism of early Gothic style; a refinement in detail and open, spiny, elegant arabesques have replaced monumentality and a sense of structure. In this flamboyant Gothic statement, so-called because of the flamelike tracery of the ornamentation, the structural reality of the building has been totally obscured by a web

of decoration that merely creates a picturesque tangle of lines.

The major forms of pictorial illustration during the Gothic period were stained-glass windows and manuscript illuminations. In Italy, however, Giotto, whose major work was done in the early fourteenth century, brought to fresco painting some of the natural proportions, solidity, and sense of space noted in the figures from the south portal at Chartres (Figure 4–11). He also revived the use of highlight and shade to give a sculptural mass to his people that prevented them from having the swaying, decorative elegance of most later Gothic figures. Giotto was never decorative

Figure 4–13 Church of St. Maclou, Rouen. Begun in 1434. A late Gothic church in which refinement of detail and open arabesques of spiny, elegant tracery have replaced unity, simplicity, and monumentality of structure. Photo courtesy of the Archives Photographiques, Paris.

and elegant but strong, simplified, dramatic, and natural. Even more important for students of the theatre, he made the mansions used in the performance of medieval plays into solid little houses for framing or backing the stories he wished to present. For example, the mansion in *The Angel Appearing to St. Anne* is a true stage for dramatic action, indicating an outdoor scene when all the curtains about it are open and an indoor scene when the curtains behind the action are closed (Figure 4–14). In true medieval fashion, the mansion is a strong organizer and frame for the action, without creating a sense of natural space and distance.

Figure 4–14 Giotto, *The Angel Appearing to St. Anne*, Scrovegni Chapel, Padua, c. 1306. Illustrates the use of a theatrical mansion to stage a scene from the Bible. Photo courtesy of Alinari, Florence.

The later medieval manners and customs among the nobility were completely colored by the cultural ideals of this late Gothic period. An account by a young Castilian, Guittierez de Gomez, who visited a castle in Normandy in 1405, gives a very vivid picture of the enviable pattern of life on a medieval barony.

The noble Spaniard first commented on the castle set on the banks of a river amidst orchards and ponds, noting the many additions to the castle that gave it slimmer lines, larger windows, conical and peaked roofs, and delicate lacy carvings. He also dutifully praised the beautiful and charming great lady of the house and her ten well-born daughters who surrounded her and kept her company. That her daughters were at home was unusual since noble families usually sent sons and daughters to other castles as maids-in-waiting and pages to be trained in the sophisticated manners and customs of the age. Apart from the immediate family, pages, maids-in-waiting, and guests, the house swarmed with servants, minstrels, trumpeters, grooms, kennel men, falconers, gardeners, valets, and menials to do the cooking and cleaning.

Later Medieval Life and Cultural Ideals

In the morning, the Spaniard noted that the maids-in-waiting assembled with their books of hours and rosaries and accompanied the countess to a nearby grove for meditation and prayer, before gathering flowers and attending mass in the chapel. After this, servants served the ladies silver platters heaped with roast thrushes, pigeons, and other small birds, which they ate daintily while sipping wine. Then the grooms brought up the horses—the gentle ones for the ladies and the more spirited ones for the gentlemen. The party then rode into the country, stopping to gather greenery for garlands, while singing songs in parts. The young Castilian thought that these French songs were the music of paradise.

Back at the castle the tables were set, and the old count, who could no longer ride, greeted the horsemen with a courteousness that impressed the young Spaniard. The count, countess, and the young guest were seated at a small table, while the others were paired off at a larger one. The main meal of the day began with artful, polished, elegant conversation on love and war engaged in while jongleurs provided music. At the close, grace was said; it was followed by an hour of dancing that included court *rondes* and *bourrées* in which the partners held hands and executed complicated figures, meeting and parting, and bowing and circling. At the end every gentleman kissed his partner, and wine was served along with candied and spiced fruits.

All now retired to their rooms for a siesta, although some girls evidently did not rest but discussed the new visitor, the dancing, and stories of chivalry and love while others bathed and changed their clothes. After the heat of the early afternoon, the party rode out once more with their falcons on wrists protected with heavy gloves. The countess showed great style in handling her bird, though all were connoisseurs of hawking. Talk centered on the fine points of rearing and training the predators as well as on the design of the falcons' hoods and their different temperaments. Each bird's flight and battle with its quarry were discussed as if it were an artistic spectacle. Then, after the falcons had been transferred to the care of pages, the party dismounted and walked through the wood to where servants had unpacked baskets of roast chicken, pheasant, fruit, and wine. The party ate, drank, sang songs, wove new green garlands, and then returned to the castle as the sun sank lower in the west.

If it had been winter, there would have been a late supper by the fire; but since it was fine weather, the company had an early snack and played outdoors at bowls until dark. Then in the great hall, lighted by torches, the group listened to minstrels, danced, had fruit and wine, and finally retired about midnight. In his journal the young Spaniard wrote: "And thus it was every day we spent there and whenever [I] came on a visit to the castle."

This idyllic country life of the nobles sharply contrasted with that of the lowly serf and those in the lower depths of a city like Paris. The city records of this time show many ordinances against the tribe of:

> crocodiles and rogues who pretend to be crippled, hobbling on canes and simulating decrepitude; sporting open wounds, sores, scabs, swellings; smearing themselves with salves, saffron, flour, blood, and other false colors, and dressing in muddy, filthy, evil-smelling, and abominable garments even when they go into churches; who throw themselves down in the busiest street, or when a large group such as a procession is passing, discharge from their noses or mouth blood made of blackberries, of vermilion or other dyes, in order dishonestly to extort alms that are properly due to God's real poor.

Thus here, as in most ages of man's historical development, there was a tremendous discrepancy between the lives and customs of the aristocrats and those at the bottom of society. For the student of period style, the manners and customs of the upper classes are the primary concern simply because their life style is more frequently dramatized and was more sophisticated, artificial, and unrelated to natural body movement.

Later Medieval Ornament, Interiors, and Furniture

To analyze Gothic ornament, breaking it down into its various components, often seems impossible because it is so rich and complicated. Yet from its early beginnings in the late twelfth century up to its flamboyant profusion in the fifteenth century, it was based on four key patterns. First, there were the many varieties of the pointed Gothic arch; the later ones were often either depressed or extended upward in a rising point to create a more graceful serpentine line for the arch. Second, there were a number of clover leaf patterns in what were called *trefoil* and *quatrefoil* groupings. Third, there were the *crockets*, or curling leaves, adorning the cotton-ball-puff points of these groupings. These leafy bumps on the outside of Gothic arches were responsible for the lacy arabesque decoration characteristic of all later Gothic architecture, furniture, and ornamentation (Figure 4–13). Finally, at the top of the point of many Gothic arches, one sees a *finial* similar to a complex multiple cross or leafy *fleur-de-lis*. The finial gave a sense of movement and lightness to the flowing, lacy serpentine lines of the Gothic ornamentation.

In many ways, the castle interiors were merely a refinement of those built at the end of the early medieval period. Ceilings were either vaulted in wood or stone or flat and crossed by many large beams. Windows, either single or in groups, were still relatively small but now had pointed arches; fireplaces were shallow and high, culminating in ornamented, hooded chimneys that projected into the room; and the bare stone walls were usually decorated with tapestries telling the stories of legendary and historical heroes and heroines. Rich cushions and draperies on chairs and couches added other accents of warmth and color. In addition, heraldic banners and shields were often hung from the beams or were fastened to the walls of the great hall to give a feeling of courtly grandeur. The lord and his family still dined on a raised dais at one end of the great hall while musicians played in a carved gallery at the other end. To gain an idea of the size of the hall and the revelry that occurred there, look at the drawing of a performance of a mummer's play at Haddon Hall from the close of the Gothic period (Figure 4–15).

Figure 4–15 Drawing of the interior of Haddon Hall, a late medieval English manor house. Illustrates the living conditions in the great hall of an aristocratic house during the late medieval period. Here we see a festival banquet at which a mummer's play is being performed. From Nash, *The Mansions of England in Olden Times,* 1849.

The clothing of later medieval times can be classified into three fairly distinct periods: early, middle, and late Gothic. The first covers the development of High Gothic art and architecture and runs from roughly 1200 until the second quarter of the fourteenth century. The second lasts until about 1425, or the time of Joan of Arc; and the last extends until 1485, when the ideals of the Renaissance began to dominate all European dress. Italian clothing in the late Gothic period was quite different from that in northern and western Europe simply because the Italians had abandoned Gothic artistic ideals by the middle of the fifteenth century.

In the early Gothic period, the longer Byzantine male tunic, which had in the past been reserved for royalty and special occasions, became the *cote*, with wide sleeves cut into the shoulder and narrowing to the wrist and usually covered by a sleeveless tunic, or *surcote*. Sometimes, the surcote had hanging sleeves or caped sleeves, or it was lined in fur and called a *peliçon*. As a military garment it was emblazoned with a coat-of-arms and was worn over the *hauberk* of chain mail. The hooded cloak was a favorite outer garment, and the hood with a short collar cape was also very fashionable. The female costume looked very similar to the male dress, having an undertunic, or cote, an overtunic, or surcote, a *wimple* draped over the head, and a *gorget* tightly draped under the chin. Sometimes the hair was placed in a pillbox or *toque* with chinstrap, sometimes coiled over the ears and held by jeweled nets, or loosely confined by a gold circlet or coronet (the style for very young women).

A very good example of this early style can be seen in the superb polychromed statues of Ekkehard and Uta, life-size figures from the west choir of the Cathedral of Naumberg, dating from about 1250 (Figure 4–16). Their civilian dress has the same simple draping found on religious statues of the period. The fashions also project a sober, balanced view of self in relation to this life and the next. The most striking characteristics are the great he-

Later Medieval Costume and Accessories

raldic shield and sword of Ekkehard and the muffled beauty of his wife. The shield and sword symbolize the husband's place within the feudal order and the accepted ideal of chivalry. The hidden female form of the wife symbolizes the woman as a queen of chivalry linked to the worship of the Virgin.

By the second quarter of the fourteenth century, these ideal and spiritual clothing forms were replaced by slim, close-fitting garments sometimes overlaid with full robes that stressed the grace and movement of the body while displaying rich decoration and ornament. The basic male body garment was the

Figure 4–16 *Ekkehard and Uta,* Cathedral of Naumberg, life size, c. 1250–60. Illustrates the heavy, muffled clothing of the early Gothic period, which consisted primarily of tunics and mantles trimmed with simple jewelry. Photo courtesy of Bildarchiv Foto, Marburg.

close-fitting hip tunic called the *cotehardie,* sometimes coupled with a hood and caped collar having richly cut edges of scallops or foliage shapes reminiscent of the crockets of Gothic architectural decoration. Often the cotehardie had cuffs on the sleeve, or *tippets,* that also flared into foliations; the bottom of the garment was also *dagged, foliated,* or *scalloped.* Later in the century, a voluminous overgown, or *houppelande* with trailing bell sleeves and high collar also decorated with foliated edges, was worn over the cotehardie. The hood of the cotehardie was worn with the band of the face opening placed around the head and the dagged edges of the collar falling to one side. A long tail, or *liripipe,* wrapped about the head and draped on the shoulder. This fantastic headdress known as a *chaperone* was one of the more exotic effects that made men look as if they were wearing turbans. The woman's version of the cotehardie was a close-fitting princess-line gown with a low neckline and a full skirt; it was often covered with an outer gown whose sides had been cut away to the hips. These sideless gowns were often emblazoned with the family coat of arms and continued as official court dress throughout the fifteenth century. Toward the end of the fourteenth century, the houppelande was also worn by women and had the same foliated and dagged edges as on the male's garment. Headwear, like clothing and architectural decoration, became more and more ornate and included turbans, *reticulated* headdresses with ornate metal cages holding the hair over the ears, small horn-shaped headdresses with veils, and heavily ornamented heart-shaped rolls.

The famous manuscript illuminations done for the *Très Riches Heures de Jean Duc de Berry*—probably by the Limbourg brothers about 1415—are beautiful resources on the courtly styles at the close of the fourteenth and the opening of the fifteenth centuries (Figure 4–17). In the scene depicting a lavishly dressed betrothed couple exchanging rings in front of their parents, we have the elegant, fairy-tale idyll that was the goal of aristocratic life during the period. There is the

Figure 4–17 *The Exchange of the Rings,* from *Très Riches Heures de Jean Duc de Berry,* early fifteenth century. Illustrates the elegant fantasy fashions at the turn of the fifteenth century with their dagged and foliated edges, turbans, flowing lines, and sprinkled ornamentation. Musée Condé, Chantilly. Photo courtesy of the Bibliothèque Nationale, Paris.

same decorative fantasy here as in the architectural decoration of this period—the same scalloped edges, serpentine lines, and light interplay of forms that make this and the following period of Gothic style so exactly right for illustrating the medieval fairy tale.

Beginning about 1425, two distinct styles developed in fashion: one based on the blossoming of the Renaissance in Florence and interested in sculptural form (which will be discussed in the next chapter); the other based on the Burgundian court centered in Flanders and projecting a final Gothic richness and splendor. This Burgundian style is represented in the illuminated manuscript *The Betrothal of Renaud de Montauban to Clarisse, Daughter of King Yon of Gascoigne* (Figure 4–18). Shoes for the men were now elegantly pointed, and broad-shouldered pleated doublets replaced the cotehardie and the houppelande, though an occasional long, slim gown was seen as well as a few hanging sleeves. The majority of the hats had a sugar-loaf shape, though the padded doughnut-shaped *roundlet* with draped liripipe was still used occasionally. Hose, sometimes still particolored, were now frequently sewn together at the top of the legs because of the shortness of the doublets, and this single tightslike garment was fastened to the *jupe* or vest under the doublet with ties or *points*. A voluminous mantle occasionally lined in fur emblazoned with heraldry for ceremonial occasions was the chief outer garment, although loose gowns were also worn for this purpose.

The woman's gown now had a slightly lifted waistline, a train that was quite voluminous, a deep V-shaped neckline partially filled in with the top of the undergarment and corset, and a wide belt just above the waist. The wide shawl collar rolled back from the neck was usually trimmed in fur, as were the cuffs. The sideless gown over the cotehardie was now reserved for purely ceremonial occasions, as was the half-circle heraldic mantle. The heads were now usually topped with the steeple-shaped *hennin* with its floating veil, but there were other variations such as the

Figure 4–18 *The Betrothal of Renaud de Montaubon and Clarisse, Daughter of King Yon of Gascoigne,* from the *Roman de la Violette,* mid-fifteenth century. Illustrates the taller figures, padded clothing, and three-dimensional form found in the Franco-Burgundian style of the fifteenth century. Photo courtesy of the Bibliothèque Nationale, Paris.

heart-shaped headdress, the high, rounded *escoffion*, and the butterfly hennin with its wired, winglike veils. The women's headdresses were the most flamboyant aspect of this later style, which in many ways was beginning to experiment again with form rather than mere lacy decoration—but form that was distorted rather than natural. Only in northern Italy did one find a simpler natural silhouette with an emphasis on pleated short and long gowns, natural headdresses, and limited ornamentation.

The most important thing to remember about body movement in Gothic dress is that it must appear easy and natural to an audience. The actor or actress must study the art of the period and then practice moving in Gothic costumes. In general, movement in Gothic clothing must be larger and more sweeping than movement in modern dress, because of the amount of fabric that must be manipulated effectively.

Later Medieval Manners and Movement

Until the fifteenth century and the invention of the printing press, little was written about deportment and etiquette. Despite the gracefulness of many male figures in the illuminated manuscripts, one can assume that the early gallant cut a better figure on the battlefield and at the chase than in a ballroom. Thus, the typical movement was probably that of an athlete—easy and buoyant from the hips with braced knees and an erect head position.

Because gallants were particularly proud of their legs and always displayed them to their best advantage, an actor should put on a pair of wrinklefree tights and practice walking and standing in front of a large mirror. He should carefully study his every movement in order to remove any self-consciousness, weakness, or huddling together of the knees. Drooping languidly and gracefully in order to create an elegance of line like that seen in the figures from the famed *Très Riches Heures de Jean Duc de Berry* (Figure 4–17) comes from adopting an athletic pose, not a sagging slouch.

When sitting, the actor should always turn his feet outward, not in, particularly when one remembers the emphasis placed on the long pointed toes in later medieval footwear. Crossed legs should be avoided, and hands should not be placed on the knees but kept either above the waist or gracefully between the thighs, one slightly higher than the other. To display the wide pictorial sleeves of later medieval male dress, and to wear them gracefully, the actor should make broad, sweeping arm gestures.

As far as greetings were concerned, family members kissed one another with full feeling, whether men or women, and knights often kissed one another on meeting. However, since it was difficult to know friend from foe, strangers usually approached each other warily by grasping each other with both hands gripped tightly above the elbows. This insured that one would not be stabbed since no hands were free to reach for a dagger. The hat or headdress was never removed when greeting, and a gentleman removed his hat only in the presence of his equals. In making a bow, one moved back the left foot as if about to kneel on it, while the weight was still on the right foot. After a half bend, both knees were straightened; and the body was once again brought to an erect position. If the hat was removed, it was held in the left hand close to the hip while bowing. If there was no hat, then both arms could move the full-bell sleeves backward. If the gentleman wore elaborately pointed shoes, he could make a flourish with the right foot as the bow was completed.

Ceremonial actions, such as swearing allegiance, being knighted, paying homage, and "taking seizin," were simple gestures done slowly and with great solemnity. To pay homage to his sovereign, the subject had to kneel, raise his right hand palm downwards in order to lift the sovereign's hand on the back of his wrist while he placed his forehead on it. The subject then stood and bowed before backing slowly away. When a man had knighthood conferred on him, he took out his sword with his right hand, holding the center of the blade with his left, and then offered the sword to the monarch with the hilt resting on his right forearm. The king then lightly touched the blade to the knight's left shoulder, after which the knight took back the sword between his two hands and, while standing, resheathed his weapon. To "take seizin," the vassal accepted in a formal manner a piece of earth as a token of the lands held in fief by his lord or king.

Though women by virtue of their sex did not have to worry about a proper ceremonial decorum, the wearing of full skirts after about the middle of the fourteenth century and the swaying, pregnant movement (much affected by ladies attempting to match the pose in later Gothic statues of the Virgin) demanded much practice. In order to present a graceful appearance, one had to keep the folds of the dress in vertical, draped lines rather than allowing them to fall to the side. In addition, because of its fullness, the front of the dress was lifted with one hand in order to bring the toes forward under the lifted area for ease in walking.

An actress unused to coping with the amount of material in later Gothic gowns tends to move slowly and heavily. When required to exit with speed, she usually appears quite clumsy since she does not control her waist firmly and tends to stride forward from the thigh. Control of waist and diaphragm is essential for all movements quick or slow, and a fast walk is easily executed if steps are fairly small and the skirt is held away from—not above—the knees. By lifting the front folds of the skirt with care and precision, the actress can always be stepping through the space created by the upheld folds even when she is turning to the right or to the left. Also, actresses should consider making circular movements in these full skirts since they are very effective in giving a picturesque swirl of weighty folds to a sharp turn or exit (Figures 4–17 and 4–18).

The actress faces another challenge in sitting so that the skirts seem to arrange themselves in beautiful folds around the feet or, when very long, spread themselves out in a pool of color. The skirt should be smoothed under, and the surplus folds draped gracefully so that when the actress arises, the folds allow freedom of movement and do not look bunched or pulled tightly about the legs. The actress should always sit with a very straight back.

There are many positions for the arms and hands that the actress can learn by studying portraits and pictures of the later medieval period. When she is in repose, the hands can be clasped on the girdle, whether it is worn low or just under the bust. The left hand can hold the elbow of the right arm, while the right hand rests against the right or left shoul-

der or holds the locket on the neck chain. Both hands can hold the skirt against the waist, though it is frequently easier to drape the skirt folds over the wrist or forearm so that the hands are free. In sitting, the hands may be dropped at the side, resting in the folds of the skirt, or be laid on the lap with wrists crossed. Wrists can also be crossed with the hands clasping the forearm, or they can merely rest on the arms of a chair. Positions to be avoided when portraying ladies of noble birth include hands clasped behind the back, crossed arms, hands fixing the hair, or hands on the hips. When portraying maids, actresses can swing their hips and put their hands on them. When portraying peasant women, they can spread their legs and clasp the knees. The portrayal of a medieval lady, however, must emulate the beauty of the statues and illuminations of the period. Since the bow, or curtsy, was not fully developed for women in the Gothic period, gentle bending of the knees is usually sufficient. When great respect has to be shown, the actress should sink her body perpendicularly within the skirt without spreading the skirt folds to the side.

At the beginning of the Gothic period, the Church moved the dramatized episodes to the square in front of the cathedral; and a specific week, known as the Feast of Corpus Christi, was set aside for the performances of religious dramas. At first, the scenes were arranged in the same way as they had been inside the cathedral, and the *platea*, or open space, was also treated the same. Gradually, however, the placement and use of mansions expanded to take advantage of the greater space and flexibility offered by the open-air square or marketplace. The mansions, like the other visual arts, became larger and more elaborate, though they still maintained the compartment or framing niche that surrounded religious scenes and characters inside and outside the Gothic cathedral. The exciting dramatizations that took place in front of them are often reflected in the sculptural scenes decorating the cathedrals.

Later Medieval Theatre

Other variations besides the open layout in the marketplace or cathedral square included a rectangular platform on which mansions were placed in linear progression from left to right; a pageant wagon that carried a two-storied mansion from square to square throughout a city; and the use of ancient amphitheatres for arranging the mansions around a central platea. There were, however, definite constants: mansions surrounded by generalized space; short playlets tied together only by their religious subject matter and employment of three planes of action—Earth, Heaven, and Hell; and the attempt to make frightening and miraculous effects as convincing and realistic as possible (Figure 4–19). It is this type of mansion, similar to that depicted in the scene from the Valenciennes Passion Play, that was probably occasionally used in front of the inner above and inner below in Shakespeare's theatre (Figure 6–12).

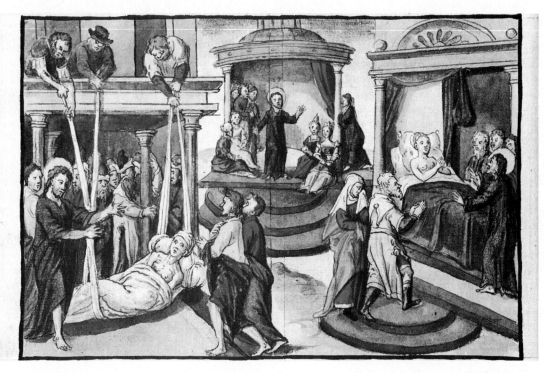

Figure 4–19 Scene from the Valenciennes Passion Play showing the depiction of several scenes framed against little set pieces or mansions. *Left,* Christ curing the paralytic; *right,* Christ curing a woman with dropsy. Photo courtesy of the Bibliothèque Nationale, Paris.

The mansion in the left of the scene would have been very useful in Shakespeare's *Antony and Cleopatra* as a guide to how to lift Antony up to the monument in which Cleopatra has taken refuge. It makes the second level lower than the second level of the Elizabethan stage, pushes the action closer to the audience, and actually demonstrates the physical method that may have been used in this scene in the Elizabethan theatre.

Special effects usually concentrated on portraying a fiery and smoky Hellmouth and realistic devils with terrifying masks, tails, claws, hoofs, and exploding fireworks. The costumes for medieval plays were a mixture of everyday dress and overlaid accessories; when saints or important biblical personages appeared, they usually carried a specific symbol identifying them throughout the presentation. The costumes of heavenly figures were supposed to inspire awe and reverence, while those of demons were intended to evoke fear and terror. Only the ordinary citizen appeared in everyday dress as a symbol of man caught between the supernatural forces of good and evil.

The Plays

The major dramatic form during the late medieval, or Gothic, period was the liturgical cycle or mystery play based on stories from the Bible. Probably the most widely known playlet from the four great English mystery cycles is *The Second Shepherd's Play* from the Wakefield cycle. It is the thirteenth in a long group of thirty-two playlets dramatizing biblical events from Creation to the Last Judgment, all arranged and dramatized to create that simple, linear progression found in the illuminations of a medieval manuscript. Based on a simple statement in Luke about the shepherds who watched over their flocks at the birth of Christ, the playlet enriches this biblical moment with comic detail, farcical humor, and a strong feeling for medieval peasant life. Involving opposing ideas of spirituality and farcical reality, the playlet typifies the unselfconscious religious thought of the medieval peasant mind and vividly illustrates the duality of outlook in medieval art.

All seven roles would have been played by men; the actor playing Gil may have doubled as the Virgin, while the Christ child was probably a doll. The shepherds have one or two specific personal traits; all are generous, and it is this generosity that finally unmasks Mak as a thief. Mak is portrayed as a wily, henpecked rogue, who communicates with expert timing one thing to the shepherds and another to the audience. Gil, his clever,

shrewish wife, is a close comic supporter of her husband, while the religious figures are religious stereotypes without personality. The dialogue is simple and naïve, illuminating a scene or a character with a minumum of effort; the theme is man's sinfulness and need for redemption. The play first demonstrates Mak's sinfulness and then follows with the birth of the Redeemer. There are other parallels between the two parts of the story: a comic mother, father, and "child" set against holy ones. The child is a real lamb in the first part and a symbolic lamb of God in the second. Also, the shepherds present gifts in both parts of the story.

The rhythm of the play constitutes an unrolling linear progression as in all medieval art; the physical requirements are limited to a field, Mak's house, and a manger. The same mansion was probably used for the house and manger; only the curtain was changed. A curtain was needed to hide Mak and Gil when

Figure 4–20 Banquet scene from *The Salzburg Everyman* by Hugo von Hofmannsthal produced by the Goodman Theatre, Chicago, 1957. Translated and directed by John Reich. Illustrates the rich costumes, properties, and accessories frequently required in very late medieval religious drama. Photo courtesy of John Reich.

they were not supposed to be on stage and to obscure the cradle and the bed. If the mansion were placed on a pageant wagon, another flat-bedded wagon or stationary platform would have been needed to serve as the open field. Costumes for Mak and the shepherds would have been simple medieval peasant tunics and hose; Gil would have worn the skirt and blouse of a lower-class woman, and only Mary and the angel would have required richer symbolic garments.

In addition to the cycle dramas, other play forms developed in the late Gothic period. The most important of these were the miracle plays, about the lives of the saints; morality plays like the famous *Everyman;* and secular farces like *Master Pierre Pathelin.* All were short and included only one or two major incidents. All are more important for learning about the transition to the Renaissance than for gaining an understanding of medieval thought and culture.

The most famous of these later medieval dramas is probably the morality play *Every-man* in its various national variations. Morality plays were allegories about the moral temptations that beset man on his journey from life to death; the protagonist, usually Mankind or Everyman, was advised by personifications of good and evil like the seven virtues, the seven deadly sins, Mercy, Good Deeds, Knowledge, and Death. Though many morality plays cover man's entire life, *Everyman* deals only with the preparations for death as the protagonist asks former companions (including Goods, Beauty, Strength, Discretion, and Five Wits) to accompany him to the grave. Because only Good Deeds will go with him, Everyman comes to understand the meaning of life on earth in relation to salvation. It is a moving drama with universal appeal. In the German version, dramatized anew by Hugo von Hofmannsthal in 1911, there is a brilliant theatrical banquet scene during which Death calls Everyman to his final Judgment (Figure 4–20). As can be seen, this version allows a full display of late Gothic costumes, properties, manners, and customs.

Acting and Directing the Plays

Obviously, there is a tremendous difference between acting in religious dramas and farces from the late medieval period and in the nineteenth- and twentieth-century plays set in this period. Medieval religious plays and secular farces demand a naïveté and directness of performance not found in the sophisticated dramas about Gothic times written in the past century and a half. The majority of actors in medieval cycle plays were drawn from the local community and were chosen by audition as in modern community theatre. Though there was much doubling of minor roles, a full company usually consisted of seventy-five to one hundred actors. There were initial readings of the script and fines for missing rehearsal. The longer cycle sequences were rehearsed section by section over about an eighty-day period, with sponsoring guilds usually supplying food and drink at rehearsals. The quality of acting probably varied enormously. A good voice was highly valued, as were actors who had the timing and physical agility for the important comic roles. By the close of the Gothic period, a number of actors were paid as coaches, while others were actually paid performers in leading roles.

Thus, the modern actor and director tackling these plays should strive for simplicity and directness and the unselfconsciousness and exuberant enjoyment still found in village community theatre. To feel superior to the material or to comment on it is to lose the straightforward results desired. In a morality play like *Everyman*, the characters are more vivid and meaningful if they are not presented as symbolic stereotypes; as in the cycle dramas, a direct, simple, strong realism is best. In farces like *Master Pierre Pathelin*, the actor should be agile and able to handle much acrobatic action and physical byplay.

The problem changes abruptly in presenting plays about the medieval period written in modern times. In a play set in the early or High Gothic period of the thirteenth century, the simple semidraped garments and relaxed poses found in statuary would dictate a simple approach in the use of costumes even while presenting the nineteenth- or twentieth-century sophistication of character. But in a play set in the middle of the fourteenth century onward, the costume, manuscript illumination, sculpture, and architecture dictate a great emphasis among the upper classes on artificiality, sophistication, exaggerated grace, and a decorative, ornamental use of body and gesture. The gestures must be strong and bold, and the body movement must be rather exaggerated so that the costumes and accessories will not seem excessive and burdensome to the actor.

Designing the Plays

Those producing *The Second Shepherd's Play* should try to approximate the vivid, personal, naïve, decorative reality achieved by the medieval craftsmen who first produced it. (Many times the artisans who worked on the medieval mystery plays also decorated the great cathedrals.) The difference between character size and background size, between the reality of personality and the unreality of the story—all should be carefully stressed to capture the duality of the worldly and the unworldly that exists in these plays.

The lines, textures, and colors of Gothic art can be studied with profit in preparation for a modern production of one of the mystery plays. Color could reflect either the chalky fresco color of Giotto or the bright, clear, undiluted color of the stained-glass windows and illuminated manuscripts. Line might reflect either the simple lines of Giotto's frescoes or the fascinating arabesques of the international Gothic style. Texture, which is usually subordinate to line and color in Gothic art, could reflect the rough surface of stone, the soft texture of wool, the carved texture of wood, or the brilliant transparency of stained glass.

Since the most important visual idea in the medieval mysteries is the unrolling processional progression from playlet to playlet, with all scenes visible at the same time, some arrangement should be made in presenting *The Second Shepherd's Play* so that the open fields, Mak's house, and the manger are seen together, possibly using a single mansion (with a change of curtains) set in a small open space as the setting for both Mak's house and the Nativity. This mansion could be a decorative Gothic framework for action (as in many illuminated manuscripts), or it could suggest a specific miniature house as in the paintings of Giotto (Figure 4–14). If the play is to be produced as one in a series of cycle dramas, then a decorative architectural framework, which could appear in many of the playlets, would be a good design choice.

Properties should obviously be realistic and simple, and costumes should be limited to the medieval peasant hoods, tunics, cloaks, and hose that are worn, for example, by two shepherds on the royal portal of Chartres Cathedral. Here we have an excellent example of the fit and drape of two, simple, lower-class costumes that would be exactly right for the mood of the play. The draping of the hoods, the wrinkles in the hose, the folds on the sleeves—all make a decorative linear statement that could be achieved in actual costumes by the correct choice of soft woolens and the right cutting and fitting of the garments. The Virgin and the Angel should be clothed in the religiously symbolic colors and garments found in illuminated manuscripts, statues, and paintings of the period (Figure 4–14). A balance of simplicity and casual beauty can be adapted to the costumes for the shepherds in the play to bring out the naïve charm of the early scenes, the farcical humor of the middle scenes, and the religious beauty of the final tableau.

PROJECTS AND PROBLEMS

1. Stage a scene from the tomb of Junius Bassus (Figure 4–1). What are your problems? What effect will an audience get from the scene?

2. Now stage the entire sequence of scenes one after another. How will you frame them? What transitions will you make from one to the other? How will you indicate which are from the Old Testament and which from the New Testament? What kind of dramatic rhythm is obtained from presenting the entire group of scenes?

3. Think of the Theodora grouping as part of a staged scene (Figure 4–2). If you were a director, what would you tell your actors about their roles, the effect they are to create, and the reason for their downstage and frontal blocking?

4. Design the makeup for the participants in the mosaic of Theodora and her retinue (Figure 4–2).

5. Describe the weight, texture, and feel of the costumes in the Theodora mosaic (Figure 4–2).

6. Describe the properties in this mosaic (Figure 4–2). What does each item contribute to the scene, and what is its symbolism?

7. Design an appropriate setting within which the mosaic scene (Figure 4–2) could take place.

8. After reading the Book of Job, then design a Byzantine church setting for a dramatization of the story.

9. What other plays or stories can be presented in Byzantine dress against a Byzantine background?

10. Devise a design and a directorial plan for presenting the first and last scenes of *The Winter's Tale* within a Byzantine setting.

11. Within a Byzantine perspective, how would you develop and treat the transformation scene at the end of *The Winter's Tale* when Hermione changes from a statue into a person?

12. List the attributes of the Roman versus Byzantine dress. Briefly summarize the differences.

13. After studying the animal interlace patterns in the *Animal Head from the Oseberg Ship Burial* (Figure 4–4), create your own interlace pattern. How did you feel while you were developing it? What aspects of your personality does this kind of

doodling invoke? What does the final result look like?

14. After studying the *Animal Head from the Oseberg Ship Burial* (Figure 4–4), describe the motivations, thought processes, and world outlook of the warriors who would have sailed in a ship with such a head.

15. Choose a theatrical scene from a particular play or invent a scene that could play inside the chapel at Aachen (Figure 4–5). Describe the scene. What is the mood? Describe the lighting, the blocking, and the feelings of the clothing in texture, line, and color.

16. What is the mood created by the gathering around Charles the Bald in the manuscript illumination of that name (Figure 4–6)? If you were to play this grouping as part of a staged scene, what would be the nature and effect of the scene?

17. Imagine yourself in the costumes of the earlier medieval or Carolingian period (Figure 4–6). What do they do for your feeling about yourself? For your movement? For your senses when you feel and look at the textures?

18. Borrow, or even make, some simple tunics like those in the *Bible of Charles the Bald* (Figure 4–6). Put them on, draping them to suggest the clothing ideal in the scenes. What is the feeling? What happens to your movement?

19. Design a simple layout for a series of simple religious playlets inside a cathedral. Do a ground plan and describe the sequence of action.

20. Describe the arrangement of the mansions in a cycle series and their relation to the *platea* in an early medieval theatrical production.

21. Imagine yourself in the makeup and costumes worn by an actor in *Romans by St. Paul*, produced by the Everyman Players (Figure 4–9). How would you move? How would you speak? How realistic a character would you create?

22. After studying the pictures in Chapter 4, explain Henry Adams's famous statement that the Romanesque style is primarily masculine while the Gothic is more feminine.

23. Imagine yourself dressed to look like the statues on the west portal of Chartres (Figure 4–10). In what kind of play would you be appearing? How would you move? How would you feel?

24. Compare the figures on the west portal of Chartres (Figure 4–10) with those on the south portal (Figure 4–11). What has happened? Why would it be easier to play one of the figures from the south portal?

25. Describe the personality, goals, and ideals of the Christian knight, St. Theodore, from the south portal of Chartres (Figure 4–11). How would you present him on stage? How do his clothes differ from those worn in earlier medieval times?

26. What mood would a setting representing Notre Dame Cathedral (Figure 4–12) give to a scene in a play?

27. Imagine yourself in front of the Church of St. Maclou (Figure 4–13). Describe your feelings and the kind of play that might include the ornamental effects at St. Maclou as a part of the design.

28. Imagine a large theatrical scene played out against the interior of Haddon Hall (Figure 4–15). What would be the character of the scene? Describe the characteristics of plays having such a scene.

29. Imagine playing the role of either Ekkehard or Uta (Figure 4–16). What kind of people are they? How would they relate to one another? To their position in life? To the outside world? What would your movement be like in either of their costumes?

30. Now compare the costumes in *The Exchange of the Rings* (Figure 4–17) with those worn by Ekkehard and Uta (Figure 4–16). What has happened to fashion and personal appearance in the century and a half or so that separates the two works? Describe the movement and manners that you would adopt in playing one of the characters in *The Exchange of the Rings*.

31. Finally, compare the costumes in *The Betrothal of Renaud de Montaubon and Clarisse, Daughter of King Yon of Gascoigne* (Figure 4–18) with those in *The Exchange of the Rings* (Figure 4–17). What has happened to dress in the short forty years that separate these two works? What kind of play would contain a scene like the betrothal scene?

32. Why is there no conflict in the medieval mind between the episodes of farcical horseplay and sheep stealing and the final nativity scene in *The Second Shepherd's Play*?

33. Explain how you would develop contemporary productions of *The Second Shepherd's Play* and of *Everyman*. Discuss costumes, sets, blocking, makeup, lighting, and stylistic interpretation.

BIBLIOGRAPHY

Aubert, Marcel. *The Art of the High Gothic Era.* New York: Crown, 1964. An excellent survey of the basic qualities making up the art of northern and western Europe during the late twelfth and early thirteenth centuries.

Brantl, Ruth, ed. *Medieval Culture.* The Culture of Mankind Series. New York: Braziller, 1966. An excellent compilation of writings from original sources on early and late medieval culture.

Brooke, Iris. *Medieval Theatre Costume.* New York: Theatre Arts, 1967. An excellent volume on costume for the medieval theatre.

Chambers, E. K. *The Medieval Stage.* 2 vols. Oxford: The Clarendon Press, 1903. This standard work is still useful in establishing the basic facts of medieval staging.

Evans, Joan. *Art in Medieval France.* New York: Oxford University Press, 1948. A classic study by one of the acknowledged experts in the field.

Focillon, Henry. *The Art of the West in the Middle Ages.* Translated by Donald King. 2 vols. New York: Phaidon, 1964. An excellent and au-thoritative study on art in western Europe from pre-Carolingian times through the Gothic period.

Fremantle, Anne. *Age of Faith.* The Great Ages of Man Series. New York: Time-Life Books, 1965. Covers the intellectual, artistic, and cultural developments in Europe from the Romanesque through the Gothic periods.

Gardiner, Harold C. *Mysteries' End: An Investigation of the Last Days of the Medieval Religious Stage.* New Haven: Yale University Press, 1946. An excellent scholarly study of the staging methods for religious drama at the close of the Gothic period.

Grabar, André. *Christian Iconography: A Study of Its Origins.* Translated by T. Grabar. Princeton, N.J.: Princeton University Press, 1968. Useful for the student in finding out the nature of early Christian symbolism in art.

———. *The Beginnings of Christian Art*, 200–395. Translated by Stuart Gilbert and James Emmons. London: Thames and Hudson, 1967. A very good study of catacomb art in Italy and of the earliest Christian artistic remains in the eastern Mediterranean area and Near East before the final fall of Rome.

———. *Byzantine Art in the Middle Ages*. Translated by Betty Forster. London: Methuen, 1966. An excellent study of Byzantine art after the iconoclastic controversy.

———. *Romanesque Painting from the Eleventh to the Thirteenth Century*. Translated by Stuart Gilbert. New York: Skira, 1958. The companion volume to the study of early medieval painting, this volume covers the high period of Romanesque art.

———. *The Golden Age of Justinian, from the Death of Theodosius to the Rise of Islam*. Translated by Stuart Gilbert and James Emmons. New York: Odyssey Press, 1967. An excellent study, beautifully illustrated by this master of the arts of the early Middle Ages; very useful for the theatre student reconstructing the life and times of Justinian.

Grabar, André, and Nordenfalk, Carl. *Early Medieval Painting*. New York: Skira, 1957. Containing tipped-in plates, this book is an excellent overview of medieval fresco and manuscript art from early Christian times to the early Romanesque period.

Hardison, O. B. *Christian Rite and Christian Drama in the Middle Ages: Essays in the Origin and History of Modern Drama*. Baltimore: Johns Hopkins Press, 1965. A fascinating discussion of the beginnings of theatre and dramatic art within Christian ritual and of how Christianity affected the moral tone of later dramatic art.

Hinks, Roger P. *Carolingian Art*. London: Sidgwick and Jackson, 1935. Though a little dated, this is still the standard classroom survey on the art of the Carolingian period.

Houston, Mary G. *Medieval Costume in England and France*. London: A. & C. Black, 1959. An excellent technical explanation of the cutting and wearing of medieval garments from pre-Carolingian through Gothic times; contains a few color plates and over 300 line drawings.

Kahrl, S. J. *Traditions of Medieval English Drama*. London: Hutchinson, 1974. A useful update to go along with Chambers's *The Medieval Stage*.

Katzenellenbogen, Adolf. *The Sculptural Programs of Chartres Cathedral*. Baltimore: Johns Hopkins Press, 1959. An excellent book from which to develop a sense of the immense human and technical changes that took place in sculpture from the transitional to the High Gothic style.

Kernodle, George. *From Art to Theatre*. Chicago: University of Chicago Press, 1944. One of the seminal books on the relationship between visual arts and the theatre. Traces this relationship from early medieval times through the Renaissance.

Kidson, Peter. *The Medieval World*. Landmarks of the World's Art Series. New York: McGraw-Hill 1967. Deals with medieval art from pre-Romanesque times through the Gothic period.

———. *Sculpture at Chartres*. London: Tiranti, 1958. An excellent companion volume to the one by Katzenellenbogen.

Lassus, Jean. *The Early Christian and Byzantine World*. Landmarks of the World's Art Series. New York: McGraw-Hill, 1967. Covers all aspects of eastern Mediterranean art in the thousand years following the acceptance of Christianity in Rome. Excellently illustrated with many color plates.

Mâle, Émil. *The Gothic Image: Religious Art in France of the Thirteenth Century*. Translated by Dora Nussey. New York: Harper, 1958. A beautifully written book on the religious thought that infused the art of the High Gothic period.

Martindale, Andrew. *Gothic Art*. New York: Praeger, 1967. A fine survey on all aspects of Gothic art.

Morey, Charles Rufus. *Early Christian Art*. 2nd ed. Princeton, N.J.: Princeton University Press, 1953. A very good survey on the development of early Christian art in Rome and related areas before the reconquest of Italy by the Byzantines. Contains some illustrations.

Nicoll, Allardyce. *Masks, Mimes, and Miracles*. New York: Harcourt Brace Jovanovich, 1931. Another standard work by one of the great historians of the theatre. Although slightly dated, it is still a useful volume for studying medieval play production.

Nordenfalk, Carl. *Celtic and Anglo-Saxon Painting*. New York: Praeger, 1977. A very useful and well-illustrated volume on the manuscript paintings in Ireland and England in the years before 1000.

Norris, Herbert. *Costume and Fashion: The Evolution of European Dress through the Earlier Ages*. London: J. W. Dent & Sons, Ltd., 1947. A very useful book, with some colored plates and many drawings, tracing the development of clothing and ornament from Greek to early medieval times. Especially helpful information on early Christian and Byzantine dress.

Rice, David Talbot. *Art of the Byzantine Era*. New

York: Praeger, 1963. An excellent and beautifully illustrated survey on the visual arts of the Byzantines.

Saalman, Howard. *Medieval Architecture*. New York: Braziller, 1942. An excellent survey on the growth and development of all phases of medieval architecture from pre-Carolingian times to the Renaissance.

Sherrard, Philip. *Byzantium*. The Great Ages of Man Series. New York: Time-Life Books, 1966. Intended for the average reader, this beautifully illustrated book, with extensive color photography, covers the major intellectual, cultural, and artistic developments in the Byzantine Empire.

Simons, Gerald. *Barbarian Europe*. The Great Ages of Man Series. New York: Time-Life Books, 1968. Intended for the average reader, this beautifully illustrated book with extensive color photography discusses the major artistic, intellectual, and cultural developments in Europe during and after the fall of Rome and until the beginning of the Romanesque period.

Southern, Richard. *The Medieval Theatre in the Round*. 2nd ed. London: Faber & Faber, 1975. An interesting study by a theatrical historian and designer on the staging of plays in the round in medieval times.

Volbach, Wolfgang F., and Hirmer, Max. *Early Christian Art*. New York: Abrams, 1961. An excellent, well-illustrated survey of the beginnings of Christian art and its eventual absorption into Byzantine and Carolingian art.

Wickham, Glynne. *Early English Stages* 1300–1660. 3 vols. New York: Columbia University Press, 1959–1980. A superb and very detailed history of drama and play production in England during medieval and Elizabethan times.

Williams, Arnold. *The Drama of Medieval England*. East Lansing: Michigan State University Press, 1961. A good summary of the structural elements in medieval drama in England.

Winston, Richard and Clara. *Daily Life in the Middle Ages*. A Horizon Book. New York: American Heritage, 1975. Discusses life during the great cultural moments in Mediterranean and Western history. Gives interesting insights into medieval life and contains excellent and infrequently published illustrations.

Early and High Renaissance Style

At the height of the flamboyant late Gothic style flourishing in Europe after the middle of the fourteenth century, a new classical Golden Age developed in Florence. It made both scholars and artists compare the city to Athens of the fifth century B.C. Like the Athenians after their repulse of the Persians, the citizens of Florence, after their similar defeat of the Duke of Milan's attempt to subdue Tuscany, responded with new patriotic pride in their city. They made it the center of an exploding artistic and cultural development that has come to be called the Renaissance. Though this cultural development had its origins in the early fourteenth century, it was cut short by the Black Plague of 1348 that swept all Europe. The plague was particularly deadly in Tuscany, and Florence took almost a half-century to regain its pride and self-confidence. By the opening of the fifteenth century, however, the city had once again become a center of vast trade and wealth in the hands of a few illustrious families interested in being patrons of art and learning.

The most influential of these patrons was the Medici family, whose clever manipulation of local politics made it the virtual dictator of the Florentine Republic. The most outstanding member of the family was Lorenzo the Magnificent; in the late fifteenth century he acted as patron to numerous artists and intellectuals, who to this day symbolize the highest cultural development that a city and an art patron can achieve. Lorenzo also extended the Medici Library, revitalized the academy for instruction in the arts, established the Platonic Academy of Philosophy, and lavished sizable personal and city funds on buildings, festivals, and many other forms of public art. By the time of his death in 1492, Florence had passed through its golden age. In the period that followed—which saw the invasion of Italy by the French, the loss of the Medici family's power in Florence, the shift in the center of art and power to Rome, and a change in artistic ideals—the tradition of art patronage was carried on in Rome by the

Medici Pope Leo X, the patron of Michelangelo and Raphael.

The artistic outlook of the fifteenth century in Florence can be considered the youth of Renaissance culture—an age of experimentation with the natural world. Particularly in his use of mathematical perspective to set man in a real space in a specifically calculated position, the Early Renaissance artist demonstrated a new idea about man's place in the scheme of things and about man's control over his own destiny. Naturalism had been at work to some extent in early and High Gothic art, but never in a coherent and organized manner. The naturalism of the fifteenth century in Florence was consciously scientific and mathematical in origin. The decorative, curving lines and flat patterns of the international Gothic style gave way to tactile forms, mathematical precision, and the simple dignity found in the works of the great Florentine triumvirate: Masaccio, Donatello, and Brunelleschi. This early Renaissance ended about the time of the death of Lorenzo the Magnificent and was gradually replaced by a High Renaissance art of more maturity, nobility, strength, power, and unity—an art symbolizing the absolute authority and power of the Catholic Church and its popes in Rome.

To see this distinction between the Early and the High Renaissance, let us compare *David* by Donatello, dating from 1430 to 1432, with the even more famous one by Michelangelo dating from 1501 to 1504 (Figures 5–1

Figure 5–1 Donatello, *David,* bronze, approximately 62″ high, c. 1430–32. The first life-size fully free-standing nude statue since antiquity, it symbolizes the adolescence and youth of Italian Renaissance culture in the first three-quarters of the fifteenth century. Museo Nazionale, Florence. Photo courtesy of Alinari, Florence.

Figure 5–2 Michelangelo, *David,* marble, approximately 18′ high, 1501–04. Illustrates the heroic scale, monumental grandeur, and unified emotional power of the High Renaissance. Galleria dell'Accademia, Florence. Photo courtesy of Alinari, Florence.

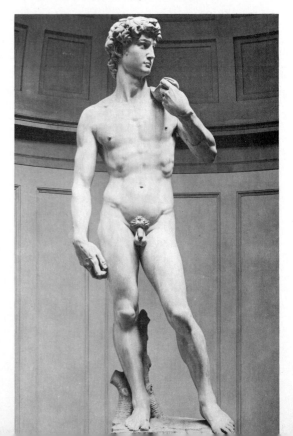

and 5–2). Donatello's *David* is the first free-standing nude statue since classical times, with a contrapposto pose and radiant sensuous charm impossible in Gothic art. One need only examine the figures on the south porch at Chartres to see the striking difference (Figure 4–11). But this David is involved in a complex psychological drama that would have been unknown in classical times. The glance of this adolescent hero is directed not at the severed head of Goliath but at his own graceful body as if his heroic deed has made him aware of the strength, vitality, and beauty of his own body. In many ways the figure is the perfect symbol of youthful self-discovery, a key theme of the early Renaissance.

In contrast, Michelangelo's *David* no longer represents the adolescent world of the Early Renaissance but has a maturity, power, and strength symbolic of the High Renaissance. Bursting with confidence and vitality and no longer willing to copy antiquity, artists like Michelangelo took the ideals of the Greek and Roman past, absorbing, mastering, and surpassing them. This *David* depicts the moment of perfect muscular tension and balance just before the body is released into action. The rugged torso and limbs, large hands and feet, and fierce gaze are unified into a powerful mood of tense expectation. We feel in the presence of a monumental, superhuman hero symbolic of the new cultural and artistic ideals of the High, or Roman, Renaissance. The student of the theatre should be able to identify easily with these two figures and see in them patterns of movement, gesture, and outlook characteristic of the two cultural-artistic styles.

To complete the comparison between the Early and High Renaissance, let us look at two small chapels—architectural cameos of the design principles found in larger buildings of the time. The first is the Pazzi Chapel, begun between 1430 and 1433, next to the Church of Santa Croce in Florence (Figure 5–3). Its creator was Filippo Brunelleschi, an artistic genius who was a founder of the early Renaissance style in Florence both in sculpture and in architecture. A small structure with a

Figure 5–3 Filippo Brunelleschi and others, Pazzi Chapel, Church of Santa Croce, Florence, c. 1430–33. Note the slender classical arcading, simple geometric forms, and delicate decoration in the colonnaded loggia and dome. Photo courtesy of Alinari, Florence.

central dome and a *narthex*, or porch, it repeats at the center a smaller version of the larger dome. The façade is delicate and quite flat, consisting of an entablature supported by slender columns broken in the middle by a large central arch with flat decoration consisting simply of geometric squares, rectangles, and circles. Like Donatello's *David*, it is a delicate, youthful, simple, and very cool intellectual plan whose mathematical design creates its own thin ornamentation. Each larger section is a multiple of smaller ones, and the whole is a series of clearly defined and quite separate compartments. How different this is from the ever-changing skeletal openness of Gothic structures (Figure 4–13).

The second small chapel is the Tempietto (Figure 5–4). Designed by Donato Bramante in 1502, who was later to design St. Peter's Cathedral, it represents the arrival of Renaissance maturity much as does Michelangelo's *David*. The Tempietto is the perfect prototype of classical domed architecture for the High Renaissance and many subsequent periods. Its sculptured muscularity—the feeling of having been carved out of a great mass of masonry—gives it monumental weight despite its small size. Its round volumes seem to move and remain still at the same time, and there is a marvelous harmony among its parts. The controlled play of light and shade around the columns, balustrade, niches, and lip of the cupola enhances this harmony. In every way, the chapel fulfills the High Renaissance demands for the ideal church, based on the perfection of the circle. An actor against this setting would feel nobler and more mature than against the Pazzi Chapel; his clothing would also be fuller and heavier with thicker textures and more rounded lines.

The High Renaissance was both a maturation of Early Renaissance style and an amalgam of new ideals of grandeur, unity, and dramatic effectiveness. The Early Renaissance has the mood and character of light chamber music, while the High Renaissance is closer to a full-bodied symphony. Yet, despite the overpowering genius of High Renaissance artists like Michelangelo, Bramante, Raphael, and Leonardo da Vinci, the style lasted only about twenty-five years, from about 1495 to 1520. External conditions created by big power politics and the rise of the Reformation caused the style to decline after 1520, though it might have come to an end

Figure 5–4   Donato Bramante, the Tempietto, Church of San Pietro, Montorio, 1502. Illustrates the architectural design ideals of the High Renaissance with sculptured muscularity, swelling rounded volumes, unity and harmony of parts, and controlled use of light and shade. Based on the perfection of the circle, it demonstrates the mature Renaissance love of unity, balance, grandeur, and nobility. Photo courtesy of Alinari, Florence.

of its own accord shortly thereafter, since its reach for an impossible harmony and grandeur was inherently unstable. A precarious balance of basically divergent qualities was maintained only by the genius of leading artists; when the majority of these died, the style was lost amidst the instability of the times and the lesser ideals of minor artists.

Music

Popular music making in Florence and in other Italian cities was very much a part of the good life; but, because few pieces were actually written down, it was mainly a performer's art. However, the Flemish musician Heinrich Isaac, organist and choirmaster of Florence

Cathedral and appointed Lorenzo the Magnificent's concertmaster in 1475, did compose some musical settings for Lorenzo's verses. One of the surviving pieces shows a tendency away from complex counterpoint toward simple harmonic texture. This emphasis on simplicity characterizes the musical development of the Italian Renaissance; the intent was to take the northern Burgundian "chanson" and simplify it, to remove all artificiality, and to enliven a rather stiff form with graceful folk melodies and rhythms.

When the focus of the Italian Renaissance shifted to Rome in the early years of the sixteenth century, the center of musical development became the Sistine Chapel Choir under its esteemed Flemish director, Josquin des Prez, who was described fifty years after his death "as a natural prodigy in music." The *Capella Sistina* was devoted to the Italian High Renaissance ideal of perfection, even though dominated by musicians from Burgundy, Flanders, and France. In Josquin's compositions, the stark and rather hard intervals of Gothic polyphony, as well as all harshness in the use of the voice, were eliminated; all rhythms and forms were based on strict symmetry and mathematically regular proportions. This musician was at home in all Renaissance musical forms, and his unique abilities were perfectly combined with the warmth and fluidity of Italian lyricism. For example, his "Ave Maria," like Michelangelo's early *Pietà,* has a perfectly self-contained form, great emotional restraint, and luxuriantly full-flowing lines. His was undoubtedly the greatest musical mind of the early sixteenth century.

Life and Cultural Ideals

Despite its new-found love of the classical past and the civilized qualities of ancient Greece and Rome, the Renaissance was still a period of violence and brutality. The upper classes, however, did go to remarkable lengths to be polite and agreeable when they were not at each other's throats. In the typical, and in many ways, ideal city-state of Urbino in the mountainous area northeast of Rome, an enlightened Renaissance ruler, Federigo Montefeltro, established one of the most admired and cultured Renaissance courts in Italy during the later years of the fifteenth century. At his palace, filled with fine art, he entertained famous artists, philosophers, and intellectuals. In *The Book of the Courtier,* written by a young Mantuan, Baldassare Castiglione, who settled at the court in the reign of Federigo's son, we have excellent descriptions of how the perfect gentleman and lady should behave in Renaissance society.

Castiglione began by describing how the gentlemen of the court gathered about the duchess after dinner to participate in dancing, music, games, and discussions about the responsibilities of the ideal courtier. For four centuries Castiglione's definition of the perfect gentleman, though extremely class-conscious, has remained an admired ideal:

> I would have our Courtier born of a noble family . . . for noble birth is like a bright lamp that makes manifest and visible deeds both good and bad. . . . And since this luster of nobility does not shine forth in the deeds of the lowly, they lack that spur, as well as that fear of dishonor. . . . [The Courtier is] endowed by nature not only with talent and with beauty of countenance and person, but with that certain grace we call an "air." . . .

The courtier was to be handsome, manly, full of grace, and acquainted with all weapons as well as to be able to swim, jump, run, play tennis, and ride horses expertly.

> But above all, let him temper every action with a certain good judgment and grace . . . let him laugh, jest, banter, frolic, and dance in such a manner as to show always that he is genial and discreet; and let him be full of grace in all that he does or says. [He must] exhibit a certain *sprezzatura,* or nonchalance, so as to conceal all art and make whatever is done or said appear to be without effort and almost without any thought about it.

. . . the true profession of the Courtier ought to be that of arms; which I would have him follow actively above all else, and be known among others as bold and strong, and loyal to whomsoever he serves. . . . And just as among women, their fair name once sullied never recovers its first lustre, so the reputation of a gentleman who bears arms, if it once be tarnished with cowardice or disgrace, remains forever infamous before the world and full of ignominy. . . . Whenever the Courtier chances to be engaged in a skirmish . . . or a battle in the field . . . he should discreetly withdraw from the crowd, and do the outstanding and daring things that he has to do in as small a company as possible. . . . Whereas, if he happens to engage in arms in some public show— such as jousts, tourneys, stick-throwing, or in any other bodily exercise . . . he will strive to be as elegant and handsome in the exercise of arms as he is adroit, and to feed the spectators' eyes with all those things that he thinks may give him added grace.

There is no doubt that many noblemen of the period tried to live up to Castiglione's standards not only in the arts of warfare but also in social conversations about philosophy, music, and art, which were sprinkled with references to Michelangelo, Raphael, Ovid, and Livy. Discussions were supposed to have wit, charm, and frankness; the gentlemen, as can be seen in the portraits of the period, were to wear an air of gravity, elegance, nonchalance, and self-assurance. Castiglione definitely projected a man of learning as well as a warrior:

I would have him more than passably learned in letters, at least in those studies which we call the humanities. Let him be conversant not only with the Latin language but with Greek as well, because of the variety of things that are so divinely written therein. Let him be versed in the poets, as well as in the orators and historians, and let him be practiced also in writing verse and prose, especially in our own vernacular. . . . [In dancing] I think he should maintain a certain dignity, though tempered with a fine and airy grace of movement; and . . . let him not attempt those quick movements of foot and those double steps . . . which would perhaps little befit a gentleman. . . .

The proper dress for the Courtier was another topic of discussion:

[It should] not be extreme in any way, as the French are sometimes in being over-ample, and the Germans in being over-scanty. . . . I prefer [clothes] always to tend a little more toward the grave and sober rather than the foppish. Hence, I think that black is more pleasing in clothing than any other color; and if not black, then at least some color on the dark side. I mean this of ordinary attire, for there is no doubt that . . . it is appropriate for gala dress to be trimmed, showy, and dashing. . . . [But] who of us on seeing a gentleman pass by dressed in a habit quartered in varied colors, or with an array of strings and ribbons and bows and cross lacings, does not take him to be a fool or a buffoon?

In setting down the ideal character of the Renaissance gentleman, Castiglione described a man who seems without much substance, believing in little, and having no burning convictions or goals other than his urbane worldliness.

As far as the Renaissance woman was concerned, Castiglione had Giuliano de Medici, son of Lorenzo the Magnificent, describe the ideal court lady:

I think, that in her ways, manners, words, gestures and bearing, a woman ought to be very unlike a man. . . . It is seemly for a woman to have a soft and delicate tenderness, with an air of womanly sweetness in her every movement. . . . Now if this precept be added to the rules which these gentlemen have taught the Courtier, then I think she ought to be able to follow many such and adorn herself with the best accomplishments. . . In a Lady who lives at the court a certain pleasing affability is becoming above all else, whereby she will be able to entertain graciously every kind of man with agreeable and comely conversation to the time and place and to the station of the person with whom she speaks. . . .

I think there is none here who does not recognize that, as for bodily exercises, it is not seemly for a woman to handle weapons, ride, play tennis, wrestle and do many other things that are suited to men. . . [But intellectually the Lady should have] a knowledge of letters, of music, of painting and . . . how to be festive, adding a discreet modesty and the giving of a good impression of herself to those other things that have been required of the Courtier.

Clearly, the ideals of freedom were in conflict with tradition, and contradictions were inevitable. The Renaissance woman was certainly freer than her medieval counterpart, even though her role was still defined by the male. Certainly the Renaissance attitude toward both men and women persisted as a Western ideal until the early twentieth century.

Let us now look at the social organization of upper-class family life typical of Italy in the hundred-year period between 1420 and 1520. The Doria family in Genoa, whose male population numbered over four hundred, can serve as a model. This family resembled in many ways a modern Mafia "family." The fact that a crime committed by an individual Doria was a crime committed by the entire family explains why Renaissance family feuds were so frequent. The father or head of the family had absolute authority, though his decisions often were based on consultations with uncles, cousins, and sons. In contrast, women were not consulted on matters of importance; their only role was to bear children and supervise the domestic scene. Male children were a necessity, but female children were also helpful in establishing a certain social upward mobility through arranged marriages. No negotiation was more important than the marriage contract with its careful arrangement of a girl's dowry. The haggling of the parents over the dowry often took months, and the procedures involved were much like those of a corporate merger. The wedding feast itself lasted for days with scores of relatives involved, and the food consumed was enormous. When Lorenzo the Magnificent was married, the guests consumed 800 calves, 4,000 chickens, 5,000 pounds of sweetmeats, and 100 kegs of wine.

Daily fare was quite different. The poor ate bread and soup and had meat only a few times a year, while the upper-middle class ate milk, butter, cheese, and had meat every Sunday. Breakfast included bread, fruit, and cheese; the main meal consisted of salad, bread, fruit, cheese, soup, and occasionally sausage and vegetables with large amounts of pasta.

The town houses, or palaces of the fifteenth century, were larger than those in the past so as to give some privacy from the flock of relatives; despite this fact, little space was allotted for living quarters. There were shops or storage areas on the ground floor; the family lived on the middle floor in a dozen or so rooms without connecting corridors, each room opening to the next. The central gathering place, except for formal occasions, was the kitchen, where a fire burned all day. The two meals of the day were at ten in the morning and at five in the evening. Furnishings were sparse. People often sat on stools and chests, and tables were frequently made by placing boards on trestles. The most important pieces of furniture were carved beds with great mattresses and bolsters, while the most ornate piece was the *cassone*, or wedding chest, intricately carved and containing all the wife's clothing and possessions. The objects of real value in an urban town house were not the pieces of furniture, but rather the jewelry, pitchers, goblets, books, tapestries, and works of art.

Even the wealthy families had only three or four servants; thus, life was relatively simple except for festive occasions. Typical of most capitalist family traditions, the husband was seldom at home; his home was merely a base from which to launch business trips and political forays. Women spent their time in church or at home with the children, who often numbered in the teens. For example, the household of Otto Niccolini in 1470 consisted of one bastard son and two sons by a former wife, a pregnant second wife, and thirteen other children ranging in age from twenty-four to one. To support such a family and to ensure the comforts of living typical of his level in society, the Renaissance father was ever after money. Money was the mainspring of the Italian Renaissance, and those who did not have it borrowed it. This society set in motion the economic machine that eventually created the modern world.

Though many houses, such as the Davanzati Palace in Florence, have been refurnished in the style of the period, some of the best examples of Renaissance ornament, interiors, and furniture can be found in paintings of the time. *The Birth of the Virgin* by the Florentine Domenico Ghirlandaio, dating from about 1490, shows the clothing of upper-class women, ladies-in-waiting, and servants and a palace interior of the time (Figure 5–5). The columns are covered with urns and acanthus leaf decoration based on Roman sources, while

Ornament, Interiors, and Furniture

the walls are embellished with fine *intarsia,* or wooden mosaics. Though a bit excessive, the decoration represents the excitement of discovery and display that gripped Italy in the later fifteenth century. The foreground column with its profusion of urns and acanthus leaves looks Roman only at first glance, since it is organized in a very Renaissance way. In its organization and excessive richness, this column marks the end of the Early Renaissance and the beginning of the High Renaissance. Nowhere does the youthful simplicity

Figure 5–5 Domenico Ghirlandaio, *The Birth of the Virgin,* fresco, Church of Santa Maria Novella, Florence, c. 1485–90. Illustrates the growing weight and richness of interior decoration at the end of the Early Italian Renaissance and the female fashions of the time. Photo courtesy of Alinari, Florence.

at work in Donatello's *David* and in the façade of the Pazzi Chapel appear (Figures 5–1 and 5–3). The room even seems a bit overpowering and oppressive in its display of *nouveau riche* wealth.

Costume and Accessories

Renaissance clothing, like the art of the time, showed an interest in simplicity, balance, and natural form. While Gothic costume was approaching its final development at the courts of Burgundy in Bruges, Ghent, and Brussels, the first stirrings of the Renaissance in Florence revived classical concepts of dress. Because the Gothic style had never really been at home south of the Alps, the Florentines integrated certain classical ideals with silhouettes inherited from the late Gothic period. The new style stressed the horizontal over the vertical, the simple and geometric over the complexly decorative, blond or earth-colored tonality over bright heraldic color, and a natural silhouette over exaggerated and artificial clothing forms. This new Renaissance dress developed from the concept that perfection lay in the rational and harmonious relationship of all the separate parts of the costume rather than in decoration for its own sake.

In masculine dress after the middle of the fifteenth century, the undergarment was usually a sleeveless doublet to which long hose could be fastened with ties or "points." These hose of cloth or leather were sometimes sewn together at the top and became a single garment with a separate piece of material, or *codpiece*, tied over the front opening. If they remained separate, they were drawn up over white diaperlike underdrawers; and the top was hidden under the outer doublet. There was a collarless shirt under the doublet, with sections of a matching or contrasting doublet sleeve laced loosely over it and slashed or cut to show much of the shirt sleeve beneath. The doublet front was laced loosely across the shirt that bloused casually at the waist between hose and doublet, if the doublet was short. Eventually, the doublet was cut low at the neck and finished with embroidery or a ruffle. The general effect was very loose and casual, as if the costume would drop off when lacings were untied. Overgowns were either short, calf length, or ankle length and were worn loosely and casually. They had wide lapels and square or horizontal lines rather than the more vertical lines found at this same time in the late Gothic costume of France or at the Burgundian court in Brussels. The thick, square gowns of the middle-aged and elderly had large cuffs, wide collars, and thick pleats. The headgear of the period favored wide, flat, slightly turned-up brims decorated with plumes and jewels, skull caps, simple truncated cones, fur hats with turned-up brims, and tiny pillboxes. Young men usually wore their hair quite long, while older men wore it shorter. Shoes were like slippers without the exaggerated toes of the later Gothic period. In general, the Italians favored loose and natural lines (Figure 5–6).

After 1510, with the arrival of the ideals of the High Renaissance, men's clothing began to reflect the change to nobility, gravity, and grandeur noted in Michelangelo's *David* (Figure 5–2) and in Bramante's Tempietto (Figure 5–4). Fabrics became thicker; sleeves and doublet skirts were fuller; rounded beards were prominent; and rounded berets made the face seem larger and fuller. Men, in general, looked twenty pounds heavier than they had at the close of the fifteenth century. One need only compare two portraits to see this remarkable change. The *Self-Portrait* by Albrecht Dürer, painted in 1498, shows him in dashing garb based on the dress of the Venetian youths that Dürer had observed during his trip to Italy in 1495 (Figure 5–7). The effect is a casual, loose, easy, and sensual one. In contrast, Raphael's *Portrait of Baldassare Castiglione*, author of *Il Cortegiano*, done in 1516, shows a full, rounded, solid-clothing silhouette in textures of fur and velvet that gives the count an aloof self-assurance and gravity (Figure 5–8). Again, one is strongly reminded of the fact that the people of a culture attempt to dress, move, and pose exactly as portrayed in art.

In feminine dress, the same precepts per-

Figure 5–6 Vittore Carpaccio, left detail and center section of *The Arrival of the English Ambassadors,* from the *The Legend of St. Ursula,* 1490–95. Illustrates the looser, natural, draped lines of Italian Renaissance garments during the late fifteenth century, as opposed to the exaggerated, artificial fashion lines of late Gothic clothing. The Accademia, Venice. Photo courtesy of Alinari, Florence.

tained. The lacing characteristics of male dress also appeared in women's costume at the breast, under the arms, and at the shoulder, where long, tight-slashed sleeves were laced to the armhole of the bodice over the looser sleeves of the chemise. The gown was frequently divided into bodice and skirt and worn under a sleeveless outer gown slit below the waist on each side or in the front. Sometimes, the outer gown was loose and flowing, but more frequently it was fitted smoothly to a slightly raised waistline and cut away in a V-shape in front to show the lacing of the undergown. Older women, servants, and ladies-in-waiting still wore kerchiefs, but younger women preferred the hair uncovered so that the complex knots and twists of the hairdressing, set off with jewels or nets of gold, could be seen. Sleeves were the most complex part of the costume with their many ties and slits through which the fabric of the chemise could be loosely pulled to make interesting puffed effects. Such sleeves marked the beginning of slashing, which was to grow in importance and decadent complexity during the whole of the sixteenth century. Again, the general effect was loose, casual, and natural. Look again at the painting by Domenico Ghirlandaio that also illustrates female dress between 1485 and 1490 with its relaxed harmony, richness, simplicity, and naturalness (Figure 5–5).

Like the male costume, female dress in the early years of the sixteenth century took on weight and fullness as did the actual women themselves. By the year 1514, when Raphael painted his *La Donna Velata* (Figure 6–7), the circular forms, full sleeves, and rich, soft, expanding fabrics matched the fullness and sculptural roundedness found in all the arts of the High Renaissance.

Figure 5–7 Albrecht Durer, *Self-Portrait*, c. 1498. Illustrates the youthful, loose, easy, sensual dress of the Italian Renaissance at the time of Dürer's visit to Venice in 1494–95. Photo courtesy of the Prado, Madrid.

Figure 5–8 Raphael, *Portrait of Baldassare Castiglione*, c. 1515. Illustrates the expanding, rounded forms and thick, solid textures of clothing in the High Renaissance. The Louvre, Paris. Photo courtesy of Alinari, Florence.

Manners and Movement

As with all manners and movement, those of the Renaissance were closely connected to what was worn as well as to what were the ideal images of gentleman and lady. Because few books on etiquette were written, most of the information on deportment, manners, and movement must be inferred from paintings or taken from other written sources.

As with medieval dress, the walk and stance of the male was based on the easy athletic movement of the warrior, leading from the hips with knees braced and an erect head position. The gentleman of this period, like his medieval counterpart, was particularly proud of a good leg and always posed to show it off to the best advantage. The contrapposto stance of Donatello's *David* is a natural one for the youthful costume of the Early Renaissance, while a divided stance with feet further apart is more appropriate to the heavier, bulkier costume of the High Renaissance. Another favorite pose was to stand with one foot raised on a step or footstool with one hand on the raised knee, the other on the hip. Arm and leg positions frequently employed were: arms folded loosely across the chest; hands on the hips; hands on the belt, dagger, or sword hilt; a hand fingering a locket, medallion, or order; and one hand fingering the beard or chin while the other supported the elbow.

This easy, swaying, relaxed full movement is expressed in Raphael's *The School of Athens* (Figure 5–9). By looking at this painting and relating its gestures and poses to the little advice we do have about salutations and bows, an actor can gain some sense of the movement style practiced at the time in which Castiglione formulated his ideals for the perfect gentleman. For example, we know that greetings between close friends involved a warm handclasp; a short bow was employed for mere acquaintances. This bow involved a graceful lunge forward, with the right foot. It was similar to the movement of a swordsman aiming his weapon at his opponent. While bowing, the gentleman held his hat across the body. An actor should particularly study portraits and experiment with movement in costume before he can hope to make Renaissance movement a part of his stage technique.

The Early Renaissance female dress was similar to the late Gothic female dress except that the amount of fabric to be controlled was less and the lines of the costume were more natural. Movement still originated from the center of the body; steps had to be small; and the skirts were lifted only when absolutely necessary. One can deduce from certain paintings by Fra Filippo Lippi that a variety of pace was important and that the transitions from slow to rapid movement were smoothly controlled.

The actress playing a Renaissance court lady may feel unsure about what to do with her hands. There are many possibilities. For example, when she is in repose, the hands may quietly rest in front of the abdomen just below the waist, as in the central figure of the

Figure 5–9 Raphael, *The School of Athens,* fresco, from the Stanza della Segnatura, Vatican Palace, 1510–11. The balanced organization here is analogous to the dramatic composition of the forum scene in Shakespeare's *Julius Caesar.* The grand, swaying, rounded gestures and movement are typical of the High Renaissance. Photo courtesy of Alinari, Florence.

daughter of the Tornabuoni family in *The Birth of the Virgin* (Figure 5–5). Hands can also be clasped at the waist or on the girdle, if one is worn. The left hand may hold the elbow of the right arm, while the right hand rests on the shoulder or holds a locket or chain. In sitting, the hands can be held in the lap, clasping the forearm, or they can be rested on the arm of the chair.

When sitting, an actress should smooth her skirt fabric under her body, allowing the folds to drape gracefully at her side. Then, when she rises, the folds will open smoothly and easily to give both freedom and grace of movement.

The bow, or curtsy, for a Renaissance lady was similar to the late medieval one, though simpler and more natural in execution. Both knees were bent; the head remained erect; and the skirt was held as its fullness demanded. To give interest to the bow, the head was sometimes tilted to the right; the right shoulder was inclined forward; and the right hand was placed lightly on the breast. When curtsying to a king or overlord, the lady swept her arms back with the palms forward in a show of submission. Such a curtsy would be very appropriate for Kate at the close of a production of *The Taming of the Shrew*. All curtsies are individualized to show differences in personality and social station.

The seating at a banquet was arranged by social position and rank. The banquet table was sometimes still placed on a raised dais, but even when on the floor, it was symmetrically arranged so that the person of highest rank sat at the very center. If there were many guests, the table might have been extended into a U-shaped arrangement; yet the guests were seated on only one side of the table so as to leave room for the entertainers to perform nearby.

The Theatre

With the revival of Greek and Roman artistic ideals in the fifteenth century also came an interest in the classical plays of antiquity and their staging. By the beginning of the sixteenth century, a book by the Roman architectural author Vitruvius—first published in 1486 and devoted to Greek and Roman staging methods—had stimulated interest in classical staging and attempts to approximate it in court performances. As early as the late fifteenth century, the princes and dukes of the various Italian states were presenting festivals of plays against perspective scenery. In the major cities and courts, academies of intellectuals organized solely for the purposes of studying the arts of antiquity and of producing classical plays, which they also wrote, translated, or adapted. For their performances, the courts and academies used their own members rather than professional actors, and costumes and scenery were usually the responsibility of a local painter or architect and his assistants.

The staging quite naturally stemmed from two sources—the admiration for the permanent Roman theatres described by Vitruvius and the contemporary fascination with perspective painting. Plays were usually performed in a banquet hall in which the stage was specifically designed and erected for each new production. Though many designs and sketches of such staging survive, the first treatise on the subject by Sebastiano Serlio did not appear until 1545, or well into the later Renaissance, or mannerist period. Serlio's street scenes for classical tragedy and comedy were the street scenes of Roman comedy translated into a perspective setting, while his scene for the satyric or pastoral play was a sylvan landscape. Since the stage was not permanent, there was no proscenium frame or provision for shifting from one perspective scene to another; the background was the same throughout each production of a play.

The first permanent theatre built in classical Roman style was the Teatro Olimpico at Vicenza, designed by Andrea Palladio and opened in 1585. Though following Vitruvius's designs, it also incorporated the ideas of Vincenzo Scamozzi, Palladio's assistant, in the sloped perspective of the alleyways behind the five doors of the proscenium façade. These perspective streets were fixed and immovable, although by the time this theatre was completed, the demand for changeable scenery was very strong. In many ways this theatre was old-fashioned even at the time it was built—a relic in many ways of the ideals of the High Renaissance.

Costumes for classically inspired plays, particularly those used for the popular pastorals, were based vaguely on Roman and Greek theatrical styles, with a great overlay of Renaissance ornamentation. The costume for a classical Greek or Roman hero consisted of a tunic, a very decorated *cuirass*, or breastplate, laced boots, a vaguely antique helmet with plumes, and decorative *labels* or tabs at shoulder and waist that were supposed to remind one of the leather straps worn at the waist and shoulders of Roman armor. Classical heroines wore short court dresses over an underskirt that was reminiscent of the Greek chiton; there was much overlay of decoration and labels, and the hair was adorned with plumes and jewelry. The pastoral costumes were even more exotic, with labels turned into foliage and hanging decoration based on meadow and woodland motifs. In a delightful sketch by Leonardo da Vinci of such a pastoral figure, we have an excellent example of the Early Renaissance ideal of youth and exposed physicality (Figure 5–10).

Figure 5–10 Leonardo da Vinci, a pageant costume for a male masquer, c. 1506–07. A pastoral shepherd's costume for an entertainment produced at the opening of the High Renaissance. Note the rich use of foliage ornamentation in the hanging sleeves. Windsor Castle. Photo reproduced by the gracious permission of H.M. Queen Elizabeth II.

The Plays

The only truly Renaissance play that still has a genuine appeal for audiences today is *Mandragola*, written between 1513 and 1520 by Niccolò Machiavelli. It combines elements of the medieval farce and classical Roman comedy in a story about a jealous old man who is tricked into approving an adulterous relationship between his wife and a young man. Although rather offensive in its obscenity, the play is an accurate comment on many of the customs, morals, and standards of the times, seen through the eyes of a cynical realist.

It is the plays of Shakespeare, however—though written three-quarters of a century after the close of the High Renaissance—that are considered the greatest works of the Renaissance period. The early comedies and even tragedies, like *Romeo and Juliet*, do seem to portray the nature of the Italian Renaissance spirit found in his literary sources. Endowed with great powers of observation, identification, and human compassion, Shakespeare managed to absorb and reflect in two decades of work in the theatre the entire cultural development of Europe from the medieval and Early Renaissance ideals of the fifteenth century to the Baroque concepts of the early seventeenth century. This could be done in England because the country was emerging from a late medieval past at the very moment that it was absorbing the complex ideals of the Renaissance and its later development into mannerism. Unlike the rest of Europe where this development took a century and a half, England, from the defeat of the Armada through the early years of the reign of James I, was in a golden age, a meeting ground for more than a century of European cultural ideals.

Although Shakespeare's works do not follow a simple pattern of development, they do roughly parallel the European cultural development of the Renaissance. The earliest plays are medieval in organizational structure and subject matter; the early comedies reflect the youth, optimism, exuberance, and simplicity of Early Renaissance culture; and the mature works are marked by the probing personal unrest and ambiguities associated with the later mannerist Renaissance. Although Shakespeare was always too free and informal to relate to the noble, formal, classic grandeur of the High Renaissance ideal, his handling of mood and subject matter in *Julius Caesar*, due to his use of Plutarch as a source, is somewhat classical. Especially in the forum scene, the effect is analogous to the feeling and balanced organization of Raphael's *The School of Athens* (Figure 5–9). In his very last plays, there is even a reconciliation between artistic and personal forces that we now associate with the thought and art of the Baroque period.

Romeo and Juliet, in particular, gives evidence of Shakespeare's instinctive understanding of the spirit of the Early Renaissance. One is immediately struck by the symmetrical placement of the major figures against a background of town square, orchards, and rooms that suggest the recessional planes of fifteenth-century Italian perspective painting. The figures tend to group themselves like those in Botticelli's *The Adoration of the Kings* (Figure 5–11). In all the big scenes—the opening, the banishment, and the conclusion—the opposing enemy families balance themselves to the left and right of the central figure of the Prince, who stands above the quarrel dividing Capulet and Montague (Figure 5–12). Also in the ball scene, the figures arrange themselves into planes of depth like a Ghiberti bronze panel, with Romeo and Juliet in the immediate foreground against a middle plane of dancers and a background of servants and observers.

The principal characters are also neatly balanced, with Romeo placed against Paris and Mercutio, the Nurse against Lady Capulet, Juliet against the invisible Rosaline, and the father Capulet against the father Montague. The players are also organized into three planes that recede gradually into the background as in early Renaissance paintings. Romeo and Juliet are strongly placed in the foreground; the Nurse, Friar Lawrence, and Mercutio occupy a middle ground; and the rest are background figures.

Even the ideas of the play are based on symmetrical opposition: love versus hate, rashness versus caution, courtly love versus passionate love, purity versus sensuality, night versus day, and sleep versus death. In his development of the play's language, Shakespeare relied heavily on the tightly balanced symmetry of the sonnet. Many poetic pieces can be lifted from the play and admired in their own right, and one tends to admire the play's language for its symmetry, polished beauty, lightness, and youthful sparkle rather than for its psychological profundity.

In addition, the rhythmic mood of the piece is also developed around a contrast of opposites. It moves from lightness to heaviness, from a measured pace in early scenes to a breathless rush in the later ones. Time is the villain, and Shakespeare uses every rhythmic device at his disposal to make haste and speed the central factor in the play's tragic denouement. The scenes of the play remain in the imagination because each occupies a clearly delineated boxed-in space. Even on the Elizabethan stage, the scenes were securely localized: the upper stage was used for the bedroom, the window for the balcony scene, the inner stage for the tomb, and the doors at each side for the homes of the two opposing families.

Figure 5–11 Sandro Botticelli, *The Adoration of the Kings,* c. 1478. The balanced symmetry and rich simplicity here are analogous to the compositional method in Shakespeare's *Romeo and Juliet.* The Uffizi, Florence. Photo courtesy of Alinari, Florence.

Because there are no direct sources, the acting style in the classical comedies, tragedies, and pastorals of the Italian Renaissance must be determined from looking at costume sketches, scenic designs, and paintings of the period. One can assume that the formal symmetry

Acting and Directing the Plays

found in the paintings and the scene designs must have been operative in the blocking. Certainly, Leonardo's *The Last Supper* and Raphael's *The School of Athens* illustrate the dignified, grand, and beautifully choreographed gestures employed for subjects dealing with

Figure 5–12 Act III, scene i from *Romeo and Juliet* by Shakespeare; produced by the Royal Shakespeare Company; Stratford-on-Avon, England, 1954. Directed by Glen Byam Shaw, scenery and costumes designed by Motley. A simple, symmetrical, youthful, light production of the play set in the Italian Renaissance. Photo reproduced by permission of the Governors of the Royal Shakespeare Theatre, Stratford-on-Avon.

the Bible or antiquity (Figure 5–9). Thus, gestures were apparently studied statements that expressed in a fairly obvious manner the intentions and personality of the character portrayed.

The contemporary actor is unlikely to be faced with performing any of the classical Renaissance comedies and tragedies except *Mandragola,* and there the comic action is close to Roman comedy and the Commedia dell'Arte. Of primary concern to the modern actor is the proper style to use for such plays

as *Romeo and Juliet, Two Gentlemen of Verona, The Taming of the Shrew, The Merchant of Venice,* and *Much Ado About Nothing.* All these plays set in Italy seem to represent Shakespeare's fascination with the tales, atmosphere, and romantic mythology that had developed throughout Europe in response to the wonder and excitement generated by Italy during the Renaissance. In other words, Shakespeare viewed the youth and early maturity of European Renaissance culture from much the same perspective that we today view the youth and early development of the United States from the late eighteenth century to World War I. Rather than try to analyze what the performances of Burbage and his actors were like or whether Elizabethan acting was realistic, formal, presentational, or representational, one should focus on understanding how Shakespeare interpreted the Italian Renaissance from the sources available to him when he was still young enough to identify with them in a very direct, open, and excited personal way. Once directors and actors understand the nature of the Renaissance and Shakespeare's interpretation of it, they can be true to his play and characters regardless of the period in which the script is set. Though Shakespeare's own company may have presented *Romeo and Juliet* in straight Elizabethan costume, for very practical reasons, it is much better for contemporary productions to capture with their costumes and stage properties the early Italian Renaissance spirit that lies within the play.

As for later plays set in the Italian Renaissance, those like Shelley's *The Cenci* and de Musset's *Lorenzaccio* are effective only when the Italian Renaissance is treated from a richly romantic, nineteenth-century point of view or from a very abstract modern psychological approach. Certainly, they would be weakened by a purely early Italian Renaissance approach because the characters and the structure are not developed in that way. There is no rule for actors and actresses approaching a play written in or about the Italian Renaissance. They must depend on the director, their own interpretations of the play's characters, and their study of Renaissance art.

Designing the Plays

In staging *Romeo and Juliet*, the very localized nature of each scene might lead a director to choose a series of enclosed spaces (as Zeffirelli did in his famous production of 1960), but such a choice detracts from the haste and speed of the play's rhythm. An approach needs to be devised that gives both speed of action and a clearly defined sense of separate areas of stage space. The basic areas of the Elizabethan stage are not only useful as a guide but also, in one respect, almost essential: the dramatic irony of Juliet's "death" after the potion scene is not fully absorbed unless her body, laid out on the bed, is fully visible above the action of the subsequent scenes, which involve the arrival of the musicians, the display of flowers, and the richly dressed wedding figure of the Count Paris. Steps, doors, windows, and platforms can usually be arranged to provide an upper area for the bedroom and the balcony, a raised area for the appearance of the Prince, side doors or arches leading into the central square, a large area for the ballroom, and a small forward area for Friar Lawrence's cell. Within such an arrangement (which should involve minimal changes during the action), the designer will want to suggest the symmetrical forms, the simplicity of line and ornament, and the light, bright color that we associate with the early Renaissance (**no matter** what the period in which the play is to be set). These abstract qualities are so much a part of the play's construction and mood that they should always be in the mind of the designer when working on this script. For example, if the play is set in the 1590s, when it was written, the twisted complexities and grotesque ambiguities of mannerist sixteenth-century art should be put aside in favor of the simplicities of the Early Renaissance.

The most natural period in which to costume this tragedy is in some version of the Early Renaissance, but it is often done in other periods. In the nineteenth century the play was often produced in a heavy romantic manner with great ornamentation and richness. This missed the lightness and youthfulness of the earlier Renaissance paintings and absolutely defied the mood and structure of the play. Rich brocades should be put aside in favor of soft, supple fabrics, with an emphasis on the beauty of draping rather than on heavy, complex surfaces. Fabrics with a soft, subtle sheen, leathers, suedes, soft woolens—these are the fabrics appropriate to the youthful physicality of the play (Figure 5–12). Much can be learned from the paintings of Botticelli, even to the accent of transparencies that can be found in his work (Figure 5–11). Simple lines that show off the body lines of the human figure are more appropriate than are complicated, body-distorting fashions, and the light, blonde colors of Botticelli are superior to the heavy richness of a Titian or Tintoretto. *Romeo and Juliet* is both a play about youth and a youthful play, and it partakes in its very manner of creation of the youthfulness of Renaissance culture.

PROJECTS AND PROBLEMS

1. Why did the Florentines of the fifteenth century consider themselves citizens of a modern Athens?

2. In what ways was the Medici family a patron of the Renaissance?

3. Compare St. Theodore from Chartres (Figure 4–11) with *David* by Donatello (Figure 5–1) and then explain the difference in outlook, attitude, and technique between High Gothic and Renaissance artistic approaches.

4. Explain the different feeling conveyed by Donatello's *David* (Figure 5–1) and Michelangelo's *David* (Figure 5–2). What do these differences communicate about the cultural outlooks of the Early and the High Renaissance? If you were playing these conceptions of David in different plays, what would be the difference in the plays? In your approach to the roles?

5. Compare the Pazzi Chapel (Figure 5–3) with the Church of St. Maclou (Figure 4–13), both begun at the same time. Aside from difference in size, what are the striking contrasts? What do these differences communicate about the cultural outlooks of Italy and France? Imagining yourself in front of each, describe your feelings, clothing, and movement.

6. What kind of play (think of blocking, scene organization, characterization, and rhythm) would take place in front of each structure (Figures 4–13 and 5–3)?

7. Now compare the Tempietto (Figure 5–4) with the exterior of the Pazzi Chapel (Figure 5–3). Why are they different, although only about seventy years separate their construction? What is the mood of each? The cultural ideal expressed? The type of play that would use each as a background?

8. Why did the High Renaissance style last less than twenty-five years?

9. How does the music of the Early and the High Renaissance relate to the theatre?

10. How does Castiglione define the role of the gentleman courtier in the period of the High Renaissance?

11. What are Castiglione's views on clothing for the perfect gentleman?

12. How does Castiglione have Giuliano de Medici define the role of the perfect Renaissance lady?

13. What is your first response to the interior scene in Ghirlandaio's *The Birth of the Virgin* (Figure 5–5)? How is it organized? How is the room decorated? What is the nature of the ornament used? What kind of play would be performed in this setting?

14. Look closely at the persons in *The Birth of the Virgin* (Figure 5–5). What are they like? Describe their individual personalities and their life in this type of town palace.

15. Compare the clothing in Carpaccio's *The Arrival of the English Ambassadors* (Figure 5–6) with the clothing in *The Exchange of the Rings* (Figure 4–17). What are the differences in movement? In attitude? In cultural ideals? In the use of clothing in relation to the body?

16. What aspects of dress are most striking in Dürer's *Self-Portrait* (Figure 5–7)? What is the mood of the clothing? What is its relationship to the movement of the body and to the personal psychology of the wearer? Does this costume answer Castiglione's disapproving description of a habit with an array of strings and cross-lacings? Why or why not?

17. Compare the *Portrait of Baldassare Castiglione* (Figure 5–8) with the *Self-Portrait* (Figure 5–7). Why do you think they are so different? What does each communicate about the wearer? What kind of role does each costume demand? What does each say about the cultural changes occurring between the last decade of the fifteenth century, when the Dürer painting was done, and the second decade of the sixteenth century, when the Raphael painting was done?

18. What characteristics of Renaissance female dress are expressed in *The Birth of the Virgin* (Figure 5–5)? How would you feel if you were an actress wearing such costumes? What kind of movement does such clothing require?

19. Compare the upper torso and head of the major female figure in *The Birth of the Virgin* by Ghirlandaio (Figure 5–5) with the portrait of *La Donna Velata* by Raphael (Figure 6–7). What has happened to the concept of woman and to female dress between the last decade of the fifteenth century and the second decade of the sixteenth century? How would you feel wearing the costumes of each period? How would your movement and concept of self differ?

20. Make an assessment of the movement, blocking patterns, and gestures in *The School of Athens* by Raphael (Figure 5–9). What kind of performance would result from using all these effects? How would you feel if you were one of the char-acters in this scene? What kind of play could profit from being directed this way? How is space used in this scene?

21. Describe the costume designed for a court entertainer by Leonardo da Vinci (Figure 5–10). What does it do for the actor's movement? How would you feel wearing it? How does its shape relate to the stage space in a Renaissance perfor-mance?

22. Why does *Romeo and Juliet*, written by Shakespeare a century or more after the close of the Early Renaissance, still give evidence of this period's use of space and structure?

23. How does *The Adoration of the Kings* (Figure 5–11) by Botticelli relate to *Romeo and Juliet*? Why does the clothing worn by many of the foreground figures in this painting seem related to what one would imagine in *Romeo and Juliet*?

24. How does the blocking in Raphael's *The School of Athens* (Figure 5–9) relate to the forum scene in *Julius Caesar*?

25. What are the best ways to find visual sources for supporting the direction, acting, or de-sign in Shakespeare's plays? Why is it difficult to use a straight Elizabethan approach to costume and setting in Shakespeare's plays?

BIBLIOGRAPHY

Antal, Frederick. *Florentine Painting and Its Social Background.* London: Kegan Paul, 1948. Although a little dated, this is an excellent study of the relationship between painting in fifteenth-century Florence and the social environment.

Beckerman, Bernard. *Shakespeare at the Globe, 1599–1609.* New York: Macmillan, 1962. An excellent summary of theatrical performances at the Globe during the ten-year period in which Shakespeare wrote his major plays.

Berenson, Bernard. *Italian Painters of the Renaissance.* Rev. ed. London: Phaidon, 1957. One of the great studies by the renowned scholar of Italian Renaissance art.

Burckhardt, Jakob C. *The Civilization of the Renaissance in Italy.* 3rd ed. New York: Phaidon, 1950. The classic nineteenth-century introductory work on the Renaissance by one of the most distinguished nineteenth-century historians. Although Burckhardt's capitalist-mercantile outlook pervades the book, he brilliantly introduces the reader to Renaissance culture.

Campbell, Lily Bess. *Scenes and Machines on the English Stage during the Renaissance.* Cambridge: Cambridge University Press, 1923. Reprint ed., New York: Barnes and Noble, 1960. A great classic on the development of staging in England during the Renaissance. Despite its age, it is still very useful.

Castiglione, Baldassare. *The Book of the Courtier.* Translated by L. E. Opdycke. New York: Charles Scribner's Sons, 1903. The great classic of high Renaissance manners and ideals written by one of the great gentlemen of the Renaissance. The quotations in this chapter on life and cultural ideals in the Renaissance have been taken from his work.

Chastel, André. *The Age of Humanism: Europe 1480–1530.* Translated by Katherine Delavenay and E. M. Gwyer. New York: McGraw-Hill, 1964. An immensely useful study of the meaning of humanism in the period of the High Renaissance.

Dewald, Ernest T. *Italian Painting 1200–1600*. New York: Holt, Rinehart and Winston, 1961. A very useful survey on the development of a new order in painting in Italy.

Freedberg, Sydney J. *Painting of the High Renaissance in Rome and Florence*. 2 vols. Cambridge, Mass: Harvard University Press, 1961. An excellent and in many ways indispensable study of Italian Renaissance painting.

Hale, John R. *Renaissance*. The Great Ages of Man Series. New York: Time-Life Books, 1965. A beautifully illustrated book with extensive color photographs, covering the major intellectual, artistic, and cultural developments of the Renaissance.

Herrick, Marvin. *Italian Comedy in the Renaissance*. Urbana: University of Illinois Press, 1960. An excellent scholarly study of classical and popular comedy in Italy during the fifteenth, sixteenth, and early seventeenth centuries.

———. *Italian Tragedy in the Renaissance*. Urbana: University of Illinois Press, 1965. An excellent companion volume tracing the development of tragedy in Italy.

———. *Tragicomedy: Its Origins and Development in Italy*. Urbana: University of Illinois Press, 1955. The final study on Italian Renaissance dramatic development that demonstrates the rise of this semimusical form and its eventual absorption by the Baroque form of opera.

Kennard, Joseph S. *The Italian Theatre*. 2 vols. New York: William Edmund Rudge, 1932. The standard work on the nature of the Commedia dell'Arte in Italy during and after the Renaissance.

Kernodle, George. *From Art to Theatre*. Chicago: University of Chicago Press, 1944. One of the seminal books on the relationship between the visual arts and the theatre. Traces this relationship from early medieval times through the Renaissance.

Klein, Robert, and Zerner, Henry. *Italian Art 1500–1600*. Sources and Documents in the History of Art. Englewood Cliffs, N.J.: Prentice-Hall, 1966. An interesting look at the written theories and ideas about art during the High Renaissance and in the late mannerist Renaissance.

Lowry, Bates. *Renaissance Architecture*. New York: Braziller, 1962. An excellent survey on Renaissance architecture and its relationship to culture and society.

Martindale, Andrew. *Man and the Renaissance*. Landmarks of the World's Art Series. New York: McGraw-Hill, 1966. An excellent and beautifully illustrated survey, with many color plates, on the development of all the arts during the Renaissance. The text is secondary to the plates.

Mates, Julian, and Cantelupe, Eugene, eds. *Renaissance Culture*. The Cultures of Mankind Series. New York: Braziller, 1966. An excellent compilation of writings from original Renaissance sources on the Renaissance view of life and its culture.

Mee, Charles L., Jr. *Daily Life in Renaissance Italy*. A Horizon Book. New York: American Heritage, 1975. A very fascinating and useful book concerning all aspects of daily living in Renaissance Italy; contains excellent illustrations.

Murray, Peter. *Architecture of the Italian Renaissance*. New York: Schocken Books, 1966. Another useful pictorial and written survey on all aspects of architecture during the Renaissance in Italy.

Nicoll, Allardyce. *Masks, Mimes, and Miracles*. New York: Harcourt Brace Jovanovich, 1931. Another standard work by one of the great historians of the theatre. Although slightly dated, it is still useful for studying medieval play production.

———. *Stuart Masques and the Renaissance Stage*. New York: Harcourt Brace Jovanovich, 1938. A highly regarded, excellently illustrated work that presents the development of the court stage in Italy and its influence on the masque presentations of the English court during the early seventeenth century.

Pope-Hennessy, John. *Italian Renaissance Sculpture*. London: Phaidon, 1958. An excellent survey by a highly recognized authority of the nature of sculpture in Italy during the fifteenth century.

Schoenbaum, Samuel. *Shakespeare, The Globe and the World*. Washington, D.C.: The Folger Library, 1979. A catalogue of a lovely traveling exhibition devoted to Shakespeare; profusely illustrated.

Symonds, John A. *The Renaissance in Italy*. 7 vols. London: John Murray, 1909–37. One of the great studies of the Italian Renaissance, this massive work is an invaluable reference.

Sypher, Wylie. *Four Stages of Renaissance Style*. Garden City, N.Y.: Doubleday-Anchor, 1955. Although written with a rather heavy hand, this is a brilliant work. It weaves together the stylistic characteristics operating in art and literature during the fifteenth, sixteenth, and seventeenth centuries.

Trewin, J. C. *Going to Shakespeare.* London: George Allen & Unwin, 1978. A gathering of reviews and notes by the elder statesman of London drama criticism; gives rare insights into many productions of the past half-century.

Vasari, Giorgio. *Vasari's Lives of the Artists.* New York: Noonday Press, 1957. The great contemporary Renaissance work by an artist and early art historian who recorded the facts and legends about the great artists of the Renaissance.

Wickham, Glynne. *Early English Stages 1300–1600.* 3 vols. New York: Columbia University Press, 1959–80. A superb and very detailed history of drama and play production in England during medieval and Elizabethan times.

Wittkower, Rudolf. *Architectural Principles in the Age of Humanism.* New York: Random House, 1965. An impressive scholarly work by one of the twentieth century's leading art historians on the nature of Renaissance architecture in relation to the theories and ideals of humanism.

Wölfflin, Heinrich. *Classic Art: An Introduction to the Italian Renaissance.* New York: Phaidon, 1952. The classic introduction to the artistic principles of the Renaissance.

Late Renaissance Mannerist Style

The period between 1520 and 1620 that followed the death of Raphael in Italy, the meeting on the Field of the Cloth of Gold in France, the accession of Charles V in Spain, and the rise of Martin Luther in Germany used to be labeled the late Renaissance. Today, however, art historians and cultural psychologists frequently use the term *mannerism* to refer to the art and cultural outlook of this period. Originally the term was used in a deprecatory way, and negative connotations still remain; however, if one can abandon the idea that something "mannered" is necessarily shallow, inferior, and arbitrary, then the term is a convenient label for the late, or postclassic, Renaissance.

Sociologically and politically this was an age of crisis, loss of faith, and political cynicism—an age summarized by the political and cultural mood in *Hamlet*. The unleashing of the military powers of France and Spain, caught up in the power struggles that accompanied the Reformation, led to the sack of Rome in 1527 by the German mercenaries of Emperor Charles V. Because of Italy's loss of economic and cultural supremacy and the deep shock and loss of faith sustained by the Church, a mood of impending doom predominated. This cultural and spiritual malaise gradually spread through all Europe—particularly as the wars of religion engulfed France, Flanders, and areas of the German Empire. It was an age of ambiguities, contradictions, bizarre contrasts, and highly self-conscious taste. The overriding atmosphere was one of inwardness and retreat from the sensuous, natural values of the real world. It was also an age in which printing and the written word began to dominate the visual arts and produced works of genius by men like Cervantes and Shakespeare.

In adherence to Michelangelo's declaration that rules were less important than the artist's inspiration and interpretation, artists turned away from the logic of nature and the classic rules inherited from antiquity to so-called *desegno interno*, or inner caprice and

113

personal ideals of design. Art moved from unity, balance, and logic to personal invention, self-conscious stylization, and bizarre fantasy. The result was ambiguous, unsettling, elegant, precocious, and complex—anything but logical, natural, and simple.

This movement did not suddenly arrive with the Reformation and its politics but was inherent in the strain placed on artists of the High Renaissance in their attempts to portray a unified, heroic conception of man in relation to the universe. Even Raphael, the sunniest and most balanced of those great geniuses, showed signs of strain and a desire to shock (to break out of his pattern of classic rules and unified logic) in some of the later frescoes painted in the Vatican chambers.

Even Michelangelo found the strain of his grand conceptions too great to maintain and began to project an inner psychology that disrupted the outer logic of form. Look at the peaceful, unified, gentle beauty of his famous *Pietà* from St. Peter's Cathedral, done in 1498 (Figure 6–1). The round lines of the Virgin's body encompass and enfold the relaxed form of Christ. The compositional lines are triangular and circular, one balancing the other exactly, and the outer surface seems polished until it glows with a soft natural beauty. It is one of the most appealing and beautiful interpretations of the Virgin grieving over the crucified Christ. Compare this with the *Pietà* that Michelangelo finished about 1550 and then partially defaced because of his dissatisfaction with it (Figure 6–2). Though the work is marred by the figure of the Magdalen finished by one of Michelangelo's pupils, it is still a shocking contrast to the earlier *Pietà*. The figure of Nicodemus is brooding and hooded, creating a sad and depressing father image (rather like the ghost in *Hamlet*) above a zigzag composition that stresses the painful, broken body of Christ. Though a few rules and rhetoric of the High Renaissance are still at work here, the hovering, inward, painful, devotional image is very private and almost medieval in its religious feeling. The work is a very strong symbol of the changed cultural

Figure 6–1 Michelangelo, *Pietà*, marble, 69″ high, St. Peter's, Rome, 1498. Note the peaceful, soft, rounded forms and smooth texture of this unified, quietly beautiful High Renaissance sculpture depicting the dead body of Christ surrounded and enfolded by the Virgin. Photo courtesy of Alinari, Florence.

outlook that dominated Europe by the middle of the sixteenth century.

Michelangelo also experimented with mannerist ambiguity and the concept of *desegno interno* in architecture. One of the most brilliant products of this approach is the Laurentian Library vestibule begun in 1524 (Figure 6–3). The library itself is a long horizontal hall, while the vestibule has a contrasting vertical emphasis. It has a compressed, ominous, shaftlike feeling with a vast, flowing three-part stairway that seems to move down into the room as if forcing the visitor against the wall. Michelangelo seems totally indifferent to classical rules in his use of orders and proportions; paired columns lock back into wall niches and are supported only by ornamental brackets; eyeless, blank windows float above

Figure 6–2 Michelangelo, *Pietà*, marble, life size, Florence Cathedral, c. 1550. Illustrates the zigzag broken forms, deliberately unfinished surfaces, and painful brooding mood in many late religious works by Michelangelo. The ideals of the High Renaissance have given way to a pessimistic, private inward feeling. Photo courtesy of Alinari, Florence.

Figure 6–3 Michelangelo, vestibule of the Laurentian Library, Florence, begun in 1524, stairs designed in 1558–59. The vestibule has a cold, compressed, ominous, shaftlike feeling with a three-way staircase that seems to engulf the small room. Here Michelangelo begins to play with the rules and forms of High Renaissance architecture and gains individual, unsettling effects. Photo courtesy of Alinari, Florence.

the visitor's head; columns break around corners; and contrasts of light and dark create an almost physical stress—a feeling of anxiety and fear. Again, like Shakespeare in *Hamlet* and *King Lear*, Michelangelo moves from outer rules and techniques to inner feelings and psychological truths.

By the second decade after the death of Raphael and the excommunication of Martin Luther, a group of younger artists appeared in Italy. Understanding implicitly what Michelangelo had done with the artistic rules of the High Renaissance in a work like the Laurentian Library, they declared their right to personal interpretations in keeping with the social and psychological outlook of the times. The artist became a *divino*—a virtuoso who cultivated not the study of nature but the fascinating intricacies and possibilities within art itself.

Let us compare *The Last Supper* by Tintoretto (Figure 6–4) with the far more famous work by Leonardo. Tintoretto, who appeared as an important painter in Venice toward the middle of the sixteenth century, said that his aim in painting was to paint like Titian and design like Michelangelo. However, his *Last Supper* projects a feverish emotionalism, an unreal flickering light, a ghostly sense of mystery, an unsettling imbalance and instability, and a self-conscious, choreographed

Figure 6–4 Tintoretto, *The Last Supper*, 12' × 18', 8", Church of San Giorgio Maggiore, Venice, 1592–94. Exaggerated perspective, brilliant night light, and self-conscious choreographed action create a sense of mystery and theatricality in this late sixteenth-century mannerist version of the Last Supper. Photo courtesy of Alinari, Florence.

movement. It denies all the symmetrical, classical values responsible for the unity and quiet profundity of Leonardo's painting. Christ is still more or less at the center of the canvas, but the table is positioned on a sharply tipped diagonal angle. There is an oppressive, cave-like atmosphere here with no connection to the natural world. The many extra guests and attendants create a partylike atmosphere, the light from the lamps and Christ's halo is a mysterious, sulfurous explosion of supernatural origin, and the whole event has a fantastic, dreamlike quality of unreality.

Of course, Tintoretto portrays a very different moment in *The Last Supper* than did Leonardo. Whereas Leonardo was interested in the psychological responses to Christ's statement "One of you will betray me," Tintoretto is interested in portraying the transubstantiation of the bread and wine into Christ's body and blood. Each artist has succeeded brilliantly in interpreting the particular moment he has chosen, and each painting brilliantly represents the difference between the High Renaissance and the mannerist Renaissance cultural outlook.

An actor, director, or designer need only look at the Tintoretto painting for a moment to realize its affinity to Shakespeare's dramatic outlook in plays like *Macbeth*, *King Lear*, and *Hamlet*. It has the same ambiguity, mystery, supernaturalism, and nighttime darkness found in these plays as well as the same minor characters, like those in the right corner of the painting. This painting could easily be a model for the mood and compositional arrangements of the banquet scene in *Macbeth*, whereas Leonardo's could not because of its direct and balanced symmetry.

Another very important aspect of the mannerist Renaissance, less laden with dark, violent, subjective emotion, was an elegant, artificial, sophisticated approach to art. The result was an exquisitely crafted product that suited the rarefied tastes of those aristocratic patrons who frequented the elegant European courts at mid-century. This aspect of mannerism became the first European international style since the late Gothic period.

Music

Similar shocking developments in music occurred during the sixteenth century. In the late sixteenth century, the center of musical development shifted from Rome to Venice, which adopted the musical ideals of the Flemish masters at the Sistine Chapel and was epitomized by the *ars perfecta* in the polyphonic style. Venice now became an innovator in musical development, while Rome remained the bastion of tradition. The experimentation of the Venetian school with individualized tones reached a high point after the famous Giovanni Gabrielli was appointed first organist of St. Mark's in 1585. The domed Greek-cross plan of St. Mark's, with its separate choir lofts in each of the transept wings, suggested to Gabrielli some unusual acoustical possibilities that would have been impossible in the traditional Latin-cross church, with its unified choir arrangement. By placing the choir in two or more widely separated groups, Gabrielli developed the so-called "polychoral style," or *chori spezzati*—literally broken choruses that added spatial contrasts to Venetian music and a new sense of color and drama.

These new experiments, which soon ripened into a *stile moderno* as opposed to the older and very unified *stile antico*, included the echo effect, the alternation of two contrasting bodies of sound with chorus against chorus, a single chorus line on top of a full choir, a solo voice opposed to a full choir, instruments against voices, and instrumental group against instrumental group. There were also other contrasts such as high against low voices, softness against loudness, fragmentary effects against continuous ones, melodies against melodies, and blocked cords against flowing counterpoints. Like mannerist literature, painting, sculpture, and architecture, these sharp musical contrasts produced a shocking effect. The new form was the *concertato* derived from *concertare*, meaning "to compete with or strive against."

Life and Cultural Ideals

While the Reformation was reshaping Europe's religious values, an economic revolution was reshaping the daily lives of citizens from Italy to the Baltic. Old concepts of barter and land-based wealth gave way to an economy in which money was used to create more money; anything could be bought for a price. The era has often been called the final defeat of chivalry and an age of cynicism and political realism. Wherever one looked, gold and silver had become, as Sir Thomas More said, "the blood of the whole body social." The supply of metals available for coinage doubled and redoubled as ships returned laden with gold and silver from Africa, the Orient, and the New World; and with this influx of gold and silver came increasing prices. By the middle of the century, people everywhere were caught up in that phenomenon that we now call inflation.

To increase efficiency and profits merchants and bankers pooled resources and founded great trading firms that were, in many ways, like modern corporations. Their operations were diversified and complex; through income on loan interest, trade profits, mining, and real estate, some larger firms became so powerful that even kings were helpless in carrying on wars without their support. For example, Jacob Fugger, a powerful banker of Augsburg, had the temerity to ask the most powerful ruler in Europe, Emperor Charles

V, to make immediate payment on a loan, reminding the monarch that "Your Majesty could not have secured the Roman Crown without me."

The loss of faith engendered by the shredding of the Church's authority during the Reformation and the total cynicism sponsored by the new moneyed economy led to many attempts at establishing new religious and spiritual values. No real changes occurred, however, until the triumph of the Counter Reformation and the stabilization of Protestantism in the early seventeenth century. Erasmus's cry in the early sixteenth century, "When did avarice reign more largely and less punished?" remains a true description of the times until Church and State were reestablished along with the new Baroque style.

The ideal manners and customs described in *The Courtier* were still outwardly admired but really served only to cover up man's basic corruption. Political manners, in particular, were now based more and more on *The Prince* by Machiavelli, whose reputation had grown to the point where the character of the "machiavel" became the standard archvillain in literature and drama. Stage characters like Shakespeare's Iago and Iachimo were meant to personify the Machiavellian personality. Machiavelli, of course, did not really invent his prince but modeled him on the political realism and double morality of the times. Because few read *The Prince*, its basic ideas were often grossly distorted; nevertheless, "Machiavellism" was the common property of all. By the time that Shakespeare wrote his plays, every liar seemed to speak the language of Machiavelli, and all shrewdness and cleverness were suspect.

Since *The Prince* did have such a psychological and emotional impact on the culture of the late Renaissance, a few key passages from it appear in the following section. They describe the actions of one Oliverotto, who was determined to take power from his uncle, Giovanni.

After waiting some days to arrange all that was necessary to his villainous projects, Oliverotto invited Giovanni Fogliani and all the principal men of Fermo to a grand banquet. After the dinner and entertainment usual at such feasts, Oliverotto artfully introduced certain important matters of discussion. . . . To which discourses Giovanni and others having replied, he all at once rose, saying that these matters should be spoken of in a more private place, and withdrew into a room where Giovanni and the other citizens followed him. They were no sooner seated than soldiers rushed out of hiding-places and killed Giovanni and all of the others. After which massacre Oliverotto mounted his horse, rode through the town and besieged the chief magistrate in his palace, so that through fear they were obliged to obey him and form a government, of which he made himself prince. And all those being dead who, if discontented, could injure him, he fortified himself with new orders, civil and military, in such a way that within the year that he held the principality he was not only safe himself in the city of Fermo, but had become formidable to all his neighbors. . . .

Whence it is to be noted, that in taking a state the conqueror must arrange to commit all his cruelties at once, so as not to have to recur to them everyday, and so as to be able, by not making fresh changes, to reassure people and win them over by benefitting them. . . . For injuries should be done altogether, so that being less tasted, they will give less offence. Benefits should be granted little by little, so that they may be better enjoyed.

Though this bald and cynical opportunism was not new, the openness with which such political precepts were practiced in the century after the death of Machiavelli, coupled with the Reformation confusions, led fearful conservative thinkers by the close of the sixteenth century to stress the absolute importance of adhering to the natural order and "degree" found in the universe. Shakespeare, in *Troilus and Cressida*, included a famous speech brilliantly suggesting the terrible evils and horrors that can occur without such order:

The heavens themselves, the planets and this
   center,
Observe degree, priority and place,

Insisture, course, proportion, season, form.
Office and custom in all line of order.
And therefore is the glorious planet Sol,
In noble eminence enthroned and sphered
Amidst the other, whose medicinable eye
Corrects the ill aspects of planets evil,
And posts like the commandment of a king,
Sans check to good or bad. But when the
   planets
In evil mixture to disorder wander,
What plagues and what portents, what
mutiny,
What raging of the sea, shaking of the earth,
Commotion in the winds, frights, changes,
   horrors,
Divert and crack, rend and deracinate,
The unity and married calm of states
Quite from their fixture! Oh, when degree is
   shake'd
Which is the ladder to all high designs
The enterprise is sick! How could communi-
   ties,
Degrees in schools and brotherhoods in cities,
Peaceful commerce from dividable shores,
The primogeniture and due of birth,
Prerogative of age, crowns, scepters, laurels,
But by degree, stand in authentic place?
Take but degree away, untune that string,
And hark, what discord follows! Each thing
   meets
In mere oppugnancy. The bounded waters
Should lift their bosoms higher than the
shores,
And make a sop of all this solid globe.
Strength should be the lord of imbecility,
And the rude son should strike his father
   dead.
Force should be right, or rather, right and
   wrong.
Between whose endless jar justice resides,
Should lose their names, and so should jus-
   tice too.
Then everything includes itself in power,
Power into will, will into appetite,
And appetite, a universal wolf,
So double seconded with will and power,

Must make perforce a universal prey,
And last eat up himself. . . .

The end of the sixteenth century also in-cluded a new belief in the supernatural. One of the dark fears that arose amid the turbulence of the Reformation was a violent obsession with witchcraft, so brilliantly expressed by Shakespeare in *Macbeth*. Though even the more skeptical fifteenth-century humanists accepted the existence of witches, it took the religious zeal of the sixteenth century to turn witchcraft and witch hunting into a frenzied hysteria. The spiritual awareness engendered by the Reformation brought about a corresponding sensitivity to the powers of Satan, and the mania spread until any misfortune— a tree struck by lightning, a calf born dead— set off a witch hunt. In Spain and Italy, where the Inquisition functioned, witchcraft was treated as a heresy. Though a penitent witch was sometimes spared death by burning, the prevailing attitude was expressed by Jean Bodin, an eminent French jurist:

> Whatever punishment one can order against witches by roasting and cooking them over a slow fire is not really very much and not as bad as the torment which Satan has . . . prepared for them in hell, for the fire here cannot last more than an hour or so until the witches have died.

At least 10,000 "witches" were killed in Germany during the sixteenth century. The obsession with witchcraft was symbolic of the cultural outlook and temper of the times, analogous to the smoky, midnight supernaturalism of Shakespeare's *King Lear* and *Macbeth* and Tintoretto's *The Last Supper* (Figure 6–4) and opposed to the balanced High Renaissance view of man and nature seen in Raphael's *The School of Athens* (Figure 5–9).

Ornament, Interiors, and Furniture

One of the most influential interiors in northern Europe is the gallery of Francis I by Rosso Fiorentino, a colleague of the artist Primaticcio at the Palace of Fontainebleau in the 1540s (Figure 6–5). Its tunnel-like plan is reminis-cent of the space arrangements in Michelangelo's Laurentian Library in Florence. This basic spatial organization, the tunnel-like shape, was adopted for walking and picture galleries in many palaces and manor houses

Figure 6–5 The Gallery of Francis I from the Palace of Fontainebleau; c. 1530–1540. Illustrates the tunnel-like proportions, oppressiveness of decoration, tension in ornamentation, and ambiguity as to where sculpture, painting, and architecture meet that was the hallmark of the new European international mannerist style of the sixteenth century. Photo courtesy of the French Government Tourist Office.

throughout Europe. The result was the creation of an oppressive atmosphere of great tension caused by the extreme length, the relatively low ceiling, and the tight intertwining patterns in the woodcarved furniture and decoration. The decoration of the walls of the gallery of Francis I combines painting, sculpture, and twisting stucco ornament into a vibrating mass of tense decoration that caters to the rarefied, overelegant, rather unnatural tastes of European aristocrats of the time. The interpenetrating scrolls in the upper corners of the paintings, in which tongues from one stucco scroll pass through slits in the other, are analogous to the forcing of lining fabric through slashes in the clothing of the period, to the interweaving story threads of *Hamlet* and *King Lear,* and to the contrapuntal effects in music.

Costume and Accessories

In the century following the beginnings of the Reformation, fashion was divided into roughly two periods—from 1520 to 1560, when German influences were predominant, and from 1560 to 1600 or 1620, when Spanish styles were the major source of inspiration. The major attributes of each style were an artificial distortion of the human body into an often grotesque but extravagantly ornamental padded and stiffened encasement and a fantastically varied display of linings pulled through slits or slashes in the outer fabric. These were analogous to the interpenetrating plot lines in plays and the scrollwork of interior decoration. The earlier period emphasized a broad, horizontal, rather square silhouette, especially for men, while the later period emphasized a more vertical line.

The most distinctive upper-class male garment in the early period was a short gown, usually fur-lined, with puffed or hanging sleeves, ample folds, and a very wide fur collar that accentuated the breadth of the figure. The open front framed a jerkin cut away to show the doublet, usually heavily padded and slashed or cut to show the lining. A separate, formally pleated skirt, or *bases*, covered the hips and the upper thighs. At the beginning of the period, the neckline was low, but as the shirt rose to a ruffle at the base of the neck, the doublet also was cut with a small standing collar to support this ruffle. At first, hose with slashed tops were worn but seen only on dashing young gallants since they did not wear the bases, or skirt; later, the slashed tops were replaced by *slops, melon hose, trunk hose,* or separate upper *stocks* slashed or fitted with panes of fabric over puffed lining fabric. Shoes were broad-toed with slashes; hats were moderately wide, flat-brimmed caps finished with jewels and feathers; hair was cut relatively short; and beards were very popular. The major characteristics, however, were the heavily padded bodies and the slashing, with its tight forcing of lining fabric through holes made with scissors or a red-hot iron.

The extreme difference in outlook taking place between the first and middle part of the sixteenth century and reflected in fashion can be seen by comparing the portrait of Castiglione by Raphael, painted about 1516 (Figure 5–8) with the famous portrait of Henry VIII by Hans Holbein, painted about 1540 (Figure 6–6). Raphael's *Castiglione* still exists in a real world of beautiful, curved, rounded forms, natural fabrics, and relaxed easy grandeur. In contrast, Holbein's *Henry VIII* is a rich, exaggerated, artificial, grotesque symbol of authority. The work creates an overpowering

Figure 6–6 Hans Holbein the Younger, *Henry VIII,* oil panel, 1540. Creates through distorted body lines, excess ornamentation, and linings tightly pushed through slits in the outer garments an artificial, immobile, almost grotesque authority that is both fascinating and repellent. Photo courtesy of the Galleria Nazionale, Rome.

portrayal of an immobile, ruthless, commanding physical presence in which humanity and personality are totally abandoned in favor of an excessive richness that is both fascinating and repellent.

Now let us look at two portraits of women. Raphael's *La Donna Velata,* painted about 1514, shows simple, full, rounded lines and rich natural fabrics (Figure 6–7). In contrast, there is a shocking cultural difference in the portrait of Eleanor of Toledo, wife of the Duke of Florence, painted by Agnolo Bronzino about 1550 (Figure 6–8). This difference cannot be explained simply by the fact that Raphael's subject was a rich upper-class lady and Bronzino's a member of the court. Eleanor is not an individual personality, but an exemplification of position as she sits con-

Figure 6–7 Raphael, *La Donna Velata,* Pitti Palace, Florence, c. 1515. Illustrates the full, rounded lines and rich, natural fabrics admired in fashion during the High Renaissance. Photo courtesy of Alinari, Florence.

Figure 6–8 Agnolo Bronzino, *Eleanor of Toledo and Her Son Giovanni de Medici,* c. 1550. Illustrates the unnatural, grotesque, artificial fashions worn by the upper classes by the middle of the sixteenth century. Decorative patterns are overly large; under fabric is forced through slits in the outer garment; shoulders are distorted; the bust line is absent; and the lines of the costume are reinforced with braid and pearls. The Uffizi, Florence. Photo courtesy of Alinari, Florence.

gealed into immobility behind the barrier of her lavish, ornate costume. Her body is made unnatural and grotesque by the alarming scale of the dress pattern. Tight puffs of fabric are forced through slits in the sleeve and then choked off by braid and jewels; the shoulder netting is hammered down with pearls; the hair is confined by a tight net of pearls, and the breasts are completely removed by the rigidities of corseting. The work has both a frightening sense of masochistic self-torture and a lavish brilliance. In every way it indicates that the ideals of mannerism had triumphed in all phases of European society by mid-century.

In the North the female silhouette was a little heavier than in Italy because of the thicker fabrics trimmed much more frequently with fur. Skirts were pleated to the bodice over a heavy V-shaped front panel that was richly ornamented; sleeves were usually fur-lined, bell-shaped appendages folded back over a slashed and puffed undersleeve; and head-dresses were usually gable or crescent-shaped hoods that framed the face. Though Italian ladies throughout the sixteenth century were loath to accept the added rigidities of the *far-thingale,* in the North this funnel-shaped stiff-boned petticoat, which gave a rigid triangular line to the lower part of the female figure, was much admired.

By the close of the reign of Emperor Charles V and the accession of his son Philip II to the throne of Spain, style ideas began to come from Spain rather than from Germany. The Spanish tailors elongated the figure, exaggerated the shoulders and hips, extended the length of the waist, and held the body in a tense, elegant, formal envelope. The wearer was encased in an armor of ornament and adorned like an idol with gold, pearls, and precious stones; the dark-colored silk and velvet fabrics were like the rich linings of a jewel case.

In male dress, a bag-shaped cap with a narrow brim replaced the flat cap, and a short circular cape with a stiff collar was frequently substituted for the short gown. The short puffed breeches or upper hose were frequently stuffed with horsehair and had a stuffed and decorated *codpiece* at the front. Stuffed shoulder wings or crescents were appended at the armhole of the doublet, which was now extremely long-waisted and severely pointed, the front being frequently padded into a *peascod*. The legs were usually enclosed in tight hose of soft cloth, though knitted silk stockings became more prevalent toward the end of the century. The stockings were pulled up and gartered over tight knee pants, or *canions,* that came from beneath the puffed *melon* or *trunk hose.* In Italy and elsewhere, there was a fuller style of knee pants known as *Venetians.* Shoes were narrower and had soft soles until the beginning of the seventeenth century, when moderately high heels and shoe rosettes became popular. Of all these fascinating artificialities, the most distinctive was the *platter ruff,* starched and pleated into a band on top of the doublet collar. It was often matched by ruffs at the cuffs. These grotesque fantasies finally ended at the opening of the seventeenth century in a flat, starched collar, or *whisk,* for men and a feathery lacy collar that framed the face for women.

In many ways, the female costume followed the male silhouette with the exaggerated width of the hips, the long waist, the horizontal stress at the shoulders, and the stiffening of various parts of the body. The cone-shaped farthingale of the earlier sixteenth century was often replaced by a stuffed *hip roll,* an even wider *hip cage,* or a *wheel*

farthingale. Sleeves were padded, puffed and slashed; necklines were low cut, framed by a spreading starched collar filled with a soft *partlet* or finished with a great platter-shaped ruff. Hair was done in a heart-shaped roll away from the face and frequently framed by a heart-shaped cap.

For two examples of late sixteenth century dress, let us look at the famous portrait of Charles IX of France by François Clouet, painted about 1565, and the famous portrait

Figure 6–9 François Clouet, *Charles IX,* c. 1565. Illustrates the longer line of late sixteenth-century Spanish male fashions with padded trunk hose, high ruff, and the usual stiffened and padded body lines. Photo courtesy of the Kunsthistorisches Museum, Vienna.

of Queen Elizabeth by an anonymous artist in England, painted about 1592 (Figures 6–9 and 6–10). Each is an artificial, padded, and grotesque perversion of the natural lines of the human body. Each involves tightly controlled, tense, vibrating decoration inside rigidly controlled limits, like the controlled decorations and tense space arrangements in the gallery of Francis I (Figure 6–5), a perfect frame for the groups of courtiers who gathered there. Both Clouet and the anonymous artist who painted Queen Elizabeth present their subjects as fashion mannequins rather than as individuals.

Figure 6–10 Anonymous, *Queen Elizabeth I*, c. 1592. Illustrates the grotesque perversion of the natural lines of the human body through padding, stiffness, excess decoration, and the use of white makeup and wigs. Photo courtesy of the National Portrait Gallery, London.

Manners and Movement

Though the rules of polite behavior inherited from the medieval period had stressed tradition and monarchical and aristocratic precedence, in the sixteenth century, more stress was placed on a personal individualized projection of courtesy. For example, a treatise on manners published in 1581 underlined the difference among them from country to country and area to area. The Italians and other Mediterranean people were supposed to move quicker and gesture more frequently since they were from a warmer climate, while northern Europeans were supposed to be heavier, weightier, and less animated in movement and gesture. Even costume followed this precept, since Italian costume was less rigid and confining than northern European dress.

Male movement was still swaggering and virile, though controlled and confined by the rigidities of the costume. There was so much stiffening and padding that body stance no longer had a gracious ease; a man had to as-

sess continually the space he would need to execute all courtesies. Giovanni Della Casa, in his comments on men and their manners published in London in 1576, denounced those who flung their arms about as if they "were sowing corn in a field," those who walked splay-footed, fidgeted too much with their clothes, stroked the wrinkles from their hose, or posed like a peacock with hands on hips. Like all commentators, he felt that the costume dictated the movement and that affectation and excess were wrong.

In walking, movement was slow since shoes were soft and had no heel until the opening of the seventeenth century. The gait was a kind of rolling curve with the hips leading and the feet sliding forward to the right or left (Figure 6–11). When outdoors, the gentleman wore double-soled, very awkward overshoes that made rapid movement even more impossible. Moreover, the fullness of the trunk hose demanded a medium-wide

Figure 6–11 French School of the sixteenth century, *Ball for the Wedding of the Duc de Joyeuse*, c. 1581–82. Illustrates the processional walk of the late sixteenth century in which the body leads with the hips, thus creating a slow, rolling curve. The Louvre, Paris. Photo courtesy of the French Musées Nationaux.

stance. A striking, sober, yet dazzling artificial sense of "beauty" was the aim of the courtier in all that he did. As Tommaso Buoni said in his discussion of male beauty in a treatise published in 1606: "[all men] endeavor by art to seem that they are not. And for this cause proceedeth their exquisiteness, their art . . . their care in apparel, their Gate, their speech."

In sitting, the gentleman perched tensely on the edge of a chair or stool with artful grace. He placed both feet on the ground almost side by side, never crossed or spread wide apart. A chair with arms presented a very tight frame for the gentleman and was sometimes impossible for him to master because of his fully padded trunk hose. The left arm rested along the chair arm; the right rested on the elbow; and the right hand often held a handkerchief or gloves. A gentleman never removed his hat in sitting except to greet a friend or to defer to a superior. Similarly, he never removed his rapier, which gave him a military and decorative look. When the gentleman was seated, the point of the rapier could protrude behind the chair, thus causing someone passing by to stumble and start a fight. It was, therefore, the courtier's duty, according to F. Caroso in his book of manners, "to give a slight bow to those who are near," then with the cap in the right hand, "with your left you will put your sword point forward, and sit down with every grace on your chair or bench; when settled, you will put on your gloves if you think fit." Also, when in a crowd or dancing, the gentleman lifted the hilt of the rapier so that the point hung perpendicular beside his leg.

Gloves, tight-fitting and often worn with rings on the outside, were troublesome since a gentleman had to remove them constantly in the presence of ladies; it was considered bad manners to offer a gloved hand to a lady. Some gloves were so tight that a gentleman took a long time removing them, during which the lady hid her annoyance or amusement behind her fan.

Pomanders, which were small round balls of gold or silver containing musk, ambergris, or other perfume, were carried by the dandies of the period and by the ladies. Women carried them on a chain about the neck or waist, but a man usually carried them in his hand. Sometimes, a hollowed-out orange was carried to ward off infection as well as to perfume the air. Dandies also carried stiff flag fans before they became the sole property of women in the seventeenth century. Although pipe smoking and snuff taking were not common in the late sixteenth and early seventeenth centuries, they created much comment when indulged in.

The most common bow for men in the late sixteenth century had many small variations, but the basic moves were as follows. The left foot was drawn backward with leg and foot turned outward slightly and the knee straight. Both heels remained on the ground, and the body and head were held erect. Then, without pausing, the gentleman bent both knees and bowed forward from the hips. The head followed the line of the body without the chin's sinking into the chest. As the knees bent, the weight of the body moved partially to the back foot so that this weight could be evenly distributed to both feet. The knee of the back leg was turned out *slightly* as the knee bent; if this movement were exaggerated, it looked ugly. Throughout the bow, the front and back heel remained on the ground if the knee bend was slight; if the knee bend was deep, the back heel was raised, thus keeping the weight of the body partially on the ball of the back foot. In a very deep bow,

the back knee nearly touched the floor; the body returned to an erect position at the completion of the bow, and the weight moved to the front foot, thus releasing the back one.

Though the costume for women was equally artificial and inhibiting in its allowance for movement, ladies were admonished to act and move with discretion, to avoid foolish mannerisms that would draw attention to them. Walking indoors was also a problem for the lady, since the base of her shoe was very soft and often not an appropriate platform for supporting the massive width and padding of the costume. Walking outdoors was even more of a problem, especially if the lady wore the high platform *chopines* or *pianelle* so popular in Venice. Caroso commented that to "keep one's pianelle properly on one's feet so that one does not sprain an ankle or become a mockery or drop them" was a real problem. He noted how some ladies dragged their pianelle as they walked, making a very unpleasant noise. He suggested lifting the foot gracefully but firmly a full three fingers from the ground at each step.

It was even more difficult to move gracefully in the Spanish conical farthingale. The first precept was to move smoothly to keep from having an ugly bobbing or swaying effect. Also, short steps had to be taken so that the lady appeared to glide along the floor. When moving through a restricted space or in sitting, the lady had to exercise great control. Caroso commented on how frequently the train of a gown remained outside the chair, thus getting in the way of those passing. He described how ladies used the foot to bring the train nearer—"just what cats do with their tails." He also disapproved of lifting the farthingale and pulling it under the chair as he believed this was a deliberate attempt to show off the richness of the petticoat. Approaching a chair, the lady was to turn slightly, using the farthingale to put the train between the legs of the chair, and then was to sit only halfway into the seat. Sitting further back would have raised the farthingale and gown halfway up the leg. In fact, the custom was not to show the feet at all when seated. The correct sitting position was similar to the male's—an erect body with the left arm along the chair arm and the right resting on the elbow with the hand holding a fan, pomander, handkerchief, or muff. If seated on a stool or chair without arms, the lady put her hands in her lap, as in the portrait of Eleanor of Toledo (Figure 6–8).

Salutations followed much the same format as in the late medieval past except that the actual movements were quite different because of the changes in fashion. A man bowed and swept his hat down to his side, while the lady made a deep curtsy. In its execution, the curtsy was very similar to the man's bow except that the lady kept her feet close together while bending her knees and bowing usually much lower than a man. Though kissing a lady's hand was noted in books of manners, this practice was often ridiculed as either being an excessive affectation or something that should be reserved for ecclesiastics. When the lady's hand was kissed, the right hand was brought toward the mouth but kept at a discreet distance with the salutation accompanied by a bow.

By studying the many books on deportment and etiquette written during the sixteenth and the opening years of the seventeenth centuries as well as the art and clothing of the period, actresses and actors should be able to emulate appropriate gestures and movement. In particular, the famous anonymous painting *Ball for the Wedding of the Duc de Joyeuse* in the Louvre offers a wealth of information about manners and movement of the period (Figure 6–11).

The Theatre

Theatrical design during the sixteenth century showed little of the oppressive distortions found in the other arts and dress. In Italy, theatrical design of the Early and High Renaissance had stemmed from two traditions: one emulated the permanent theatres of Rome and was based on the recently published architectural treatise of the Roman architect Vitruvius; the other derived from a fascination with perspective painting. The theatre lagged far behind the other arts in absorbing and integrating these two traditions in performance. It was well into the later part of the sixteenth-century mannerist Renaissance before the two traditions were fully merged in the Teatro Olimpico at Vicenza, designed by the famed northern Italian architect Andrea Palladio, with additional perspective additions by his assistant and collaborator, Vincenzo Scamozzi. This combination of the Roman ideals of Vitruvius with the Renaissance ideals of perspective was an uncomfortable wedding of two dissimilar traditions that today gives this theatre a touch of mannerist ambiguity. Though Shakespeare's theatre was medieval in conception and could make little use of perspective because of space arrangements and the outdoor nature of the Elizabethan stage, it is possible that the large central door of the Teatro Olimpico influenced the development of the central pavilion used to frame important scenes in Elizabethan staging.

Costumes for the performances in the Italian theatre during the sixteenth century were again a blend of mannerist Renaissance ornament and accessories and a basic tunic design that was classically derived. In many ways the grotesque fantasy of these costumes is more reflective of contemporary artistic taste than of the impressive but reactionary high classicism of the Teatro Olimpico.

The blossoming of the Commedia dell'Arte in Italy during the sixteenth century was an even more important theatrical development whose influence is evident in contemporary theatre. Such comedy developed as groups of itinerant professional actors from the lower classes began to tour the countryside, performing on makeshift wooden platforms set up in any convenient square or marketplace. They presented improvised comedies based on stock characters very similar to those found in the farces and comedies of classical times. There were the lovers, the miserly merchant *Pantalone,* the long-winded schoolmaster *Dottore,* the cowardly, boasting soldier known as the *Capitano,* and a number of mischievous comic servants called *zanni.* All characters except the lovers wore half-masks and traditional costumes that made them instantly recognizable. Within the flexibility of the scenario, or action outline, the actors developed brilliant pieces of comic by-play, set speeches, and great acrobatic agility as they perfected their roles in the tough and demanding atmosphere of the outdoor marketplace. This popular style, which spread throughout all Europe by the close of the sixteenth century, obviously influenced Shakespeare in his writing of *The Taming of the Shrew* and *Henry IV,* parts I and II, particularly in the character of Falstaff who is clearly related to the Capitano figure.

Most important to us is the development of the Elizabethan theatre at the close of the sixteenth century, since an understanding of it helps us in producing Shakespearean drama. Like the equally popular and nationalistic theatre that developed in Spain at this time, drama in England began with amateur production and moved to the outdoor professional playhouse. Because they had a wide mixture of subject matter (late medieval interludes, folk tales, romances from Italy, and classical drama), the Elizabethans, like the Spaniards, inherited few limitations in storytelling except those created by the physical theatre for which the plays were written. Round, square, or polygonal in shape, the outdoor playhouse held about 2,500 spectators, who either stood in the central yard or pit or sat in the surrounding roofed balconies (Figure 6–12). The stage, a raised platform that projected midway into the yard, was partially covered by a roof, or "heaven," supported by carved and painted columns and backed by either a wall with doors or a curtained inner stage flanked by large doors. Movable pavilions, or *mansions,* may have been placed in front of this wall or curtain. An upper stage, frequently needed in Shakespeare's plays, was flanked by windows that were also used in certain scenes. A third level for musicians was sometimes used for supernatural appearances. The stage had great flexibility,

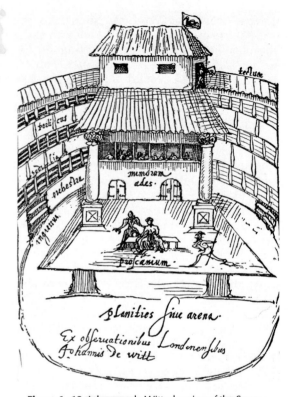

Figure 6–12 Johannes de Witt, drawing of the Swan Theatre, London, 1596. The only contemporary drawing of the Elizabethan stage, showing a partially covered platform projecting into a circular yard surrounded by balconies for spectators and backed by two doors and a stage balcony. From Johannes de Witt's sketch as copied by Arend van Buchell.

and plays could be blocked to take advantage of the theatre's basic symmetry or arranged to give asymmetry, instability, and even incongruity if such effects were needed—as in the case of *Hamlet.*

The property lists of a theatre businessman of the time, Philip Henslowe, indicate some of the minimal scenic pieces necessary for the Elizabethan stage: rocks, trees, furniture, Hellmouths, and a backcloth representing Rome. Machinery housed below the stage allowed for the appearance of ghosts through trap doors, and ropes and pulleys permitted objects and actors to be raised to the upper stage. Such special effects as fire, smoke, the

Figure 6–13 Sketch, known as the Peacham print, from a production of *Titus Andronicus* by Shakespeare, 1595. Illustrates the mixture of classical and contemporary dress worn in classical plays presented on the Elizabethan stage. From the original drawing in the possession of the Marquess of Bath.

sounds of cannons and bells, and thunder were also employed.

Lighting was unnecessary since the performances were held during the day, but torches, candles, and lanterns were used to indicate night. There were two kinds of costumes: the symbolic and the contemporary. The symbolic costumes represented gods, classical figures, supernatural beings, animals, foreign figures, and special characters like Falstaff. Some classical costumes were made specifically for the wardrobe; but, more often, the costumes were a combination of Elizabethan and classical Roman dress, as is the case in the famous Peacham print of a performance of *Titus Andronicus* (Figure 6–13). Contemporary costumes were worn in the majority of plays and were often donated by the aristocratic sponsors of the theatrical troupe. The acting company usually consisted of ten to twenty members; some were shareholders who received a percentage of the profits; others were hired at a fixed fee. Boy apprentices played female roles, and "extras" or "supers" were taken on for individual productions. The audience represented all levels of society from the nobility in the balconies and on the edges of the stage to the "groundlings" who stood in the yard.

The Plays

Though many exciting and theatrical plays were written in Europe—particularly in England and Spain—in the late sixteenth century, the work of Shakespeare stands above all others. He had the compassionate humanism and sensitive powers of observation to absorb and reflect the entire range of cultural and artistic development from the late medieval to the early Baroque periods. *Hamlet*, in particular, represents the full range of his response to the forces of the late mannerist Renaissance.

Though written only six or eight years after *Romeo and Juliet*, *Hamlet* has a maturity and world-weariness that make it seem much more modern than the earlier tragedy. This may partly stem from the fact that government in England, after the Essex Rebellion, moved toward a police state; the high spirits that had followed the defeat of the Armada gradually gave way to the pessimism and malaise marking the early reign of James I. England, which had long used mannerist ideals in a decorative way, now began to accept the disturbed art of mannerism as a deeply felt, psychological expression of the social-political disturbances of the times. Even Shakespeare himself, with the death of his son, seems to have undergone major changes in his psychological outlook. It is in this new world of malaise that Hamlet resides, contemplating the "rottenness" of the state and obsessed with an almost medieval sense of death.

The drama has a complex interplay of inner and outer realities, and its multiple, shifting action leaves the audience with feelings of ambiguity and disturbance. Its interpenetration of story threads reminds one of the linings pushed through slashings in the clothing of the period or of the interwoven stucco work in Elizabethan interior decoration. The action often seems excessive and overly dramatic, and focus shifts from foreground soliloquy to background action, from high pageantry to interior monologue without adequate transition. Like mannerist art, Hamlet operates both within and outside the action, presenting the story in a manner analogous to the gesturing figures in works by Tintoretto, who speak directly to the viewer to draw him into the painting (Figure 6–4).

Hamlet's character is sometimes ambiguous because of his neurotic shifts in temperament—outward action and inward feeling at war in the same moment. The only explicit line of development is from the "to be or not to be" speech to "the readiness is all" speech in which Hamlet accepts the idea of death. The audience is never sure whether Hamlet is playacting or responding with a deeply felt malaise to the existential meaninglessness of life. Most other characters seem less vivid and dimensional than Hamlet, although they do mirror the ill health of the Danish state.

Hamlet and *Oedipus Rex* are similar in that they both invoke the need for well-being in the state; both demonstrate how the destiny of the individual and the state are intertwined; and both depict the suffering of a royal victim who must die (figuratively in the case of Oedipus) before a new beginning is possible. In addition, the theme of order within the Renaissance monarchy is a direct successor to the Greek ideal of a cosmic order in things, evident also in the speech from *Troilus and Cressida* already quoted.

The verbal and visual imagery in the play is fascinating in its sensuous sickness. Words like *blasted, mildewed, apoplex'd, ulcerous, tumour, infects, corruption, rank,* and *smells* are just a few of those that vividly conjure up a state of infection. Another phrase that describes the nature of the play and of mannerism almost as well as the famous "something is rotten in the state of Denmark" is a phrase used by Polonius in Act II, scene 1, line 666, to describe to Reynaldo how to search out the relationship of Hamlet to Ophelia. He says: "By indirections find direction out": this phrase could describe both the progression of the play and the nature of mannerist European culture in the sixteenth century. Throughout, the play uses language to build a changing, shifting, complicated image of life that carries over into the basic rhythm of the play. The play's forward movement follows this same rhythm—from inward to outward action, from soft speeches to hysterical outbursts, from slow movement to rapid.

There are three great opportunities for visual splendor in the play: the opening court scene, the scene in which the play is presented, and the final duel scene. Each of these ritual-ceremonial scenes, representing the social order of the decaying state, demands special attention to spatial arrangements in order to convey the various instabilities in the play at these particular points. In particular, the thrones must be positioned to establish the asymmetrical balances and diagonal lines of action needed to convey a basic sense of spatial instability. Only at the close, with the arrival of Fortinbras in an upstage central position, does the play return to calmness and stability. The play also requires many passageways and rooms within the castle, including a graveyard and a plain. In Shakespeare's day, these would have been represented by various areas on the Elizabethan stage. Contemporary Elizabethan costume or clothing from another period that can suggest tension, distortion, and repression is appro-priate for establishing the unnatural mood of the play.

Though *Hamlet* is the most famous Shake-spearean play expressing the compositional methods and imaginative outlook of the man-nerist Renaissance, *Measure for Measure, All's Well That Ends Well, King Lear, Macbeth, Troilus and Cressida,* and *Timon of Athens* also have strong mannerist overtones. The plays of Shakespeare's slightly younger contempor-aries, Webster and Tourneur, also evidence the dark aspects of mannerism in a more su-perficial and obvious way in order to titillate the rather jaded tastes of Jacobean audiences. In addition, the lighter side of mannerism is reflected in the tragicomedies of Beaumont and Fletcher. The problem for the modern actor and director is to create an appropriate visual metaphor for the particular Jacobean or Elizabethan play chosen.

There is little to be gained by re-creating Elizabethan acting on stage since it would seem stilted and pedantic to a modern audi-ence. What is needed is an intuitive sense of the compositional nature of mannerist art and literature and of the instability and ambiguity of the style. The artistic creation of these ef-fects will help create that sense of mystery and uneasiness absolutely necessary for pro-jecting the darker side of mannerism.

Much also depends on costume. *Hamlet* or other similar plays need not be done in Elizabethan dress; but, whatever the period chosen, the costumes must assist the actor in creating that sense of tension, unnaturalness, and distortion basic to most fully mannerist plays. If late sixteenth- or early seventeenth-century costumes are worn, an actor must make use of the stiffness, formality, and ar-tificial elegance of the dress. If costumed from a period that gives less distortion to the hu-man form, the actor must rely more on move-ment and gesture to portray the shifts from the natural to the unnatural, from the ex-pected to the shockingly grotesque. The vi-olent speech contrasts in a play like *Hamlet*—as when Hamlet moves from quiet mono-logue to the hysteria of "Get thee to a nun-nery"—can be echoed and reinforced through movement, gesture, and clothing. Only when he thoroughly understands the essence of mannerist style can the actor or director de-sign a performance to take full advantage of mannerist shock values (Figure 6–14). The di-rector, in particular, can make very effective use of asymmetrical blocking, unstable fur-niture placement, and a sharp and even con-trast between one scene and another. The triangle created in the "Mousetrap" scene of *Hamlet* by the players, the King and Queen, and Hamlet and Ophelia should always look unbalanced and unstable.

Acting and Directing the Plays

Figure 6–14 The Player King and Queen from *Hamlet* by Shakespeare, produced by the Oregon Shake-speare Festival, Ashland, Oregon; 1961. Directed by Robert Loper, costumes designed by the author. Il-lustrates the exaggerated fabric patterns, white makeup, and sinister effects found in mannerist fash-ions. Photo by the author.

Modern plays written about the period are much less of a problem, since their composition and outlook will more likely be realistic or romantic without the ambiguities of mannerism. In such cases, the actors' problems are reduced to learning how to wear the costumes and how to execute the period's manners with authority and assurance.

Designing the Plays

In presenting *Hamlet* today, the director and designer must first decide whether to approximate the spatial arrangements of the Elizabethan stage or to create some other multiple-area arrangement of stage space. Having the upper stage for the parapet, the trap door for the grave, the full width from door to door for the large court scenes, and the forestage for soliloquies has its advantages, but it also has disadvantages: there is a certain rigidity and lack of rhythmic flow from area to area unless the stage space is specifically designed to match the play's structural rhythm. A good solution is to keep those elements of the Elizabethan stage that further the play's action and to incorporate them into a stage plan that will emphasize the mannerist compositional tensions of the script.

The space arrangements for the three court scenes are crucial. Particularly for the play scene, the director must decide if the audience is to look through the backs of the King and Queen to the players, or to glance at them at one side of the stage while they watch the play, or to observe the players performing downstage in front of Claudius and Gertrude. The mannerist qualities of the script can be emphasized most successfully by an asymmetrical, unstable use of color and texture so as to give a sense of imbalance and discomfort to the scene. It is also important to have an asymmetrical placement of the thrones in the three court scenes. In each scene the position of the thrones will create the appropriate sense of instability in the action, which can be further emphasized at moments of crisis by the use of diagonal and recessional movement of the actors. At the close of the play, on the entrance of Fortinbras, an upstage center entrance is needed to return the play to symmetrical calm and stability.

The tilted composition, sharp shifts in focus, and strong eruptions of light in Tintoretto's *The Last Supper* might be read as a visual analogy for much of the compositional method in *Hamlet* (Figure 6–4). Though it cannot be used as a literal source, the painting can serve as a creative stimulus to the imagination and as a visual catalyst for the images and impressions suggested by the script. The sulfurous lamplight of the painting certainly reminds one of that moment when Claudius rushes from the court, calling for lights; the highlight, shadow, and texture in this work could be of great assistance to the designer in developing the court scenes. Claudius and Gertrude might wear rich, overlarge, brocaded robes which are similar in effect to the gown on the Bronzino painting of *Eleanor of Toledo and her Son* (Figure 6–8). The costumes of the Player King and Queen might reflect—in exaggerated and distorted patterns of black and white—the royal robes of Claudius and Gertrude (Figure 6–14).

But often *Hamlet* is not produced as taking place in the late sixteenth or early seventeenth century. If an early nineteenth-century setting were chosen, the German romantic painter Caspar David Friedrich might be an inspiration for the production (Figure 12–3). Friedrich's lonely figures silhouetted against leaden skies, seen in graveyards, glimpsed at open windows or against gnarled trees create a sense of mystery, pessimism, and melancholy that would be appropriate for a melancholy, romantic *Hamlet* or an existential one.

The success of a *Hamlet* production is not in its novelty or its change of period but in the sensitivity with which space, fabrics, colors, textures, and ornament are integrated into an appropriate visual and rhythmic support for the play's action.

1. Into what three distinct periods can the Renaissance of the fifteenth and sixteenth centuries be divided?

2. What is the derivation of the term *mannerism?* What does it mean today?

3. How do the French invasions of Italy, the beginning of the Reformation, and the sack of Rome relate to the rise of mannerist art?

4. What is meant by the term *desegno interno?*

5. Describe the mood and character of the famous High Renaissance *Pietà* by Michelangelo (Figure 6–1). How does this work differ from Michelangelo's *Pietà* (Figure 6–2) of about a half-century later?

6. Why does the vestibule of the Laurentian Library by Michelangelo (Figure 6–3) create a mysterious, uncomfortable impression? Imagine yourself entering from an unseen door outside the photo to the left and facing this staircase. How do you feel? How do the blank wall niches affect you? What is the effect of the columns set into the wall? Of columns that do not reach the floor?

7. Consider the space arrangement in this vestibule of the Laurentian Library (Figure 6–3) from a director's point of view. What does the arrangement do to patterns of movement? What is the effect of the size of the room in relation to the height of the stairs? What is the effect of having three separate paths open for mounting the stairs?

8. Look carefully at *The Last Supper* by Tintoretto (Figure 6–4). What is the mood? As an actor in such a scene, how would you feel? Describe your movement, speech, and relationship to the other characters in the scene.

9. As a director, why would you block a scene as Tintoretto has done in *The Last Supper* (Figure 6–4)? What is the reason for having two servants take stage down at the right of the painting? What is the effect of raking the stage? Of placing the table on a diagonal? Of having no windows in the room? Of using artificial night lighting?

10. Block the banquet scene in *Macbeth* using the painting (Figure 6–4) as the basis. Develop directing instructions for the character of Macbeth in the banquet scene to be played in a setting like Tintoretto's *The Last Supper*.

11. How does the music of the so-called *stile moderno* or later Renaissance style relate to the art of the late sixteenth century and to the structure used in many of Shakespeare's later plays like *Hamlet, Measure for Measure,* and *Troilus and Cressida?*

12. Why is the period of the late Renaissance often referred to as one that experienced the second defeat of chivalry?

13. Summarize in a sentence or two the basic tenets of Machiavelli's advice to rulers in his book *The Prince.*

14. How do Machiavelli and his ideas relate to Shakespeare? Give examples of how Shakespeare uses these ideas.

15. What is Shakespeare's major point in the famed "degree" speech from *Troilus and Cressida?* How does this speech reflect the major cultural outlook of late sixteenth-century Europe?

16. Why was witchcraft suddenly resurrected in the sixteenth century? What does witchcraft tell us about the cultural outlook of the times? How does Shakespeare's use of witches in *Macbeth* reflect his sense of the times?

17. What kind of mood would be established by using the gallery of Francis I (Figure 6–5) as a setting or background for a staged scene? How does the gallery use space? How is ornament handled on walls and ceiling? What kind of effect would costumed figures have on the gallery setting?

18. How does the slashing in the costumes of the sixteenth century (Figure 6–5) relate to the scrollwork in the wall decorations? Why are they both ugly and beautiful?

19. Compare the portrait of Castiglione by Raphael (Figure 5–8) with the portrait of Henry VIII by Holbein (Figure 6–6). Why does Henry VIII have an ominous look? What are the differences in clothing, body line, and fabric texture in each?

20. Compare *Eleanor of Toledo and Her Son Giovanni de Medici* by Bronzino (Figure 6–8) with *La Donna Velata* by Raphael (Figure 6–7). How do they evidence the changes in cultural outlook that occurred in the thirty to thirty-five years separating their creation? As an actress, how would you feel playing each woman? How would your body feel in each of the costumes? Think of your movement in each case and describe it and its effect on an audience.

21. Compare Dürer's *Self-Portrait* (Figure 5–7)

with Holbein's *Henry VIII* (Figure 6–6). Aside from the different social status of the subjects, why do the two portraits seem from totally different worlds?

22. Describe the costumes in the portraits of Charles IX (Figure 6–9) and Queen Elizabeth (Figure 6–10). What do they do for the person wearing them? How would you feel as an actress or an actor appearing in them? What do they tell you about the cultural outlook of late sixteenth-century Europe?

23. How does the concept of beauty described by Tommaso Buoni in 1606 relate to the movement, manners, costume, interior decoration, and fine arts of the period?

24. Practice moving, standing, walking, and sitting in a male or female costume of this period. Describe how you feel.

25. During this period, why was it impossible for men and women to place arms at their sides?

26. What does the *Ball for the Wedding of the Duc de Joyeuse* (Figure 6–11) communicate about dance poses, movement, and groupings in large gatherings?

27. Block a scene from *Romeo and Juliet* to be played on the Elizabethan stage, using the pre-cepts of early Renaissance style that have been described in relation to this play. Now do the same thing with a scene or two from *Hamlet*. Can you capture on the Elizabethan stage the differences in staging and blocking that accompany the stylistic differences in these two plays? Why or why not?

28. Describe the different costumes in *Titus Andronicus* (Figure 6–13). What is their overall effect? Which garments or parts of garments are meant to be Roman? Which Elizabethan? Do they work together? What effect would they create on the Elizabethan stage? On the modern stage?

29. Why is *Hamlet* such a different tragedy from *Romeo and Juliet*? How are the relationships of the leading characters to the audience different in each play? How are night and artificial light different in each play? Choose six to eight key words of imagery from each play and then contrast them. What are the striking differences?

30. Look at Tintoretto's *The Last Supper* (Figure 6–4). Describe elements in the painting that you could use in a production of *Hamlet*. Then, after choosing a key scene from *Hamlet*, design it to incorporate elements from *The Last Supper*.

BIBLIOGRAPHY

Beckerman, Bernard. *Shakespeare at the Globe, 1599–1609.* New York: Macmillan, 1962. An excellent summary of theatrical performances at the Globe during the ten-year period in which Shakespeare wrote his major plays.

Benesch, Otto. *The Art of the Renaissance in Northern Europe.* Rev. ed. London: Phaidon, 1965. An excellent look at the various medieval, Renaissance, and mannerist influences and trends in art in northern Europe during the sixteenth century.

Bosquet, Jacques. *Mannerism: The Painting Style of the Late Renaissance.* Translated by S. W. Taylor. New York: Braziller, 1964. An excellent pictorial and written survey on mannerist style in painting during the late sixteenth century.

Briganti, Giuliano. *Italian Mannerism.* Translated by Margaret Kunzle. Leipzig: VEB Edition, 1962. Another excellent study of the nature and development of Italian mannerism.

Campbell, Lily Bess. *Scenes and Machines on the English Stage during the Renaissance.* Cambridge: Cambridge University Press, 1923. Reprinted, New York: Barnes and Noble, 1960. A great classic of critical writing on the development of staging in England during the Renaissance.

Chambers, E. K. *The Elizabethan Stage.* 4 vols. London: Oxford University Press, 1923. One of the major references on the Elizabethan stage.

David, Richard. *Shakespeare in the Theatre.* Cambridge: Cambridge University Press, 1978. A detailed study of a series of English productions of the 1970s. Well illustrated.

Friedlander, Walter F. *Mannerism and Antimannerism in Italian Painting.* New York: Columbia University Press, 1957. An excellent discussion of the conflict between mannerist and classic Renaissance ideals in European art after the death of Raphael.

Hale, John R. *Renaissance.* The Great Ages of Man Series. New York: Time-Life Books, 1965. A beautifully illustrated book with extensive color photographs, it covers the major intellectual, artistic, and cultural developments of the Renaissance.

Hodges, C. W. *The Globe Restored: A Study of the Elizabethan Theatre.* Rev. ed. London: Oxford University Press, 1968. A beautiful book, illustrated by the author, on the Globe and other theatres.

Joseph, Bertram. *Elizabethan Acting.* 2nd ed. London: Oxford University Press, 1964. An interesting theoretical analysis of acting on the Elizabethan stage.

Klein, Robert, and Zerner, Henry. *Italian Art 1500–1600.* Sources and Documents in the History of Art. Englewood Cliffs, N.J.: Prentice-Hall, 1966. An interesting look at the written theories and ideas about art during the High Renaissance and the late mannerist Renaissance.

Martindale, Andrew. *Man and the Renaissance.* Landmarks of the World's Art Series. New York: McGraw-Hill, 1966. An excellent and beautifully illustrated survey, with many color plates, on the development of all the arts during the Renaissance. The text is secondary to the plates.

Mates, Julian, and Cantelupe, Eugene, eds. *Renaissance Culture.* The Cultures of Mankind Series. New York: Braziller, 1966. An excellent compilation of writings from original sources on Renaissance life and culture.

Nagler, Alois. *Shakespeare's Stage.* New Haven: Yale University Press, 1958. A summary of the nature of Shakespeare's stage.

Nicoll, Allardyce. *Stuart Masques and the Renaissance Stage.* New York: Harcourt Brace Jovanovich, 1938. A highly regarded, excellently illustrated work that presents the development of the court stage in Italy and its influence on the masque presentations at the English court during the early seventeenth century.

Shakespeare Survey: An Annual Review of Shakespearean Study and Production. New York: Macmillan, 1948–present. An excellent compendium of critical studies, theories, and production approaches published each year for students and teachers of Shakespeare. Illustrated with photographs of performances.

Shearman, John K. G. *Mannerism.* Baltimore: Penguin Books, 1967. Another excellent and very scholarly survey on mannerism in art during the sixteenth and early seventeenth centuries.

Sprague, A. D. *Shakespearean Players and Performances.* Cambridge, Mass.: Harvard University Press, 1953. An interesting study of acting and staging on the Elizabethan stage.

Stechow, Wolfgang. *Northern Renaissance Art.* Sources and Documents in the History of Art. Englewood Cliffs, N.J.: Prentice-Hall, 1966. A compilation of writings on northern European art during the sixteenth century.

Sypher, Wylie. *Four Stages of Renaissance Style.* Garden City, N.Y.: Doubleday-Anchor, 1955. Although written with a rather heavy hand, this is a brilliant work. It weaves together the stylistic characteristics operating in art and literature during the fifteenth, sixteenth, and seventeenth centuries.

Vasari, Giorgio. *Vasari's Lives of the Artists.* New York: Noonday Press, 1957. Discusses the facts and legends about the great artists of the Renaissance.

Wain, John. *The Living World of Shakespeare: A Playgoer's Guide.* New York: St. Martin's Press, 1980. The book is just what it says: a very good introduction to attending and responding to Shakespearean productions.

Wickham, Glynne. *Early English Stages 1300–1660.* 3 vols. New York: Columbia University Press, 1959–1980. A superb and very detailed history of drama and play production in England during medieval and Elizabethan times.

Würtemberger, Franszepp. *Mannerism: The European Style of the Sixteenth Century.* Translated by Michael Heron. New York: Holt, Rinehart and Winston, 1963. Another excellent and quite fascinating study of mannerism in Europe during the sixteenth century.

Baroque Style

Though the development of Baroque style began in the middle of the mannerist sixteenth century, it took another half century for the arts to develop fully the secular richness, sensuous glory, and worldly grandeur that characterized the new-found power of the Church during the period of the Counter Reformation. Rome became the center of this reintegration and renewal as it had a century before when Michelangelo, Raphael, and Bramante created the High Renaissance.

The origin of the word *baroque* is obscure but may have come from the Portuguese word for irregular pearl. The term was at first used disparagingly to describe the asymmetrical excess of the new seventeenth-century art, but today it is a blanket stylistic term for the art and culture of the period from 1600 until the early 1700s.

The major difference between Baroque and Renaissance art was the expansiveness and dynamics of this new style as opposed to the relatively static qualities of the earlier style. The new era itself was dynamic, brilliant, colorful, theatrical, passionate, extravagant, and ecstatic. It was an age of expansion, of rising national powers and empires with the fate of Europe decided in faraway places like India and North America. Baroque expansiveness also extended to new conceptions of man and his universe, developed from the discoveries of Copernicus, Galileo, Kepler, and Newton. Baroque thinking and art were obsessed with the infinite space of an unfolding universe. The new elliptical patterns of movement established for heavenly bodies had a direct effect on compositional patterns in art; the exaggerated theatricality, the lighting from within or beyond, and the movement leading beyond the frame of a work of art can be viewed as strivings after the infinite. Descartes made space and what occupies it the sole physical attribute of being; Pascal confessed that the infinite spaces of the universe frightened him; and Milton termed this new Baroque image of space "the vast and boundless deep." Light also became a

137

physical entity, propelled in waves through Pascal's "infinite spaces" and seen as a metaphor for truth in an age that soon developed for itself the label "The Enlightenment." Alexander Pope characterized this age perfectly in his enthusiasm for the discoveries of Newton: "Nature and Nature's laws lay hid in night, God said: 'Let Newton be!' and all was Light."

The Baroque period was an age of theatre and drama, when opera was invented as an art form to combine spectacle, music, exciting action, and human passion in expansive and overwhelming theatrical presentations incorporating all degrees of lightness, darkness, and intensity. The arts thus involved all the delights of sensuous experience. In all parts of Europe, poetry and literature acquired a richly expressive language, and stories were created that combined description, presentation, conflict, and a final resolution of human emotions. Luxurious display and magnificent splendor framed life at the Catholic courts of Europe; and even in rich Protestant countries, like Holland, there was a sober sense of expansiveness, grandeur, and display. Courtiers, aristocrats, middle-class businessmen, and even brigands and pirates were virtuoso performers in the spectacle of life presented on the expanded stage of the Baroque period.

The beginning of the Baroque period is usually tied to the development of the Counter Reformation after the closing of the famed Council of Trent; the organization at the forefront of this Counter Reformation was the Jesuit order, founded in 1534 by Ignatius Loyola. The mother church of this new order in Rome, the Gesu, was designed by Giacomo Vignola and built between 1568 and 1584. Giacomo della Porta, who had helped Michelangelo with the dome of St. Peter's, was responsible for the façade, which became a model for Baroque churches for the next two centuries.

When Carlo Maderna was asked to complete St. Peter's in 1603, he incorporated Michelangelo's idea of colossal pilasters for holding the building together from base to attic and then created an even greater crescendo of movement from the corners to the center of the structure by using pilasters and columns (Figure 7–1). He thus released the tensions locked into place within the various parts of the structure and created architectural forms and forces that have movement, drama, and climax.

This sense of movement and drama at St. Peter's was not fully realized until the great Roman Baroque sculptor and architect Gianlorenzo Bernini was asked to complete the façade with a monumental piazza (Figure 7–1). He used some preexisting structures to define his design of a long axis or oval space embraced by colonnades and connected to St. Peter's by two diverging wings. The result is a great embracing, expansive gesture that reaches out to enclose space in a dynamic thrust of movement. The entrance from the avenue opposite the façade into the great oval piazza expands from a tight opening to create a wide dramatic vista and then contracts into a trapezoid that expands a second time directly to the façade of the church. This expansion and contraction of space to create movement and climax is the basis of much Baroque design and constitutes the basis for the blocking patterns of the corps de ballet and choruses in Baroque opera and theatre.

This emphasis on dynamic movement is abundantly clear in Bernini's *David* (Figure 7–2). Completed in 1623, Bernini's version, unlike Michelangelo's powerful static version, captures a moment of action in time. Here David is in the midst of a pivoting, unwinding motion that will launch a stone against Goliath; the continuous action releases all those energies locked inside Michelangelo's statue. Moving through time and space, this David thus draws attention to the space around him and to the implied presence of Goliath. For the first time since Hellenistic art, a sculptured figure is not sufficient in itself but partakes of the physical space of the observer. The three great statues of *David* each represent and symbolize the nature of the culture producing them: Donatello's *David* (Figure 5–1) is a graceful nude youth of sixteen representing the youthful self-discovery of the early Renaissance; Michelangelo's *David* (Figure 5–2) is a heroic superhero representing the ma-

Figure 7–1 Aerial view of St. Peter's, façade designed by Maderna in 1607, colonnade and piazza designed by Bernini in 1656. The façade moves toward the center, while the colonnade expands into an ellipse, contracts sharply, and then expands again into a square or trapezoid—all to give dynamic movement and expansion to the space enclosed. Photo courtesy of Alinari, Florence.

Figure 7–2 Gianlorenzo Bernini, *David*, marble, life size, 1623. This Baroque David moves in such a way that he involves the space around him in his movements. Galleria Borghese, Rome. Photo courtesy of Alinari, Florence.

turity, power, and balanced unity of the High Renaissance; while Bernini's *David* (Figure 7–2) represents the release of energy into space, the opening out to the infinite that is the major theme in Baroque art.

The extreme differences within the Baroque style throughout Europe during the first half of the seventeenth century may be seen by comparing the expansive opulence of any of the religious works by Peter Paul Rubens with similar religious subjects painted by Caravaggio, Rembrandt, or Velasquez. Rubens had studied in Italy during the formation of the new style and, upon his return to Flanders

139

in 1608, displayed the same opulent, sensuous, flamboyant outlook that Bernini later developed in Italy. Rembrandt and Velasquez, however, were influenced by followers of the lower-class figure method in Caravaggio's realistic religious works. Using shafts of artificial light to focus viewer attention and feeling, they created works that were closely focused, compassionately real, and richly tactile.

Rubens's *The Garden of Love* is an ideal example of the full flamboyant, early Baroque style used to depict figures in contemporary clothing. Here is a grand, swelling, intense explosion of action, founded on recessional compositional lines (Figure 7–3). The painting has a sense of immediacy, theatricality, energy, space, and lighting control that are completely Baroque.

Figure 7–3 Peter Paul Rubens, *The Garden of Love*, c. 1632–34. Illustrates the operatic, or flamboyant, Baroque style. Here, there is a pulsing vitality, a grand, swelling, intense explosion of action that sweeps the viewer into the dramatic spectacle portrayed. Photo courtesy of the Prado, Madrid.

It was not long before the contradictions and ambiguities in sixteenth-century church music were attacked by those Counter Reformation churchmen who wanted music and the other arts to convey feeling and passion rather than to remain "filled to overflowing with barbarisms, obscurities, contrarieties, and superfluities. . . ." Giovanni da Palestrina was one of the first to undertake the reform; by his death in 1594, prayers-in-song had achieved a fluid and transparent texture and a spiritual and organic unity of feeling reminiscent of the ideals of the High Renaissance *ars perfecta*. But it was Claudio Monteverdi who was truly to understand the inner spirit of the new style. Appointed master of music of the Most Serene Republic of Venice in 1613 after many years as a court composer in Mantua, Monteverdi brought sixteenth-century mannerist Renaissance counterpoint into a new relation with true human emotion. Removing music from the realm of the exquisite and artificial game, he brought it back to the service of human passions. Of his "Madrigals of Love and War," he said that he intended to depict anger, warfare, entreaty, and death and to simulate the passions expressed in the words. For example, in a madrigal, "Return, O Zephyr," he used a rippling melody to suggest waves and rising and falling lines of music to suggest mountains and valleys.

In his preface to *Tancred and Clorinda*, Monteverdi also requested his singers and instrumentalists to render their parts in imitation of the passions of the words; the score contains a fascinating rhythmic figure that represents a galloping horse and a tremolo on the strings that represents a trembling shudder. Monteverdi is, of course, primarily remembered today as having written the first full-length, complete opera—the most popular musical media of the Baroque style that was to sweep all Europe. A number of these early Monteverdi operas, including the famous *Coronation of Poppea* (1642), are still performed in opera houses today. Monteverdi truly brought passion, real feeling, movement, action, and expansive grandeur back to the world of music.

The worst of the religious conflicts unleashed by the arrival of the Reformation—the terrible Thirty Years War—actually occurred during the formation of the new Baroque style in the first half of the seventeenth century. In many ways it was a last terrible rending of the old medieval, social, and political order in Europe. During the entire time of this conflict, intellectuals, artists, and politicians were attempting to develop a new set of relationships between restless, forward, expanding motion and enduring order. Baroque art and culture were a heroic attempt to transcend the innate contradictions between motion and order or, to put it the other way, to find a pattern and an order within the apparent disorder of a changing world.

Europe's traditional machinery of government had been designed to deal with the affairs of an essentially static, feudal society that was agrarian, land based, and bound by a uniform religion. It just could not cope with the tensions and problems of an expanding commercial society sharply divided in matters of religion. The new social order of the Baroque period, first in the church-dominated lands in Italy and later in France, was absolutism, and for a brief time this new order dazzled Europe with the stability it brought to the social-political scene. With all power concentrated in king or pope and an administrative bureaucracy responsible only to the ruler, anarchy, revolution, religious conflict, and civil war were banished for a time to permit tremendous gains in stability, national power, and intellectual and artistic creativity.

The image of the gentleman that now emerged differed in some ways from the one portrayed by Castiglione during the High Renaissance at the beginning of the sixteenth century. There was now an emphasis on a studied carelessness and casual freedom. The new and rapidly accepted image of the ideal man represented by the French phrase *honnête homme*, which really defies translation, was summed up by Nicolas Faret in his work *Honnête Homme*, written in 1630:

> First of all, it seems to me absolutely necessary that he who wishes to enter court society be of noble birth and of a family marked by some noble distinction. . . . As for his profession, there is none more respectable or more essential for a gentleman than that of bearing arms.
>
> The greatest ambition of one who carries a sword should be to be considered a generous and brave man, and consequently he ought to be a man of good conduct and of virtue. And, indeed, those who join malice to valor are usually feared and hated like ferocious beasts, because, having the power to do evil, they also have the will to do so. But those whose great courage is accompanied by good intentions are loved by everyone and considered as guardian angels whom God has sent among us to oppose the oppressions of the wicked.
>
> Since everybody is concerned about his reputation, especially where his profession is involved, a gentleman has all the more reason to watch over the reputation of his weapons, which are truly the means of his nobility. In this respect he must be rigorous without being ostentatious, for, just as the reputation of a lady once

blemished can never regain its original purity, so it is impossible that the esteem enjoyed by a soldier once tarnished by a lack of courage may be so completely re-established as to be above reproach.

> One of the greatest gifts consists in a certain natural gracefulness which in all his movements, in his slightest actions, must shine forth like a divine ray of light, a feature that is found in all those who are born to please courtly society. . . .
>
> I feel that rather than get entangled in all the quarrels of philosophy which would consume the entire life of a man, he would be wiser to study in the great book of experience than in Aristotle. It suffices for him to have a general idea of the most interesting matters that occupy the conventions of good society. I would rather have him be tolerably well informed in several subjects than solidly profound in only one. The reason is that life is too short to attain perfection in even the slightest of those specialties within our reach and that one who can speak only of one thing is too frequently obliged to keep silent.
>
> In consequence of all the efforts one must make to present a pleasant appearance, the first and foremost incumbent on one who wants to please women is to honor them with all the respect and all the submission that he is capable of and that are proper.

Ornament, Interiors, and Furniture

The ornament and decoration of the new Baroque style adopted typical Renaissance forms and added expansion and movement. Even an Italian Baroque chair feels as if it were expanding around and out from the sitter. Arms undulate, backs spread out at the top, stretchers ripple and expand with carving and decoration. An actor seated in full costume in such a chair has the illusion that he is going to rise slowly off the floor, to the sound of great choruses and orchestras, into heaven. This is exactly what happens, of course, in Baroque opera when clouds containing

Figure 7–4 Grand staircase from the Archepiscopal Palace, Würzburg, c. 1720–50. Illustrates the exaggerated, theatrical grandeur of the great staircases of Baroque Europe. Photo courtesy of A. Ohmayer, Rothenburg-o.-Tauber.

thrones are lifted to heaven. Richness, grandeur, opulence, and expansion into space are the key descriptive words for a Baroque chair as they are for architecture, sculpture, and decoration.

Let us now envision ourselves parading up one of the great staircases of the Baroque era. These staircases, symbols of power and grandeur, were often given more space and decoration than any other section of the palace. Some of the best staircases come from the end of the Baroque era when the style was softening into the more delicate colors and lines of the Rococo. One of the most impressive of these architectural complements to authority and power is in the Archepiscopal Palace in Würzburg, Germany. The staircase was designed by Balthasar Neumann and decorated with frescoes by Giovanni Battista Tiepolo (Figure 7–4). The grandeur of the scene when the staircase was lit by candlelight to receive a procession of guests must have been overpowering. An actor, director, or designer will readily appreciate that the scene is totally theatrical, closely related to the spectacle in seventeenth-century opera and heroic drama and to the lavish and fantastic architectural stage designs executed by the famed Bibiena family.

Costume and Accessories

Though Baroque costume went through at least three distinct changes in style, its release from the tensions and rigidities of mannerism into the expanding, full, loose clothing of the first half of the seventeenth century is the most interesting to analyze. Compare, for example, the clothing in the *Ball for the Wedding of the Duc de Joyeuse* with that in *The Garden of Love* by Rubens (Figures 6–11 and 7–3). In Rubens's painting, the ruffs have lost their tension and stiffness and have relaxed into soft lace collars; the boning, padding, and forcing of the human body have been abandoned in favor of an easy expansion of the clothing out and away from the natural contours of the body. The tortured, ornamented, excessively decorated surfaces of fabrics have given way to a natural interest created by the fabric itself. Like the architecture, sculpture, and painting of the Baroque period, the costumes move, expand, and spread out to create a sense of size and rich grandeur. The men's hats have bigger brims and are worn more casually; the women's skirts blossom out from the body without the inhibiting controls of braid and jewelry; and the natural surfaces of fabrics shimmer and move with a new sense of freedom.

The prints of Abraham Bosse, who recorded the Parisian social scene around 1630, provide the best sources of information on the new costume style, which was more quickly accepted in Flanders, France, and England than in Italy, the birthplace of the Baroque period. A look at his print *The Costume Ball*, dated 1635, gives much information on overall fashion as well as on individual variations (Figure 7–5).

In male dress, the doublet was now unstiffened with a slightly raised waist, and skirts were either cut into the top or casually added as peplum tabs at the waist. The waistline was frequently decorated with points—metal-tagged ribbons made into bows that had originally been drawn through eyelets in the waist to hold up the knee-length breeches. Breeches lost their padding and were either loose or baggy or long and tapering, often with buttons or bows on the sides. They usually ended in loose ribbon garters tied about the leg below the knee, the end hanging loosely at the outside. Sometimes the bottoms of the trousers were loose and finished with a row or two of ribbon loops, a style that was to gain great importance by the middle of the century. High, soft leather boots were worn, indoors as well as out, over silk boot hose that fell gracefully and widely over the boot cuffs. Sleeves were full, usually with one or more slashes the length of the arm to expose the rich material of the shirt beneath; these openings were frequently set with buttons and holes down the length of the arm. Cuffs, like collars, were made of exquisite starched lace.

Figure 7–5 Abraham Bosse, *The Costume Ball*, engraving, c. 1635. Illustrates the looser, softer, more relaxed fashions that succeeded the tense, artificial grotesque dress of late mannerism. Photo courtesy of the Bibliothèque Nationale, Paris.

Circular, half-length cloaks were worn over one shoulder and under the other arm, falling diagonally across the back. Wide-brimmed hats, made of soft felt or beaver and trimmed with ostrich plumes, were worn at a jaunty angle.

In feminine dress the corset and the farthingale disappeared; the waistline rose and was no longer pointed in front. Several full skirts, often draped over each other, gave the female form a full, healthy, sensuous, expansive silhouette. The bodice, usually low cut, with a rich lace collar to cover or frame the bosom, ended in a raised waistline finished with square tabs. Like the male's, the woman's sleeves ended in wide lace cuffs and were full and large, sometimes slashed down the

full length to show a lining or undersleeve and caught at the elbow with silk ribbons. Sometimes the waistline was also finished with a silk ribbon sash or with points as in the male doublet. The hair was worn with a fringe of bangs on the forehead and two long shoulder-length ringlets falling over the ears. Masculine hats were worn for riding, while the hooded cloak was the standard outer wrap for evening and travel.

To sum up the attributes of the new style, let us look at the famous Anthony Van Dyck portrait of Charles I, painted as if the king were returning from an outdoor canter on his favorite horse (Figure 7–6). Once again after a hundred-year lapse, the natural body is seen outdoors against a natural landscape in easy,

Figure 7-6 Anthony Van Dyck, *Portrait of Charles I Hunting*, c. 1635. Illustrates the simple, rich fashions of the early Baroque period, which gave the body an aristocratic assurance without the use of heavy artificial decoration. The Louvre, Paris. Photo courtesy of the French Musées Nationaux.

natural clothing. The frozen, immobile mannequins that passed for royal portraits during the mannerist Renaissance have disappeared (Figures 6–6, 6–10). There is an easy, aristocratic assurance in the body pose, the tilt of the head, the way the eye contacts the viewer. The king does not need the heavy, distorting, artificial trappings of power to establish his position; he seems to accomplish this solely through his self-knowledge. The excessive sense of place and "degree," fanatically described by Ulysses in *Troilus and Cressida* (see pp. 118–119), has been put aside in favor of an easy, personal, direct sense of position and power. The jaunty tilt to the expanding outline of the hat; the soft, rich, and strikingly simple satin surface of the doublet; the lovely, natural, tactile surface of the suede trousers; the rich lace of the collar and cuffs, and the soft doeskin of the boots are all calculated to appeal subtly to the senses in a natural way, suggesting richness and taste without overstating it. This portrait symbolizes the youth and early maturity of the new Baroque style just as a similarly posed portrait of Louis XIV, painted about sixty-five years later, represents the stultified, heavy, hot-house, interior atmosphere that marked the end of the late Baroque style before it relaxed into the delicacies of the Rococo style.

Manners and Movement

Because of the nature of the costume, the movement of this period was grander and easier than in the preceding mannerist Renaissance. As the century progressed and costumes and etiquette once again became more formal and complex, the affected nonchalance of the "Cavalier" period gradually gave way to a more planned self-assurance and studied informality. As much attention was paid to a man's bodily carriage as to the instruction of his mind. One of the most studied effects frequently noted in portraits of this age is that of a standing figure with toes turned outward ninety degrees from each other. This stance, which became a necessity for an elegant bearing, was achieved by turning out one leg from thigh to foot. It was developed from the clas-

sical ballet steps of this time, since deportment and dancing went hand in hand in the training of the court gentleman. In walking, the gentleman was advised by James Cleland, a tutor to young gentlemen in 1607, to "take very good heed unto your feet and consider with what grace and countenance ye walk, so that ye go not softly tripping like a wanton maid, nor yet striding with great long paces. . . . Walk man-like with a grave, civil pace, as becometh one of your birth and age. Away with all affectation." The gentleman was also advised to avoid the manner of those who find it difficult to "go forward one step without looking down to the rose upon their shoes; or lifting up their head to set out their band or setting up the brim of their hat." In accompanying a person of quality, a gentleman gave the other person the "upper hand," that is, stayed slightly behind him. Since the wallside of the street was also given to a person of superior quality, the gentleman was admonished not to change street sides too frequently lest his companion keep shifting his side "like a managed horse." To greet people on the street, a mere salutation without physical contact was considered sufficient. The youthful gallant, of course, always placed his lady on the inside of the street while he walked on the outside. In a garden stroll, the superior person or lady was always kept on the right side, but indoors, the side toward a bed or away from the main entrance was considered appropriate for the lady or the person of superior position. When three people walked, the superior position was in the middle, but when all were of equal rank, there was an almost dancelike change as each changed place with his companion at every turning.

Hats, worn indoors as well as out, were an important accessory in conveying the exact deference due a man of social standing. Whether and when the hat was to be removed were matters of serious consideration, and the least blunder was long remembered by others. Subtle degrees of social distinction were tied in with the rules for handling the hat. In general, one always removed his hat in the presence of his superior until requested to put it on again. For the superior to forget this showed great arrogance and ill-breeding. If the men were of equal position, they either did not remove their hats or, if they did, put them on again at the same time. No one, not even the king's own followers, remained covered in the presence of royalty except for a royal ambassador who might keep his hat on while performing ceremonial duties for his absent master. Such subtleties caused much gossip as when the son of Charles I, later Charles II, was instructed by his father to cover while dining, but a visiting ambassador was allowed to continue through the dinner with his hat removed.

When the hat was removed with the right hand in a graceful sweep, it was not held on the thigh, as in the late mannerist Renaissance, but at the waist or sometimes with a negligent gesture under the left arm. For the bow that accompanied this, the man swept off his hat, stepped back on either foot, and bent his back knee while sweeping his hat across the chest. He then straightened his knee and placed his hat back on his head.

Gloves, or gauntlets, were less tight fitting than in the previous period and were either worn or carried during all social occasions. Unlike in the past, the gloved hand was now offered to a lady in a dance; sometimes the gentleman waited for the lady to extend her hand before donning his glove. When giving or receiving an object by hand, one was expected to remove the right-hand glove, and the same was true when the hand was to be kissed.

The major change in both male and female clothing was toward an ease and casual elegance as the immobile rigidities of the mannerist Renaissance disappeared. For the first time in European fashion, a woman's arms often showed below the elbow, and the bodice was often extremely low in its décolletage. Good manners and deportment were still a paramount concern, and the conventions of the day specified, according to a treatise on the education of ladies published in 1673, that "women ought to be brought up to a comely and decent carriage, to their Needle, to Neatness, to understand all those things that do particularly belong to their sex [though] merely to teach Gentlewomen to Frisk and Dance, to paint their faces, to curl their Hair, to put on a Whisk, or wear gay Clothes, is not truly to adorn . . . their Bodies."

Richard Braithwaite, who wrote about the training of the gentlewoman in 1641, stressed that carriage should neither be too precise nor loose; smiles should be pleasing and a little bashful; walks should be graceful and not too active; and posture should not possess a seemly carelessness. He scorned women who indulged in affectations and artificial extravagance. As with men, much stress was placed on dance as an appropriate training for female deportment; particular attention was given to the holding of the head since this was the part of the body that would first draw the attention of the courtier. The dancing master also taught the lady the correct art of walking: to "put her feet close to one another, the toes outward . . . sedately and in a straight line."

For the first time, the female curtsy differed from the male bow. With the body held erect and inclined slightly forward, the lady gently and steadily bent her knees outward, lifting her heels off the ground only if the curtsy was to be very low. The hands remained easily at the sides, and the eyes were first directed at the person receiving the curtsy and then were lowered on the knee bend and raised as the body returned to an upright position. Because greetings and conversation curtsies were not usually deep ones, both heels

remained on the ground, particularly since ladies now wore moderately high heels.

Both men and women embraced and kissed on special occasions when feeling was more important than formality and decorum. In France, ladies were usually kissed on the cheek. In England and often in Italy, they were kissed on the mouth.

In sitting, the body was relaxed and comfortable; and, unlike the late sixteenth century—when men and women perched stiffly on the edge of a chair or stool—the body was allowed to expand over and outside the frame of the chair. In an anonymous painting based on *The Five Senses*, an engraving by Abraham Bosse, we can see the relaxed poses affected by courtiers and their ladies at a domestic social gathering (Figure 7–7).

Figure 7–7 Anonymous painting based on *The Five Senses,* an engraving by Abraham Bosse, c. 1636–45. Illustrates the relaxed, seated postures affected by upper-class individuals at a domestic social gathering. Note how the bodies expand over and outside the frames of the chairs. Photo courtesy of the Fine Arts Museum, Tours.

Theatre in the Baroque era was heavily influenced by opera, that new theatrical form from Italy sweeping through Europe during the first half of the seventeenth century and remaining a most popular form of entertainment for the next hundred years. By 1650 the basic physical structure for drama and opera was fully established in Italy, as were the designs for settings and costumes. The auditorium was most commonly a U-shaped structure lined with tiers of boxes and sometimes with a gallery at the very back for servants and apprentices. Visibility was excellent only from the center of the house. The floor of the auditorium usually had no seats, only standing room, though benches sometimes were used in smaller theatres. Here aspiring gentlemen and middle-class theatre devotées congregated, as it was not nearly as costly as buying a seat in one of the boxes. This floor area, easily accessible by stairs from the stage, was also used for grand promenades, spectacular ballets, and large balls and parties.

The auditorium was divided from the stage by an ornate frame, or proscenium arch, and the stage itself sloped upward and was usually much deeper than the auditorium. There was a considerable amount of room below the stage for machinery and lifts to the trap doors, and there was enough room above the stage for painted sky borders. The sides of the stage were equipped with overlapping rows of painted wings that could be moved out of sight behind the proscenium by hand or by machinery. Lighting came primarily from chandeliers hung over both the stage and the

Figure 7–8 Cosimo Lotti, *Apollo Enthroned,* pen and ink with gray wash, c. 1641. Illustrates the full, operatic Baroque spirit with architectural wings framing a cloud machine ready to move upward into the heavens. From the G. P. Baker Collection, owned by Donald Oenslager. Photo courtesy of Mrs. Donald Oenslager and Viking Press.

auditorium, though there were sometimes footlights behind reflectors and lights set against reflectors behind the downstage wings.

The settings consisted of painted canvas flats, representing either nature or architecture, which were set one behind the other in groups up each side of the raked stage. There were as many flats in each group as there were locations in the play or opera; the back wall was composed of a series of large flats, or shutters, that met center stage. Thus, at every change of scene, a set of wings, shutters, and sky borders was drawn away from the stage in full view of the audience to reveal the next painted scene (Figure 7–8).

Costumes, as might be expected for the grand spectacles that made up most classical tragedies and operas, were rich, fantastic, ornamental garments of great formality. They were based on contemporary fashions com-

bined with items from nature, classical antiquity, or the exotic East. A Roman or Greek male wore a plumed helmet or headdress, a breastplatelike tunic, a short skirt covered with ornamental tabs, a mantle, and short, very tight-fitting calf-high boots. A lady of classical times wore what appeared to be a court gown often with a hip-length overskirt and labels or tabs at the waist and shoulders. Sleeves were usually bell-shaped and caught back at the elbows with hanging points finished in tassels; the hair or headdress was richly adorned with plumes. From this basic structure ingenious designers invented variations suggesting Turks, Indians, mythological beasts, and demons of the underworld. Only in comedy were the rich fashions of contemporary dress allowed to appear without the basic structured silhouette and ornamentation of the "costume antique" or "costume à la Romaine."

The Plays

It is difficult to find a truly Baroque play since the dominant theatrical form was opera. However, since the modern actor is more interested in the subtle characterizations found in a play than in the broad emotional patterns of opera, it is important to find a drama of some depth that includes strong Baroque characteristics. A heroic tragedy might seem the natural choice; but such plays, written during the mid-seventeenth century and filled with ranting heroics in rhymed couplets against a background of changing spectacle, lack all subtlety of characterization. Or one might use Milton's *Samson Agonistes*, which is rich in Baroque imagery, but it is not truly a play for the stage. We do have, though, Shakespeare's *Antony and Cleopatra*, which, while not fully participating in the Baroque style, does have the depth and subtlety of a truly great tragedy and the sweep and grandeur of the Baroque era. It transcends the bounds of this world like the great Baroque palace ceiling paintings of the time (Figure 8–4).

The play emerges into Baroque grandeur from mannerist darkness and half-light. While

King Lear, Macbeth, and even *Othello* are plays taking place both in literal night and the nighttime of the soul, *Antony and Cleopatra* is a drama of bright and expansive magnitude. The figures are so multiple and varied, the canvas so vast, and the imagery so rich that they lead our imagination beyond the confines of Egypt and Rome to an infinite, cosmic level.

The opening scene sets the mood of physical richness and emotional grandeur within which the transcending love of Antony and Cleopatra flourishes. The play still has some mannerist tendencies in organization, since it demands continuing shifts and changes in audience reaction as the lovers' passion fluctuates between attraction and repulsion and as the scene shifts throughout the Mediterranean world. But unlike the mannerist style, the play is not locked within the inner reaches of the soul. The fluctuations in love and war and in attitude and outlook are continually linked through soaring, cosmic imagery to a view of life that lifts reality to an infinite realm where cause and effect merge with the universal flux of the universe. This imagery of reaching out to the heavens and to a larger, cosmic world can be experienced visually in Pietro da Cortona's *The Glorification of the Reign of Urban VIII* with its apocalyptic rise of swirling figures through an illusionistic opening in the ceiling of the Barberini Palace (Figure 8–4).

To understand *Antony and Cleopatra* is to realize that superficial characterizations of Cleopatra as an intriguing courtesan and Antony as an aging playboy are impossible. Even the down-to-earth Enobarbus sees the contradictory, mysterious extremes of greatness in Cleopatra and combined grandeur and foolishness in Antony. Throughout both characterizations runs the idea that *all* is both lost and won. The whole play is one great paradox that cannot be resolved within the limits of this world. Antony and Cleopatra are the Baroque hero and heroine; only Enobarbus with his richness of personality and warm humanity approximates their Baroque complexity. All the other characters remain ciphers surrounding this trio's sunbursts of character and personality, like swirling angels in a Baroque ceiling.

In his thematic development, Shakespeare does retain more mannerist ambiguities than single-minded Baroque assertiveness. He will not directly state whether the passion at the center of the play is destructive or a glimpse of something greater than temporal power and death. He will not tell his audience, as would a high Baroque artist, whether Antony or Caesar has made the correct choice in the worldly game of fortune. In his use of language and imagery, however, he deliberately underlines images of the firmament, the world, the ocean, and the vastness of the universe. Antony says that to measure his love one must "needs find out new heaven, new earth." Cleopatra says that Antony's face is like "a sun and moon, which kept their course and lighted the little O, the earth." At his death Cleopatra says that there is "nothing left remarkable beneath the visiting moon," and Lepidus describes Antony's faults "as the spots of heaven, more fiery by night's blackness." The word *world* occurs almost twice as many times in this play as in any other of Shakespeare's dramas, and it is always used to increase the audience's sense of vastness, sweep, and grandeur.

The rhythm of the play is closely tied to the shifting contrasts in the play's structure as well as to the sweep of its imagery; but, unlike the shifts in other more mannerist plays of Shakespeare, the transitions are not as abrupt. They remind one of the rhythmic movements in Baroque architecture established by the expansion and contraction of space as in the layout of the Bernini piazza in front of St. Peter's Cathedral (Figure 7–1).

The physical requirements for *Antony and Cleopatra* would be enormous if the play were presented within the style of Baroque opera. Within the open conventions of the Jacobean stage, however, the only absolute necessity is an upper level for the monument. The play actually has few definite localizations of scene. To enable the play to move with the speed and flow written into its structure, it should be presented on a basically open stage with furnishings, costumes, properties, and decorative accessories used to reinforce the action and to assist the audience in capturing the imagery of the Baroque style.

Acting and Directing the Plays

Most of what we know about Baroque acting in the early and middle years of the seventeenth century comes from a study of the art of the period. We know from the very nature of opera and its costumes that the emphasis was on presence, grandeur, expansiveness of gesture, and disciplined control of the body. In order not to be dwarfed and intimidated by the spectacle that surrounded him, the actor or singer had to command attention and feel in control of the space surrounding him. In the larger chorus scenes, the choreography had to be as disciplined and as carefully worked out in its symmetrical patterns of expansion and contraction as the expanding and undulating piazza of St. Peter's Cathedral designed by Bernini (Figure 7–1). The individual performer, too, undoubtedly would have mastered this alternating expanding and contracting movement so that his performance would have achieved a climax through increasing speed, movement, and size of gesture—a tremendous crescendo, supported appropriately by music, costume, and scenery. The great "tirades" of heroic tragedy were also based on this sense of movement and were achieved in the same way—an increasing volume, pitch, and tempo to the climax and then a gradual contraction and fall to the conclusion of the speeches. Training in this acting method, called Heroics, is given at the American Conservatory Theatre Training Program in San Francisco. It is excellent training even today for actors developing voice and diction for the larger-than-life classic plays of the past.

In those cases where great spectacles and large-scale costumes are not required in a Baroque opera, heroic tragedy, or high comedy, the actor can learn much from studying Baroque art. Look again at the portrait of Charles I by Van Dyck (Figure 7–6). Note how without mantles, robes, crowns, and accoutrements, Charles commands our attention with a look, slight lift of the head, pose of one arm on the hip and the other on a walking stick, and a stance that seems to move him slightly forward. The clothing is rich but simple, and the whole figure is elegant but casual. The surrounding scene is natural but subordinate. Charles *is* a king and *does* command the scene without the forced accessories needed by a mannerist Henry VIII or Queen Elizabeth (Figures 6–6 and 6–10).

Designing the Plays

If one were to use some approximation of the spatial arrangements of the Elizabethan stage for a production of *Antony and Cleopatra*, the sense of the movement, expansiveness, and richness of the Baroque would have to come from swagged drapes, ornate set pieces, the placement of furniture, the use of heavily fringed canopies, and the suggestion of rich-

ness and variety in textures (Figure 7–9). The ideal should be to create a collage of Baroque shapes, colors, and textures suggesting movement, expansion through the judicious use of convex and concave effects, and an overall sense of size, grandeur, and richness. If the arrangement of space is not that of the Elizabethan stage, the setting must still re-

Figure 7–9 Scene from *Antony and Cleopatra* by Shakespeare, produced by the Oregon Shakespeare Festival, Ashland, Oregon; 1959. Directed by James Sandoe, costumes designed by the author. Illustrates Baroque theatricality within the classical conventions of the early seventeenth-century stage. Photo by the author.

main primarily a symbol of the Baroque rather than a suggestion of various places, since the action must move rapidly through forty-two different scenes. Possibilities are a turntable with a great baroque collage of columns, steps, canopies, and ornament or an open thrust stage with, again, a judicious arrangement of forms and rich, tactile ornament. Useful images from the preceding illustrations could come from the Piazza of St. Peter's (Figure 7–1), the background in Rubens's *The Garden of Love* (Figure 7–3), and the grand staircase from the Archepiscopal Palace of Würzburg (Figure 7–4).

In a production of *Antony and Cleopatra* the costume designer's ideal should be the Renaissance-Baroque ideal of the classic painted by Veronese and Rubens in which certain conventions of helmets, breastplates, plumes, and labels at waist and shoulder are combined with contemporary dress to create a rich, sophisticated, opulent view of antiquity as seen through the contemporary Baroque mind's-eye. Rich fabric swagged and draped in a pseudo-classical manner over the male and female form, trained gowns and trailing mantles, and large, opulent ornaments should be the key to the costumes, with a mixture of the classical corselets and the near-Eastern turbans found in contemporary paintings of antiquity. In every way the designer should probably shun the actual facts of Roman and Egyptian clothing of the time of Antony and Cleopatra in favor of the rich, fantasy vision of antiquity seen in Baroque paintings. In every way possible the costumes should support the images of "the world," "the firmament," "the ocean," and the "new earth" that give an image of vastness and expansion to the entire production.

PROJECTS AND PROBLEMS

1. What was the role of the Council of Trent in laying the foundations for the Baroque era?

2. What are the main characteristics of Baroque art?

3. What new scientific views of the cosmos greatly influenced the use of space in Baroque art?

4. Explain why the use of light and infinite space is a fundamental characteristic of Baroque style.

5. Why are Baroque art and culture usually labeled "theatrical"?

6. Look at Maderna's façade of St. Peter's (Figure 7–1). What are its qualities of rhythm and movement? Why is the central balcony, on which the Pope appears to give speeches and blessings to the public gathered in the piazza, so strong theatrically?

7. When Bernini designed the piazza in front of St. Peter's (Figure 7–1), what visual and spatial effects did he use to dramatize the approach to the steps of the church? Use these spatial concepts to work out a floor plan for a set or a blocking pattern for a chorus in opera or heroic tragedy.

8. Look closely at *David* by Bernini (Figure 7–2). What are the major differences from Michelangelo's *David* (Figure 5–2)? From Donatello's *David* (Figure 5–1)? Why is space more involved in Bernini's *David* than in Michelangelo's?

9. What theatrical qualities in Rubens's *The Garden of Love* (Figure 7–3) remove it sharply from the work of Rembrandt? How does it relate to the work of Cortona (Figure 8–4)? How does it differ? Describe the spatial arrangement and movement in *The Garden of Love*.

10. What characteristics of opera by Monteverdi complemented the style of the Baroque Era?

11. What is meant by the statement that the Baroque style was a heroic attempt to transcend the innate contradictions between motion and order?

12. Why was absolutism the primary political answer to the needs of the Baroque era?

13. What is your opinion of Faret's description of the perfect gentleman during the Baroque era? Why is it typically Baroque to speak of the perfect gentleman's manners as shining "forth like a divine ray of light"?

14. Imagine yourself making a grand entrance on the staircase of the Archepiscopal Palace in Würzburg (Figure 7–4). How would you feel? How would you be dressed? What would you want to support your grand entrance? Describe how you would use such a staircase in a design for a play or opera.

15. Compare the costumes in the *Ball for the Wedding of the Duc de Joyeuse* (Figure 6–11) with those in Rubens's *The Garden of Love* (Figure 7–3). What are the major differences? How would you feel wearing costumes from each painting? How would the costumes from each affect your movement? How do the lines of the clothing in the Rubens work relate to Baroque ideals in sculpture and architecture?

16. Imagine yourself wearing the costumes in *The Costume Ball* by Abraham Bosse (Figure 7–5). How would you feel? What would be the colors and textures? Describe the movement depicted here.

17. Study the famous Van Dyck portrait of Charles I (Figure 7–6). Why does Charles seem so unregal? How does this work differ from the Holbein portrait of Henry VIII (Figure 6–6)? What does the portrait of Charles I communicate about the movement and manners of this period?

18. Block an intimate at-home scene based on Abraham Bosse's *The Five Senses* (Figure 7–7). How do you feel about the way you would have to sit? About your relationship to others at the table? Describe your feeling and response to the scene as a whole.

19. Imagine yourself in a performance of *Apollo Enthroned* in front of the setting by Cosimo Lotti (Figure 7–8). Describe your feelings and movement and the audience's reaction to the performance.

20. Imagine a Baroque production of *Antony and Cleopatra* on an open nonoperatic stage. Describe the costumes, blocking, properties, use of voice, rhythm of the play, and the overall effect of the performance.

21. Describe how you would use the Baroque images in *Antony and Cleopatra* that relate to the cosmos, the heavens, the infinite, the sun and moon, and the world in a design for a production.

BIBLIOGRAPHY

Baur-Heinhold, M. *Baroque Theatre*. New York: McGraw-Hill, 1967. The finest pictorial compendium published to date on the theatre of the seventeenth and eighteenth centuries.

Bjurstrom, Per. *Giacomo Torelli and Baroque Stage Design*. Stockholm: Almquist and Wiksell, 1961. An excellent study of the Baroque scenic innovations created by this first famous master of the Venetian operatic Baroque scenic style.

Blitzer, Charles *Age of Kings*. The Great Ages of Man Series. New York: Time-Life books, 1967. Intended for the average reader, this beautifully illustrated book, with extensive color photography, is a concise and useful text on the major artistic, intellectual, and cultural developments in Europe during the seventeenth century.

Bode, Willhelm von. *Great Masters of Dutch and Flemish Painting*. Translated by M. C. Clarke. London: Duckworth, 1909. Although published almost eighty years ago, this is still an excellent study of northern Baroque style in Flanders and Holland during the seventeenth century.

Campbell, Lily Bess. "A History of Costuming on the English Stage between 1660 and 1823." *University of Wisconsin Studies in Language and Literature*, 1918, pp. 187–223. A useful scholarly study of the changes in theatrical dress on the English stage from the time of Shakespeare to the beginning of the nineteenth century.

Fokker, Timon H. *Roman Baroque Art: The History of a Style*. London: Oxford University Press, 1938. An excellent study of the foundations of the Roman Baroque style.

Hempel, Eberhard. *Baroque Art and Architecture in Central Europe*. Pelican History of Art Series. Baltimore: Penguin Books, 1965. A very good survey of the expansion of the Baroque ideal in architecture to central Europe during the late seventeenth and early eighteenth centuries.

Hibbard, Howard. *Bernini*. Baltimore: Penguin, 1965. A very fine survey of the contribution to Baroque architecture and sculpture made by this seventeenth-century giant of Italian art.

Kitson, Michael. *The Age of the Baroque*. Landmarks of the World's Art Series. New York: McGraw-Hill, 1966. This beautifully illustrated book, with many color plates, deals with the art of Europe from the beginning of the seventeenth century until the middle of the eighteenth century.

Mayor, A. Hyatt. *The Bibiena Family.* New York: Bittner, 1945. The best-known study on the history and methods of this famous Italian family of theatrical designers during the Baroque period.

McComb, Arthur. *The Baroque Painters of Italy.* Cambridge, Mass.: Harvard University Press, 1934. A slightly dated yet excellent study of the painters in Italy who established three types of Baroque art: realistic, classic, and flamboyant.

Millon, Henry A. *Baroque and Rococo Architecture.* New York: Braziller, 1961. A very useful and well-illustrated study of Baroque and Rococo architecture throughout Europe during the seventeenth and early eighteenth centuries.

Spurgeon, Caroline F. E. *Shakespeare's Imagery.* Boston: Beacon Press, 1958. A necessary reference for designers and directors interested in visual imagery.

Stechow, Wolfgang. *Rubens and the Classical Tradition.* Cambridge, Mass.: Harvard University Press for Oberlin College, 1968. A fine scholarly study of Rubens's relation to the classicism of the High Renaissance.

Tapié, Victor L. *The Age of Grandeur.* Translated by A. Ross Williamson. New York: Praeger, 1957. A fascinating account of the rise of Baroque art and architecture in Italy and its move to France during the seventeenth century; also contains some information on art and architecture in England, central Europe, and the European colonies.

Waterhouse, Ellis K. *Italian Baroque Painting.* London: Phaidon, 1962. Another excellent study of the development of Italian Baroque painting; discusses the variations in, and interrelationships among, the realistic, classic, and flamboyant Baroque styles.

Weinstein, Leo, ed. *The Age of Reason.* The Cultures of Mankind Series. New York: Braziller, 1965. An excellent compilation of writings from original seventeenth-century sources on the Baroque view of life and culture.

Wittkower, Rudolf. *Art and Architecture in Italy, 1600–1750.* Baltimore: The Pelican History of Art Series, Penguin Books, 1958. Another solid survey on the development and change in Italian architecture during the seventeenth and early eighteenth centuries.

Wölfflin, Heinrich. *Principles of Art History.* Translated by Mary D. Hottinger. New York: Holt, 1932. One of the great seminal books on art history that discusses the important differences between Renaissance and Baroque art.

Worsthorne, S. T. *Venetian Opera in the Seventeenth Century.* Oxford: Clarendon Press, 1954. An excellent and very useful illustrated study for the theatre student wishing to gain an insight into the creation and expansion of opera in the seventeenth century.

Classic Baroque Style

At the same time that the high Baroque "operatic" style originated in Italy under the guidance of artists like Bernini, another level of Baroque art developed in Italy in the work of Domenichino, Guercino, and the Carracci family that we have come to call the classic Baroque style. This style reached its fullest statement in France during the reign of Louis XIV. At the opening of the seventeenth century, a development in French art, literature, and education caused the rules of classical art and writing to supersede the freer medieval and Renaissance methods. Similarly, an atmosphere of comparative freedom gradually gave way to one of strict regimentation during the later years of Cardinal Richelieu's power, and this centralization of the government was increased to a grand, political imperialism by Louis XIV. The impetuous, exuberant nobleman now became the tame, well-bred courtier living under the king's roof at Versailles, and all the arts were harnessed to propagandize the disciplined, ordered, tightly controlled life of pomp and grandeur that was the ideal of the Sun King.

The many ideas propounded to control and circumscribe French art and literature during this age can be condensed into the following five: One, every aspect of a painting or character in a play should possess decorum by maintaining a balanced and appropriate relationship to every other character or aspect of composition. Two, all art should be composed on a high plane in an elevated style. Three, subject matter for all serious art should be taken from mythology, the Bible, or Greek or Roman history. Four, the individual aspects of nature and personality should be subordinated to a generalized universal portrayal, emphasizing the beautiful as opposed to the irregular. Five, all artistic techniques should be based on the rules of the Ancients as exemplified in the art and literature of the best classical artists of Greece, Rome, and the High Renaissance.

These were exactly the precepts followed by Racine in writing his classical tragedies and by Nicolas Poussin in developing his paintings on classical and biblical history. Poussin was, in many ways, directly responsible for the basic tenets of the style, since Charles Lebrun, who became Louis XIV's dictator of the arts, used an analysis of this artist's work in formulating the rules that were propagated by the newly created Academy of Art. Poussin, who spent most of his life in Italy and based his work in great measure on the work of Annibale Carracci at the Farnese Palace, believed in cool, rich color, strongly modeled figures, frozen action, complexly balanced compositions, and a severe intellectual approach (Figure 8–1).

Though the grandeur of the Italian Baroque period remained, it was now locked into rigid rules and regulations for life and art, which exemplified the reign of the Sun King. To make the distinction vivid and immediate, let us look at the Church of St. Agnese in Rome by Francesco Borromini, dating from the middle of the seventeenth century, and the Church of the Invalides in Paris by Jules Hardouin-Mansart, dating from the last years of the century (Figures 8–2 and 8–3). The Borromini church has movement, several points of focus, and a sense of easy grandeur. The concave-convex juxtaposition of its lower façade gives dramatic height to the dome; there is also an elastic connection between the two towers, which have their own

Figure 8–1 Nicolas Poussin, *Holy Family on the Steps*, c. 1656. Illustrates the elevated style, cool precision, ideal beauty, and restrained decorum of the classical Baroque style. Photo courtesy of the National Gallery of Art, Samuel H. Kress Collection, Washington, D.C.

Figure 8–2 Francesco Borromini, Church of St. Agnese in the Piazza Navona, Rome, 1653–63. Illustrates the Italian flamboyant Baroque style of architecture with its multiple points of focus and use of concave-convex effects to create movement and elasticity between the various architectural parts. Photo courtesy of Alinari, Florence.

Figure 8–3 Jules Hardouin-Mansart, Church of the Invalides, Paris, 1680–91. Illustrates the classical, late Baroque style admired in France with its single, unified focus; measured discipline; monumental form; cold, carefully articulated structure; and slow, sonorous upward movement from base to cupola spire. Photo courtesy of the French Government Tourist Office.

"in and out" concave and convex movement. The Hardouin-Mansart structure is colder, without a sense of elastic movement, with the dome decoration locked into massive frames, and with one single, unified, monumental sense of focus. It beautifully represents the measured, disciplined, restrained grandeur that was the ideal of the court of Louis XIV; it is also a visual image for the grandeur and restraint of the tragic actor in a Racine play.

Finally, let us take two interiors that fully exemplify the Italian high Baroque sensibility versus the French classic sense of ordered grandeur. The Italian one is the ceiling in the Barberini Palace designed by Pietro da Cortona, and the French one is the Salle des Gardes at Versailles designed by Charles Lebrun, Louis XIV's dictator of fine arts (Figures 8–4 and 8–5). The Barberini ceiling is an operatic crescendo of twisting, swirling, excited movement opening out in its expanded perspective to an infinite world of the heavens beyond. It reflects a taste for excessive emotional climaxes, and though it has some underlying structural control, the overall impression is one of triumphant, unrestrained emotion. The mood created by the Salle des Gardes, except for a similar sense of

grandeur, is entirely different. Here the richness and ornamentation are tightly controlled within strong and rigid geometric frames. The room does not open to another world but is circumscribed, measured, and closed. The spirit of absolutism and control is strikingly apparent in the geometric regularity imposed on this rich chamber.

Even before one looks at the clothing, manners, and customs of this period, it is obvious that individuality was not admired and that all courtiers had to dress, act, and fill a place according to the rules of "le Grand Monarque." The French classic style became the international style for all Europe by the close of the century. Louis XIV prided himself on his universal, cosmopolitan outlook just as Racine stressed a universal outlook and never included an individualized portrait of a Frenchman in his tragedies.

Figure 8–4 Pietro da Cortona, *Glorification of the Reign of Urban VIII*, portion of a ceiling fresco, Barberini Palace, Rome, 1633–39. An operatic crescendo of twisting, spiraling movement opening out through an expanded perspective to an infinite, heavenly world above. Illustrates the Italian Baroque taste for excessive emotional climaxes in art, literature, and theatre. Photo courtesy of Alinari, Florence.

Music

The musical-dramatic productions at the court of Louis XIV were as lavish, tightly organized, and grand as the other arts. During Louis's minority, the court ballet that developed in the early years of the seventeenth century was challenged by the Italian opera, so admired by Cardinal Mazarin, prime minister of France and an Italian by birth. In 1660, when the noted Venetian composer Cavalli was invited to Paris to produce a full-fledged Italian Baroque opera, it had a mixed reception, even though the new style of opera in its French form was soon to challenge the old court ballet. Another challenge soon came from Molière who united the elements of comedy, music, and dance into a form he called *comédie-ballet*. The best known of these today is the popular *Le Bourgeois Gentilhomme*, first performed at the Palace of Chambord and later at the court in 1670.

It was Jean Baptiste Lully, however, a Florentine by birth but a Frenchman by education, who remade Italian opera into the great French version, the *tragédie-lyrique*. Lully, who collaborated with Molière in supplying the musical portions of the *comédie-ballets*, entered the serious musical dramatic field with a performance of *Alceste* at the marble court of Versailles in 1674. Lully truly understood Louis XIV's love of discipline and organiza-

Figure 8–5 Charles Lebrun, Salle des Gardes de la Reine, Versailles, c. 1671–81. Illustrates a restrained sense of grandeur in which ceiling paintings and wall decorations are locked into rigid geometric frames. Unlike Italian Baroque rooms, this chamber does not open to another world but is circumscribed, measured, and closed. Photo courtesy of the French Musées Nationaux.

tion. Using the traditional "twenty-four violins" of a chamber group, supplemented with wind instruments for hunting, battle, and climactic transformation scenes, he developed an opera orchestra that had tight discipline and control.

The form of Lully's lyric tragedies, with texts by Quinault, was also exact and very formal. They opened with an instrumental number, known as the French overture, that began with a dignified and sonorous march and closed in a much livelier tempo. Next came the prologue. In *Alceste* the prologue is set in a garden of the Tuileries where the Nymph of the Seine is discovered reciting poetry alluding to the current war in very flowery, high-flown, mythological phrases. Glory then enters, supported by a triumphal march, and a duet and solo follow. Entering eventually is a chorus of naiads and pastoral gods, whose songs and dances assure the audience that France will be victorious under its great hero-king. The overture is repeated, followed by five acts of a full classical tragedy based on Racine and the precepts established in the prologue.

In his lyric tragedies Lully insisted that music and dance always be the servants of drama and poetry, and he encouraged his singers to follow the grand, noble declamation found in the tragedies of Racine. Gradually, his work so pleased Louis XIV that Lully was made head of the Académie Royale de Musique, which exists today as the Paris National Opera Company. The fame of the group soon spread throughout Europe, especially because the orchestra was noted for its discipline, pure intonation, uniform bowing of strings, accurate tempo and measure, and elegant melodic ornamentation. Lully's work was considered superior to Italian Baroque opera in its precision and standardization of effects. In every way it reflects the dramas of Racine. There is the same observance of classical proprieties, the same dignified declamation, and the same polished correctness. What is lacking is a resonant human sensibility. Like the paintings of Poussin, Lully's work remains aloof, restrained, and aristocratic even though presenting beautiful language, restrained emotional appeal, rich splendor, majestic movement, and great visual elegance.

Life and Cultural Ideals

When Louis XIV declared that he *was* the state in France, he also admitted that his dominant passion was the love of glory. In his wars, architectural plans, court etiquette, pleasures, and sponsorship of theatrical entertainments, his overriding consideration was whether his and France's glory were being served. Once he was able to house all his court at Versailles, the king pursued both business and pleasure relentlessly. No matter how exhausted he or his courtiers were, there was daily hunting or tennis, and every evening was devoted to parties, dances, and plays.

Though Louis thrived on this regimen, the courtiers often found it tortuous. For example, a lady invited to Versailles was expected to arrive at six in the evening in full court dress and might not have been allowed to depart until eight the following morning. During those fourteen hours, she attended a comedy, a ballet, or a ball; she probably partook of two suppers and a roulette of cards, and, throughout it all, she had to observe the most rigid rules of etiquette. One such lady who broke these rules by sitting at the gaming table was never received at court again.

Even greater demands were placed on courtiers who were expected to attend the rising of the king in the morning and his retiring at night. It was considered a great honor to hand the king his nightshirt or his stockings, and this had to be done in a certain prescribed order and way. Though Louis never seemed to tire of this routine, many of the courtiers found it trying in the extreme. Mme. de Sévigné in a letter to her daughter has left a picture of some of the games that were played at these *levées*. The following describes one that took place in the bedroom of Louis XIV's sister, Mademoiselle:

> A circumstance took place yesterday at Mademoiselle's which gave me no small pleasure. Who should come in but Madame de Gêvres, in all her airs and graces! I fancy she expected I should have offered her my place; but to say the truth, I have owed her a little grudge for her conduct the other day, and now I have paid her with interest, for I did not stir. Mademoiselle was in bed; Madame de Gêvres was obliged to place herself at the lower end of the room, a provoking thing to be sure. The princess called for drink; somebody must present the napkin. I perceived Madame de Gêvres drawing the glove from her withered hand, upon which I gave Madame d'Arpajon, who was above me, a push, which she understood; and pulling off her glove, with the best grace in the world, advanced a step, got before the duchess, took the napkin, and presented it. The duchess was perfectly embarrassed; for she had reached the upper end of the room, and had pulled off her gloves, only to have the mortification of being a nearer witness of Mme. D'Arpajon's presenting the napkin before her. My dear child, I am very wicked; this pleased me infinitely: it was uncommonly well done. Would anyone have thought of depriving Madame d'Arpajon of a little piece of honour, which is naturally her due, as being one of the bedchamber? Madame de Puisieux was very much diverted at it. As for Mademoiselle, she did not dare look up, and my countenance was not the most settled. After this a thousand things were said to me about you; and Mademoiselle was pleased to order me to tell you, that she is very glad that you escaped drowning and are in good health.

Though the letters of Madame de Sévigné may not be known to contemporary actors, the plays of Molière certainly are. In them we find strong support for society as representative of a golden mean and stern warnings against excess, obsession, and extremism. Though it is sometimes difficult in *The Misanthrope* to know if Alceste or Philinte is Molière's spokesman, certainly it is Philinte who sounds like the typical rational man of the period in his view of society:

But, while we're of the world, we must observe
Some outward courtesies that custom calls for. . . .
There's many a time and place when utter frankness
Would be ridiculous, or even worse;
And sometimes, no offence to your high honour,
'T is well to hide the feelings in our hearts.
Would it be proper, decent, in good taste,
To tell a thousand people your opinion

About themselves? When you detest a man,
Must you declare it to him, to his face? . . .
Don't take the manners of the time so hard!
Be a bit merciful to human nature;
Let us not judge it with the utmost rigour,
But look upon its faults with some indulgence.
Our social life demands a pliant virtue;
Too strict uprightness may be blameworthy;
Sound judgment always will avoid extremes,
And will be sober even in its virtue.
The stiff unbending morals of our times
Clash with our modern age and common usage;
They ask of mortal men too much perfection;
We must yield to the times, and not too hardly;
And 'tis the very utmost height of folly
To take upon you to reform the world.
I see a hundred things each day, as you do,
That might be better, were they different;
And yet, whatever I see happening,
I don't fly in a passion as you do;
I quietly accept men as they are,
Make up my mind to tolerate their conduct,
And think my calmness is, for court or town,
As good philosophy as is your choler.

Ornament, Interiors, and Furniture

Although the ornament in the interior of Versailles is grandiose and rich, it is strongly disciplined and controlled in organization and placement (Figure 8–5). Despite all the use of gilded wood and plaster, richly painted walls and ceilings, grand tapestries, and heavy ornamental furnishings, the overall effect is one of monumental grandeur tightly reined in by the geometric rules restraining the overall design. Especially in the ceiling from the Salle des Gardes, one can see that the excessive movement and expanding action that pours over and out of the frames in the Barberini Palace in Rome has been firmly locked into place and slowed in its movement (Figures 8–4 and 8–5).

The ornamental designs most frequently associated with Versailles include concave ellipses framed in scroll patterns and surrounded by sculpted or molded plaster acanthus leaf patterns; circular disks framed in garlands and housing classical busts; monumental classical helmets surmounted by plumes, garlands, or mythological monsters; and enormous vases with dragons and mythological beasts symmetrically placed with acanthus leaves and garlands. In short, though the subject matter is strictly classical, its size, grandeur, and movement are truly Baroque.

The primary characteristic of French classic Baroque furniture was its weight. Every chair was like a throne and thus difficult to move. Unlike the games played with furniture of the eighteenth century, French Baroque chairs and stools were not arranged to enhance conversation or to give a personal touch to an interior grouping (Figure 8–12). In every way, furniture reflected the grandeur, weight, and control found in interior decoration and, as we shall see, in the manners and movement of the courtiers inhabiting such grand settings.

Costume and Accessories

The dress of this period may be completely misunderstood by students who understand romanticism in the theatre but not Baroque control. At first glance, the sensuality of the ribbons, bows, long hair, and excessive ornament may cause one to miss the precise arrangement and intellectual structuring of these decorative elements. Only when the clothing is viewed as an extension of the architecture and the interiors is the structured basis for the decorative excess discernible.

For example, look at the typical male figure during the early years of Louis XIV's reign (1660–1675), as exemplified in a portrait by Gerald Terborch of an aristocratic though restrained gentleman from Holland (Figure 8–6). In many ways, the structure of the clothing is more visible in this sober black costume than in the more ornate and frivolous garments worn by the courtiers at the court of the Sun King (Figure 8–9). Though the costume looks frivolous and less dignified than the later styles of the reign because of its short-line harmonies, it is a very carefully structured affair. Note the carefully planned layering of the costume from top to bottom and the diamond-shaped silhouette created by the whole. Like interior decoration, all richness and decoration are channeled into a controlled silhouette and structure. The same is true of the rounded "boat" neckline, triangular-shaped bodice, and contour-draped overskirt of the woman's gown in the costume plate by J. D. de St. Jean depicting Madame la Dauphine in 1670 (Figure 8–7). The lines expand up and down from the waist in a carefully controlled manner with brooches (more

Figure 8–6 Gerard Terborch, *Portrait of an Unknown Man,* c. 1665–70. Illustrates the emphasis on geometric structure and carefully related short lines of harmony in male dress between 1660 and 1675. Photo courtesy of the National Gallery, London.

Figure 8–7 J. D. de St. Jean, *Madame la Dauphine,* c. 1670. Illustrates the carefully controlled rich costume, punctuated with jewels or ribbon bows, of the third quarter of the seventeenth century. Photo courtesy of the Pierpont Morgan Library.

often ribbon bows) acting as points of carefully calculated punctuation within the lines of the gown. Also, the movement of the overskirt as it is lifted up and back over the underskirt falls in a train carefully calculated to give elegance, richness, and grandeur within a disciplined control.

After 1685, the costumes were much heavier and reminiscent of a great upholstered chair, as can be seen in *Louis XIV and His Family,* painted by Nicolas Largillière about 1711 (Figure 8–8). A heavy, fitted coat with rich braid and grand cuffs, surmounted by a monstrously large, full-bottomed wig, was

balanced on perfectly posed legs that were firmly and carefully placed in their high-heeled, square-toed shoes in the famous third ballet position. When decorated by a chest-high walking stick, dress sword, muff, ostrich-trimmed hat, and other smaller accessories, the male figure was grand, imposing, encumbered, and weighty. When a hat was worn over the great wig, each slight movement of the head was portentous; the neck, swathed in a great cravat and accented with a large bow, tilted itself imposingly above the body; the arms with their great cuffs gestured with a sense of importance; and the uphol-

Figure 8–8 Nicolas Largillière, *Louis XIV and His Family,* 1711. Illustrates the pretentious dignity and encumbered body stance that marked the end of Baroque fashion. Note that the king sits overlapping his chair with his feet in the third ballet position. Photo courtesy of the Trustees of the Wallace Collection, London.

stered torso with its long waistcoat under a full-skirted coat suggested the weight and substance of the Louis Quatorze *fauteuil.*

The clothes of women were equally imposing. The hair was built up to support the many-tiered *fontanges* that nodded from the top of the head like an imposing, partly closed fan. The neck was accented with a jeweled choker and framed in a square neckline on top of a triangle of bows that diminished in size down the corset to the pointed waist. The arms, cuffed at the elbows, gestured impos-

ingly through a froth of tiered lace, while the lower torso, covered by the expanding weight of the underskirt, ended in heavy layered trim that gave a firm base to the silhouette. The overskirt was looped back into a most impressive mass of material that spread out into a sweeping train, thus giving each lady the grandeur of an empress. Dressed in these costumes, a man and a woman made an imposing couple entering any room side by side and certainly expressed the ideal of grandeur that Louis XIV espoused above all else.

Manners and Movement

Obviously the test for the actor in wearing the clothes of this Louis XIV period is whether he moves in them with the assurance of a true courtier. Portraits and paintings of this period should be studied in great detail, brought to rehearsals, and discussed. An excellent visual source is the Gobelin tapestry, designed by Charles Lebrun, depicting the meeting of Louis XIV and Philip IV of Spain in 1660 (Figure 8–9). Concentrating on the overall mood of the clothing and the total effect created by the costume silhouette, one should practice, before a mirror, wearing and moving in such dress.

Male movement in this period was primarily influenced by the high-heeled shoes worn; the poses and many steps were like those in a ballet, an art highly respected by Louis XIV, who prided himself on his perfect legs and on his own ballet performances. Fencing was the other major activity that affected male movement. Movement based on certain ballet positions and fencing stances has grace, simplicity, and, if understood, a classic and structured beauty. It is a complete mistake for an actor to think that the heavy beribboned costumes betoken fussy and frivolous movement. In fact, the contrast between the simplicity of the movement and the frivolity of the costume trim gave this period its dignity and theatricality.

The tapestry showing Louis XIV greeting Philip IV (Figure 8–9) reveals three important stances for the courtier. The first, a simple and rather heroic posture not acceptable in

the presence of one's superior, was the second ballet position, with feet about a foot apart and slightly spread and hands gracefully on the hips. The second was the third enclosed ballet position; that is, feet perpendicular to one another with the weight on the rear foot and with the heel of the front foot against the hollow of the rear foot. Since the front foot bore no weight, the knee was slightly bent. Hands were placed between the folds of the coat or the waistcoat if it were partially unbuttoned, or one hand rested lightly on the sword and the other on the head of the high walking stick. The third was to have the enclosed foot open sideways, bearing no weight and with toes pointed out. The hat was placed under the arm that was on the same side as the foot that took the weight; the head turned toward the free foot; and the other arm rested easily but low on the hip.

One always walked with "toes handsomely turned out." Pointing the toes forward with each movement, with the heels raising the body up and forward, was very important in capturing the calculated beauty of movement that was so much admired. In fact, the feet remained in an almost ninety-degree relationship to one another as the courtier stepped forward, carefully pointing his ribboned, high-heeled shoes as he moved.

The appropriate movements for removing the broad-brimmed hat were as follows: The arm was brought to shoulder level and then the elbow was bent as the hat was grasped firmly, lifted from the head, and al-

Figure 8–9 Charles Lebrun, *History of the King: Interview of Louis XIV and Philip IV of Spain at the Isle of Pheasants,* from a Gobelin tapestry, 1660. Illustrates the contrast between the outdated styles of Spanish royalty and aristocracy and the more fashionable ones of French nobility, consisting of petticoat breeches, carefully layered effects, and masses of ribbons. Note also the precise ballet positions of the French gentlemen. The National Museum of Versailles. Photo courtesy of the French Musées Nationaux.

lowed to fall easily to the side with the head hole to the front. The head itself did not move, and the hands never covered the face. If the hat were large and thus not easily lifted away from the wig, the other hand was sometimes used to help remove it or put it on again. The hat could be worn or carried under the arm at all times except in the presence of the king.

In sitting, one foot was usually placed well ahead of the other with the toes well turned out, and a little tap was given to the sword hilt on its hanger under the coat in order to flip the skirts of the coat out of the way. Seldom did the man push fully back in the chair; he sat squarely in it or a bit to one side and kept an alert yet relaxed pose with one arm usually overlapping the chair's arm as if to dominate the chair and the scene that he surveyed. Unlike the sixteenth-century man who perched uneasily on the chair and seemed locked in by it, the seventeenth-century man dominated the chair as if it were a throne (Figure 8–8).

The walking sticks of the period were frequently a good forty inches high, topped with ribbons and usually equipped with a loop through which one passed the hand. Many elegant poses were possible, but almost always the stick was held at arm's length away from the body to widen the pose and give controlled dignity to the ballet stance. The walking stick was used to achieve an unaffected grace and interesting variations in movement and pose rather than an excessive dignity as in this portrait.

Another major male accessory was the handkerchief, which was large, beautifully trimmed in lace, and held between the index and second fingers with the four corners falling down the back of the hand. Other accessories that enhanced the gentleman's sense of importance were round, egg-shaped watches hung from the neck by a ribbon or put in the waistcoat pocket; large square or round muffs, with ribbon bows and frills of lace, hung from the neck or waist; and dress swords hung by a shoulder hanger under the coat.

Probably the most important ritual movement for the modern actor to master from this period is the courtly bow. In many ways, mastering the "best" bow is more a matter of personality and an instinctive feeling for the movement of the costume than it is a matter of following precise rules. Though there were numbers of variations, three very stageworthy bows can be abstracted for modern performance. The first is to step back with knees bent and then bow with the hand swept over the heart. Then straighten the body and drop the hand, bringing the front foot back to the third position. The second is to place the feet in the third position, heel to the hollow of the rear foot; draw the body up again; and put the hand to the heart as if to say "My heart is yours." Then step back and bow as suggested in the first bow, bringing the hand down in front of the body with palm uppermost as if to say "I lay it at your feet." Finally, straighten up by drawing back the front foot to the third position, with the hand sweeping up at the side so as to conclude the process with a flourish. The third involves bowing as described with a hat carried under the left arm. While completing the bow, take the hat in the right hand and sweep it back and down low at arm's length on the right side of the body. Pause for a second before straightening up and returning the hat to under the left arm.

In addition, the *bow en passant* was used during receptions and balls to acknowledge people when one did not wish to pause for a conversation. It consisted of bowing from the waist while dragging one foot from behind to in front of the body without stopping the onward movement of the walk. The same bow was used by ladies, although they also waved their fans gently.

Female movement was also like that of a trained ballet dancer, graceful and vital with the center of motion at the waist, which was both flexible and yet firmly controlled at all times. The gown often had to be lifted and set down again; this was accomplished by making a graceful sweeping curve, not by merely picking up and dropping the skirt. A grand manner had to be adopted in walking in order to carry the heavy looped-up skirts and the high headdresses of the later French Baroque style. A lady learned to walk in high-heeled shoes with a firm but graceful step rather than an unsteady mincing one. In dancing, the skirt was firmly picked up on one side or even on both sides, and the insides of the wrists were always turned out when the lady was in repose so as to display the line of the hands and arms to the best advantage. In addition, when sitting on the grand furniture of the period, the lady had to gracefully but firmly ensure that her skirt was smoothly placed under her while she sat straight and tall, conveying a combination of queenly authority and feminine charm.

Probably the most vital weapon for the lady of this age was the fan, which was used in the "pitched battles" and "absolute surrenders" of love and conversation. The lady always handled it with technical proficiency, never fluttering it in a rapid or random way. Because the first folding fans were not developed in France until about 1670, the rigid fans of the earlier period lacked many subtleties of movement possible with the later collapsible fans. The fan was usually held away from the body with very flexible movements of the arms, wrists, and shoulder socket. The modern actress should begin with exaggerated movements and then, after mastering them, attempt more subtle and delicate gestures.

In their book *Manners and Movements in Costume Plays*, Chisman and Ravenhart suggest some exercises that might be useful. Hold the fan in front of the body, not too close to the face, with the painted side facing the audience; then bring the arm straight down in front of you and to the side. With the fan toward the ground, turn the wrist sharply so that the fan is turned up to its original position; then swing it in toward you to the starting position. Then practice running all these movements together into a rhythmic swing. Once you have accomplished this with deftness and elegance, try dropping the fan open and then twisting it into position with a quick turn of the wrist.

The earlier noncollapsible fan was wafted back and forth with movements of the wrist and forearm; the same was done with the collapsible fan. There was no fluttering of the fan as in the nineteenth century, and all movement was controlled and subtle—used to emphasize a point or accent an idea rather than to create a picturesque effect.

The curtsy was the basic movement of female reverence from the sixteenth century onward, and variations developed, based on the costume worn or the amount of reverence shown. Basically, the lady slid back on the instep of the right foot with the instep pressing the ground, behind and slightly to the left of the left leg; the instep of the sliding foot took the weight, and the lady gradually sank down sitting on the bent right leg, arms falling to the side, and head lowered. The important point was the crossing under of the sliding right leg, this movement being supported by crossed thighs. The lady then rose with her weight on the left foot since this foot did not move during the entire sequence of the curtsy.

For entering a room, the curtsy *en avant* was in order. Here the lady paused on the foot that made the last step, slid the disengaged foot into the fourth position, or to the front, and bent the knees with weight equally distributed and without bending the body or shaking. The lady rose with the weight on the front foot. For leaving a room, the curtsy *en arrière* was appropriate. Stepping aside, the lady curtsied in the first or third position with the weight evenly distributed and then rose with the weight on the rear foot. A compliment in conversation might also be acknowledged in this way. In walking, the curtsy *en passant* was appropriate. To accomplish this, the lady positioned herself parallel to the person being greeted, made a step on the left foot and half turned to the person, and then bent her knees, bringing forward the right foot and coming up with the weight on the right foot. This was repeated to many different individuals in a group or receiving line. The lady might have also waved her fan gently while curtsying. In all of this, the gentleman led the lady, walking slightly ahead and turning slightly toward her.

The Theatre

The physical structure of the theatre during these years was becoming a picture-frame stage primarily built to house the grandeurs of the new theatrical medium of opera. The auditoriums were usually rectangular or U-shaped, lined with rows of boxes. A gallery was sometimes placed above the top row of boxes for servants and apprentices. Sight lines from the side boxes were poor, and the flat floor usually held only standees, though sometimes there were benches at the back half of the auditorium. The stage, framed in an ornate proscenium arch, was frequently raked upward and was very deep. For productions of opera, there was considerable space below the stage for machinery and trap doors and above for hanging sky borders. The sides allowed space for the side wings to move out of sight behind the proscenium. Lighting was generally provided by chandeliers hung in the auditorium and over the stage and sometimes from footlights set behind reflectors along the stage edge or from lights set against reflectors behind each set of wings. The wings usually moved on masts attached to little chariots beneath the slits in the stage floor, and there were as many sets of wings as there were locations in the production. The back was usually formed of two large flats or shutters that met in the center. Changes were made in full view of the audience by removing shutters, wings, and borders from the stage to reveal the next setting (Figure 8–10).

The most admired plays of the period were the classical tragedies of Corneille and Racine, operas, and the comedies of Molière. The costumes for tragedy and opera differed considerably from those for comedy. Those for operas and classical tragedies were rich, ornamental, formalized garments—a combination of contemporary clothing and items modified from classical antiquity. A plumed helmet or headdress, breastplate-shaped tunic, a flaring skirt or *tonnelet* to above the knee, a mantle, and soft, short boots to the calf completed the standard male silhouette, as they had since the late sixteenth century. Variations suggesting near-Eastern characters were made with robes, turbans, and other fanciful headdresses (Figure 8–10). The woman's costume was a court gown with a corsetlike front, trimmed with tabs at the waist and sometimes at the neckline and edge of the shoulder. Sleeves, often finished with tassels, usually flared at the elbow, and the hair or headdress was adorned with plumes. From this basic structure, ingenious designers, like Jean Berain, were able to develop variations

Figure 8–10 Scene from *Thésée* by Lully. Designed by Gaspare Vigarani after an engraving by François Chauveau. Illustrates the staging methods and costumes designed for the lyric classical tragedies of Jean Baptiste Lully. From a contemporary engraving in the possession of the author.

suggesting Turks, Indians, and mythological gods.

In the comedies of Molière, however, the costume style was basically contemporary dress accented by an exaggerated silhouette, trim, and other accessories for comic comment. It is important to realize that, despite portraits of the period indicating excessive ornamental decoration, the basic structure of the costume was very carefully organized. As in the Baroque architecture of the age of Louis XIV, the basic design was simple, geometric, and direct; rich ornamentation was then poured into that strong basic structure.

The Plays

The more excessive early Baroque style, which the French gradually abandoned in favor of the French classicism of Louis XIV, is evident in an early tragedy like Corneille's *Le Cid*. The later work of Corneille, however, adheres to the classical unities; and by the time that his supremacy as a tragic writer was challenged by Racine, the French tragic style was fully developed.

Racine adhered to the concept of a single action developed in a single place during a single day. He interpreted action to mean its psychological results, not the portrayal of physical events on the stage. Thus in his plays, the external action is very simple, while the psychological action and character relationships are very complex. For example, in refashioning Euripides' *Hippolytus* as *Phèdre* for seventeenth-century court audiences, Racine eliminated the chorus, reduced the influence of the gods, and substituted for the natural, religious world view of the Greeks a limited, artificial, ceremonial world based on the strategies and rules found at the court of Louis XIV. Though there is a diminished sense of man's relation to nature, there is an increased emphasis on rational perfection and polished organization.

Racine was a master of psychological characterization, particularly of the female personality. In *Phèdre*, every shift in the emotional climate must be underlined by the acting without loss of subtle nuances and details. All the characters attempt to act rationally but are swayed by the forces of emotion. In addition, all are patterned after the ideal gentleman or lady of the period. Of noble birth, they act with the dignity and decorum of courtiers and abide by the rules of personal honor. The stateliness and magnitude that we feel in the characters undoubtedly were mirrored in the acting, and the movement and action must have been measured, deliberate, and carefully limited. Poses and postures for supporting the classic Baroque ideals of beauty, dignity, and grandeur were specifically formulated in the same way that Lebrun's treatises on art formulated exact rules for facial and bodily beauty.

The themes are like those in the historical and biblical paintings of Poussin (Figure 8–1); namely, that duty, honor, and a severe sense of personal integrity must triumph over passion and that tragedy results when passion is allowed to usurp the power of reason, decorum, and good breeding in society. The language supporting these themes is ordered in a most logical musical manner by the controlling precision of the French *alexandrine*, which can be built line by line to towering climaxes that then ebb away to devastating quietness like a storm at sea. When brilliantly performed, such great speeches or "tirades" can bring an audience to its feet in tumultuous applause. All actors who perform in Racinian tragedies agree that to do justice to the language takes tremendous vocal technique and emotional control.

The rhythm or musical progression of *Phèdre* derives directly from the rise and fall of this carefully ordered verse form. Since there are no abrupt breaks in the action, the progression throughout the play is as clear and inexorable as the rhythm of the sea. It is this ebb and flow that establishes the very essence of the neoclassic tragic rhythm.

As far as physical presentation is concerned, nothing is indicated except that the play takes place in the Palace of Troezen. In seventeenth-century presentations, furnishings would have been minimal or non-existent; the setting simple, grand, and monumental; the costumes reflecting the station and importance of each character; and the lighting remaining constant throughout the production (Figure 8–11).

In many ways the comedies of Molière, as distinct from his farces, demand much the same sense of symmetry, simplicity, precision, and concentration of focus that one finds in Racine. Now, however, the setting is contemporary bourgeois society, and there is no need for Poussin's classic, historical background. The paintings of Vermeer, who presented the late seventeenth-century middle-class interior in a classical manner, may be useful in providing furniture and interior details but are even more helpful as a guide to the mood of precision, cool concentration, and careful organization found in Molière (Figure 8–12).

In a play like *Tartuffe*, for example, Molière uses borrowings from the Italian comedy combined with the classical story line and writing method of Terence. He adheres to the classical unities, and the play progresses without subplot or numerous minor characters. There is an exaggerated bias and eccentricity in both protagonist and antagonist that is countered by the man of reason, Cléante, who comments on the action and represents the playwright's belief in common sense. Tartuffe is the evil catalyst in the action whose character is developed by others until he enters in the third act and proceeds to demonstrate himself as a repressed sensualist in his two love scenes. Orgon, the protagonist, is a man of foolish good nature whose gullibility allows Tartuffe's plans to mature and flourish. He is the prosperous businessman who

Figure 8–12 Jan Vermeer, *A Lady and Gentleman at the Virginals,* c. 1664. Illustrates the cool, carefully composed, classical, bourgeois interiors painted by this Dutch artist. Royal Collection, London. Photo courtesy of the Lord Chamberlain, St. James's Palace, London. Copyright reserved.

Figure 8–11 Scene from *Phèdre* by Racine, produced by the University of Kansas City, 1958. Directed by Patricia McIlrath, costumes designed by the author. Illustrates the use of modern costume designs based on the stage dress of the late seventeenth century. Photo by the author.

feels guilty about his money and so gives impulsively and overgenerously to the man he feels is worthier than he. Even when Tartuffe is exposed, Orgon cannot distinguish between hypocrisy and piety and wants to turn his back on all religion. It is Cléante who stands between the antagonist and protagonist with his balanced view.

All the humor derives from the psychological relationship of characters to situation, and all deviations from the ideal of common sense established by Cléante and Dorine are sharply ridiculed. The major theme is the importance of the balanced life; the secondary theme is the folly of a forced marriage.

Though Molière usually wrote in the alexandrine of twelve feet with a rhyme at the end, the results are essentially realistic prose. His verse is clever, witty, and fully able to express idiosyncrasies of character but seldom attempts idealized poetry. To play the plays in prose translation is to miss the witty comment made on the traditional alexandrine form; only the polished symmetry and precision of English rhyming couplets can approximate this verse style. The rhythmic flow of the action is closely tied to the polished delivery of the verse, which evidences a sprightly, direct, onward movement from beginning to end without sharp contrasts, abrupt breaks, or strong shifts of mood. It is this rhythm that gives Molière's plays their urbane, classical clarity of mood.

The visual requirements are limited to a room in Orgon's house with a table, several chairs, a closet, a door, and possibly a staircase for Tartuffe's first entrance; the blocking should make use of the dynamic, geometric symmetries so much admired in all Baroque art. The play can be produced in almost any period from the seventeenth century to the present as long as costumes, setting, and the social scene are subordinated to the personality and social standing of each character (Figure 8–13). The lighting need not be varied at all, since in Molière's day, chandeliers hung over the acting area, giving an appropriate general illumination to the play.

Acting and Directing the Plays

It should be obvious from the discussions of Racine and Corneille and of neoclassic tragic costume that the acting style for these playwrights must convey stateliness and grandeur. The ordered cadence and rhythm of the lines and the inexorable step-by-step unraveling of the single, simple plots dictate a certain static yet strangely magnificent style of movement.

It is safer for the director to choose a modification of neoclassic theatrical dress than the Greek or Roman dress suggested by the stories of the plays. A perceptive actor can then visualize the grand and sweeping movement of the arm that is required to make appropriate use of the open sleeves that end in a tassel or of the cloak also weighted at the corners and finished with tassels. Such tassels are meant to make beautiful and sweeping arabesques in space in support of the actor's emotion and mood. If they are shaken, whipped about, and moved in an abrupt and arbitrary fashion, they destroy the stately grandeur of the actor. All accents in such Baroque classic costumes should be carefully chosen to stop the eye at points of focus in the dress like punctuation in a sentence. They also should underline and support gesture and movement. The tilt and nod of the head should control the plumes, pointed headdress, or tasseled turbans that act as the climax at the top of these exotic but controlled costumes. Each step that is taken must move all parts of the costume—robe, gown, mantle, sleeves, or headdress—in a perfect harmony of stateliness and grandeur.

With Molière this stateliness and grandeur is not important, since the subject matter is bourgeois and the mood is comic. But deft, controlled, almost acrobatic precision of movement *is* necessary. One cannot forget Molière's long apprenticeship with the Commedia dell'Arte style, even though he more often than not put that experience at the service of a classical structural development. In *The Impromptu at Versailles*, Molière certainly denounces excess and bombast in favor of a clear, clean, deft presentation of character and action. Much of his own ability as a comic actor was based on his sudden shifts in voice and face in order to project in a sharp clear way varied emotional responses to the action. Just as the costumes and sets for Molière should be buoyantly comic but direct and simple, so the gestures and movement should be exaggerated for comic effect, yet remain simple and uncluttered.

The director of Molière's plays can make much of the triangular symmetry of those scenes in which there is a rapid tennis game of short phrases back and forth between two characters finally interrupted by a third character. These are Molière's favorite set pieces of comic dialogue and should be blocked as such, in order to call attention to their triangular symmetry and game-plan construction.

Designing the Plays

In the design of a stage setting for a Racinian tragedy such as *Phèdre,* the essential ingredient is a simple, balanced grandeur. It is useful to have a set of stairs at the back for grand entrances, while the specifics of the columns, lintels, arches, and architectural ornamentation should probably be kept relatively abstract in order to create the "palace of the will" or of the mind that is the essence of a Racine setting. A difficult decision is whether to do the play in Greek or in French Baroque stage costume. Unless seventeenth-century stage costume is sharply modified for a modern audience, it may seen humorous or comic; if Greek dress is not given the formality, the grandeur, and the sophistication of the court of Louis XIV, it will be ineffective. In either choice the classical attitudes and poses to be found in the classical paintings by Poussin will be helpful; his cool, strong primary colors—if accented in gold and silver—will be especially useful to the costume designer. Once a designer has absorbed the classical visual ideas of Poussin, he should feel much more comfortable in modifying and simplifying seventeenth-century classical stage costume for the needs of this particular play. Full-bottomed wigs can be replaced by long, full natural hair, over-ornamentation can be avoided, and complexity in color and texture can be discarded. The structure of the costume can be proportioned and accented to give a formal, rich, artificial, classical look to the play (Figure 8–11).

On the other hand, if the designer and director choose a more contemporary mode of production, an abstract "no period" approach may be taken; or modified formal wear or evening dress may be used to match the formality and classical restraint of the script. A modern design for the palace could also have the same intellectual coolness and simplicity found in the play.

What of the comparable classical visual demands in the comedies of Molière? The design of a modern production of *Tartuffe* should support the simplicity and clarity of the writing and not be a display of rich period detail. In most contemporary productions the play is either placed in a semi-abstract setting suggesting the architecture of the period or in a realistic bourgeois interior. If the director wishes to stress the symmetry and balance of the play's structure and the universality of the characters, then an abstract setting is appropriate; if he or she wants to stress Orgon's bourgeois temperament and taste, then the setting is more appropriate if realistic. In either case the production should not be loaded with decorative accessories; only those items clearly revealing character and personality should be used. In costume, if a somewhat realistic mood is wanted, then the costumes should be varied in line, texture, and color; if an abstract architectural background is used, the color and texture of the costumes should be limited, with the shape and structure of the costume having the focus (Figure 8–13).

As has been stated, one of the best sources for designing Molière's comedies is the work

Figure 8–13 Scene from *Tartuffe* by Molière, produced by the Stanford Repertory Theatre, 1965. Directed by Robert Loper, costumes designed by the author. The strong unity, simplicity, and structure shown in the costumes and settings here relate closely to the structure of this classical comedy. Photo by the author.

of Vermeer, whose classical spirit is in tune with Molière's sense of structure (Figure 8–12). His subtle and simple use of color, line, and texture can give the designer great insight into how to translate Molière's verbal methodology into visual designs. For example, a designer can make use of Vermeer's cool and limited color palette by restricting the color palette in his costume; a basic hue accented by another color or a neutral is much more effective than many hues, values, and intensities. The same is true of texture: a few similar textures for most costumes, accented with a contrasting texture, will give clarity and simplicity to the production and allow the focus to be on the comic silhouette of each character. Useful textures might be silk taffetas, satins and failles with accents of velvet ribbons and bows. With this simplicity in texture and color, line is then all important. The width of a cuff, the flair of a bow, the fall of pleated lace, the shape of a wig—these are the important things when the method is so spare and intellectually planned. If the individual, satiric character of the costumes and the simple balanced setting match the polished acting required by the script, then a performance of the play will be as pleasing visually in its directness and simplicity as it is verbally.

Look, for example, at a costume for Elmire in a 1984 Stanford University production
of *Tartuffe* (Figure 8–14). It has simple, strong
lines based on the styles of the 1660s with
outlines in black velvet framing the enlarged
and simplified decorations on skirt and bodice
in the same way that the richness is contained
in strong geometric frames in the Salle des
Gardes at Versailles (Figure 8–5).

Figure 8–14 Costume worn by Elmire in the 1984
Stanford University production of Molière's *Tartuffe.*
Note the simple, strong silhouette with outlines in
black velvet which frames enlarged, simplified dec-
orations—a design concept based on the Salle des
Gardes at Versailles (Figure 8-5). Photo by the author.

PROJECTS AND PROBLEMS

1. Why did France look to the classical Baroque style for inspiration in the first half of the
seventeenth century?

2. What goals for the development of France
did Cardinal Richelieu and Louis XIV share?

3. Summarize the five rules governing classical French art during the Baroque period.

4. Summarize the characteristics in Poussin's
Holy Family on the Steps and explain why they are
labeled classic (Figure 8–1). Think of yourself as
an actor or actress in such a staged scene and describe the kind of performance that would be required.

5. What qualities in a Racine script are similar to those found in *Holy Family on the Steps* (Figure 8–1)?

6. Why does the Church of St. Agnese (Figure 8–2) evidence an operatic or flamboyant Baroque style and the Church of the Invalides (Figure
8–3) a classic Baroque style? After looking at the
Church of St. Agnese, diagram its lines of structural force. Then do the same for the Church of
the Invalides and describe the differences.

7. Think of the Church of the Invalides (Figure 8–3) as a theatrical background for a stage ac-

tion. What kind of action would it be? How would
it be blocked? What would be its rhythm? What
kind of costumes and costume lines would be used
for the participants?

8. Imagine yourself at a ball in the Barberini
Palace (Figure 8–4). How would you feel about the
room, the ceiling, and the occasion? What effect
would the ceiling have on those gathered in the
room? Why can the ceiling painting be labeled representative of the flamboyant or operatic trend in
Baroque art?

9. What is the difference in feeling between
the Salle des Gardes from Versailles (Figure 8–5)
and the Barberini Palace (Figure 8–4)? How would
a scene staged against this setting differ from the
one in the Roman ballroom? Describe the differences in blocking, costume, color, and movement.
Despite the differences, why are they both Baroque
works?

10. Why was the Italian love of opera not immediately accepted in France? Describe what Lully
did to make opera suitable for late seventeenth-
century French taste.

11. Why were the tragedies of Racine so closely
connected with the operas of Lully and Quinault?

Why did the musical style developed by Lully spread throughout the rest of Europe by the end of the century?

12. What did Louis XIV gain socially, culturally, and politically by having all the nobility of his realm spend a good part of the year at Versailles? Describe the king's *levée* when he rose in the morning and his *couchée* when he went to bed at night?

13. From Madame de Sévigné's letter to her daughter, what happened to interpersonal relationships at the court of Versailles?

14. From the selection taken from *The Misanthrope* by Molière, what was Molière's view of society and how it should operate?

15. Why can the ornamental designs popular in France in the late seventeenth century be considered "classical" when compared with the simple, direct effects of Greek Golden Age art? How could such complex ornamentation be organized to create a "classical" effect?

16. Look closely at Terborch's *Portrait of an Unknown Man* (Figure 8–6). Describe the structure of the costume, and your feelings wearing it. Describe how it could be transformed into a court costume for the retinue of Louis XIV. Describe the movement required by this transformed costume.

17. What are the basic characteristics of the costume in J. D. de St. Jean's engraving of Madame la Dauphine (Figure 8–7)? Imagine yourself as an actress in such a costume. What happens to your movement? To your bearing? To your sense of yourself? How does this dress relate to the male costume of the period (Figures 8–6 and 8–9)?

18. What changes occurred in court costumes after 1685 (Figure 8–8)? What do these changes communicate about the changes in society? In Louis XIV? How would you feel as an actress or actor wearing these later costumes?

19. Look carefully at the feet and body poses in the tapestry showing the meeting of Louis XIV and Philip IV (Figure 8–9). Think of yourself as playing one of the persons in the tapestry scene and describe your sense of yourself, your movement, and the effect of your costume on your body.

20. Compare the Spanish costumes in this tapestry scene with the French ones (Figure 8–9). Why are the Spanish costumes outdated? What do all the ribbons on the male costumes of the French do for their movement? Why do the French look frivolous and carefully structured at the same time?

21. Reread the section in this chapter on bows and practice the bows in front of a mirror. What was the bow *en passant?* The curtsy *en arrière?* The curtsy *en passant?*

22. Work with the costume properties of this period (walking stick, muff, fan, and hat) before a mirror until you can easily manage them. Borrow costumes of the period and practice moving, sitting, standing, and gesturing in them.

23. Describe the physical construct for the theatre in France in the late seventeenth century (Figure 8–10). How was the scenery arranged? How did it change from one scene to the next? What kind of lighting was used?

24. Describe the stage costumes of the time. What were movement and gesture like in these costumes (Figure 8–10)?

25. Read a scene from Racine's *Phèdre* aloud and then describe what demands are made on you. What kind of costume would you wear for this play and how would you move and gesture in it? Summarize your reaction to this play.

26. What characteristics of movement and costume were emphasized in the University of Kansas City production of *Phèdre* (Figure 8–11)?

27. How do Vermeer's paintings (Figure 8–12) relate to Molière plays? What elements in Vermeer's work are totally opposed to the spirit of Molière's plays?

28. What design and production qualities in the Stanford production of *Tartuffe* (Figure 8–13) reinforce the structural methods in the play? After reading *Tartuffe* or doing a scene from the play, what would you say are the ways in which Molière tells the story?

29. What are the similarities in acting in a Molière and a Racine play? The differences? What are the differences between acting in a modern play about the Louis XIV period and in a classical tragedy written in the seventeenth century?

BIBLIOGRAPHY

Baur-Heinhold, M. *Baroque Theatre*, New York: McGraw-Hill, 1967. The finest pictorial compendium published to date on the theatre of the seventeenth and eighteenth centuries.

Bjurstrom, Per. *Giacomo Torelli and Baroque Stage Design*. Stockholm: Almquist and Wiksell, 1961. An excellent study of the scenic innovations created by this first famous master of the Venetian operatic Baroque scenic style.

Blitzer, Charles. *Age of Kings*. The Great Ages of Man Series. New York: Time-Life books, 1967. Intended for the average reader, this beautifully illustrated book, with extensive color photography, is a concise and useful text on the major artistic, intellectual, and cultural developments in Europe during the seventeenth century.

Blunt, Sir Anthony. *Art and Architecture in France, 1500–1700*. The Pelican History of Art Series. Baltimore: Penguin Books, 1957. An excellent and comprehensive survey on the development of French architecture from late medieval and mannerist Renaissance forms to the close of the classical Baroque era.

———. *The Paintings of Nicolas Poussin*. London: Phaidon, 1968. An excellent study of Poussin and his art by a great authority on Baroque seventeenth-century art in France.

Chisman, Isabel, and Ravenhart, Hester. *Manners and Movements in Costume Plays*. London: H. F. W. Deane & Sons, n.d. A useful if somewhat eclectic and dated booklet devoted to period manners and movement.

Friedlander, Walter. *Nicolas Poussin: A New Approach*. New York: Abrams, 1966. Another excellent study by an esteemed American academician on the painting of Poussin and its influence on French art in the late seventeenth century.

Hubert, Judd D. *Molière and the Comedy of Intellect*. Berkeley: University of California Press, 1962. A very useful study on the comedy technique of Molière.

Kitson, Michael. *The Age of the Baroque*. Landmarks of the World's Art Series. New York: McGraw-Hill, 1966. This beautifully illustrated book, with many color plates, deals with the art of Europe from the beginning of the seventeenth century until the middle of the eighteenth century.

Lancaster, H. C. *History of French Dramatic Literature in the Seventeenth Century*. 5 vols. Baltimore: Johns Hopkins Press, 1929–1942. An exhaustive study of dramatic literature during the rise and climax of the Golden Age of French dramatic writing.

Lawrenson, T. E. *The French Stage in the Seventeenth Century: A Study in the Advent of the Italian Order*. Manchester: University of Manchester Press, 1957. A very interesting study of the change in French plays from a late medieval and "romantic" form to a more sophisticated classical form imported from Italy.

Lockert, Lacy. *Studies in French Classical Tragedy*. Nashville: Vanderbilt University Press, 1958. An excellent study of the nature and content of French classical tragedy during the age of Racine, Corneille and their followers.

Lough, John. *Paris Theatre Audiences in the Seventeenth and Eighteenth Centuries*. London: Oxford University Press, 1957. A very interesting look at the changes in the makeup and attitude of Parisian theatre audiences over the two centuries that marked the rise of France as the cultural center of Europe.

Tapié, Victor. *The Age of Grandeur*. Translated by A. Ross Williamson. New York: Praeger, 1957. A fascinating account of the rise of Baroque art and architecture in Italy and its spread to France during the seventeenth century; also contains information on art and architecture in England, central Europe, and the European colonies.

Tilley, A. A. *Molière*. Cambridge: Cambridge University Press, 1936. Another excellent study of the dramatic method of Molière, even though it has been superseded in some of its details by more recent criticism.

Turnell, Martin. *The Classical Moment: Studies in Corneille, Molière, and Racine*. New York: New Directions, 1948. An excellent study of the classical outlook in the work of these three playwrights.

Weinstein, Leo, ed. *The Age of Reason*. The Cultures of Mankind Series. New York: Braziller, 1965. Writings from original sources on the Baroque view of life and culture.

Wiley, W. L. *The Early Public Theatre in France*. Cambridge, Mass.: Harvard University Press, 1955. An excellent study of the development of public theatre in France from the opening of the Hotel de Bourgogne in 1548 until the end of the seventeenth century.

Wright, C. H. C. *French Classicism.* Cambridge, Mass.: Harvard University Press, 1920. One of the outstanding studies of the nature of French classicism.

Restoration Baroque Style

At first, one might think that the Restoration style that developed in England after 1660—with the return of Charles II—would have been similar to the French classic Baroque style. Charles and his fellow aristocrats had spent the majority of their exile at the French court, and on their return to England they prided themselves on their newly acquired French manners and tastes. Yet for all its French borrowings in clothing, theatre, architecture, interior decoration, painting, and furniture, Restoration style had an unmistakable English tone. It never aimed at the single-minded precision, order, and structural unity characteristic of French art and theatre during the late seventeenth century. It also lacked the excessive grandeur and complex ceremonial style that prevailed at the court of the Sun King. Despite the French influences, the English approach was more pragmatic, eclectic, comfortable, and human.

To investigate British Restoration eclecticism, let us look at Christopher Wren's design for the east façade of Hampton Court and compare it with the east façade of the Louvre (Figures 9–1 and 9–2). The east façade of the Louvre is coldly formal and rigidly symmetrical, while that of Hampton Court is sober but pleasingly comfortable, lightly classical but also warm and human because of Wren's decision to keep the red brick from the original construction of the palace in the early sixteenth century. Interruptions take place naturally in the ornamentation emphasizing the doors, and the white stone trim that accents the brick work looks decorative rather than structural. In every way, Hampton Court is less impressive and more comfortable than the garden front of Versailles or the east façade of the Louvre.

Now look at an elegant interior, the famous Double Cube Room at Wilton House, designed by John Webb under the influence of Inigo Jones and furnished during the early years of the Restoration (Figure 9–3). In comparison with the Salle des Gardes in Versailles (Figure 8–5), this Restoration interior is just

Figure 9–1 Christopher Wren, east front of Hampton Court Palace, 1689–1701. A pleasingly comfortable English Baroque design without the tightly structured formality of similar French structures. Photo by the author.

Figure 9–2 Claude Perrault, Louis Le Vau, and Charles Lebrun, east façade of the Louvre, Paris, 1667–70. Illustrates the coldly formal, rigidly symmetrical, and tightly structured organization of classical Baroque architecture in late seventeenth-century France. Photo courtesy of Giraudon, Paris.

as aristocratic and grand, but without the cold formality and structural unity of the French interior. The room in Wilton House owes something to the Italians, something to the French, and something to the British past; and it is charmingly ornamented by lovely portraits by the Flemish artist Van Dyck. It is a rich and comfortable pastiche of decorative Baroque elements.

Music

Though Restoration England did not develop the solid musical tradition found in France and Italy during the Baroque era, it did produce a composer who might have become one of the great operatic composers of all time if he had had a truly worthy collaborator on operatic libretti. Henry Purcell was a diligent, unassuming professional composer, technically capable of fulfilling any commission that came his way; unfortunately, however, most of his early work was incidental music for a series of undistinguished plays. Finally, in 1689, he was invited by a dancing master for a London theatre to write a short opera to be performed at a boarding school for young girls at Chelsea; the result was the operatic masterpiece *Dido and Aeneas*.

As might be expected of a countryman and contemporary of Christopher Wren's, Purcell was fully conversant with the latest

Figure 9–3 John Webb (under the influence of Inigo Jones); the Double Cube Room, Wilton House, near Salisbury, England, c. 1650. Illustrates the more eclectic and less formal Baroque style that was admired in England during the Restoration. Photo courtesy of the Earl of Pembroke; Wilton House; near Salisbury, England.

the recitatives and airs employ what Monteverdi and his successors in Venice called the "representative style" in which word painting is done with music and the descriptive imagery of the text is reflected in the melodic line. The choruses and dances are based on the English court masque tradition developed by Ben Jonson and Inigo Jones. In Act III, when Aeneas is preparing to sail from Carthage, there is a musical description of a typical English seaport in which the sailors' dances mingle with the earthy comments of the common people. Here the crudities of hornpipe rhythms are set against the formal *courantes* danced by the courtiers. The result is a perfect blend of native and foreign sources that distinguishes the best in English Baroque art, literature, and music. Like Dryden, Purcell was trying, despite a poor libretto by Nahum Tate, to educate his countrymen in the latest continental developments without neglecting their English roots and English common touch. Like Wren in his design for St. Paul's, Purcell merged the richness and grandeur of the Baroque style with past English art forms and compromised high-flown Baroque ideals in order to keep in touch with his English audience.

Though Purcell did collaborate in 1691 with the famous John Dryden, playwright and poet laureate of England, on the opera *King Arthur*, his effort was not a great success. It was many years before truly recitative opera was accepted in England since English audiences simply were not interested in perpetual singing. Nevertheless, Purcell's *Dido and Aeneas* is an outstanding example of English Restoration Baroque style.

continental innovations in opera. His work, like Wren's, is a perfect blend of native and foreign elements. The opera begins with a dignified overture in the style of Lully, and

Life and Cultural Ideals

After the restoration of Charles II to the throne, London became the center of the new monarchy and of all those forces that were transforming England from a medieval state into a modern world power. There is no better firsthand source on life in London between 1660 and 1669 than the *Diary of Samuel Pepys*, written by the well-educated son of a tailor.

After his marriage in 1665 to a fifteen-year-old Huguenot refugee girl, Pepys identified with the cause of the exiled Charles II; and in the new society of the Restoration, he had a brilliant career as secretary to the admiralty. In his diary he recorded memorable events like the coronation of Charles II, the Great London fire, and the Great Plague as well as personal descriptions of living, working, and being entertained in Restoration London. He took particular delight in the street life, the gossip-filled taverns, and the ribald court manners of a city that he deeply loved.

The following entries attest to the variety in his London life:

Round the Abbey to Westminster Hall, all the way within rails, and 10,000 people with the ground covered with blue cloth. And the King came in with his crown on, and his sceptre in his hand. And many fine ceremonies there was of the Heralds leading up people before him, and bowing; and three lords coming before the courses on horseback, and staying so all dinnertime. I went from table to table to see the Bishops and all others at their dinner, and was infinitely pleased with it.

To Lambeth to dinner with the Archbishop of Canterbury; a noble house with good pictures and furniture and exceeding great cheer. . . . My cousin Roger told us that the Archbishop do keep a wench, and that he is as very a wencher as can be, which is one of the most astonishing things I have heard of.

To Whitehall into the ball this night before the King. They danced the Branle. After that the King led a lady a single Coranto. Then to country dances, the King leading the first, which he called for, which was, says he, "Cuckolds all awry," the old dance of England. When the King dances, all the ladies in the room and the Queen herself, stand up.

About eight o'clock, having got some bottles of wine and beer, and neats' tongues, we went to our barge at the Tower and set out for the Hope, all the way down playing at cards and other sports, spending our time pretty merry. Embarked again for home; and so to cards and other sports til we came to Greenwich, and there to an alehouse, and so to the barge again, having shown them the King's pleasure-boat: and so home, bringing night home with us.

To my office. Home to dinner. We had a fricassee of rabbits and chickens, a leg of mutton boiled, three carps in a dish, a great dish of a side of lamb, a dish of roasted pigeons, a dish of four lobsters, three tarts, a lamprey pie (a most rare pie), a dish of anchovies, a good wine of several sorts, and all things mighty noble and to my great content.

Being directed by sight of bills upon the walls, I did go to Shoe Lane to see a cock-fighting at a new pit there, a sport I was never at in my life: but Lord! to see the strange variety of people, from Parliament-man to the poorest 'prentices, bakers, brewers, butchers, and what not; and all these fellows one with another in swearing, cursing, and betting. . . .

Bought my cloth, coloured, for a suit and cloak, to line with plush the cloak, which will cost me money, but I find that I must go handsomely, whatever it costs me, and the charge will be made up in the fruit it brings.

This day I first began to go forth in my coat and sword, as the manner now among gentlemen is.

By and by comes Chapman, the periwigmaker, and upon my liking it, without more ado I went up, and there he cut off my hair, which went a little to my heart at present to part with it; but it being over and my periwig being on, I paid £3 for it; and away he went with my own hair to make another of it, and I by and by, after I had caused all my maids to look upon it; and they concluded it do become me.

I found that my coming in a periwig did not prove so strange to the world as I was afraid it would, for I thought that all the church would presently have cast all their eyes upon me, but I found no such thing.

Home to dinner where my wife having dressed herself in a silly dress of a blue petticoat uppermost, and a white satin waistcoat and white hood, though I think she did it because her gown is gone to the tailor's, did, together with my being hungry, which always makes me peevish, make me angry, but when my belly was full were friends again.

When the House began to fill she put on her vizard, and so kept it on all the play; which of late is become a great fashion among the ladies, which hides their whole face. So to the Exchange, to buy things with my wife; among others a vizard for herself.

Clearly society life in Restoration England was less pompous and formal than in France, though the English aristocrats prided themselves on their French customs and tastes.

Costume and Accessories

Though Restoration clothes followed the style of the French court, they were worn differently—with a casual, sensuous, comfortable elegance totally unlike the formal silhouette and structured layering of the French costume. The painter who best captured what Restoration aristocrats wished to see in their portraits was Sir Peter Lely, a Dutchman who, after his move to England in 1641, donned the mantle dropped by Anthony Van Dyck in portraiture. Lely captured in his portraits both the beautiful simplicity of rich fabrics and the elegant poses that Van Dyck had pioneered, as well as the new sensuality that was so much a part of Restoration society and its plays. Look, for example, at his *Portrait of the Duke of York*, brother to the king and later to become the ill-fated James II (Figure 9–4). The duke is seated in a casually elegant manner in clothing that, though like the styles worn in France, creates a far more sensuous impression because of its soft, slithery, satin texture, reflectivity to light, and loose, casual draping of the body. The garments are without the ornamentation that would add stiffness and formality; the whole effect is almost that of boudoir *deshabille* rather than costume for a formal portrait.

The *Portrait of Anne Hyde, Duchess of York*, wife of the Duke of York, has the same sensuous, silken curtains through which we catch a glimpse of a lush and fulsome natural scene (Figure 9–5). The duchess's gown resembles a morning negligée in its loose, uncorseted fit over the body and shares the slithery, light reflective, sensuous characteristics of the duke's garments. The duchess's raised eyebrows and hooded lids give a slightly disdainful, beckoning look, while the soft folds of her gown fall intriguingly between the legs in a very sensuously appealing, boudoir manner. Lely obviously captured exactly the tone

Figure 9–4 Peter Lely, *Portrait of the Duke of York*, c. 1660–75. Illustrates the sensuous, loose, silky clothing, based on French styles imported by the exiled aristocrats on their return to England, and lightened and softened by the English. Photo courtesy of the National Gallery of Scotland, Edinburgh.

Figure 9–5 Peter Lely, *Portrait of Anne Hyde, Duchess of York*, c. 1660–70. Illustrates the same sensuous, silken, soft image as in the portrait of her husband, with strong overtones of boudoir sensuality. Photo courtesy of the National Gallery of Scotland, Edinburgh.

and mood that his patrons desired, or he would not have been so successful. The fact that both these portraits stress an elegant, sensous informality, rather than an aristocratic formality, tells us much about the game of life and love played by upper-class Restoration society.

In 1680 Sir Godfrey Kneller succeeded Sir Peter Lely as the principal portrait painter to the king after executing a very successful portrait of Charles II. Kneller came to England at exactly the moment when the frivolity of the Restoration was waning and the escapades of "The Merry Monarch" were all but finished. He brought with him a sober, rather unimaginative ability to capture a likeness that suited England's gradual return to more sober, middle-class values. As court painter to James II, William and Mary, and Queen Anne, Kneller catalogued this emphasis on virtue and morality—the outward ideal of late seventeenth- and early eighteenth-century English society.

Manners and Movement

It is important to remember that the basic elements of movement and manners are the same as those described for France in Chapter 8, but early Restoration portraits tell us more about the manners and movement of this period than many of the rules set down in books of etiquette. Certainly, the ribbons and bows accenting the short soft lines of the male costume demanded elegantly controlled flourishes to give them just treatment. The Restoration gentleman of the Lely portraits needed a swaggering, elegant movement in order to carry off the full weight of the layers of fabric and ribbons. He dominated his costume with assurance and delight, from the tip of his square-toed high-heeled shoes to the great plumes of his broad-brimmed beaver hat. The lady's movement must also have had a graceful, sensuous vitality and an attractive bounce that epitomized the spirit of the times. The waist would have been flexible but firmly controlled with never a sag in the middle, since most gowns were unlike the one worn by the Duchess of York (Figure 9–5) and did contain boning and corseting. From Pepys's diary, other commentators, and artists of the period, we know that ladies preened and pranced like pigeons, fluttered their eyelashes, and manipulated their skirts and their charms with a complete knowledge and assurance about the effects they were creating.

The painting *Charles II at a Ball in The Hague* by Hieronymous Janssens, which celebrates the king's return to England in 1660, provides some good illustrations of the movement of this period (Figure 9–6). We see the six-foot Charles with his shining black hair and swarthy complexion walking forward to the center of the ballroom floor with a graceful and dignified carriage. Charles was a fine rider, dancer, and tennis player. By the position of his feet in an almost ninety-degree angle, he obviously was also fully trained in the French ballet walk and stance. Only practice in the appropriate shoes before a mirror for a long period of time can give the modern actor any sense of how this movement is executed.

The lady toward whom Charles is advancing curtsies lightly by holding her dress out to the sides, dragging one foot to the front, and crossing it slightly in front of the other foot while bending slightly at the knees. This movement is basically a variation of the bow or curtsy *en passant* discussed in Chapter 8. The only other figures of major interest are the couple at the bottom left of the picture. The man points his left foot toward the lady and drags his right foot, with knee bent, behind at a ninety-degree angle to the left. This movement gives his whole form a swinging, elegant pose even when his body is at rest. Also note that his body twists elegantly at the waist toward his feminine companion and that his arms spread out in a welcoming gesture. The entire pose is one of easy, relaxed, casual but calculated elegance. Though it is difficult to see much of the lady to whom he talks, she too has her arms delicately spread and the fingers of her left hand calculatedly set to

Figure 9–6 Hieronymous Janssens, *Charles II at a Ball in The Hague,* c. 1660. Illustrates the manners and movement of the period, especially in the poses and foot positions. Windsor Castle. Photo courtesy of the Lord Chamberlain, St. James's Palace, London. Copyright reserved.

create the right impression. Those who are seated lean lightly forward on their stools or chairs.

We know that a man of fashion had to manipulate a number of accessories such as a walking stick, muff, snuff box, and handkerchief. The fashion extremists or "fops" of the Restoration period, who especially enjoyed these accessories, exaggerated their movements, overdid their flourishes and hand gestures, and minced, rather than strode, across a reception or ballroom floor. They would turn their heads with an abrupt twist to give a flounce to the curls of their wigs; would clutch their muffs to their chests and peep over them at friends; would toy with the ribbons on their walking sticks; and would

flourish their handkerchiefs in a ludicrously ostentatious manner. These dandies must have been very much like their theatrical portraits—figures of fun and amusement.

The single most important accessory for the Restoration woman was the fan, which was used as a weapon in the game of love. Involved in skirmishes, fierce battles, and abject surrenders, it often seemed to have a life of its own. Too often modern actresses give the fan a mechanical staccato rhythm. Only practice and a knowledge of the rhythm of the Restoration period can make the modern actress handle the fan properly. Each actress should develop her own meaning for her fan gestures—to make this love weapon completely her own.

Though theatrical performances were illegal in England between 1642 and 1660 owing to Puritan laws, theatre did not disappear. Performances were given in private halls, tennis courts, inns, and even in the theatres that were supposedly closed. When the restoration of the monarchy seemed imminent, two enterprising theatrical producers, with Charles II's permission, organized two outstanding theatrical troupes. Sir Thomas Killigrew formed the King's Company, composed of experienced actors; and Sir William Davenant formed the Duke's Company, made up of younger, less experienced actors and named for the king's brother, the Duke of York. Davenant's group, because of his excellent management, was the more successful; when the King's Company plunged into serious financial trouble, the two companies united and remained together until 1695.

At first, converted tennis courts in the French style were used for production; then the Dorset Garden Theatre opened in 1671, followed by the Drury Lane three years later—the first of many theatres built on the same spot under the same name. In addition, a converted tennis court called the Lincoln's Inn Fields Theatre was used throughout the late seventeenth century.

Though the three theatres differed in size and detail, they shared common features that continued in British playhouses until the early nineteenth century. The auditorium was divided into pit, boxes, and galleries; and, unlike those on the Continent, the English pit was raked to improve sight lines and equipped with backless benches. There were two or three galleries, the lowest divided into boxes and the top undivided and set with benches. The theatres were relatively small; for example, the Drury Lane was only 36 feet from the front of the stage to the back of the auditorium and held only about 650 people (Figure 9–7). The stage, unlike that of the European theatre, had a forestage in front of the proscenium arch, flanked by two proscenium doors surmounted by balconies. Most of the entrances were through these doors just as most of the action in the plays occurred on the forestage. The stage floor sloped upward from the forestage to the back wall; and, behind the proscenium, it was set with grooves in the floor.

Figure 9–7 Christopher Wren, sectional plan of a theatre, believed to be Drury Lane, 1674. The auditorium is at the left with backless benches in the raked pit. On stage, there is a deep apron flanked by double proscenium doors. Photo courtesy of the Warden and Fellows of All Souls College, Oxford.

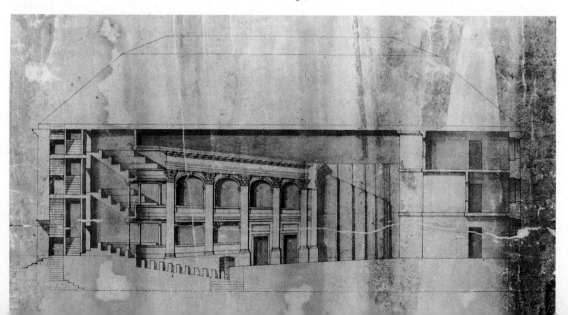

Grooves also hung from the ceiling to accommodate the various wings and shutters needed to set the action of the play.

Trap doors and flying machinery were usually available for special effects. At the Dorset Garden Theatre, a curtained box above the stage even accommodated a small orchestra. Because the front curtain was raised after the prologue and was not lowered until the end of the play, all scenery changes took place in full view of the audience. Furnishings, kept to the bare minimum demanded by the play, were either brought on by servants or set up behind a closed set of shutters and revealed when the shutters were pulled apart to disclose the next scene. Following the neoclassic ideal of generality and universality, sets were anonymous and could be used in many different plays. The common inventory for a theatre usually included temples, tombs, city gates, palace interiors, palace exteriors, streets, chambers, prisons, gardens, and rural views. Most Restoration comedies required only interiors, chambers, and gardens.

The principles governing costume were similar to those in Shakespeare's day. Since time and place were not particularly important, many productions were performed in contemporary dress made to look as sumptuous as possible in order to emphasize neoclassical ideals of beauty and nobility of character. Classical heroes wore the *habit à la romaine*, while Near Eastern characters wore turbans, baggy trousers, and long braided gowns (Figure 8–10). Actresses performing classical or Near Eastern roles merely added plumes to the headdress and a few exotic ornaments to the waist, shoulder, or hips of an otherwise contemporary gown. There were also special conventionalized costumes for certain characters like Falstaff, Richard III, Henry VIII, and King Lear. The dress of all performers in Restoration comedies was taken from the fashions of the day.

The Plays

[handwritten annotation: GEORGE VILLIERS SECOND DUKE OF BUCKINGHAM]

The dominant Restoration theatrical mode in serious playwriting until 1680 was the heroic tragedy. For its stories of heroic deeds in the service of love and honor, it was heavily indebted to French and Spanish playwrights of the early seventeenth century. These tragedies often have contrived happy endings and are filled with ranting speeches in rhymed couplets that today make them seem hopelessly archaic. George Villier's *The Rehearsal*, written in 1671 and still sometimes performed today, is a marvelous burlesque of the themes, plot devices, and staging effects of this mode of playwriting.

Heroic tragedy was eventually replaced by neoclassic tragedy in blank verse, which observed the unities and gave English audiences imitations of Racine and Corneille without the exactness of French structure and speech. The best-known work in this mode is Dryden's *All for Love*, which is a "regularization" of Shakespeare's *Antony and Cleopatra*, forcing the great, expansive, sprawling structure of that play into the narrow confines of the neoclassic rules of playwriting; however, even these rules were interpreted far more liberally in England than in France.

What is primarily remembered today, however, is the Restoration comedy of manners. This mode was rather slow to develop and was not fully established until 1676, when George Etherege wrote his masterpiece, *The Man of Mode*. This play contains all the elements of Restoration comedy: sophisticated characters from the upper classes, preoccupation with the game of love and seduction, arranged marriages, excesses of fashion, and brilliant and witty repartée.

Unlike the plays of Molière, which frequently dealt with similar themes and social excesses, the Restoration comedies lacked a clear moral point of view. The Restoration playwrights, taking their cue from the small coterie of aristocrats who surrounded Charles, "The Merry Monarch," developed an amoral tone; the only virtue was unsentimental self-knowledge. In the plays, the self-deceived are ridiculed and tricked by protagonists with cynical but superior insights into human character; the message is that man is corruptible, a fact that must be accepted with a sophisticated and worldly tolerance.

By the 1690s when William Congreve, the greatest of the Restoration comic writers, began his career, Charles was dead; his brother James, who succeeded him, had been driven from the throne because of his Catholicism; and the bourgeois William and Mary had been crowned king and queen. Society had changed to a more moral outlook, and a number of attacks were launched on the theatre, culminating in Jeremy Collier's *A Short View of the Immorality and Profaneness of the English Stage* (1698). By the last decade of the seventeenth century, Congreve and Farquhar were writing for only a small coterie of admirers who were attempting to keep alive the spirit of the Restoration. The spirit in the Restoration comedies was at its peak in England between 1660 and 1688; after that time, a resurgence in Puritan ideals caused major social changes that led to the sentimentality and surface morality of the eighteenth century.

Let us look briefly at *The Relapse,* written in 1696 by Sir John Vanbrugh, the famous courtier and architect who was responsible for the design of Blenheim Palace and several excellent comedies of manners. Though written during the reign of William and Mary when the social ideals were considerably different from what they had been under Charles II, *The Relapse* embodies the cynical spirit of the earlier Restoration period. The play was actually written as an answer to a play by Colley Cibber called *Love's Last Shrift,* which Vanbrugh thought gave a falsely moral, sentimental picture of love.

The Relapse is based on the age-old tradition of exchanged identities and has two quite separate plots. One plot follows the fortunes of Loveless and Amanda who have recently married and settled in the country; in rebuttal to Cibber's sentimentalism, Loveless does not live happily ever after but returns to his old role of seducer. The other plot follows the fortunes of Fashion and the newly ar-

ranged marriage of his excessively ridiculous brother Lord Foppington to Hoyden, the daughter of a country squire named Sir Tunbelly Clumsy. Loveless is finally seduced by the amorous Berinthia, and Lord Foppington loses his intended wife to his brother.

The characters and dialogue are more interesting than the plot, which contrasts sharply with the plays of Molière in its complexity and multiplicity of complication. Lord Foppington, the overweening and pretentious fop, is the most humorous character. Everything about him is excessive (gestures, clothing, speech, and outlook); he is thus a perfect butt for ridicule and satire on social excesses of the day. The other characters fall into one of two categories: they are either exaggerated caricatures like Sir Tunbelly Clumsy and the matchmaker Coupler or sophisticated participants in the Restoration game of love.

The witty, sharp dialogue is filled with the kind of licentious repartée expected of those involved in the game of love; in particular, Lord Foppington's speech consists of exaggerated expletives and ridiculously overblown expressions based on the fashionable speech of the day. The theme of the play is a truly unsentimental and worldly one, that of the relapse of a supposedly true love and the discomfiture of the man of excess. The parallel unrolling of the two plots gives the play a twofold rhythm; and there is no continuous line of development, only a casual balancing of individual scenes, each with its own rhythmic values. The alternating shifts in scenes between country and city, to stress the coarseness of the former in comparison to the sophistication of the latter, also contribute to the disunity of the play. Each would have been quickly set with a change of wings and shutters, and the few pieces of furniture would have been carried on and off by servants. The costumes undoubtedly would have come directly from the fashions of the day. For a modern audience, however, the costumes may have to imitate earlier seductive Restoration dress rather than the dress of the William and Mary period, in order to prevent

Figure 9–8 Scene from *The Relapse* by Vanbrugh, produced by the American Conservatory Theatre, San Francisco, 1970. Directed by Edward Hastings, costumes designed by Robert Fletcher. Illustrates a production approach to a very late Restoration comedy. Photo courtesy of the American Conservatory Theatre, photograph by Hank Kranzler.

the play from having a heavy and sober dignity. The costumes necessary for Lord Foppington, Sir Tunbelly Clumsy, and his daughter Hoyden, however, would be just as comic in the style of the William and Mary period as in the style of Charles II (Figure 9–8).

Acting and Directing the Plays

In describing acting in seventeenth- and eighteenth-century comedies of manners, Stark Young, an American drama critic of the 1920s, said in a review of a Restoration comedy: "The voice would be clear, finished . . . crisp, shining . . . like the satin and gold of the furniture and the costumes, the rapier at the wrist, the lace over it, the worldliness and the wit." The point emphasized by Young is that the worldliness and wit of the comedies are directly related to the costumes and furnishings. To understand fully the acting style of the period, the actor or actress must study the costumes, interiors, furniture, and properties surrounding the Restoration gentleman and lady. Restoration comedy involves a more objective approach to character than is usually required in most modern productions; the actors must study the social scene more fully and objectively than the character's subjective personality. One must remember that the relationship between actors and audience was very close; there was much direct address to the audience, since the actors often took the audience directly into their confidence. In the final analysis, it is more important for the modern actor to have a highly trained voice and body able to respond quickly and easily to the demands of Restoration dialogue, gesture, and movement than to spend time becoming psychologically attuned to the character. Depth of character is not important in these plays written for a very limited aristocratic audience; but bodily grace, a sophisticated personal magnetism, and a highly tuned vocal instrument are of vital concern. Directorial blocking patterns should be sensuous, relaxed and flowing compared to the geometric, balanced effects in Molière.

Designing the Plays

The Relapse could be produced today with a certain quaintness by using the wing and shutter system of the Restoration period, or more casually with a series of folding screens. If a presentation with full interiors is wanted, a turntable system might be useful. The designer, using Restoration interiors and the structure of the play as a guide, will achieve some of the rich imbalances and the casual and subtle asymmetries that make Restoration comedies so different from French classical comedy. Costumes could take their lead from the fashion drawings of the day and the ideals expressed in the paintings of Peter Lely (Figures 9–4 and 9–5), with their elegant sophistication; soft, sensuous textures; mellow golden-tan colors; careful yet casual sense of fit. Rich, crinkly, soft, reflective fabrics mixed with many pussy-willow soft velvets and other piles will underline the sharpness and spark of the wit amidst the sensuous, soft surrounding atmosphere (Figure 9–8).

PROJECTS AND PROBLEMS

1. Why do we need a separate chapter on the English Baroque style when two chapters have already been devoted to the Baroque style in general?

2. Summarize the character and mood of the east façade of Hampton Court (Figure 9–1). What are the differences and similarities between this structure and the east façade of the Louvre (Figure 9–2)? What do these differences communicate about the cultural and artistic outlooks of England and France? What would be the difference in playing a scene against each as a background? What would be the differences in blocking patterns?

3. What are the differences between the Double Cube Room at Wilton House (Figure 9–3) and the Salle des Gardes at Versailles (Figure 8–5) in terms of how the wall decoration and ceilings are organized? How do they affect the character of each room? The scenes that might be staged in each?

4. How is the music of Purcell similar to the architecture of Christopher Wren? How does Purcell relate to Lully in France and Monteverdi in Italy? Why is Purcell, for all his knowledge of the latest continental innovations in the Baroque style, still a very British composer?

5. Who was Samuel Pepys, and why is he the greatest single source for information about the Restoration period in England?

6. Summarize the character of Samuel Pepys

and the general character of British society during this period. What impresses you most strongly about this period?

7. Try to find out what £3 would have been worth in the 1660s and then comment on the cost of the wig that Samuel Pepys ordered for his daily wear.

8. Though the costumes of English ladies and gentlemen during the Restoration period were based on French designs, why do they look different from the French fashions (Figures 8–9, 9–4 and 9–5)? Compare the differences in the way they are worn, in the way the body seems to move in them, and in the cultural atmosphere and outlook of France and England.

9. Imagine yourself in the costumes worn by the Duke and Duchess of York (Figures 9–4 and 9–5). How do they feel? How must they be worn to be effective? What do they tell you about the manners and movements in Restoration plays?

10. How were French fashions (Figures 8–7 and 8–9) and those worn by the Dutch gentleman (Figure 8–6) modified in Restoration style clothing (Figures 9–4 and 9–5)? Imagine yourself walking and sitting in these costumes. What would be the ideal for which you would strive?

11. What happened to Restoration clothing after the death of Charles II? What does this tell us about the changing nature of British society? About the nature of the Restoration drama in relation to Restoration society?

12. Look closely at Janssens' painting *Charles II at a Ball in The Hague* (Figure 9–6). Describe the costumes and movement. Imagine yourself as a part of this scene and describe your feelings in relation to your costume, the setting, and the other people.

13. What training is needed to exhibit the full grace of movement and body control observed in the Janssens painting (Figure 9–6)? Gather a small group and present this scene in approximations of the costumes of the period. Describe the effect and the problems encountered.

14. In the appropriate costume and footwear of the Restoration, practice employing accessories from the period, such as the muff, walking stick, sword, handkerchief, hat, and fan.

15. Describe the Restoration playhouse (Figure 9–7). How did the shifting of scenery differ?

16. What kinds of settings were used in the Restoration playhouse? List the scenes that would have been available.

17. Describe the theatrical costumes for Restoration tragedy, for opera, and for comedy. What was the *habit à la romaine*?

18. What kinds of plays were popular during the Restoration period? What kind of a play is Dryden's *All for Love*? Which characters in it are typical of the Restoration comedy of manners?

19. How do the themes in Restoration comedies of manners differ from the themes in Molière's comedies of manners?

20. What problem arose in presenting the standard Restoration comedies of manners after the accession of William and Mary to the English throne?

21. Describe the characteristics of Vanbrugh's *The Relapse*. Choose a scene from the play and perform it. Critique the problems that you faced in preparing the scene.

22. Why did Stark Young compare the voice needed in playing Restoration comedy to the satin and gold furniture and costumes of the period?

23. Summarize the abilities needed by the actor or actress in order to play Restoration comedy on an accomplished professional level.

BIBLIOGRAPHY

Baur-Heinhold, M. *Baroque Theatre*. New York: McGraw-Hill, 1967. The finest pictorial compendium published to date on the theatre of the seventeenth and eighteenth centuries.

Blitzer, Charles. *Age of Kings*. The Great Ages of Man Series. New York: Time-Life Books, 1967. Intended for the average reader, this beautifully illustrated book, with extensive color photography, is a concise and useful text on the major artistic, intellectual, and cultural developments in Europe during the seventeenth century.

Boas, Frederick S. *An Introduction to Stuart Drama.* London: Oxford University Press, 1946. An excellent survey on drama written between the period of Shakespeare's late plays and the deposition of James II.

Campbell, Lily Bess. "A History of Costuming on the English Stage between 1660 and 1823," *University of Wisconsin Studies in Language and Literature*, 1918, pp. 187–223. A useful scholarly study of the changes in theatrical dress on the English stage from the time of Shakespeare to the beginning of the nineteenth century.

Dobrée, Bonamy. *Restoration Comedy, 1660–1720.* Oxford: Clarendon Press, 1924. Still a standard study comparing Restoration comedy to the comedies of Molière and his followers.

———. *Restoration Tragedy, 1660–1720.* Oxford: Clarendon Press, 1929. A survey on the tragedies written in England during the Restoration period.

Hotson, Leslie. *The Commonwealth and Restoration Stage.* Cambridge, Mass.: Harvard University Press, 1928. This survey, by a famous expert in the field of late sixteenth- and seventeenth-century British drama, gives a full picture of drama between 1642 and 1720.

Kitson, Michael. *The Age of the Baroque.* Landmarks of the World's Art Series. New York: McGraw-Hill, 1966. Deals with European art from the beginning of the seventeenth until the middle of the eighteenth century.

The London Stage, 1660–1800. 11 vols. Carbondale: Southern Illinois University Press, 1960–1968. A year-by-year detailed survey of the plays produced on the London stage during the late seventeenth and eighteenth centuries.

Nicoll, Allardyce. *History of the English Stage, 1660–1900.* 6 vols. London: Cambridge University Press, 1955–1959. The first part of this detailed history of the English stage is particularly useful and illuminating in understanding Restoration drama.

Odell, George C. D. *Shakespeare from Betterton to Irving.* 2 vols. New York: Charles Scribner's Sons, 1920. An excellent picture of Shakespearean production on the Restoration stage.

Palmer, J. L. *The Comedy of Manners.* London: Bell and Sons, 1913. A standard study on the comedy of manners and why it became an almost universal European art form in the late seventeenth century.

Rothstein, Edward. *Restoration Tragedy.* Westport, Conn.: Greenwood Press, 1978. A welcome antidote to all the books on Restoration comedy; helps to give the modern reader a wider perspective on the period.

Southern, Richard. *Changeable Scenery: Its Origins and Development in the British Theatre.* London: Faber & Faber, 1952. A standard, widely read study of the development of scenery during the seventeenth and eighteenth centuries on the English stage.

Styron, J. L. *Restoration Comedy in Performance.* New York: Cambridge University Press, 1986. A new book that is a must for actors and directors doing Restoration comedies.

Summers, Montague. *The Playhouse of Pepys.* London: Paul, Trench, Trubner and Co., 1935. An excellent and very readable study of the Restoration playhouse.

———. *The Restoration Theatre.* London: Paul, Trench, Trubner and Co., 1934. A companion volume to *The Playhouse of Pepys.*

Summerson, John. *Architecture in Britain 1530–1830.* Pelican History of Art Series. Baltimore: Penguin Books, 1963. Presents a very clear picture of how English architecture of the late seventeenth century fitted into the overall plan of historical development.

Tapié, Victor. *The Age of Grandeur.* Translated by A. Ross Williamson. New York: Praeger, 1957. A fascinating account of Baroque art and architecture in Italy and its spread to France during the seventeenth century; also contains information on art and architecture in England, central Europe, and the European colonies.

Waterhouse, E. K. *Painting in Britain 1530–1790.* Pelican History of Art Series. Baltimore: Penguin Books, 1966. A companion volume (in this history of art series) to those on architecture and sculpture. Relates British painting in the seventeenth century to that of the sixteenth and eighteenth centuries.

Weinstein, Leo, ed. *The Age of Reason.* The Culture of Mankind Series. New York: Braziller, 1965. Writings from original sources on the Baroque view of life.

Whinney, Margaret. *Sculpture in Britain 1530–1830.*

Pelican History of Art Series. Baltimore: Penguin Books, 1967. Presents a good picture of British sculpture and painting in the seventeenth century.

10

Early Eighteenth-Century Rococo Style

In the period between the death of Louis XIV (1715) and the outbreak of the American Revolution (1775), the power of the Church and State in France declined. By the end of his reign, Louis XIV's exercise of power had become so unbearable that even his aristocratic supporters finally longed for his death. As Marshal Richelieu said to Louis XVI: "Under Louis XIV no one dared open his mouth, under Louis XV everyone whispered, now everyone speaks aloud and in a perfectly free and easy way." This comment is a brilliant and succinct picture of the changes that occurred in Europe during the eighteenth century.

The period saw a release from the dynastic wars waged by the great Baroque rulers. The wars fought in the eighteenth century were gentlemanly affairs—balancing maneuvers among the various states carried out by professional soldiers with a gamelike formality. The ruling aristocrats, sensing their waning importance in the historical scheme of things, turned to frivolous activities and left administrative and executive functions to the ambitious members of the upper-middle class. During this period, as they slowly became obsolete, royalty and nobility devoted themselves primarily to the arts. The arts of this age brilliantly expressed the aristocrats' boredom, escapism, and pursuit of pure pleasure. In the sixty years from the death of Louis XIV until the outbreak of revolution in the American colonies, art was luxurious, frivolous, sensual, clever, and charmingly artificial. The great religious and secular themes of the Baroque era were abandoned in favor of refined, elegant, intimately charming views of mythological and courtly love.

Rococo art was the denouement of Baroque art, which had been devoted exclusively to the monarchy and an aristocratic way of life. Throughout monarchical Europe, there was a slackening of personal discipline, a pulling away from responsibility, a growing skepticism and atheism, and a move from masculine to feminine sensibility in social outlook and attitudes. The aristocracy gradually began to accept middle-class ideas, though still clothing them in elegant trappings. In many ways the delicate, elegant curvilinear decoration reminds one of the feminine imagery in the late Gothic period. The succession of mistresses to Louis XV had far more influence on social and artistic matters than did the king himself, and the age developed a strong feminine bias in its tastes and attitudes.

The paintings of Antoine Watteau—many of them painted before the death of Louis XIV—illustrate this abrupt change in style and the development of an entirely new set of cultural ideals. Watteau abandoned the grand Baroque "machines," developed and sponsored by Charles Lebrun, in favor of delicate

fêtes galantes. He surrendered the majesty of the old order to joys and pleasures touched with melancholy and nostalgia—a yearning for a lost Arcadia that merged civilization and nature, physical beauty and spirituality, seriousness and frivolity. Let us compare *Les Plaisirs du Bal* by Watteau with *The Garden of Love* by Rubens on which the Watteau painting is based (Figures 10–1 and 7–3). In the Rubens painting, there are expanding, grand, solid forms and lovers whose clothes expand from their bodies with the sensuous richness and dimension found in grand Baroque pageantry. The artist enriches his surfaces and textures with a splendor and vigor that makes the entire painting vibrate with the energy and blood-pulsing vitality of life lived and felt to its fullest measure. Rubens has created an

Figure 10–1 Antoine Watteau, *Les Plaisirs du Bal,* c. 1719. Illustrates the aristocratic dream world created by this eighteenth-century French artist who gave definition and character to the new Rococo style. Photo courtesy of the Governors of Dulwich College, London.

enchanted realm where myth and reality have become one. In contrast, Watteau has created a world of memory and nostalgia. The figures have lost their robust vitality, rich colors, expanding body fabric, and sense of an inner life force. Elegant, slim, and graceful, they drift effortlessly to distant music in a poetic, theatrical world of airy, parklike landscapes. Even the architecture is different; the ringed columns are slim and decorative without the muscular vitality and expansion into space found in the Rubens work. In Watteau's work, a casual, mannered elegance now surrounds court life in its major pursuit during the years of the reign of Louis XV—the game of love.

This lightening of the Baroque style into a less formal, more elegant, and less majestic and pompous form occurred not only in France but also in other countries, particularly in Italy, southern Germany, and Austria.

In sculpture, the move was similar—toward playfully elegant small pastel figures that have lost the cold formality of the French classic Baroque style. Compare, for example, a mythological grouping of Apollo and nymphs, by François Girardon, dating from the late seventeenth century, with a small pink terra cotta grouping of young ladies sacrificing at the altar of Bacchus, by Clodion, dating from the early eighteenth century (Figures 10–2 and 10–3). The Girardon work is coldly self-conscious, classical, and formal despite its harmonious arrangement of females positioned around Apollo, who obviously is meant to symbolize Louis XIV. In the Clodion work the figures are charming, simpering, undeveloped females with cute, rounded faces and forms, who playfully pay homage to Bacchus. The work is designed to be viewed at close range for its play of coquettish eroticism rather than for its actual subject matter; its Rococo

Figure 10–2 François Girardon, *Apollo Attended by the Nymphs,* marble, Garden of Versailles, c. 1668. Illustrates the coldly formal and self-conscious classical style admired by Louis XIV in the late seventeenth century. Photo courtesy of Giraudon, Paris.

Figure 10–3 Clodion, *Sacrifice to Pan, God of Gardens,* c. 1750. Illustrates charming, soft, adolescent female figures paying playful homage to a simpering Bacchus. This coquettish eroticism was an admired Rococo style. Private collection. Photo courtesy of Giraudon, Paris.

charm is like a miniature Baroque exercise— a playful echo of the ecstasies of Bernini. Note also that the god in the Girardon sculpture is Apollo, the deity of enlightenment and reason, whereas in the Clodion work, the deity is Pan or Bacchus, the god of wine, women, and song.

By the middle of the eighteenth century, this playful, elegant, and basically aristocratic style was challenged by the bourgeois sentimental tastes of the commercial aristocracy. First in England and later in France, a group of artists and writers waged war on the decadence of aristocratic Rococo taste in the name of middle-class morality. During the 1730s in England, William Hogarth made a strong attack on upper-class immorality with a series of paintings that were like tableaux from a play. These "morality plays" were intended to teach by terrible example the solid virtues espoused by the English middle class. Though he borrowed some technical aspects from Rococo artists, Hogarth ushered in a new kind of realistic, moral storytelling reflected in the eighteenth-century literature of Richardson and Fielding, the realistic dramas of Lessing and Diderot, and the stage melodramas of Kotzebue.

Jean-Baptiste Greuze, a French artist, though inferior to Hogarth, also perfectly ex-pressed this transition from Rococo frivolity to moral storytelling and the later ideals of romanticism. He represented the interest, championed by the encyclopedist Denis Diderot and Jean Jacques Rousseau, in abandoning Rococo decadence and luxury in favor of serious moral subjects that could be related to sensibility and natural feeling. Diderot and Rousseau exalted the simple virtues found in uncorrupted "natural" people, and Greuze won great acclaim with paintings that projected the melodramatic emotions and excessive sentimentality then admired in art and literature.

The Rococo period thus saw the gradual denouement of the old aristocratic ideal in art and the gradual establishment of middle-class romanticism that lasted in various forms until World War I. It marked the fall of the Baroque interest in an intellectual structure beneath even the most excessively ornamental composition and its replacement with eclectic forms borrowed from the past and organized around theme and emotion. The Rococo era has often been called the last unselfconscious, cohesive, cultural-artistic period in the history of Western man, the last cultural artistic statement before the onslaught of the Industrial Revolution.

Music

The art of music blossomed suddenly in the eighteenth century with the development and acceptance of more musical modes and more variety in musical expression. Though the Baroque musical style remained in force until the middle of the eighteenth century, the weighty *opera seria* gradually became less and less popular as the *opera buffa* became more acceptable. Operatic overtures changed from the stately, disciplined, French style in one movement to the more vivacious Italian operatic form in three movements, more readily fitting the temper of the times. The new elegant, aristocratic tastes demanded a simpler form of music in which clear-cut melodies in a lively rhythm were supported by a simple harmonic accompaniment. In fact, an entirely new form of orchestration made its appearance: wind instruments, which formerly had independent musical lines, now provided harmonic background. Also, keyboard instruments were no longer essential to the orchestra and were eventually dropped. Keyboard music in its own right became more popular, and instrumental music unrelated to an operatic story became very important.

In short, the modern age of music was slowly being born, with greater stress on feeling than on pure technical display and with a greater synthesis of musical modes.

Though Mozart's most mature operatic work reflects dramatic themes that could have been written only in the decade before the French Revolution, his early work is a synthesis of Rococo musical forms. While still very young he came under the diverse influences of Christian Bach, Gluck, Haydn, Pergolesi, and the German *Singspiel,* all the while composing music for aristocratic salons and an occasional chamber opera for the court. Like Shakespeare, Mozart was a great synthesizer of diverse influences, and no composer better understood that opera is not a drama with music but a drama in music. Even his earliest operatic overtures reflect the use of chroma-

ticism as a means of emotional expression, the dramatic dualism of the sonata form, and the social, ceremonial, *buffa* character of the Italianate operatic style of the day. His early work has the pastel charm of a Watteau painting or a Clodion statue; it is even more surprising, then, that he was able to create such great universal dramatic triumphs as *Don Giovanni* and *The Magic Flute* in the stirring years before and during the French Revolution.

Life and Cultural Ideals

The period leading up to the American Revolution is called the Age of Enlightenment more frequently than it is called the Age of the Rococo; it is probably true that, in the eighteenth century, people examined the world with less dogma and preconception than they had at any time since the fifth century B.C. in Greece. This pursuit of science, philosophy, and literature was carried on largely by amateurs—aristocrats who studied or wrote as a hobby and who developed a particular field of interest as an important part of their being cultured people. Ladies, too, had a great influence on art and taste and were involved in literature, philosophy, and science. Madame Pompadour studied astronomy; Mademoiselle de Coigny pursued anatomy; and Voltaire's mistress wrote about gravitation.

The major result of female influence in Rococo art was to create a culture that had few such masculine attributes as strength, weight, vulgarity, or aggressiveness. It was a society of exquisite taste, quick wit, gaiety, lightness, and elegant charm. The lady of Rococo French society, like Louis XIV in the late seventeenth century, was involved in an elegantly elaborate ceremonial of living. The following is a brief outline of a typical day in the life of an eighteenth-century French lady of fashion, based on the engravings of Sigmund Freudenberg and Moreau le Jeune (Figure 10–4).

The lady was awakened late in the morning by her maids, who prepared their mistress for another day in which each moment was

an excuse for elaborate formality and exquisite manners. The lady's toilette was a long and protracted affair during which she read or was read to, welcomed visitors, was entertained by a singer or musician, and was frequently surrounded by pets, including cats, dogs, monkeys, and parrots.

After a *petit dejeuner*, the lady took a promenade on the boulevard or in the parks and gardens of the Louvre to display her fashion and style to the admiring onlookers. Later in the afternoon, she might have a music lesson, often attended by a male admirer. The harp was a favorite instrument because it allowed the lady to appear both graceful and talented in the presence of her equally elegant companion. Still later, a game of whist allowed the lady to indulge in witty gossip as well as in gambling, which had become an obsession by this period. Time also had to be set aside for pure conversation. Talk was an art or, as Montesquieu said, "a gay dialogue in which each listens but little, yet speaks . . . in a rapid, prompt, and vivacious manner." If dinner were informal, it usually was limited to one or two couples who lingered on after the repast to read a love letter, to discuss the latest court scandal, or to pursue the complex game of love.

Brilliant balls and theatrical entertainments were also common, and much was made of the elegant masquerades and disguises used to attract attention and admiration. Often, the lady slipped away from such large-scale entertainments with her latest gentleman admirer to indulge in, amid Cupid

(a)

(b)

(c)

(d)

(e)   (f)

Figure 10–4 Scenes depicting social life in France in the third quarter of the eighteenth century: (a) *Le Lever* by Sigmund Freudenberg, (b) *La Promenade du Matin* by Sigmund Freudenberg, (c) *Le Partie de Whist* by Jean Moreau le Jeune, (d) *Les Confidences* by Sigmund Freudenberg, (e) *Oui ou Non* by Jean Moreau le Jeune, and (f) *L'Accord Parfait* by Jean Moreau le Jeune. Photos courtesy of the Metropolitan Museum of Art, Harris Brisbane Dick Fund, 1933.

and other classical statues in the garden, the complex formulas of pursuit and retreat before capitulating to the demands of love. On other occasions, the lady might occupy a private box with an elegant admirer at the opera, or she might participate in a philosophical salon hosted by one of the ladies of the court. Here she would discuss with intellectual celebrities the newest ideas of the moment. Some of the talk was very interesting and quite serious, but much of it was witty and superficial, masquerading as intellectualism.

Sometimes, the lady might have taken a festive carriage trip to a chateau outside Paris, like Rambouillet, Saint Germain, or St. Cloud, where she would have been served a lovely picnic by a corps of liveried servants amid the lush foliage and lovely ponds of the gardens and taken a pleasant stroll with a young admirer before returning to town or staying the night at the chateau as an invited ·guest. Though this life of pleasure was elegant and varied and seemingly casual and natural, it was as carefully planned and controlled as the heavy-handed protocol of the Louis XIV period. This return to natural forms and to a love of nature was in truth pure illusion; the immorality and artificiality of this Rococo society of the Enlightenment brought sharp criticism from bourgeois moralists like Denis Diderot, William Hogarth, Voltaire, and Gotthold Ephraim Lessing. Voltaire summed up the intellectuals' growing annoyance with the aristocracy in his essay "On Commerce":

In France anybody is a marquis who wants to be; and whoever comes from the obscurity of some remote province with money in his pocket and a name that ends with "ac" or "ille" can say "A man of my quality and rank"; and hold merchants in the most solemn contempt. The merchant hears his profession spoken of scornfully so often, that he is foolish enough to blush because of it. I do not know, however, which is the most useful to his country, a powdered lord, who knows to a minute when the king rises or goes to bed, perhaps to stool, and who gives himself airs of importance in playing the part of a slave in the anti-chamber of some minister; or a merchant, who enriches his country, and from his office sends his orders to Surat or Cairo, thereby contributing to the happiness of the world.

Ornament, Interiors, and Furniture

The elegant artificiality that surrounded every waking moment of the aristocratic person's day was also evident in the interior decoration of the time. For example, compare the Salon de la Princesse from the Hôtel de Soubise in Paris, decorated between 1737 and 1740 by Germain Boffrand, with a room at Versailles designed by Lebrun for Louis XIV (Figures 10–5 and 8–5). The strong, geometric, organizational architectural lines of the earlier Lebrun room are softened into gentle, flexible curves in the Salon de la Princesse. The walls melt imperceptibly into the ceiling; solid edges are replaced by irregular, meandering shapes and sculpture; and architecture and painting blend together into an elegant and aristocratic world of make-believe. The curving lines, sprays of delicate foliage, and light, pastel co-

Figure 10–5 Germain Boffrand, Salon de la Princesse. Hôtel de Soubise, Paris, begun in 1732. Illustrates the elegant, intimate curving architecture with delicate foliage ornamentation that characterized aristocratic interiors during the early eighteenth century in France. Photo courtesy of the French Cultural Services, New York.

loration create an artificially "natural" atmosphere.

A room like this—with its gilded moldings, dainty relief sculpture and delicately colored ornamentation of flowers and garlands—was a perfect setting for the elegant games of love and daily life already described. The chamber music developed to be heard in these surroundings must have harmonized perfectly with the lustrous satin and brocade costumes and the witty conversations that would have occupied a visitor's attention on first entering such an elegant salon. When lit by the candles of the chandelier, which would have been reflected in both the mirrors on the walls and in the satin clothing, the room must have been breathtaking indeed. A modern actor who can imaginatively think and feel his way into this atmosphere will have understood implicitly what is required of him in manners, dress, and movement.

The actor studying a role in a play set amid the aristocratic world of this period would do well to look closely at the furniture in the Salon de la Princesse (Figure 10–5). Two things are noteworthy in comparison to the furniture during the Louis XIV period: the chairs are smaller, lighter, with lower backs, and lack arms; they also have no complex stretchers between the curved cabriole legs. There is hardly a straight line in the entire ensemble, in keeping with those gently curving, serpentine rhythms so much admired by early eighteenth-century French society. The chairs and the settee reflect the easy, elegant, and charming artificiality of the room, and the actor can see very quickly that one does not sit in such furniture but lounges gracefully against it.

In fact, since the chairs lacked arms, gentlemen were able to effect many complex sitting positions. They sat sideways while leaning the arm elegantly over the back; they straddled the chair facing its back and chatted with a lady while leaning on the back with the forearms; or they leaned over the back of the chair, placing their weight on one foot while balancing with the toe of the other, thus creating an elegant but casual pose while talking with a lady in her boudoir (Figure 10–6).

Figure 10–6 François-Hubert Drouais, *Group Portrait*, 1756. Illustrates the new emphasis on casual elegance with a family's choosing to be painted in the mother's boudoir; note that the father leans casually on the back of the chair while crossing one leg lightly in front of the other. Photo courtesy of the National Gallery of Art, Samuel H. Kress Collection, 1946.

Elegant invention to achieve novel, asymmetrical positions was the key. Even the ladies, not to be outdone by the gentlemen, used the settee as a couch on which they lounged against pillows set against one of the arms, while holding a book of philosophy or poetry. Always the aim was a studied, aristocratic elegance and artificiality subtly disguised as casual nonchalance.

The fashions of this period were the perfect counterpart to the elegant interiors and furnishings. The pompous weight and organized structure bequeathed to the male figure by Louis XIV was abandoned in favor of a smaller, more natural form with loose lines. The most striking difference was the change from the full-bottomed periwig to a white, powdered wig worn with a few curls draped over the ear and with a small black bag at the back of the neck in which the remaining hair was tied in a queue with a black ribbon. The ladies also powdered their hair and, at the close of the period, indulged in an orgy of excessive hair styles. The dominant fashion image from this period is that of gentlemen

Costume and Accessories

and ladies with elegant white hair clothed in complementary pastel satins and brocades.

The painting by François de Troy entitled *The Declaration of Love*, dated 1731, is a brilliant evocation of the Rococo period and its fashions (Figure 10–7). The setting, typical of this time, is an elegant park or garden outside the chateau. The ladies wear the loose-fitted gown with Watteau pleats known as *la robe volante*, or flying gown, derived from the housecoat or morning gown. The kneeling gentleman has a delicately powdered wig, a flaring skirted coat and waistcoat, tight breeches buttoned over his silk stockings, and low-heeled buckled shoes. Though the overall effect is one of richness, nothing seems heavy-handed or

Figure 10–7 François de Troy, *The Declaration of Love,* 1731. Illustrates the flowered, loose-fitting Watteau-pleated gowns worn by ladies and the short white wigs, flared coats, long vests, and low-heeled buckled shoes worn by men in the second quarter of the eighteenth century. Photo courtesy of Staatliche Schlösser und Garten, Berlin.

excessive. The major interest comes from the delicately sensuous textures of satin, velvet, and flowered brocade. Note the deliberate choice of floral patterns and motifs to complement the garden setting.

The *Group Portrait* by Drouais, dated 1756, may be used to summarize male fashion at mid-century (Figure 10–6). The coat has some stiffening in its skirt but does not flare as much as does the coat in the de Troy painting (Figure 10–7), since the skirts of the coat were gradually cut away after the middle of the century. The vest was originally coat-length and flared, but it, too, became shorter after mid-century. The sleeves that ended in large, turn-back cuffs to reveal the lace of the shirt also gradually diminished in size. Stockings were most frequently rolled up over the tight breeches in the early years but, after mid-century, worn under them; shoes had a relatively low heel and were finished with a buckle. The neckcloth frequently had a ribbon known as a *solitaire* that came around from the wig to

the front and tied in a bow above the ruffle of the shirt. The hat was three-cornered, usually trimmed with gold braid or white ostrich feathers; the coat and vest were also heavily embroidered with gold, silver, or silk thread.

At the end of this period until the last years of the 1770s, fashion became excessive, especially in female dress. The *paniers*, originally used to spread the skirts away gently from the body, became very wide, giving an ungraceful and exaggeratedly artificial line to the body. The use of garlands, flounces, ribbons, and floral decoration increased, as did the height and complexity of the powdered hairdos. This excess was the last desperate attempt to retain the artificial elegance of the Rococo style, but it soon disappeared as the image of the "natural man" promulgated by Jean Jacques Rousseau and the democratic ideals created by French interest in the American Revolution came to dominate the imagination of French society.

Manners and Movement

The English periodical *The Spectator*, written in the early eighteenth century, deftly summed up the new sense of manners and movement: "At present . . . an unconstrained Carriage, and a certain openess of Behaviour are the height of Good Breeding. The Fashionable World is grown free and easie; Our Manners sit more loose upon us. Nothing is so modish as an agreeable Negligence. . . . Good Breeding shows itself most where . . . it appears the least."

All the books and letters of the period dealing with manners and behavior emphasized a disciplined movement of the body, developed and practiced from childhood. A dancing master was hired by all families to tutor their young in the physical graces demanded in society. Leaving nothing to personal caprice, the dancing master carefully trained his young male and female charges in walking, standing, sitting, bowing, embracing, removing the hat, and many other details. The studied pose of casual elegance of the gentleman in the *Group Portrait* could have

come only from such an extended education in body grace and control (Figure 10–6).

In *The Rudiments of Genteel Behaviour*, written in 1737 primarily for gentlemen, Frederick Nivelon stressed the absolute importance of the head held erect without stiffness, shoulders placed in the proper position, chest expanded, back straight and light, hips poised and easy, knees flexible, and feet turned out to support the body with a springy balance. He insisted that a gentleman holding his head correctly was capable of performing any genteel exercise in a graceful manner.

Probably the most striking effect in the paintings and engravings of the period was the male stance (Figure 10–4). It lacked the stiffness and formality of the preceding age, though the feet still turned out in a modification of the third ballet position. As Nivelon commented: "Always turn out your feet, because that makes you stand firm, easy and graceful." In addition, the arms and hands were never allowed to hang loosely at the side of the body—a pose that was deemed suitable only for merchants and servants. Consequently, the gentleman placed his hands on his sword, in his pocket, or inside his waistcoat. It was fashionable to wear the waistcoat unbuttoned except for the last three buttons below the waist. A common pose was to hold the hat loosely under the left arm while one leaned elegantly against a mantelpiece, chair back, or door frame. Always the standing male figure was in the process of moving from one elegant pose to another (Figures 10–4 and 10–6).

In walking, the posture was supposed to be erect and relaxed without affectation, the steps moderate with the heel touching the ground first, and the knee positioned forward and straightened just before the foot touched the ground. The whole leg from the hip down was turned slightly outward.

A good deal has already been said about the sitting posture in the Rococo period and the use of chairs as a prop to gain a studied and elegant nonchalance. Almost all seated poses were meant to create an elegantly asymmetrical effect. Thus the gentleman seldom sat erect in the center of the chair, but reclined to the left or right on the chair arm with one leg casually resting over the other at the knee. If the chair had no arms, the gentleman sat sideways or faced the back with legs straddling the seat of the chair. In both of these cases, the arms leaned elegantly on the chair back.

The graceful performance of the bow no longer depended on flowing gestures and deep obeisances but a polite reserve in which careful technique was concealed by art. First, the hat was gracefully removed from the head by holding the front point of the tricorne with the right hand and carrying it gracefully to the knee with the inside of the hat turned out. In a passing bow, the hat was merely lifted from the head without being carried to the side of the body. When the hat reached the side with the arm fully extended, the gentleman, whose right foot was now extended forward, bowed gently from the waist. Another version of this—considered even more ceremonious and usually done when

the hat was not worn or carried—was a bow to the side, in which the right foot (instead of being extended forward) was extended out to the side, with the right toe pointed quite sharply to the right.

A common habit at this time was snuff taking, the eighteenth-century equivalent of cigarette smoking. From an article written by Richard Steele in *The Spectator* and from manuals of deportment from the period, we have the following information about the practice to be observed when one indulged in this habit. Because snuff was extremely expensive, the lid of the snuff box was usually tapped before use so that the grains of snuff that clung to the lid would drop back into the box. The box was usually held in the left hand, tapped with the right, and the spring in the lid pressed with the left thumb. A pinch of snuff was taken with the right thumb and second finger; the box was then closed with the left hand; and the snuff now on the back of the left hand was lifted carefully to each nostril to ensure that none of it was spilled. Finally, the cuff and cravat were flicked with the handkerchief since snuff stains were difficult to remove if they settled on the clothing. Occasionally, a pinch of snuff was applied directly to the nostrils, but regardless of method, it was considered very bad breeding to sneeze at the completion of the operation. The snuff box was kept either in the waistcoat or coat pocket.

Another new ritual of polite society, prized because it fostered the ideal of a homelike and cozy group intimacy, was the serving of chocolate or coffee. (Tea was introduced very late in the eighteenth century.) These refreshments were placed on a tray with the cream and sugar already in them and then served to each guest. *The Cup of Chocolate* by L. M. Van Loo, dating from about 1755, pictures this increasing interest in bourgeois ideals after the middle of the century (Figure 10–8). It also illustrates the seemingly effortless yet calculatedly elegant finger positions and poses that were involved in even such a quiet group ritual as this.

Since the Rococo age was dominated by

Figure 10–8 L. M. Van Loo (Charpentier), *The Cup of Chocolate*, Versailles, c. 1755. Illustrates the elegant overtones of the new domestic manners borrowed from the bourgeois and adopted by the aristocracy during the middle of the eighteenth century. Photo courtesy of the French Musées Nationaux.

feminine taste, the manners and movement of the aristocratic lady were highly cultivated and commented on throughout the nearly sixty years of Louis XV's reign. The most important new item of dress that had to be mastered was the hoop and later the panier; neither looked elegant unless it was managed with dexterity—not an easy task, especially in a high wind. The lady learned to walk with short, smooth steps so that she looked as if she were floating across a room amid other pastel-tinted, satin-clad companions. In standing and walking, the head was held erect; the shoulders were relaxed; and the hands were held in front at the point of the boned bodice, with the palms turned upward and a little inward toward the body.

Since the bodice was stiffly boned, the lady experienced great discomfort unless she held her body upright when seated. In her own chambers, the lady could recline in loose garments with Watteau pleats, but once formally dressed, she had no relief from her stiff position. Though in one of her portraits Madame de Pompadour seems to recline, she would have done so only from the hips because under the profusion of bows on the front of her gown, she would have been heavily corseted.

The one great costume property and

weapon of the age was the folding fan. Though used to create a breeze, to shield the face from the fire, and to ward away insects, it was primarily considered an instrument for expressing personal feelings. All the lady's agreeable manners of high breeding would have been wasted if she used her fan in a bourgeois manner. The fan was used to punctuate a story, to beckon to a gentleman across the ballroom, and to express subtlety, in the language of love, inner emotions that could not be spoken. *The Young Gentleman and Lady's Private Tutor*, written in 1771, summarizes perfectly the purpose of the fan: "What grace the Fan can convey in the hands of a Lady who knows how to use it! It weaves, it twists, it snaps shut, opens, rises, falls—to suit occasion and circumstance. . . . So, too, a woman vulgarly got up, rather dull and plain, becomes supportable if she knows how to wield a Fan and guides its movements knowledgeably."

The decorum of fashionable good manners was so absolute that every young girl spent years preparing for society with the help of her dancing and music master. The most practiced movement was that of the curtsy, which in many ways was similar to the man's bow but with the added problem of gracefully handling the spreading skirts over a hoop or panier. It involved sliding the disengaged foot, usually the right, into the fourth, or front position, pointing the foot slightly outward, bending the knees with the weight evenly distributed; then, without bending the body or shaking, the lady rose onto the extended front foot. The curtsy could be oriented to the left or right, *en passant*, as a type of walking curtsy in which the bending of the knees was merely a pause in the forward movement down a receiving line.

In general, the ladies, like the gentlemen, found excessive formality old-fashioned. The true art of a lady's education in the eighteenth century was, according to the May 15, 1711, issue of *The Spectator*, "to make the Mind and Body improve together . . . to make Gesture follow Thought, and not let Thought be employed upon Gesture."

The Theatre

The staging methods of the eighteenth century were generally like those developed in the preceding Baroque period, although the size of the theatres tended to be larger to accommodate the increased middle-class audience that now attended the theatre. On the Continent, where the tradition of the large Elizabethan theatre had never developed, the forestage was narrow and had no proscenium doors. The action took place on a relatively narrow plane to the front of the raked stage that contained perspective scenery, whose sight lines vanished either center stage or symmetrically to the left or right. The theatre curtain, which closed off the proscenium arch from the auditorium, was raised and lowered only at the opening and the close of every performance; thus, all changes of scenery or "transformations" were made in full view of the audience. The wings and shutters making up the scenery were moved on and off the stage by a chariot system in which small carts, or chariots, on tracks in the basement supported masts moving in slits in the stage floor. The various wings and shutters were then lashed to these moveable masts. The best example of this sytem still working today is found in the Royal Theatre in Drottningholm, Sweden (Figure 10–9). In British theatres— where the action took place on a deeper forestage with most exits and entrances through the two proscenium doors on either side of the stage—wings and shutters were moved on and off the stage by means of tracks or grooves set into the stage floor.

As the eighteenth century developed, scenery gradually moved from the conventionalized temples, palaces, gardens, and prisons of the Baroque theatre to more picturesque and individualized settings painted to look asymmetrical and more historically accurate. Stage lighting also progressed from the conventional placement of chandeliers over the acting area toward more atmospheric effects in both the chiaroscuro of the scene painting and the actual illumination of the

Figure 10–9 Interior of the Royal Theatre, Drottningholm, Sweden, c. 1765. One of the few surviving stages that remains completely equipped with scenery and machinery of the eighteenth century. Photo courtesy of Drottningholm Teatermuseum.

stage. Individual set pieces, drops, and cut-out wings were added to give variety to the stage scene.

Costumes also moved slowly toward more historical accuracy and appropriateness to character. The old-fashioned, stiff-skirted *tonnelet* for classical heroes, ludicrously portrayed in a 1749 engraving of James Quin as Coriolanus, gradually gave way to more nat-ural classical effects of armor and draping. In England, Charles Macklin introduced plaids in a costume for Macbeth, and David Garrick performed Richard III in an approximation of Elizabethan dress. In France, Voltaire working with the famous actor and actress Henri-Louis Lekain and Mademoiselle Clairon brought about many realistic changes in stage dress.

The Plays

In an age in which ideals of casualness, ease, elegance, and sophistication dominated society, comedy, not tragedy, was the primary mode practiced by aspiring playwrights. Though classical tragedies—like those penned by Voltaire—were still written, they tended toward sentiment and melodrama rather than true tragedy; only marginally do they reflect the cultural and artistic outlook of the time. The true representation of the period was found in sentimental comedy whose tone was sharply different from the balanced moderation of Molière and the amoral cynicism of Restoration comedy.

There are many eighteenth-century comic playwrights, like Holberg in Denmark and Goldoni in Italy, whose works are still occasionally performed. Because these playwrights owe a great debt both to the Commedia dell'Arte and to the work of Molière, their work only occasionally reflects the basic characteristics of the Rococo age and its ideals. English sentimental comedies do reflect the bourgeois interest in sentiment that was developing at the time, but only the work of Pierre Carlet de Chamblain de Marivaux captures that mixture of sentiment, delicate love, and pale memories of commedia clowns found in the paintings of Watteau, the true founder of the Rococo style.

In the work of Marivaux, society is in transition. Love, which in Molière played only a secondary role in comedy, now moves into a central position. The characters are no longer symbols of an idea or an attitude but are socially conditioned human beings acting on impulses derived directly from their social

position. Critics have commented that Marivaux was interested in the metaphysics of lovemaking. Certainly his elegance, delicacy of expression, and refined analysis of character place him beyond the erotic dalliance of Rococo artists like Boucher and firmly in the nostalgic, poetic tradition of Watteau. There is no laughter at the expense of love, and always there is an edge of sadness. The action in the plays is less involved with events than with the delicate probing of the characters' emotions, which tell us not only what they feel but also what others think they should feel. The central figures, as in French Rococo theatre, are feminine. This delicate kind of theatre is for the salon, not for the mass public.

Les Fausses Confidences, written and produced in 1737, is typical of Marivaux's work (Figure 10–10). It portrays the scheming servant Dubois working subtly to arrange a marriage between his former master, Dorante, and the beautiful and wealthy Araminte. Dubois informs Araminte that Dorante is madly in

Figure 10–10 Scene from *Les Fausses Confidences* by Marivaux, produced by the Comédie Française, 1977. Simone Eine as Dorante, Jean-François Rémi as Monsieur Rémy, and Paule Noëlle as Marton. A modern production of this famous Rococo play. Photo courtesy of the Comédie Française, photograph by Agence de Presse Bernand.

love with her. Araminte laughingly suggests that if he works for her as a steward and sees her every day, maybe he will be cured of his infatuation. From this point on, Marivaux portrays the gradual awakening of a reciprocal love in Araminte with marvelous skill and exquisite delicacy. Her ambitious mother, a mercenary count, and a comic maid add charming complications, but the major concentration is on the sparkle and interplay of the tender sentiments of love. Though many characters are related to those in Italian comedy, none is a stock figure. All have a graceful life of their own amid the refined atmosphere of upper bourgeois and lower aristocratic society.

The sparkling, glittering, and delicately nimble dialogue, often called *marivaudage,* was often condemned as affected when the plays were first produced. In retrospect, it exactly fits the Rococo style, as does the major theme of all Marivaux's plays—the delicate awakening of love in the hearts of the young. The rhythm of the plays has the same gentle flow found in the compositional line in Watteau's *Les Plaisirs du Bal* (Figure 10–1), and the settings are delicate salon interiors or soft green gardens. Though his plays are difficult to place as comedies, no other playwright devoted to the comedy of love has ever portrayed with more insight and delicacy the subtle shifts of the human heart.

Acting and Directing the Plays

Acting in the eighteenth-century Rococo comedies of manners demanded mastery of the fashionable manners and customs of the day. The actor had to display a perfect body grace, clear, precise speech, and a magnetic, perfectly controlled personality. Since plays during this period were performed on the forestage with the set as background, the actor had to keep the audience in close personal touch with the proceedings on stage. In addition, because stage furniture was used only if absolutely necessary, the actors did most of their performing from a standing position, and there was little attempt at realistic stage pictures. Moreover, because rehearsals were limited, the players seldom gave a full portrayal until after opening night. There were many surprises for both the actors and the audience as the individual players developed their roles subsequent to the first performance.

Acting at the time was a mixture of tradition and innovation, with roles being passed down from one generation to the next. Actors were thus truly innovative when they developed a new approach to a role or made major costume changes. This held true even for new plays, since each actor tended to play a character type rather than an individual.

As the century progressed, acting moved toward greater realism and less traditional formality. Yet certain acting conventions never disappeared: for example, always facing one's audience, exchanging stage positions after a long speech, passing to the right of the person with whom one conversed, holding on to certain vowels in a speech, and intoning verse dialogue. Actors also sought and expected applause after high points in a role, and they emphasized the great speeches by projecting them with greater exaggeration than the dialogue required.

One point should be absolutely clear by now: the comedies of manners of the eighteenth century were quite different in feeling and tone from Restoration comedies, despite certain similarities in setting and subject matter. Too often, eighteenth-century comedy is treated as part of the Restoration style. The best approach for actor and director before settling on a production style is to become immersed in the visual arts of the period until feeling comfortable with, and closely relating to, the interiors, furnishings, and costumes. Then, preferably in costume, the actor should practice the manners of the period before a mirror or a friendly critic. Only when the manners begin to mirror those shown in the pictures of the time is the actor ready to develop fully the personality and character of the role.

In setting the single salon interior for *Les Fausses Confidences,* the designer could use as a source a simplified version of the Salon de la Princesse of the Hôtel de Soubise (Figure 10–5) or any combination of French doors and flats that would give a soft and delicate interior without sharp angles. It is because of the sophisticated delicacy and feminine ambiance of this period that so many interiors are oval or curved rather than square or rectangular. Such shapes would subtly shape the movement of this very feminine play along such appropriate lines. The play could also be done on a very small stage with folding screens placed so as again to give curving and delicate movement patterns to the action. It is also appropriate to have a soft, impressionistic, nature garden *à la Watteau* seen through the French doors that might ring the rear of the set. Such a background, similar to the one seen through the arch in Watteau's *Les Plaisirs du Bal,* would capture perfectly the delicate love sentiment punctuated by pale memories of commedia clowns that is the essence of the work of both Watteau and Marivaux (Figure 10–1).

For costume, Watteau is again a perfect source. The mood in *Les Plaisirs du Bal* would be perfect for the clothing of this play, using soft *peau de soie* or panné velvet to capture the shimmering wrinkles of the Watteau painting (Figure 10–1). Here is the faded melancholy and sweet-sad sentiment that a director wants in the mood for this play, and the soft, delicate colors are exactly right for the lovers and the other lesser characters. Watteau's various melancholy clowns in their pale reflections of the Italian commedia would also be ideal sources for the comic characters in Marivaux, and any number of the costumes and color combinations to be found among the poetic participants in *Les Plaisirs du Bal* would be useful costume sources for this play (Figure 10–1).

If the director wants the mood of the play to come from the acting and language of the production rather than from the visual support, absolute simplicity—a very light touch—is probably the answer, as can be seen in the 1977 production photo from the Comédie Française (Figure 10–10).

PROJECTS AND PROBLEMS

1. Summarize the change in cultural outlook between the reign of Louis XIV and the reign of Louis XV.

2. Why has Rococo art been called the dying fall of monarchy and absolutism?

3. Why has the Rococo period been called an age of feminine sensibility? How does Rococo feminine imagery relate to that in the late Gothic period? Explain the artistic relationships between late Gothic and Rococo styles.

4. What is a *fête galante?* Why was it not used as a subject in late seventeenth-century Baroque paintings? Why are Antoine Watteau's paintings the precursor of a totally new order in art and cultural outlook?

5. Compare Watteau's *Les Plaisirs du Bal* (Figure 10–1) with Rubens's *The Garden of Love* (Figure 7–3). What has happened to most of the Baroque ideals developed by Rubens in the Watteau painting? How would you play each scene? What would be the differences in your movement, performance, and feel and weight of your clothing?

6. Compare *Apollo Attended by the Nymphs* (Figure 10–2) with *Sacrifice to Pan, God of Gardens* (Figure 10–3). What does each say about the cultural ideals and outlook of the patrons who commissioned each? What is the difference in the ideal feminine form depicted in each? How does this form relate to the fashions for women in each of these periods?

7. Why did operatic tastes in the eighteenth century gradually shift from the *opera seria* to the *opera buffa?* How did orchestrations change in the eighteenth century from the methods practiced in the seventeenth century? Why does the early work of Mozart represent the Rococo spirit?

8. After looking at Figure 10–4, describe a typical day in the life of an aristocratic lady during the middle of the eighteenth century. From a careful study of these six engravings, what can you say about the clothing, the movement, the manners, and the personal deportment admired in this period?

9. Describe the game of love during the eighteenth century. What was its relationship to nature?

10. What would be your strongest feeling on entering the Salon de la Princesse in the Hôtel de Soubise (Figure 10–5)? Characterize the social event that might have taken place here. How would it differ in feeling from a similar gathering held in the Salle des Gardes at Versailles (Figure 8–5) during the reign of Louis XIV? Characterize the Rococo ornament in the Salon de la Princessse.

11. How would you sit in, and rise from, the furniture in the Salon de la Princesse (Figure 10–5)? What are some ways that you could capture a truly Rococo feeling in your relationship to the furniture? How is the chair used in Drouais's *Group Portrait* (Figure 10–6)?

12. What was the most dramatic difference between the Baroque clothing styles of the seventeenth century and the Rococo styles of the eighteenth century? How does *The Declaration of Love* (Figure 10–7) differ from the tapestry of Louis XIV meeting the Spanish King Philip IV (Figure 8–9) in clothing, cultural outlook, and background setting? What kind of a play would contain a scene like *The Declaration of Love*? Is it possible to do some of the romantic plays of Shakespeare—such as *As You Like It, Love's Labour's Lost,* and *Twelfth Night*—in Rococo clothing styles? Why or why not?

13. Look closely at the clothing in *The Declaration of Love* (Figure 10–7) and in the *Group Portrait* (Figure 10–6). How would they feel to wear? How can they be worn most effectively? What do they do to shape, movement, and gestures? Why are they similar to, yet quite different from, Restoration clothing (Figures 9–4 and 9–5)?

14. Why was ease in movement and manners so often emphasized in books of deportment and etiquette in the eighteenth century? Why was the dancing master the key figure in teaching the aristocrat proper deportment?

15. Describe how a gentleman took snuff during this period. Look closely at Van Loo's *The Cup of Chocolate* (Figure 10–8) and then act out the process of accepting and drinking a cup of chocolate.

16. What problems for a woman did the panier and high coiffure present? Describe how a lady of the times used a fan. How would a fan help you to act a scene from a play of this period?

17. Draw a diagram of the spatial arrangements in the typical eighteenth-century theatre (Figure 10–9). How did theatres in England differ from those on the Continent? What were the problems in viewing the action on stage from various positions in the auditorium? What were the problems in designing scenery for the various areas of the auditorium?

18. How were transformations handled on the eighteenth-century stage? Why was symmetry such an important part of scenery design? How was it broken and varied to suit the Rococo love for asymmetry? How did lighting methods differ from the seventeenth-century Baroque methods?

19. What happened to stage costume after the middle of the eighteenth century? Why was the older Baroque stage "uniform" gradually discarded? Explain the difference between the old and new forms of stage dress and the difference in how they affected movement and overall performance.

20. Why are the plays of Marivaux so much like the paintings of Watteau?

21. What was *marivaudage*? How do the characters in a Marivaux play differ from those in Molière's comedies or Restoration comedies? Why are Marivaux's plays difficult to perform for a modern audience?

22. How was the audience included in the action of an eighteenth-century play? How much was furniture used in eighteenth-century productions? What were some acting conventions practiced in the eighteenth century?

23. Find a scene from an English or French comedy of the Rococo period and prepare it with some approximations of the props, clothing, and furniture that would have been used in the play's original production. How does the scene differ from one in a Restoration comedy of manners? From one in Molière's comedies?

BIBLIOGRAPHY

Beijer, Agne. *Court Theatres of Drottningholm and Gripsholm.* Translated by G. L. Frolich. Malmö: J. Kroon, 1933. The standard authoritative account of eighteenth-century court theatres in Sweden.

Bernbaum, Ernest. *The Drama of Sensibility: A Sketch of the History of Sentimental Comedy and Domestic Tragedy, 1696–1780.* Cambridge, Mass.: Harvard University Press, 1915. An excellent study of Rococo, with special emphasis on English drama.

Boas, Frederick. *An Introduction to Eighteenth Century Drama, 1700–1780.* Oxford: Clarendon Press, 1953. A fine introductory work on the shift from tearful to high comedy during the eighteenth century.

Burnim, Kalman. *David Garrick, Director.* Pittsburgh, Pa.: Pittsburgh University Press, 1961. An excellent presentation of the directorial innovations of this famous eighteenth-century English actor-manager.

Campbell, Lily Bess. "A History of Costuming on the English Stage between 1660 and 1823," *University of Wisconsin Studies in Language and Literature,* 1918, pp. 187–223. A useful scholarly study of the changes in theatrical dress on the English stage from the time of Shakespeare to the beginning of the nineteenth century.

Faniel, Stéphane, ed. *French Art of the Eighteenth Century.* New York: Simon and Schuster, 1957. An excellent pictorial survey on all aspects of the visual arts during the eighteenth century, with particular attention to the minor arts.

Gay, Peter. *Age of Enlightenment.* The Great Ages of Man Series. New York: Time-Life Books, 1965. Beautifully illustrated with extensive color photography, this concise text for the non-academic reader covers the major artistic, cultural, and intellectual developments of this period.

Goncourt, Edmond and Jules de, eds. *French Eighteenth Century Painters.* New York: New York Graphic Society, 1948. A classic study of eighteenth-century painting in France by two great nineteenth-century critics and novelists.

Green, Frederick C. *Eighteenth Century in France.* New York: Frederick Ungar, 1965. An excellent historical and cultural survey of France during the eighteenth century.

Guérard, Albert. *The Life and Death of an Ideal: France in the Classical Age.* New York: Braziller, 1956.

An important study of the creation of the classical ideal under Louis XIV and its slow death during the eighteenth century.

Havens, George R. *The Age of Ideas.* New York: Holt, Rinehart and Winston, 1955. A very clear summary of the ferment in ideas in the eighteenth century that led to the name Enlightenment and to the first experiments in American and European democracy.

Hawkins, Frederick. *The French Stage in the Eighteenth Century.* 2 vols. 1888. Reprint. Westport, Conn.: Greenwood Press, 1969. An old but still useful book on French theatre during the age of Voltaire.

Kimball, Sidney Fiske. *The Creation of the Rococo.* Philadelphia: Philadelphia Museum of Art, 1943. One of the best books, beautifully illustrated, on the development of this last aristocratic and elegant style before the triumph of bourgeois taste.

Krutch, Joseph W. *Comedy and Conscience after the Restoration.* New York: Columbia University Press, 1949. An excellent look by a famous New York critic at the comedy of conscience in England in the early eighteenth century.

Lancaster, H. C. *French Tragedy in the Time of Louis XIV and Voltaire, 1715–1774.* Baltimore: Johns Hopkins Press, 1950. An excellent study of the decline of the tragic element in serious drama during the age of Voltaire.

The London Stage, 1660–1800. 11 vols. Carbondale: Southern Illinois University Press, 1960–1968. A year-by-year detailed survey of the plays produced on the London stage during the late seventeenth and eighteenth centuries.

Nicoll, Allardyce. *History of the English Stage, 1660–1900.* 6 vols. London: Cambridge University Press, 1955–1959. The first part of this detailed history of the English stage is particularly useful and illuminating in understanding Restoration drama.

Odell, George C. D. *Shakespeare from Betterton to Irving.* 2 vols. New York: Charles Scribner's Sons, 1920. An excellent picture of Shakespearean production on the eighteenth-century stage.

Pedicord, Harry. *The Theatrical Public in the Time of Garrick.* New York: King's Crown Press, 1954. A very readable book on the nature of theatrical audiences in England during the third quarter of the eighteenth century.

Rude, George. *The Eighteenth Century.* New York:

Free Press, 1965. An excellent general history of the period.

Schneider, Isidor, ed. *The Enlightenment*. The Cultures of Mankind Series. New York: Braziller, 1965. An excellent compilation of original eighteenth-century sources on life and culture during the Enlightenment.

Schonberger, Arno, and Soehner, Halldor. *The Rococo Age: Art and Civilization of the Eighteenth Century*. Translated by Daphne Woodward. New York: McGraw-Hill, 1960. A solid and authoritative study of the meaning of art in relation to culture during the eighteenth century.

Smith, Preserved. *Origins of Modern Culture: The Enlightenment, 1687–1776*. New York: Collier Books, 1962. Another excellent study of the cultural and intellectual outlook during the Enlightenment.

Snyder, Louis L. *The Age of Reason*. New York: Van Nostrand, 1955. A very good short survey of the philosophers and intellectuals of the eighteenth century.

Sypher, Wylie. *Rococo to Cubism in Art and Literature*. New York: Random House, 1960. Heavy reading, but an excellent discussion of artistic and literary stylistic methods from the eighteenth century through the early years of the twentieth century.

Thaler, Alwin. *Shakespeare to Sheridan*. Cambridge, Mass.: Harvard University Press, 1922. A standard and still very useful study of performance on the English stage from the early years of the seventeenth century to the close of the eighteenth century.

Turberville, Arthur Stanley, ed. *Johnson's England: An Account of the Life and Manners of His Age*. 2 vols. London: Oxford University Press, 1953. A very useful book that immerses the reader in the life and times of eighteenth-century London.

Neoclassic and Empire Style

The end of the eighteenth century was filled with contradictions in art, philosophy, and cultural outlook. At first glance, it seems that the visual arts and philosophy were traveling in mutually exclusive directions—one emotional and romantic, the other rational and classic—in those years between the decline of the Rococo style and the rise of the more rationally based neoclassic style of the Revolution and the Napoleonic Empire. On closer observation, one discerns that the styles (there was no single style) within European culture in the late eighteenth century were basically *romantic.* The term originated among German critics in their attempts to distinguish between art based on medieval tales of romance and that derived from classical sources. The term was imprecise and vague in its eighteenth-century application and became even more so in the early nineteenth century. The one attribute common throughout all eighteenth-century neoclassic and early nineteenth-century romantic art was the concept of *associationalism*—the rendering of an artistic work, even a classical Greek or Roman one, so that it makes connections through personal or public emotion with the past, the self, or the deeper realities of life. This idea, as demonstrated in a popular comedy of the day, *The School for Scandal;* was also linked to the concept of the "natural man" buried beneath the conventions of society—a concept that is still with us today.

After the American Revolution, the concept of freedom was much discussed in Europe. In artistic circles these discussions led to a great emphasis on inquiry and free expression and to energetic debates about "good" and "bad" art. Especially in architecture, this emphasis on freedom brought about a new criterion of stylistic or aesthetic judgment. Architecture was no longer necessarily good because it was harmonious, proportional, exacting, and carefully structured after the precepts of antiquity. It was now admired because of the emotions it aroused in the viewer. This explains why the same architect

219

could design both a medieval and a classical structure and why the neoclassic arts of the period of Louis XVI are associated in their emotional connections with Greek and Roman rationalism rather than being based on the design precepts of Greek and Roman art.

Let us look at two miniature structures built in the Gardens of the Petit Trianon at Versailles for Marie Antoinette, wife of Louis XVI. *The Temple of Love,* designed by Richard Mique in 1778, was set within the natural *jardin anglais* laid out for the queen so that she could escape from the stultifying formality of Louis XIV's Versailles (Figure 11–1). The garden, with its winding paths, streams, lakes, and grottos, also contains an artificial village, or *hameau* in rustic style, and a mill planned by the painter Hubert Robert and executed by Richard Mique (Figure 11–2).

Though *The Temple of Love* was borrowed directly from classical sources, it was not built primarily as an example of the classical rules of structure, balance, and proportion. It was constructed to stimulate the imagination, to be a place for a rendezvous with love, a haven in the forest where lovers could place their vows before the statue of Cupid. It was associationally rather than structurally conceived and is, therefore, a form of romantic architecture. The mill in the hameau of Marie Antoinette has a totally different architecture. It is asymmetrical with a variety of complex textures and seems vaguely derived from medieval English peasant architecture. Here, escaping from the formalities and traditions of

Figure 11–1 Hubert Robert and Richard Mique, *The Temple of Love,* Gardens of the Petit Trianon, Versailles, 1778. A charming structure based on classical sources to create an association with Venus and Cupid. Photo courtesy of the French Cultural Services, New York.

Figure 11–2 Hubert Robert and Richard Mique, mill in the *hameau,* Gardens of the Petit Trianon, Versailles, 1778. A charming, medieval, peasant structure of mixed textures used by Marie Antoinette to escape from the formalities of court life. Illustrates the beginning of romantic ideals in architecture in which association was more important than structure or design. Photo courtesy of the French Cultural Services, New York.

the court, the queen and her ladies could come for tea, pretending to be shepherdesses or milkmaids. Compared to the classic temple, this structure does look like a romantic, rustic, old mill, though both are associational and emotional in concept.

There are a number of reasons why a delicate form of neoclassicism became prominent in the interior decoration, furnishings, architecture, and paintings of the last decade of the reign of Louis XVI. One was the impetus to classical archaeology that came with the diggings at Herculaneum and Pompeii, begun in the middle of the century. Another was that the renewed interest in classical art stemmed less from concern with its method than from the fact that it represented the ideals of the Enlightenment and was an alternative to the hedonism and decadence of Rococo art. The yearning for regularity, discipline, and pure, clean-cut uncomplicated lines was a reaction against the empty, soft virtuoso Rococo art of the aristocratic courts of Europe and represented the new stoic ideals of the progressive, democratic middle class that was growing in power and importance in the decades prior to the French Revolution.

Jacques Louis David completely captured the imagination of middle-class society when he created *The Death of Socrates* in the years immediately preceding the French Revolution (Figure 11–3). When he argued that art must contribute to the education of the public, he was fully aware that his paintings were associational—propaganda for the political ideals that led to the Revolution. Compare *The Death of Socrates* with Hubert Robert's *The Pont du Gard*, both painted in 1787 (Figures 11–3 and 11–4). The Robert painting, like his work for Marie Antoinette in the Gardens of the Petit Trianon, is picturesque, showing a classical structure in ruins under a romantic sunset, with peasants interestingly placed in the foreground. By depicting the ruins of antiquity, Robert hoped to evoke a pleasant melancholy as one associates the subject matter with the power of the passage of time, the rise and fall of great civilizations, the conti-

Figure 11–3 Jacques Louis David, *The Death of Socrates,* 1787. Illustrates the coldness and austerity of the "new classicism," which was an attempt to associate the stoic virtues of classical antiquity with the new order needed in France. Photo courtesy of the Metropolitan Museum of Art, Wolfe Fund, 1931.

Figure 11–4 Hubert Robert, *The Pont du Gard,* the Louvre, Paris, c. 1787. A painting of romantic ruins that became one of the most popular subjects in late eighteenth-century art. Photo courtesy of the French Musées Nationaux.

nuity of life, and other romantic philosophical concepts. In *The Death of Socrates,* David also appealed to associations with antiquity, but not picturesque ones. He selected a heroic subject in which the individual's principles are more important than the authoritarian forces of the state. Socrates is a Christlike figure surrounded by twelve disciples and represents the founder of the "religion of reason." It is a powerful piece of propaganda whose cold classicism is meant to appeal to the emotions rather than to an intellectual appreciation of classical compositional method.

This new use of classical ideals for fostering propaganda by association, rather than for achieving beauty of proportion and composition, increased with the advent of the French Revolution. Since republicanism and a form of participatory democracy had developed in classical Greece and Rome, the leaders of the French Revolution used all types of classical symbols to represent their political goals. At the close of the Reign of Terror during the loose-living transitional period of the Directory, Napoleon Bonaparte gradually gained total power of the state not only through his military genius but also through his brilliant exploitation of classical symbols that led the country from a republican government with Napoleon as First Consul to a rebirth of imperial Rome with Napoleon as emperor. The change in artistic style between 1795 and 1805 was amazing as weight, grandeur, and the decorative trappings of imperial power gradually replaced simplicity, delicacy, and directness in all the arts.

Napoleon's most ambitious artistic project, the *Arc de Triomphe*, is an example of associational propaganda in its use of classical sources. This structure, begun in 1805 and not completed until the 1830s, was created to dominate the entire western end of Paris of that day; even today it is a truly gigantic monument to the imperial ambitions of Napoleon. Based on the ideal of the Roman triumphal arch, it is much larger, colder, and more militaristic than its classical sources. Rather than evoke associations to Rome, it creates a new nineteenth-century image of a vast, organized military dictatorship. In many ways, it reminds one of Nazi and Soviet monuments. Its decorative ideas, loosely based on Roman methods, are transformed by scale into a symbol of one man's unrestrained ambition for total power in Europe.

Though none of Napoleon's architects was an outstanding figure, Jacques Louis David, the painter of *The Death of Socrates*, was a brilliant designer who developed, with the help of devoted assistants, a complete imperial style in costume, interior decoration, and painting that represented the propagan-

Figure 11–5 Jacques Louis David, *The Coronation of Napoleon*, 1805–07. Although David portrays a rich classical setting, the impression is still that of the nouveau riche participating in an opera ball. Also symbolizes the new eclecticism of nineteenth-century art and culture. The Louvre, Paris. Photo courtesy of the French Musées Nationaux.

distic ideals of Napoleon. David's famous *Coronation of Napoleon* was painted in 1805, the year following Napoleon's assumption of the imperial role (Figure 11–5).

A gigantic work covering five hundred feet of canvas, it consists of many individual portraits organized within a classical setting like the one David designed inside the Gothic cathedral of Notre Dame for the actual coronation. David did a portrait drawing of each head; his assistants roughed in the figures and background, which David then completed. Napoleon is appropriately shown crowning the empress rather than kneeling before the Pope. Both Napoleon and Jose-

phine are heavily idealized, and though even David was incapable of making the crowd of family and friends look like imperial nobility, he clothed the figures in costume designs borrowed from Rome, the Renaissance, and the Baroque seventeenth century; the scene thus has the attractive qualities of an operatic performance. The assignment was an impossible one to fulfill, but David acquitted himself well enough, given the demands of the commission. It may not be a stirring composition, but it does project the new richness, decorative weight, and eclectic borrowing of artistic ideas that constituted the new Empire style.

Music

This period marked a great transition in music from the formalities of the dying classical Baroque style to the tempestuous emotions of the new romanticism. In the works of Mozart and Beethoven, we have the perfect contrast between the lighter effects associated with the age of Louis XVI and the heavier, heroic effects associated with the reign of Napoleon. Mozart, whose earlier work exemplified the superficial qualities of Rococo art, demonstrated a much broader range of realistic emotions in his later operas. In his masterpiece, *Don Giovanni,* composed in 1787, he incorporated the aristocratic charm of the past with the Faustian concepts of good and evil to create an opera that synthesized the older Rococo ideals with the new outlook produced by the Storm and Stress period in German drama and literature after 1775. To those who were soon to support the French Revolution, the central character represented the dissolute nobleman who must be sent to hell before the new order could come about; to the new romantic philosophers, he symbolized the new superman in romantic heroes; and to the older classical enthusiasts, he was the reincarnation of the Promethean hero who defied the gods. Probably Mozart saw the opera merely as an opportunity to tell a marvelous musical story in a high-spirited, comedy-of-manners form with overtones of moral satire and romantic supernaturalism. The pace of the opera is

breathtaking, and the emotional life of the music, while still connected to the forms of the past, takes fire in a way that would have been impossible in the musical drama of the past.

Once the French Revolution removed the old aristocratic forms, the change in music was rapid. In 1798, only eleven years after the first performance of *Don Giovanni,* Beethoven, inspired by the ideals of the French Revolution and by Count Bernadotte, Napoleon's emissary to Vienna, began to develop his third symphony, *The Eroica,* as a compliment to Napoleon, the man he saw as the new hero of liberty. By the time the symphony was finnished in 1804, Napoleon had accepted the title of emperor, and Beethoven had erased his name from the dedication of the title page. The work remains, however, a symbol of the heroism involved in the quest for individual liberty and the cause of popular freedom. Beethoven's only opera, *Fidelio,* exhibits the same theme.

In *The Eroica,* Beethoven, without programmatic dilutions, gave shape to the aspirations of an age. The opening movement employs the sonata form, which was perfected by Haydn and Mozart and involves the reconciliation of opposites. In this sonata form an opening section, called the *exposition,* is followed by a central core of development and then a concluding section, or *recapitula-*

tion. Sometimes an introduction and an epilogue are added. In the exposition, the various antagonistic and contrasting effects are pursued, while in the *development*, the oppositions are made to interact with one another. In the recapitulation, there is a dramatic reconciliation of the opposites. In Beethoven's first movement, this is done on a previously unknown heroic scale. The second movement of Beethoven's work is a funeral march—something that had never been included before in a symphony—and it is a glowing eulogy to the heroic efforts of mankind. Also Beethoven gave the third movement a title, "Scherzo," the first time this had been done in a formal symphony. The finale is composed of monumental variations that stand like the *Arc de Triomphe* over a procession of liberated humanity passing in review. In it Beethoven used a theme he developed earlier in ballet music for *Prometheus;* the image of Prometheus remained with Beethoven throughout his life as a symbol of creative power used for the liberation of mankind from ignorance and bondage. Beethoven's work thus represents the great shift from eighteenth-century, playfully elegant music with set forms to a new dramatic musical power, with great emotional releases but without the weakened form characteristic of much later romantic music.

Life and Cultural Ideals

The end of the eighteenth century wavered between rationalism and antirationalism in its philosophic outlook and was dominated by opposing artistic ideals—one moment demanding a strict classicistic outlook, the next plunging into unrestrained emotionalism. Even the earlier neoclassicism that had developed as a cleansing antidote to the soft decadence of the Rococo style changed from a symbol of progressive, enlightened ideas among upper bourgeois society and the more progressive aristocrats to a symbol of the French Revolution. In a more Roman imperial form, it became a symbol of the French Empire. Throughout this development, romanticism, with all its attendant richness and emotionalism, continued to spread, particularly in Germany and England. In fact, Germany was almost completely dominated by the ideals of romanticism by the close of the eighteenth century.

European culture at this time gradually moved from an emphasis on rational enlightenment ideals through an evolution of sentiment and sensibility to a flood of tempestuous emotionalism. Two key late eighteenth-century essayists, Thomas Jefferson and Jean Jacques Rousseau, brilliantly illustrate the contradictions of this period in their views about education. Thomas Jefferson, though the younger man, had the older, more rational outlook when he insisted in his essay "On History" that the study of history was at the heart of education. He saw history as the record of men aspiring to power, which they used and abused, in their ceaseless attempts to achieve their purposes. He believed that through a study of history men could come to understand the meaning of freedom and thus could learn to use this freedom constructively to shape their own fate. According to Jefferson, if history was presented as dead facts, it was taught incorrectly. History that shows man only as a passive, obedient creature is one-sided and dangerous; its study must stress the active, creative process of making laws that will someday give true freedom to all men. Its purpose is to "enable every man to judge for himself what will secure or endanger freedom."

Though Jean Jacques Rousseau's *Émile* was published as early as 1762, its ideas on education and the rearing of children did not become influential until the last quarter of the eighteenth century. This book also has much talk about freedom, but Rousseau, unlike Jefferson, states that man's passions and emotions must first be cultivated before he can be taught to reason and think. Rousseau says that a child develops, as does society, from animal instincts to a reasoning social being and that education should equip the child for this step-by-step process. A child's passions and emotions must be formed first; only when the child fully understands what he sees and feels should he be taught to read and think rationally. By the time the individual reaches adulthood and is passionately involved in life—affectionate and unaffected—he will also be knowledgeable about the Greeks and Romans and civilization's past history. Thus, Rousseau believed that natural sentiment and feeling must be understood before rational thinking could be applied.

The difference between the educational views of Jefferson and Rousseau represents the gradual, subtle shift in cultural ideals from the rational to the emotional in the later years of the eighteenth century. This shift came full circle as early as 1774 when Goethe published the short epistolary novel *The Sorrows of Young Werther*. Some have said that full-fledged romanticism began with this book; others, that it ushered in the nineteenth century. In this book the outer, rational social world is put aside. Value now comes from within—from the ultimate depths of the mind's nature and structure. Subject is divided from object; the self from the role it plays in society. The true romantic, young Werther, experiences extreme metaphysical isolation and social alienation; the self alone is now seen as the source of order, meaning, value, and identity. In the letters that precede his suicide, three lines

dated October 19 may be taken as typical: "Oh this void! this fearful void which I feel here in my breast!—I often think to myself: if you could press her just once to this heart, just once, then this entire void would be filled."

The period from 1775 to 1815 experienced one of the most complex transitions in the history of Western development, as can be seen in the changing social mores and in literature, philosophy, and art. Let us compare *L'Assemblée au Salon* from the period of Louis XVI with *The Coronation of Napoleon* (Figures 11–6 and 11–5). Both depict social occasions though admittedly a conversation in a drawing room is quite different from a coronation. *L'Assemblée au Salon* has a delicacy, sophistication and elegance that is missing in the early nineteenth-century *Coronation of Napoleon*. People stand, sit, and lean on furniture in ways that still remind us of the elegance of the Rococo period, and the decorative ideals are subtle, cool, sharp, and placed in a very precise manner. In *The Coronation of Napoleon*, there is an overdressed, nouveau riche, masquerade-party atmosphere as if the participants were wearing their rich costumes for the first time. The eighteenth-century occasion seems a natural exercise for born aristocrats; the nineteenth-century scene a dress-up party for the middle class.

The interior of *L'Assemblée au Salon* (Figure 11–6) has the same elegance and sophistication found in a Rococo interior (Figure 10–5) but without the feminine curving lines. Accurately quoted classical wall pilasters frame the room; the paneling is strictly rectangular, interrupted by Roman arches; and the lunettes above the doors contain classical quotations from Greek sculptural friezes and Roman sarcophagi. Yet the effect is not really coldly classical because there is such a controlling, aristocratic delicacy of taste present in all parts of the room. In short, despite the many classical quotations, this room is closer to the aristocratic elegance of a Rococo interior.

Ornament, Interiors, and Furniture

Although the furniture in this neoclassic room also has the same elegance as Rococo furniture, it is now based on straight lines and geometric shapes rather than on the serpentine lines of the earlier part of the century. Straight trumpet legs have replaced the cabriole or curved legs, and the patterned upholstery has a delicate play of strictly symmetrical garlanded floral motifs. The elegance of this furniture matches the elegance of the people using it; an actor should study this engraving carefully in order to understand the connection between pose and furniture weight, shape, and size.

In sharp contrast with the interior of

Figure 11–6 François Dequevauviller, engraving after Lavreince, *L'Assemblée au Salon*, 1784. Illustrates the delicate, aristocratic, classical interiors of the late eighteenth century without the curving feminine lines in ornament and furniture found in Rococo rooms. Photo courtesy of the Metropolitan Museum of Art, Harris Brisbane Dick Fund, 1935.

L'Assemblée au Salon (Figure 11–6) is the bedroom of Napoleon's wife, Josephine, at Malmaison (Figure 11–7). Though there are still many quotations from classical sources, Josephine's bedroom is not delicate and subtly aristocratic but heavy, ornate, and rather oppressive. There may be some touches of noble dignity, but all delicate poetry of design has been lost. There is a nouveau riche, bourgeois touch to all this heavy elegance; and romantic symbolism, straining to break through the formalities of the neoclassic style, is everywhere. The bed reminds one of an imperial Roman military tent, as do the hangings on the walls. The imperial eagle crowns the bed; swans and cornucopias symbolizing the empress decorate the room; the rug relates to wall paintings at Pompeii; and the couch itself is a heavy, ornate version of those found in Roman homes. Not since the period of Louis XIV have interiors and furniture been as solemn and grandiose as those of the Empire style. Though more moderate in England and other countries than in France, furniture of the first fifteen years of the nineteenth century was heavier, bolder, and less subtly elegant and aristocratic than any furniture in the eighteenth century.

Figure 11–7 Percier and Fontaine, bedroom of the Empress Josephine, Malmaison, c. 1800–1810. A heavy, ornate, rather oppressive environment meant to be associated with imperial military tents on the battlefield. Photo courtesy of Giraudon, Paris.

Costume and Accessories

There were also tremendous changes in costume and fashion between 1775 and 1815. Before the American Revolution, women still wore large, complex coiffures, corsets, padding, boning, and several layers of clothing. Yet by the beginning of the Empire period, they were wearing a simple chemise and tunic dress of the softest fabrics without boning, corseting, or padding and crowned by simple classical Greek coiffures. As can be seen in *The Coronation of Napoleon* (Figure 11–5), this sense of female freedom and simplicity began to change under Napoleon, and the artistic fashion ideals of the eighteenth century never

returned. For men, the change was even greater because men had been wearing breeches and hose since the sixteenth century. Now within a period of ten to fifteen years, men adopted the long trousers that had been the garb of the peasant; cut their hair short, letting it wave naturally instead of setting it in curls; and moved to more practical woolens instead of the satins, silks, and velvets of the period before the American Revolution. These changes symbolized the abandonment of the aristocratic ideal in favor of a new bourgeois image.

After the American Revolution, the male

figure became slimmer, with a coat cut away sharply in front to rounded tails at the back. With this coat was worn a waistcoat that now reached only slightly below the waist, tight-fitting knee breeches or culottes over silk stockings, and low-heeled black shoes. The materials were usually delicately colored silks embroidered along the garment edges with silver, gold, and silk threads. The hat was usually three-cornered and edged in braid; the wig, if one was worn, was powdered white or grey and brushed into a roll up from the forehead or into rolled curls over the ears and into a tied queue at the back of the head. At home the wig was replaced by a turban or cap and the coat by a silk dressing gown. Then in the 1780s the *style anglais* made its appearance. Stockings and breeches were replaced by close-fitting riding breeches and boots. The tricorne was replaced with a flat-brimmed traveling hat, a smaller jockey hat, or a bicorne; and woolens replaced silks as the major male fabric. Coats had standing, turnover collars, with skirts cut back even more sharply or stepped back at the waist into tails. Waistcoats were short and frequently double-breasted.

In feminine fashion the *panier* and full *robe à la française* were worn only on formal occasions and then gradually disappeared in favor of various drapings of the overskirt over padding at the waist. Shoes were made of silk and had high heels; when out walking, ladies wore ankle-length skirts and carried walking sticks and parasols. In the last part of the 1770s, coiffures were enormous—built up over frames and pads, held with pins and pomades, and culminating in flowers, fruits, or a frigate in full sail.

By the 1780s, the *style anglais* also was the rage for women. Hoops disappeared, and the gown fell loosely around the body over many petticoats or a bustle pad at the back and was held loosely by a sash. The hair was arranged in loose curls on top or down the back of the head, and the shoulders were covered by a soft scarf, or *fichu*. Long, close-fitted sleeves covered the arms to the wrist, and great straw hats with many ribbons framed the face.

With the coming of the French Revolu-tion, fashion made some violent changes, always related to freedom, classicism, and proletarian ideals. The garb of the revolutionaries usually consisted of the red *Phrygian cap* of the galley slave; a sleeveless, loose-fitting peasant jacket called the *carmagnole;* and long, wide trousers called *sans-culottes*, also worn by peasants and sailors. After the Reign of Terror and during the early years of the Directory, the most radical male fashion figures were called *Incroyables*. They carried heavy, knotted walking sticks; sported unruly, wind-blown hair; hid their jaws in enormous neck-cloths; and wore coats with huge lapels, collars, and long tails; and very tight, often striped, riding breeches with short boots. This ludicrous outfit was completed with a very large beaver cocked hat. This fashion is depicted in *Point de Convention* by Boilly (Figure 11–8).

As the Directory merged into the French Empire, the male costume adopted the long trousers of today, some very snug, others looser in fit. Leather and knitted breeches, very closely fitted and ending in knee-high boots, were also popular; knee breeches and stockings were now limited to court dress. The male fashions in England during this period were known as Regency styles and were set by the dandy Beau Brummel, who prided himself on the spotless linen two-point collar that now rose above the carefully wrapped neckcloth, or *stock*. Frills decorated the shirt front and sleeves; waistcoats were usually double-breasted and showed below the buttoned coat front; and coats had a high-rolled collar, sleeves slightly gathered at the shoulder edge, and long, claw hammer tails. Hair imitated the wind-blown Roman look; headgear was based on variations of the top hat; and caped overcoats were worn for travel. Various fashionable types of the year 1809 can be seen in Debucourt's engraving titled *The Dance Mania* (Figure 11–9).

During the height of the French Revolution, the only changes in female dress came in the casual disarray of the hair, in the use of the fichu and muslin gowns, and in the addition of cockades and sashes in the red, white, and blue colors of the Republic. At the

Figure 11–8 Louis Boilly, *Point de Convention,* c. 1801. Illustrates the extreme neckwear, large lapels, wind-swept hair, and tight boots of the *Incroyables* and the exaggerated fashions of their female counterparts, the *Merveilleuses.* Photo courtesy of Alain de Rothschild.

close of the Reign of Terror, the "antique garb" of the new Republican classicism appeared. The waistline moved up below the breast; corseting disappeared; and the dress, cut very simply in white or pastel muslin or batiste, was held by a ribbon under the breast. Flat slippers replaced high-heeled shoes; the large brim of the straw hat was turned down around the face to form a bonnet; and the hair was done in a loose series of corkscrew curls ar-

ranged in the Greek manner. Women who wore these exaggerated fashions were called the *Merveilleuses* (Figure 11–8).

By 1800 the upper part of the chemise dress became a small, separate bodice with a square neckline; a tunic was frequently worn over the dress like a Greek *peplos;* and the hair imitated various Greek fashions. Heavier fabrics were introduced after the coronation of Napoleon; small, puffed sleeves appeared; and

Figure 11–9 Debucourt, *The Dance Mania,* an engraving showing the dancing of the new waltz in 1809. Illustrates the very physical, revealing fashions of the time and the breakdown of all aristocratic decorum in the animated, swaying movement demanded by the new dance form. Photo courtesy of the Metropolitan Museum of Art, Harris Brisbane Dick Fund, 1935.

for court wear, a heavy, separate train, or *courrobe,* of dark-colored velvet was fastened to trail from the waist (Figure 11–5). The short *Spencer jacket* and a longer *redingote* were worn outdoors; shawls and stoles were still popular; and the poke bonnet fitting close to the face was fashionable. Toward the close of the Empire period, long sleeves returned, and heavier trim began to adorn the sleeves, neckline, and bottom of the skirt.

Manners and Movement

In accord with the instability of the period, there were no set rules for manners and movement from 1775 to 1815. Instead, they tended to be developed by the strong personalities of the moment. Marie Antoinette, Madame de Tallien, the Empress Josephine, Pauline and Hortense Bonaparte, Beau Brummel, Napoleon, and George IV, to name a few, influenced the life of the times and had many fashionable followers. In general, good society still followed eighteenth-century precepts like those given by Lord Chesterfield; his notes on good manners were still edited and published well into the nineteenth century. By the early nineteenth century, his advice, originally aimed at the upper middle class, was also adopted by the aristocrats.

Though artificial court manners remained in France in the 1770s and early 1780s, men gradually set them aside in favor of an air of good breeding, gentility, and gentlemanly carriage. The one thing that was to be universally shunned in good society was awkwardness. Good bodily carriage came from the right training and exercise in childhood; great emphasis was placed on riding, gymnastics, dancing, and physical coordination, and the final ideal was a perfect ease, without stiffness on the one hand or a lounging casualness on the other.

The gentleman's day during the more stable Empire period in France and the Regency period in England was divided into clearly defined periods, each of which had an appropriate dress. Morning attire for the promenade usually consisted of a dark tailed coat and a patterned dark or light waistcoat, with dark trousers for winter and light for summer. Accessories were very important. Unsoiled gloves, a handkerchief, clean boots, spotless white linen, a spotless hat lining, a fashionable cane, and an umbrella for bad weather were all carefully chosen. The last two items gave much needed employment to the hands during conversation, since it was considered very bad form to gesticulate while speaking. In the afternoon, calls were usually made or the club visited, and darker clothing was usually in order. In the evening, the latest style pioneered by Beau Brummel was a midnight blue coat with white or off-white waistcoat and form-fitting trousers. Evenings were spent at parties, at fashionable gambling casinos, or at the theatre.

The rules for walking, standing, or sitting were brief. One was supposed to stand with both legs straight or possibly with one knee slightly relaxed. In walking, the leg was moved easily and firmly from the hip without swaying or rocking, and it was still thought elegant to turn the feet and legs out slightly. In sitting, the man was not to perch on the edge of the chair or lounge back into it but ease himself into a relaxed and dignified place at its center. Crossing the legs was allowed but not hugging of the knees.

Female manners during this period also moved away from formality and artificiality to greater naturalness and freedom. The new fashions were so formless that ladies appeared to be in *negligée,* and this new physical freedom was reflected in every aspect of female activity. Unaffected grace and simplicity of manner now replaced artificiality. Women even engaged in gymnastics and exercised with Indian clubs and chest expanders. The new dances of the early years of the nineteenth century also reflected the new freedom and abandon in female movement (Figure 11–9). The emphasis was on learning the dance steps and keeping time to the music, not on learning how to bow or how to enter or leave a room.

Like men, women were not to sit stiffly in a chair. The lady was advised to sink gently into the chair, neither lounging nor sitting on the edge of her seat. In walking, the lady was advised to keep head erect and chest expanded and to follow the natural rhythm of the body in motion with arms moving in opposition to the motion of the legs. The only caution was to control the length of the step. When walking with a gentleman, the lady now took his arm rather than his hand. Much of this deportment was now taught by a master of posture and movement rather than by a dancing master. A lady then practiced the precepts during her morning promenade, afternoon carriage drive or equestrian ride, sherry and dinner hour, evening ball, or theatre engagement. In addition, the formal and complex bow of the eighteenth century now all but disappeared except during a few formal dances. It was replaced by a slight bending from the waist on the part of the man making a formal greeting to a lady and with a soft sinking on the part of the lady, since Directory and Empire styles prohibited the deep curtsy. In fact, during the first two decades of the nineteenth century, the bow was more and more replaced by the middle-class salutation of shaking hands.

The Dance Mania created in 1809 during the Empire period (Figure 11–9) shows the breakdown of all aristocratic decorum not only in movement and personal relationships between male and female but also in the dance—from a classical game plan to a romantic physical closeness, from a minuet to a waltz. Body movement is physical, swaying, and exaggeratedly active, and the clothing sharply accentuates the physical attributes of both male and female. The whole scene has a swinging, inelegant, physical looseness that symbolizes the rather heavy-handed manners and customs of the Empire and Regency periods.

The Theatre

The theatre during these transitional years also experienced many dramatic changes, including a greater variety in visual effect from play to play; more realism and authenticity in settings, costumes, lighting, and acting; and a broadening of the audience base to include not only the aristocratic and upper-middle classes but also the lower-middle classes and nobility. Thus theatres became larger and larger, both on stage to accommodate the increasing visual spectacle demanded by the varying social perspectives of the audience and in the auditorium to accommodate the increased size of this audience (Figure 11–10). Scenery became more asymmetrical in order to make it more realistic, varied, and histor-

Figure 11–10 Pugin and Rowlandson, interior of Drury Lane during an 1808 performance, from *Microcosm of London* by Ackermann. Illustrates the enormous size of English theatres at the opening of the nineteenth century to accommodate stage spectaculars and the large mass audience. Photo courtesy of the Metropolitan Museum of Art, Harris Brisbane Dick Fund, 1917.

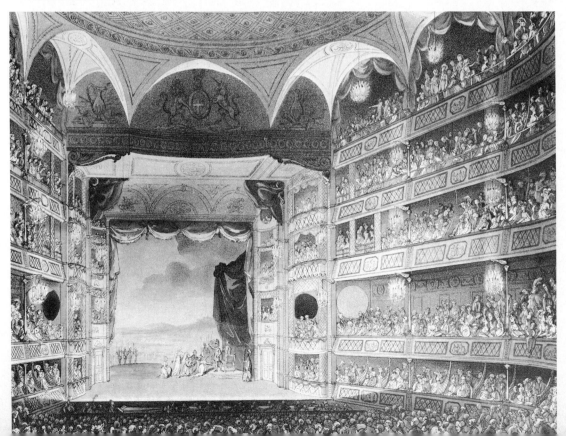

ically accurate. Asymmetry within the painted wings and even in the arrangement of the wings was more and more common. Moody lighting effects were now painted into the wings and drops to create romantic and emotional atmospheric effects; separate set pieces were frequently included on stage with the standard wing and drop arrangement, and even cut-out transparent drops were occasionally used to increase pictorial variety of mood.

A view of Drury Lane before it burned in 1809 reveals a large theatre with five levels of galleries, but relatively plain, without the decoration of the French houses of the late eighteenth century (Figure 11–10). The scene depicted on the stage is large and spectacular; the actors look small; many are needed to fill the stage; and the painted backdrop is less conventional and more realistic than any painted in the eighteenth century.

For information about costumes during the transitional period, look at the engraving based on a famous painting by G. Harlowe

Figure 11–11 Engraving based on the painting by G. Harlow showing a scene from an 1819 production of *Henry VIII*. Depicts members of the Kemble family—Charles Kemble as Cromwell, John Philip Kemble as Cardinal Wolsey, Stephen Kemble as Henry VIII, and Mrs. Siddons as Queen Katherine—in a performance dominated by the large-scale acting style that was developed to fill the large stages of the early nineteenth century. Photo courtesy of the Norman Philbrick Library, photograph by Fred English.

from the end of the Regency period in England, depicting members of the famous Kemble family in a performance of Shakespeare's *Henry VIII* (Figure 11–11). Mrs. Siddons as Queen Katherine is wearing a queenly robe with wide sleeves made of ermine that has no specific period style, though it does have an Empire waist. Stephen Kemble, who plays Henry VIII, wears a costume like that in the Holbein portraits; Charles Kemble as Cromwell, seated at the table center, wears a Byronic collar and jacket—the contemporary symbols for a romantic poet. John Philip Kemble as Cardinal Wolsey wears authentic clerical robes, but they are contemporary rather than sixteenth century. Finally, the courtiers wear a mixture of sixteenth-century Holbein, seventeenth-century Van Dyck, and contemporary fashions, blended together to create a pleasing theatrical mélange. Though great strides have been made in achieving historical accuracy in period dress, the individual actor's sense of fashion and theatricality still triumphs.

The Plays

The School for Scandal by Richard Brinsley Sheridan brilliantly illustrates the ideals of the last quarter of the eighteenth century. Though written as early as 1777, it neatly balances the old and tainted aristocratic order of life and morality with the new order based on simplicity, directness, natural feeling, and sensibility.

Sheridan's approach to play structure is closer to the nonclassical form of Elizabethan comedy than to the simple plot lines of Molière. There are major and minor plot lines, which at first have little connection but gradually entwine to a common resolution. The play carries its audience with an easy casualness and control through fourteen different scenes in four different locations. In the famous Screen Scene, all conflicts are brought together and resolved in a single comic moment. With the revelation of Lady Teazle behind the screen, all the loose ends are tied together, and the play has the expected happy conclusion.

The most fully developed characters are Joseph and Charles Surface and Sir Peter and Lady Teazle, while the scandalmongers are brilliantly suggested through their names and an attribute or two. Charles and Maria represent the new order of simplicity and directness found in neoclassic romanticism. The members of the "school" set the tone of the play, give much needed exposition, initiate much of the conflict, and supply unity and point to the plot. In many ways, they are the freshest and most humorous part of the play. Although their viciousness is too superficial to be a real threat to the leading characters, they are always available as a type of chorus to assist in complicating or untangling the action. Note also that whenever there is an ambiguity of motivation, Sheridan allows direct asides to the audience.

Like Molière's *Tartuffe*, this play deals with the unmasking of hypocrisy, though it has a much lighter tone than the Molière piece. Joseph Surface is never the threat to the other characters that Tartuffe is. This light touch reflects the difference in social outlook between seventeenth- and eighteenth-century society. The play's defense of the "natural man" against the older aristocratic order puts it squarely on the side of the present and future, not the past.

The tone of the play is one of polished wit and clever repartee. Far removed from the language of everyday life, such conversational brilliance reflects that of the sophisticated in upper-class British society, which, although wealthy and admired, was beginning to appear rather artificial and useless. The rhythm of the play, like the language, is fast-moving, depending primarily on the actors and only peripherally on the vagaries of the plot complications.

The visual requirements are not complex, as a look at the Screen Scene, recorded in an engraving of the original performance at Drury Lane in 1778, testifies (Figure 11–12). The costumes closely approximate those worn by members of the audience; the wings and shut-

Figure 11–12 The Screen Scene from *The School for Scandal* by Sheridan, produced at the Drury Lane Theatre, London, 1778. Illustrates the use of the forestage, proscenium doors, stage boxes, clearly defined wings, and contemporary dress in this comedy of manners set in fashionable London interiors of the eighteenth century. Photo courtesy of the Crown Copywright, Victoria and Albert Museum.

ters suggest a three-walled interior; and the stage has a wide apron and proscenium doors. Set pieces and properties not actually used are painted on the set. In short, at this moment in the theatre, attempts to stress realism and pictorial variety were still limited.

Acting during the last quarter of the eighteenth century and the first years of the nineteenth century was also in a period of transition. Though still reflecting the elegance and formality of the neoclassical style, it was moving toward a more natural, emotional, instinctive expression of feeling that culminated in the tempestuous performances of the succeeding romantic style. Garrick led the way

Acting and Directing the Plays in the 1750s and 1760s with his emphasis on more rehearsals, more reality, and the need for actors to listen to each other, to speak verse with natural rather than exaggerated rhythms, and to express a very individual personality rather than a generalized heroic symbol. By the turn of the century, historical accuracy in setting and dress improved, and performances attempted an uneasy balance between classical and romantic ideals as exemplified by the acting of Kemble in England and Talma in France. Kemble and Talma stressed individuality, strong emotion, and personal feeling but within a framework of stateliness, dignity, grace, and grandeur. As with architecture and sculpture, theirs was a romantic and personal version of Greek and Roman classicism. Look again at the engraving based on a painting of a performance of *Henry VIII* in 1819 (Figure 11–11). There is a certain stateliness and grandeur still at work here, but it is overshadowed by the rather exaggerated and melodramatic gestures that break through this stateliness and underline the powerful emotions projected, in particular, by Mrs. Siddons as Queen Katherine. Here we are on the threshold of the full romantic performances of the English actor Edmund Kean and the German actor Ludwig Devrient.

But how should one act in plays and performances outside the heroic or tragic tradition, particularly in *The School for Scandal*, written early in this transitional period? The actor must first remember that the Baroque concept of decorum, or the ability to act at all times within the social conventions of the day, was still active in high society in 1777, although the concept of the "natural man" was fast replacing it. In *The School for Scandal*, Charles and Maria are the strongest symbols of this new way of thinking. They must be played so that they express their natural personalities in speech and movement and stand directly against the mannered posing and artificiality of Lady Sneerwell, Mrs. Candour, Sir Benjamin Backbite, and Snake. Characters like Sir Peter and Sir Oliver who represent a balance between the old and new must be played accordingly.

Since all the characters except the servants are from the leisure class, whose aim in life was to live pleasurably, the modern actor must develop an urbanity and sophistication that may be foreign to him. This can only be done by reading about the life of the times and looking at scenes of aristocratic life. An actor must study the clothing of the day, think carefully about the gestures and poses that will project it to advantage, and imagine what it would be like to enter, move, and sit within the interior decoration of the 1770s and 1780s. Particularly important, he should practice sitting in reproductions of neoclassic furniture. Only with long and careful practice can a contemporary actor handle furnishings as if they were an extension of his manners and personality.

Designing the Plays

In presenting a contemporary production of *The School for Scandal*, the director must decide whether to echo the visual methods of the original production or to use one of a number of possible current approaches. A certain sophisticated charm often can be achieved through a combination effect: the use of wings and back shutters changed in full view of the audience by liveried servants while the painting technique on the wings and shutters reflects a contemporary approach to the architectural ornamentation.

There are other approaches, of course. The scenes could be designed as realistic, period box sets, for example; or the play could be done in the round with carefully chosen period furniture, on a thrust stage with only a suggestion of eighteenth-century decor backing the action, on an open stage with a few architectural set pieces underlining the tone of the play, or with a permanent eighteenth-century architectural framework with only the furniture shifted from scene to scene. All these approaches should aim to capture the casual elegance and light informality of the eighteenth-century English social world that is the basis for the play (Figure 11–12).

There are roughly two ways that a designer can take toward designing costumes for this play: one, a detailed, psychologically based character approach; the other, a more limited, abstract, decorative approach, in which individual designs are less important than the overall mood and period style. Whatever the approach, the casualness, elegance, and artificiality of the culture should be clearly evident. Fabrics for the most part should be crisp, shiny, and brittle with soft accents of lace and velvet. Color should be light and gay with a few darker accents in the trim. Lower-class characters should be in darker, earthier tones. The line and shape of the costumes should reflect both the soft, sentimental clothing worn by the younger women of the time and the more formal, artificial clothing of the older social leaders of the day. A designer should refer particularly to the paintings of Gainsborough, where one finds the soft lines and fabrics reflecting the new sentimental romantic ideals, side by side with the hard lines and fabrics, reflective of a more brittle and formal artificial society. By examining the conflicting styles of this period, a designer will learn how to create humor in costume through artful exaggeration. For example, Lady Teazle's naïve attempts to fit into society and the crass and overbearing personality of a Lady Sneerwell or a Mrs. Candour can be nicely illuminated by subtle exaggerations of costume line.

PROJECTS AND PROBLEMS

1. Why can we say that the neoclassicism of the late eighteenth and early nineteenth centuries was "romantic" in origin?

2. What is meant by the term *associationalism?* Why is it the basis of all romantic art?

3. How does associationalism work in architecture? How could *The Temple of Love* (Figure 11–1) and the medieval mill (Figure 11–2) have been built at the same time on the grounds of Versailles? Describe the feeling or mood each creates. What was the reason for building such completely different structures for Marie Antoinette?

4. What do *The Temple of Love* (Figure 11–1) and the mill (Figure 11–2) communicate about the cultural mood in late eighteenth-century France? Why is this period just before the French Revolution difficult to explain? How could these architectural toys be used in a play?

5. What was the associational symbolism behind the use of simple, cool, classical ornament in interior decorating and architecture in the last quarter of the eighteenth century?

6. Why was *The Death of Socrates* (Figure 11–3) considered propaganda for the French Revolution? Why was it such a shock after Rococo style paintings (Figure 10–1)? Describe the "acting" in *The Death of Socrates* and compare it to that in *The Declaration of Love* by de Troy (Figure 10–7). Describe the mood and outlook in *The Death of Socrates* and relate them to a scene in a play.

7. Compare the David painting (Figure 11–3) with *The Pont du Gard* (Figure 11–4). What is the difference in outlook, subject matter, mood, and technique? How could both have represented the cultural outlook of the time? Imagining each painting as a scene from a play, describe the story line, characters, and mood of each play. How would you act and feel in a play written by David? In one written by Robert?

8. How did the classical ideals of David become transformed into the Napoleonic ideals and outlook of the Empire period? Summarize the differences between the classicism of the pre-Revolutionary years and that of the Empire period. How did Napoleon use the classical ideal to further his own ambition?

9. Look at *The Coronation of Napoleon* (Figure 11–5). What is the mood of this great event? What kind of actors are participating in this large, operatic scene? Describe the clothing and stage properties. Do they remind you of things you have seen before? Explain.

10. What would it be like to participate in a production staged in the same manner as *The Coronation of Napoleon* (Figure 11–5)? What would be its effect on the audience? How does this painting differ from earlier royal groupings (Figures 8–9 and 9–6)?

11. Why was it possible for Mozart's *Don Giovanni* to rise completely beyond the typical mid-

eighteenth-century ideals of his early music? What is the difference between the late music of Mozart and the work of Beethoven? How is Beethoven's *Eroica* a symbol of the cultural ideals that led to the French Empire?

12. Compare the educational ideals of Jefferson and Rousseau. How are they similar? How are they different? What do they tell us about the changing philosophic ideals during this transitional period? Why did Rousseau believe that reason should be the last faculty to be trained rather than the first?

13. Why has it been said that the nineteenth century began with the publication of Goethe's *The Sorrows of Young Werther*? What problems were presented by the romantic belief that all values come from within the soul of an individual? Why are the modern feelings of isolation and social alienation associated with the development of romanticism?

14. Compare the world represented in *L'Assemblée au Salon* (Figure 11–6) with that in *The Coronation of Napoleon* (Figure 11–5). What is the major change that has taken place? Imagining yourself as an actor or actress in the drawing room scene, try to feel the personalities and cultural outlook of the people involved. Do the same with *The Coronation of Napoleon*. What differences in acting and performance are required?

15. Look closely at *L'Assemblée au Salon* (Figure 11–6). Why, even though the decoration and ornamentation are classically inspired, does the scene feel and look more like the eighteenth-century Rococo style than Josephine's Empire bedroom at Malmaison (Figure 11–7)? Describe the people, clothing, furniture, and decoration in *L'Assemblée au Salon* (Figure 11–6). Do the same for the bedroom at Malmaison.

16. Only eleven years separate *L'Assemblée au Salon* (Figure 11–6) from *Point de Convention* (Figure 11–8), yet major changes in feeling, cultural outlook, and relationship to the body have occurred, particularly for women. Describe what has happened. How would you feel wearing the costumes in *Point de Convention*?

17. Why was there a shift in personal manners from rules of conduct to mere "good taste" between the eighteenth and nineteenth centuries? What was considered the best training for children and youth in preparing them for good manners and movement?

18. Approximate the clothing of the period and then practice standing, sitting, and walking while wearing it. What great differences in movement did you experience when you wore a gown of 1785 versus a gown of 1805? What happened to the curtsy and the bow during this period?

19. How do the movements and positions differ for the persons in *L'Assemblée au Salon* (Figure 11–6) and *Point de Convention* (Figure 11–8)? Play the part of a person in each scene. Analyze the costume you are wearing, and describe exactly what it does for your movement. Do the same for *The Dance Mania* (Figure 11–9).

20. Though *The Dance Mania* (Figure 11–9) may be somewhat exaggerated, it does represent the new physical movement in the early nineteenth century. Try to approximate it by dancing the new waltz of the times. Then compare its movements with those of the minuet.

21. Characterize a theatrical performance at the close of the eighteenth century and the beginning of the nineteenth century. What has happened to stage settings since the middle of the eighteenth century (Figures 10–9 and 11–10)? How has the increased size of the theatres influenced acting?

22. Characterize acting in the early years of the nineteenth century by looking at the painting of Mrs. Siddons in *Henry VIII* (Figure 11–11). Describe the stage costume and the blocking of the scene.

23. Why is *The School for Scandal* a symbolic bridge between aristocratic classicism and the new romanticism? Do a scene from the play using a specific piece of furniture to make comic points. Do the same with a snuff box, eye glass, handkerchief, cane, or hat.

24. Why is the Screen Scene (Figure 11–12) from *The School for Scandal* so symmetrical? Would it be better if it were blocked asymmetrically into a room that was also asymmetrical? What is the relationship of the actors to each other? To the set? To the audience?

25. Why would it be difficult to change the period of *The School for Scandal* by playing it in different costumes?

BIBLIOGRAPHY

Apra, Nietta. *Empire Style, 1804–1815*. London: Orbis Publishing Co., 1972. A beautifully illustrated volume in full color depicting the ornament, fabrics, interior decorations, and furnishings of the Napoleonic era.

———. *The Louis Styles, Louis XIV, Louis XV, Louis XVI*. London: Orbis Publishing Co., 1972. Another beautifully illustrated volume in full color covering decorative design in France from 1660 to 1790, with especially good treatment of the period from 1775 to 1790.

Canaday, John. *Mainstreams of Modern Art*. New York: Holt, Rinehart and Winston, 1959. Covers European and American art from the American Revolution to the middle of the twentieth century and gives much valuable information on neglected subjects like the French salon.

Clark, Kenneth. *The Gothic Revival*. New York: Charles Scribner's Sons, 1929. A fascinating study of the change from classical to medieval sources in architecture during the middle of the eighteenth to the end of the nineteenth centuries.

Downer, Alan S. "Players and the Painted Stage: Nineteenth Century Acting," *PMLA* 61 (1946): 522–76. A fascinating article on nineteenth-century acting in relation to the theatre, architecture, and stage settings of the day.

Faniel, Stéphane, ed. *French Art of the Eighteenth Century*. New York: Simon and Schuster, 1957. Survey of the visual arts of the eighteenth century.

Friedlander, Walter F. *From David to Delacroix*. Cambridge, Mass.: Harvard University Press, 1952. An excellent picture of the shift from the cold classicism of David to the tempestuous emotion of Delacroix.

Gay, Peter. *Age of Enlightenment*. The Great Ages of Man Series. New York: Time-Life Books, 1965. Covers the major artistic, cultural, and intellectual developments of the period.

George, A. J. *The Development of French Romanticism*. Syracuse, N.Y.: Syracuse University Press, 1955. A very interesting and scholarly look at the rise of romanticism in the French theatre from the late eighteenth century until its triumph in the second quarter of the nineteenth century.

Green, Frederick. *Eighteenth Century in France*. New York: Frederick Ungar, 1965. Cultural and historical survey of France during the eighteenth century.

Hamlin, Talbot F. *Greek Revival Architecture in America*. New York: Oxford University Press, 1944. A fascinating look at the revival of Greek architecture in the United States to symbolize the republic as the inheritor of the democratic traditions of ancient Greece.

Hofmann, Werner. *The Earthly Paradise: Art in the Nineteenth Century*. Translated by Brian Battershaw. New York: Braziller, 1956. An interesting survey of some little-known works of art and architecture.

Honour, Hugh. *Neoclassicism*. Harmondsworth, England: Penguin Books, 1968. An excellent study of the revival of neoclassicism at the end of the eighteenth and the beginning of the nineteenth centuries, with a clear picture of the romantic associational basis of the style.

Lacey, Alexander. *Pixérécourt and the French Romantic Drama*. Toronto, Canada: University of Toronto Press, 1928. A dated but still interesting picture of the rise of French melodrama and its relationship to romantic tragedy.

The London Stage, 1660–1800. 11 vols. Carbondale: Southern Illinois University Press, 1960–1968. A year-by-year detailed survey of the plays produced on the London stage during the late seventeenth and eighteenth centuries.

Melcher, Edith. *Stage Realism in France from Diderot to Antoine*. Bryn Mawr, Pa.: Bryn Mawr College, 1928. An interesting study of the slow rise to realism in the French theatre at the same time as the development of middle-class industrialism.

Nicoll, Allardyce. *History of the English Stage, 1660–1900*. 6 vols. London: Cambridge University Press, 1955–1959. The first part of this study is useful in understanding Restoration drama.

———. *The Garrick Stage: Theatre and Audience in the Eighteenth Century*. Edited by Sybil Rosenfeld. Manchester: Manchester University Press, 1980. A posthumous work by the great British theatre historian that gives an excellent survey of the theatre in England in the late eighteenth century.

Novotny, Fritz. *Painting and Sculpture in Europe, 1780–1880*. Pelican History of Art Series. Baltimore: Penguin Books, 1960. Gives a clear picture of the arts in Europe during the rise of the Industrial Revolution.

Odell, George C. D. *Shakespeare from Betterton to Irving*. 2 vols. New York: Charles Scribner's Sons, 1920. An excellent picture of Shakespearean production on the Restoration stage.

Rosenbaum, Robert. *Jean-August-Dominique Ingres.* New York: Abrams, 1967. A solid study of the great traditionalist in the style of David whose underlying drives were often mannerist and romantic.

Rude, George. *The Eighteenth Century.* New York: Free Press, 1965. An excellent general history of the period.

Sypher, Wylie. *Rococo to Cubism in Art and Litera-* *ture.* New York: Random House, 1960. An excellent discussion of artistic and literary stylistic methods from the eighteenth century through the early years of the twentieth century.

Thaler, Alwin. *Shakespeare to Sheridan.* Cambridge, Mass.: Harvard University Press, 1922. Study of performance on the English stage from the early years of the seventeenth century to the close of the eighteenth century.

Romantic Style

As the culture of the old aristocratic monarchy died and was replaced by the nouveau riche imperialism of Napoleon, artists, writers, and intellectuals became extremely fearful of the instability of this new bourgeois society. The rationalism that had been growing in European society since the Renaissance and that culminated in the ideals of the Enlightenment suffered a tremendous setback during the French Revolution and the Napoleonic period that followed. With the coming of industrialization and the end of agrarian, aristocratic feudalism, intellectuals realized that a whole way of thinking about life and society was coming to an end. With this bustling, capitalistic, industrial way of life came a sense of finally being removed from the direct inheritance of Greek and Roman classical ideals. Though Greek and Roman art, literature, and philosophy were still studied, these subjects were viewed as part of past times and not as a direct and immediate inheritance. Coupled with this came a sense of loneliness and alienation from the new industrial way of life. Artists and intellectuals, cut off from the cultivated appreciation of aristocratic patrons and thrown upon the mercies of the marketplace, made a determined attempt to escape into those past times and faraway places that were the most picturesque, exotic, and emotional or into an inner world of private feeling.

In opposing the coarse formalities and banalities of the new social order, romantics set themselves up as seers and geniuses who were above and beyond society—individualistic, feeling messengers who brought, from the great cosmic universe beyond and the world within, the truths on which man should act. Just as the eighteenth-century Enlightenment had worshiped reason, so the new nineteenth-century romanticism worshiped the sublime; that is, anything that triggered in the human being emotions so powerful and ideal that they dominated one's entire personality and being. This included a more emotional identification with nature in all her moods, as well as with the ugly and the gro-

243

tesque if they stimulated powerful and dynamic responses. This sense of the inexpressible was conveyed by all possible means in art and literature, but since classical structure was frowned upon, the romantics could not use its technique and method for expressing their personal and subjective views of life. In general, inspiration now came less and less from Greek and Roman sources and more from medieval, oriental, Islamic, and barbaric cultures, since they were believed to speak to the emotions more readily than did the ancient, classical world. Romanticism thus moved from the gentle sentiment and picturesque beauty of the eighteenth century to the wild and sublime in the early nineteenth century.

An outstanding painter from the period was Eugène Delacroix, a slightly younger artist and very close friend of the painter Théodore Géricault. He became the greatest representative of the romantic style in France, despite his opposition to formlessness and excess and his refusal to surrender to the irrational and the emotional at the expense of form and composition. In his devotion to the divine and the terrible in subject matter, Delacroix was the quintessential romantic. In his depiction of themes from literature and poetry, he seemed to place himself in a strange and impulsive rivalry with the written word. In fact, in the romantic age, much painting was programmed to tell a story in much the way that romantic music was programmed to express the emotional climaxes in a piece of literature. The result in the paintings of Delacroix is a theatrical and often melodramatic staging on canvas of violent and disturbing human events, real and imaginary, for electrifying the feelings of the viewer.

For example, this grand, operatic pictorialization is evident on a colossal scale in *The Death of Sardanapalus*, painted in 1827 (Figure 12–1). The work was inspired by Lord Byron's narrative poem "Sardanapalus" and the play he derived from it. It depicts the last hour of an ancient Assyrian king who, upon learning of the defeat of his armies and the immediate

entry of the enemy into his city and palace, has all his goods and concubines brought in and then commands that they be set afire in a giant funeral pyre. The king presides over the panorama of destruction like an omen of evil, as his women are murderously dispatched by his slaves. This carnival of destruction and horror is glorified by rich, emotional color, violent poses, thick pigment, and strong contrasts of dark and light. The entire work symbolizes the stage ideals of the period with their stress on asymmetrical blocking, exaggerated theatricality, rich pictorialism, and emotionally violent acting. In mixing nude females, rearing horses, and black slaves with knives, the painting underlines the sado-masochistic tendencies of romanticism. An actor and a director, asked to undertake one of the inflated theatre pieces of the period, should study a painting like this to determine what excesses are needed in order to make the play acceptable on the stage.

Delacroix unfortunately lacked a new technique for expressing his tempestuous ideas and had to rely on the methods used by Rubens and other operatic Baroque painters of the early seventeenth century. In England, however, a landscape painter, J. M. W. Turner, invented a technique of scrubbed, "hot" pigment that seemed to create "visions painted with tinted steam." His charting of the most violent and powerful emotions within the universe is very romantic and reminiscent of the romantics' favorite scene from Shakespeare: King Lear mingling his wrath with that of the universe. Turner is thus the manic artist of romanticism, representing as he does the "highs" in one's experience of nature. *The Slave Ship*, painted in 1839–40, superficially concerns an incident that Turner had read about in which a captain jettisoned the slaves on his ship when disease broke out, since he was insured against loss at sea but not against disease (Figure 12–2). What the viewer sees, however, is an apocalyptic, cosmic catastrophe that seems to engulf us all. The moralistic story on which paintings from this period were

Figure 12–1 Eugène Delacroix, *The Death of Sardanapalus,* 1827. Illustrates the exotic subject matter, violent movement, rich color, and loose, thick brushwork found in the developed work of this leading French romantic artist. The Louvre, Paris. Photo courtesy of the French Musées Nationaux.

often based is lost here in an emotional release that is truly symbolic of the romantic love of the terrible and the sublime.

In Germany, the opposite emotional, psychological current is found in the paintings of Caspar David Friedrich, who depicted a silent, melancholy, depressing, quiet view of nature. Friedrich is thus the depressive artist of nature, while Turner is the manic. In *Cloister Graveyard in the Snow*, one sees through the leafless, wind-blasted trees in a snow-cov-

ered cemetery, a funeral cortège like the one that bore Ophelia to her burial in *Hamlet* (Figure 12–3). There is a ruined Gothic chapel in the background, the symbols of death are everywhere, and the silent melancholy of the scene sinks into one's very bones. Just as important to the romantic spirit as was the violent and the sublime was an obsession with death. Influenced by Goethe's *The Sorrows of Young Werther*, painters and poets began to create heroes and heroines who meditated on

Figure 12–2 Joseph Mallord William Turner, *The Slave Ship,* 1839–40. Illustrates the tempestuous, "scrubbed-in" brushwork of Turner through which he expressed the cosmic power behind the elements of air, fire, and water. Photo courtesy of the Museum of Fine Arts, Boston; H. L. Pierce Fund.

death in churchyards and among ruins and who viewed all history and life as a melancholy movement toward final oblivion.

Finally, a word should be said about the romantic view of architecture. Residential and public structures were no longer seen as a harmonious and unified blend of carefully structured, architectural forms but as a symbolic evocation of associations and feelings appropriate to a building's functions. A town house might use the classical accoutrements of Greece and Rome to symbolize the rational, organized character of the business or political life that flowed from this urban family

domain. In contrast, a country villa might be based on a Gothic chapel, a medieval mill house, or even a Turkish mosque in order to create exotic and escapist associations, with romance, relaxation, frivolity, or as a picturesque setting for reading and rest. For example, when the old houses of Parliament burned in 1834, a commission organized to determine a new design decreed that the new building should be either Elizabethan or Gothic in style because it was during these periods that England's national spirit had been forged. A. W. N. Pugin, who assisted Charles Barry in the final design for the new structure,

Figure 12–3 Caspar David Friedrich, *Cloister Graveyard in the Snow*, 1810. Illustrates German melancholic romanticism that concentrates on depressing moods in nature as a mirror of human emotions. From an ancient portfolio of Friedrich's paintings.

believed in the spiritual and moral purity of medieval architecture because it had been built by religious craftsmen; he, therefore, argued that the Gothic style should be employed to symbolize moral and spiritual purity for politicians. The finished product was not really Gothic in structure, only in decoration. The rectangular shapes of the building could have been decorated in any number of styles, but the Gothic mode was chosen because of the appropriateness of its associational and escapist emotions.

Let us also look at the famed Brighton Pavilion, a pleasure palace at the seashore designed by John Nash (who also designed Buckingham Palace) for the Prince Regent, later George IV (Figure 12–4). It had originally been a simple, neoclassic country villa designed along the lines of Mount Vernon and Monticello, but Nash turned it into an Islamic confection of domes, turrets, minarets, and screens that he called Indian Gothic style. This ornamentation was considered the perfect backdrop for the emotions and associations

Figure 12–4 John Nash, the Brighton Pavilion, Brighton, England, 1815–18. Illustrates the fanciful Indian Gothic style invented by Nash as an associative decorative frosting. Photo courtesy of the British Tourist Authority, New York.

felt by the gala gatherings organized by the Prince Regent in his pursuit of pleasure. The palace, which evokes images of *The Arabian Nights*, harems, and the exotic eroticism of the Islamic East, is a rather excessive yet excellent example of the escapist associationalism of romantic architecture. Structure was absolutely unimportant; only the decorative architectural frosting was admired.

Music

The one romantic composer of the first half of the nineteenth century whose music and personality stood symbolically for the most exaggerated excesses, emotional brilliance, and overwhelming power of style was Hector Berlioz. Even in the Paris of Hugo, Heine, Chopin, Liszt, Gautier, Sand, and de Vigny, Berlioz stood out as an apparition of romantic excess—a "raging bacchant" who was the terror of the Philistines and an exasperating puzzle to his fellow romantics. At the first performance of one of his overtures, when he was displeased with the orchestra, Berlioz burst into tears, tore his hair, and fell sobbing over the kettledrums. When he conducted, his expansive mane of hair, beaked nose, and ravenous eyes raked audience and orchestra alike; and when he fell in love with the Irish actress Harriet Smithson, he courted and married her under the assumption that she was Ophelia, Juliet, and the goddess Venus all rolled into one (much to his later regret). But for all his personal excesses and external flightiness, his musical loves and musical brilliance continued with him until the end of his life.

The subjects that swept his musical imagination were primarily literary, as they were in the paintings of Delacroix. First, there was Goethe's *Faust* that inspired *The Damnation of Faust*, then the poems of Byron that led to *Harold in Italy*, and finally Dante's *Divine Comedy* that was sublimated into the *Requiem*. Possibly his most autobiographical and personal work is the *Symphonie Fantastique*, which combines his passion for *Faust* with his excessive love for Harriet Smithson. In it he developed the original technical device of an *idée fixe*— a theme that changes its mood and form in each movement, thus providing a sense of unity and expressing through its mutations the dramatic progress of the work.

Goethe's *Faust* was on all romantic minds in 1830. The Paris Opera had three libretti that were awaiting music; and, though Berlioz was never commissioned to do an opera based on *Faust*, he did compose some ballet music for *Faust* that was incorporated into the first movement of the *Symphonie Fantastique*. Throughout this work, there are strong correspondences to the subject and emotions of the Goethe masterpiece. In the final movement of this symphony, the diabolical forces at work in the famed Walpurgis Night Scene in *Faust* take over Berlioz's music and turn it into a blood-curdling Black Mass, similar to the scene in Goya's famous *Witches' Sabbath*.

The *Symphonie Fantastique* is divided into three movements. The first is introductory and begins with shrieks from the woodwinds supported by the ominous rolls from the kettledrums. Then the idée fixe, representing Berlioz's underlying love for Harriet Smithson, appears in a ghostly form and continues in a nightmarish interaction with the theme of her hero and lover. The second section begins with the tolling of distant bells and proceeds with a diabolical parody of a famous Gothic liturgical melody. The final section turns into a full-fledged witches' dance, or the "Rondo of the Sabbath"; first cellos and basses are heard, then violas, and finally the entire woodwind section, thus introducing strong instrumental coloration into Berlioz's fugal musical form. Then many melodic and chromatic variations on the fugal development create a brilliant and frightening series of emotional effects. Finally, after the fugue on the dance theme has ended, the liturgical melody returns, and the two are woven together until the end of the symphony.

Berlioz was one of the first composers to build up his musical forms by using instrumental tone color, and he also developed a rich orchestral palette that is staggering for its sheer size. In every way his method reminds one of the large-scale compositions of Delacroix or the dramas of Victor Hugo. In his gigantic *Requiem*, he used a huge principal orchestra, a chorus of five hundred, a tenor soloist, and four huge brass bands, the latter placed facing the points of the compass for full acoustical effect. Berlioz was the romantic "generalissimo" of music during this period noted for its emotional excess.

Life and Cultural Ideals

No previous generation in western Europe had had such a strong awareness of being the heir and descendant of previous ages, while at the same time feeling quite cut off from those past times. This probing, dissecting, and organizing of information on the past led to a strong, self-conscious desire in all the arts to awaken this past into a new life in the present. This desire led to much execrable eclecticism and shallow surface copying of past styles in all the arts. Interiors and furnishings were often a terrible mixture of emotionally chosen borrowings from the past. Stories and plays of shockingly banal sentiment and melodramatic emotion were accepted merely because they were dressed in the superficial trappings of the Gothic or Renaissance periods, the ancient Near East, the Pacific, or the Orient. Even later in the nineteenth century, when the exacting details of realism and the psychological abstractions of symbolism were added to the artistic scene, the emotional, eclectic character of romanticism remained in the mass culture of the middle class.

In the early development of full-fledged romanticism during the opening decades of the nineteenth century, the romantic experience with the sublime was strongly developed by romantic poets. They felt that the artist should not attempt to change culture and society but should look into himself and view his emotions and feelings in conjunction with those of nature and past times. In *The Recluse*, first published in part in 1814, Wordsworth concerned himself with a turning away from ordinary society to a half-secret paradise in order to find the proper setting for the thoughts of the Visionary Artist-Poet, whose antisocietal role was to unite subject and object in the famed romantic mystical experience. The last page reads as follows:

Come thou prophetic Spirit, Soul of Man
Thou human Soul of the wide earth that hast
Thy metropolitan Temple in the hearts
Of mighty Poets, unto me vouchsafe
Thy guidance, teach me to discern and part
Inherent things from casual, what is fixed
From fleeting, that my verse may live and be
Even as a light hung up in heaven to cheer
Mankind in times to come. And if with this
I blend more lowly matter with the thing
Contemplated describe the mind and man
Contemplating and who and what he was
The transitory Being that beheld
This vision when and where and how he
    lived
With all his little realities of life
Be not the labour useless: if such theme
With highest things may mingle, then, great
    God,
Thou who art breath and being, way and
    guide

And power and understanding, may my life
Express the image of a better time
More wise desires and simple manners; nurse
My heart in genuine freedom; all pure
    thoughts
Be with me and uphold me to the end.

Wordsworth's outlook, like that of most romantics before the third decade of the nineteenth century, was not a practical one because it did not and could not come to grips with life and reality. It was replaced, after Arthur Schopenhauer wrote his *The World as Will and Representation* in 1819, with the concept that though one might not find objective meaning and value in the world, the individual could work for meaning, order, and value for himself and others; in the long run, major redemptive changes in society might be the result. This philosophy unleashed the heroic, rebellious redemption-of-the-world romanticism.

On a very practical level, Victor Hugo's Preface to his play *Cromwell,* written in 1827, illustrates the determined effort of romantic dramatists to overturn completely the classical rules of the past:

Let us take the hammer to theories and poetic systems. Let us throw down the old plastering that conceals the facade of art. There are neither rules nor models; or rather there are no other rules than the general laws of nature, which soar above the whole field of art, and the special rules which result from the conditions appropriate to the subject of each composition. The former are of the essence, eternal, and do not change; the latter are variable, external, and are used but once. The former are the framework that supports the house; the latter are the scaffolding which is used in building it, and which is made anew for each building. In a word, the former are the flesh and bones, the latter the clothing of the drama.

. . . [But] . . . we must admit, . . . or confess ourselves ridiculous, that the domains of art and of nature are entirely distinct. Nature and art are two things—were it not so, one or the other would not exist. Art, in addition to its idealistic side, has a terrestrial, a material side. . . . It seems to us that someone has already said that the drama is a mirror wherein nature is reflected. . . . [But it] must be a concentrating mirror, which instead of weakening, concentrates and condenses the coloured rays, which make of a mere gleam a light, and of a light a flame.

. . . present day literature must be cleansed of its rust. In vain does the rust eat into it and tarnish it. It is addressing a young, stern, vigorous generation, which does not understand it. The train of the eighteenth century is still dragging in the nineteenth; but we, we young men who have seen Bonaparte, are not the ones who will carry it. . . . [The so-called] defects—at all events those which we call by that name—are often the inborn, necessary, inevitable conditions of good qualities. . . .

Genius is necessarily uneven. . . . Shakespeare is blamed for his abuse of metaphysics, or wit, of redundant scenes, of obscenities, for his employment of mythological nonsense in vogue in his time, for exaggeration, obscurity, bad taste, bombast, asperities of style. . . . [Yet Shakespeare] is an oak. If you would have a

smooth trunk, straight branches, satiny leaves, apply to the pale birch, the hollow elder, the weeping willow; but leave the mighty oak in peace. Do not stone that which gives you shade. . . .

E. L. Lami's illustrations for Jules Janin's *Summer in Paris* capture perfectly the romantic mood of the time (Figure 12–5). Wearing simple but elegant summer evening gowns, the ladies stand or sit in languid poses that emphasize the rounded lines of the clothing. It is after ten by candlelight; the visiting lady to the left wears a more ceremonial evening gown as if she had been to a ball or dinner party; and the lady on the couch is in fashionable ill health that allows her a very romantic pose. The overall effect is one of rounded lines, serpentine body curves, a heavily furnished, richly textured interior, and a decorative elegance in the accessories, costume trimmings, and furnishings.

Figure 12–5 E. L. Lami, illustration for Jules Janin's *Summer in Paris,* 1843. Illustrates the elegant summer gowns, the languid poses, and the calculated, expansive opulence that was the romantic ideal even as late as 1843. Photo courtesy of the New York Public Library.

Interior decoration during the romantic period, which involved a plethora of exotic, eclectic borrowings from past or faraway sources, would have appalled the rational Enlightenment tastes of the late eighteenth century. Rooms were a mass of paintings, decorative pieces, and eclectic borrowings, and there was nothing that was not flowered or adorned with fretwork. In such rooms a bookcase looked like a choir stall, a candelabrum was often covered with Gothic saints, and a table was a composite of forms from a medieval castle. The walls were often covered

Ornament, Interiors, and Furniture

in a lush mauve striped fabric, which, in turn, was adorned with large pictures. As in all romantic interiors, the pictures portrayed members of the family, scenes of personal memory, admired personalities, and historic events for which the owners had a great affinity. All was done to suit the associations, personal emotions, and memories of the occupants.

The furniture in this period was such a mixture of shapes and sizes that it is difficult to determine any one style. Generally, furniture was upholstered in rich colors and thick textures, and the wood that framed the upholstery was polished and dark. The furniture was meant to create an emotional association with the past or with personal or literary experiences.

Let us now look at the dining room from the Brighton Pavilion (Figure 12–6). This room was completed about 1822 and is still perfectly preserved today with a full banquet setting in place on the table. The domed ceiling is partly covered by gigantic banana leaves with a silver dragon at the center. The dragon holds in his claws the chains of a vast chandelier composed of six smaller dragons that in turn support in their jaws a crystal cup in the form of a lotus flower. The walls are covered with pseudo-Chinese panels; the doors are crowned with little pagodalike forms; and the walls are ringed with large lamps of blue Spode porcelain mounted on dolphins and crowned with flowers. Only the chairs call the viewer back from fantasy to the actual Regency period. The whole effect is a nightmarish phantasmagoria of effects and forms originating from China, India, Turkey, and Regency London.

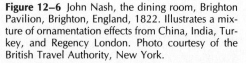

Figure 12–6 John Nash, the dining room, Brighton Pavilion, Brighton, England, 1822. Illustrates a mixture of ornamentation effects from China, India, Turkey, and Regency London. Photo courtesy of the British Travel Authority, New York.

Costume and Accessories

Like the furniture and interiors, the fashions of this period borrowed all types of shapes and accessories from past ages, particularly from the cavalier styles of the opening of the seventeenth century, the rounded elegance of the Rococo period, and minor items from the late Renaissance and Gothic periods. This eclecticism was more easily assimilated in women's dress than in men's, but even the new middle-class mercantile uniform of trousers and tailcoat, developed since the French Revolution, exhibited the hourglass lines and expanding, rounded forms that were the basis of feminine dress. Color and trim in both male and female costume were chosen for their emotional, associational values and changed with the occasion and the mood of the wearer.

In masculine dress, the trousers fastened under the instep so that they would not climb up the leg when one bent or sat down, and they were padded at the hip to emphasize the hourglass line of the male figure. The coat and

Figure 12–7 A display of winter fashions for 1837 by Scott and Perkins of New York. Illustrates the romantic, hourglasslike male and female fashions that were popular just before the styles became less expansive and more conservative. Photo courtesy of the Library of Congress.

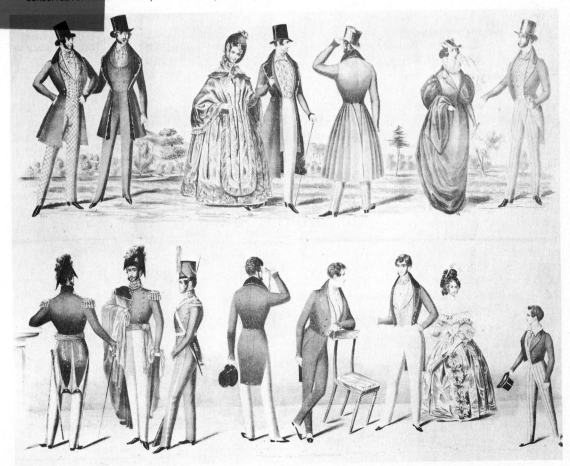

overcoat were fitted very closely with slightly leg-o'-mutton sleeves to raise and expand the shoulder line, while collars rolled high behind the head to accentuate the length of the neck and to frame the white linen shirt with its tall, pointed collar and tied scarf-cravat. Coats were fitted either with flaring tails or with the square skirts of the frock coat, and a corset or basque belt was often worn to pinch in the waist under the pigeon-breasted, padded waistcoat. Height was also given by the tall, flaring, top hat that was worn for all formal occasions except for court presentations, when the cocked bicorne was still carried under the arm. Men wore full side whiskers and clustered curls about the ears, and toward the close of the period, beards and mustaches began to appear. Rich ruffles still appeared on the front of the shirt and at the ends of the shirtcuffs, and mantles and caped overcoats were standard wear for outdoors and travel. Knee breeches, stockings, and slippers were now reserved exclusively for court presentations, and pointed boots were worn under the trousers except for riding and sporting occasions, when they were worn over skin-tight riding breeches. The dandies depicted in the display of fashions for 1837 are typical of the romantic male style (Figure 12–7).

In female dress, the gowns of the late Empire period had already added much frivolous trim, and by 1820 the high Empire waistline moved down from below the bust to the slimmest part of the waist. The corset returned, and the sleeves began to expand in size as the skirts began to flare out in many folds over layers of petticoats. Appliqué, trimming, ruching, and lace ruffles came back in style, and by 1830 the entire costume was a riot of decorative trim and accessories. The poke bonnet was still in use, but it now flared out into a huge brim decorated with plumes and ribbons framing a hairdo that had great sausage curls at the temples and a complexly curled standing knot at the back. Flat shoes, fastened with cross-lacings up the legs, continued to be worn, and shawls of all sizes and textures were seen. As the width of the costume expanded at the hips and shoulders, the collar of the low-cut bodice increased in size and formed a type of shelf over the greatly expanded leg-o'-mutton sleeves, which were now attached to the bodice well below the shoulder line.

From about 1835 on, the upholsterer, rather than the cabinet maker, dictated in matters of interior decoration. Just as the basic shape of the furniture was lost under padded fabric, tassels, and fringe, so women's fashions ceased to have a light ballet line and were weighted down with heavier fabrics and dec-

Figure 12–8 A costume plate from *Le Petit Courrier des Dames*, 1829. Illustrates the beribboned, frivolous, expansive costume and headdress that were the fashion at the height of the romantic movement. Photo courtesy of the New York Public Library.

Figure 12–9 A costume plate from *Godey's Lady's Book,* 1842. Illustrates the change in female fashion from openness and expansiveness to tighter neck and sleeve lines, flattened coiffures, and bonnets that hid the face. Photo courtesy of the New York Public Library.

oration. The skirt, lengthened to the floor, was further extended with stiffened petticoats and sometimes even had a slight train, as in the mid-eighteenth century. The leg-o'-mutton sleeve disappeared in favor of snug-fitting sleeves; exaggerated hairdos were modified to ringlets over the ears and a smooth part in the center of the forehead; and bonnets closed in about the face. The hourglass line gave way to the tea-cozy look, and heavier fabrics and trim replaced the light ruffles and flowers of the 1830s. By comparing a costume plate from

Le Petit Courrier des Dames of 1829 with a plate from *Godey's Lady's Book* for April 1842, one can see the transformation and the direction in which romanticism in fashion was heading in the 1840s (Figures 12–8 and 12–9). The most noticeable changes were from expansive to tight coiffures and from wide puffed sleeves to tight, sloping, restricted sleeves. The visual effect speaks for itself; the ideal woman in a little more than ten years had changed from a gay butterfly to a domesticated doll.

Manners and Movement

As one would expect, the manners and customs established during the Regency and Empire period became more firmly established during the years between 1815 and 1848. Society gradually began to solidify into the Victorian straitjacket of pseudo morals and domestic ethic developed by the capitalist merchants of the Western world who now dictated taste and style in society. Ostentation in any form gradually became an anathema to the polite world of good society; to be thought vulgar was to be an outcast from the world of taste and fashion. Thomas Tegg in *A Present for an Apprentice*, written in 1838, had this to say about genteel bearing:

> Next to good breeding, is a genteel manner and gentlemanly carriage, wholly free from ill habits, and awkward actions, to which, nevertheless, many very worthy and superior persons are addicted. Awkwardness of behaviour, while having nothing in it criminal . . . is such an offence to good manners and good breeding, that it is universally despised.

In England, the acquisition of a calm confidence was inculcated in young people from childhood, sometimes having the effect of making the English seem aloof. In 1833 and again in 1844, Ralph Waldo Emerson saw in the English gentleman:

> [An] incuriosity, and stony neglect, each of each other. Each man walks, eats, drinks, shaves, dresses, gesticulates, and, in every manner, acts and suffers without reference to the bystanders, in his own fashion, only careful not to interfere with them, or annoy them. If an Englishman walks in a pouring rain, swinging his closed umbrella like a walking stick; wears a wig, or a shawl, or a saddle, or stands on his head . . . no remark is made. And as he has been doing this for several generations, it is now in the blood. In short, every one of these islanders is an island himself, safe, tranquil, incommunicable.

Standing, walking, and sitting for the gentleman of this period was a further refinement of what had been developing during the last decade of the eighteenth century and the first two decades of the nineteenth century. One could stand with both legs straight or with one knee slightly relaxed. One was to walk by moving the leg easily and firmly from the hip, without swaying or rocking the body. To turn the feet and legs slightly outward was considered elegant, but this affectation was not overly emphasized. Hurrying in the streets was not recommended. As Thomas Tegg commented: "Walking fast in the streets is a mark of vulgarity, implying hurry of business; it may appear well in a mechanic or tradesman, but ill suits the character of a gentleman, or a man of fashion." It

was considered the "mark of little minds, a proof that the business we embark on is too much for us. . . . A man of sense may be in haste but he is never in a hurry." As to sitting, Tegg had this to say: "The manner in which others throw themselves back and stretch forward their legs savours too much of familiarity. You may cross your legs if you like, but not hug your knees or your toes. Straddling a chair, and tilting it up may be pardonable in a bachelor's room, but not in a lady's drawing room."

Smoking, a habit that was now firmly established for men, blossomed into a number of variations from the days when it was limited to the long-stemmed pipe. Men now smoked cigarettes, which they rolled themselves, and the more affluent smoked cigars. The pipe was now relegated to the elderly and the conservative. The unspoken regulations given by Tegg in 1838 were as follows: "One must never smoke, nor even ask to smoke, in the company of the fair." A lady who realized that a man wished to smoke a cigar might, in the summer, have tactfully asked him to withdraw to the garden. It was not proper to smoke in a room full of ladies or in the company of one's own family; it was also in very bad taste to smoke in the streets except after dark. At all public gatherings—a flower show, a promenade, a theatrical performance, or a horse race—smoking was not acceptable. As Tegg said: "The tobacco smoker in public is the most selfish animal imaginable; he perseveres in contaminating the pure fragrant air, careless whom he annoys, and is but the fitting inmate of a tavern." In a railway carriage, it was permissible to smoke after obtaining the consent of the occupants, but it was never correct to do so if ladies were present. It was also improper to smoke in a coffee house or hotel, or in the presence of a clergyman. One comic note, however, was the admonition not to offer any churchman a cigar if "over the rank of curate."

In contrast with male manners, which by the 1830s had reached some orthodoxy, female manners and movements changed with the changes in fashion from 1815 to 1848. By the end of the eighteenth and the beginning of the nineteenth centuries, there was more freedom in women's clothes and a greater emphasis on athletics to develop grace of movement; with the coming of the romantic era, women once again wore corsets and petticoats restraining their movement and gesture. Some of this new freedom for women remained at least until about 1840, and books spoke of avoiding stiffness when standing, walking, or sitting. One of the practices that was most deplored in this new romantic era was employing retired soldiers to teach ladies to walk. The anonymous author of *The Young Lady's Book* in 1829 said: "The stiffness acquired under regimental tuition is adverse to all the principles of grace, and annihilates the buoyant lightness which is so conducive to ease and elegance in the young." Also, at all times the young lady was to appear impervious to the unbecoming effects of exertion or emotion. Any hard breathing, flushing with heat, or looking blue with cold were to be avoided, since anything that distracted from the relaxed pleasures of society was in bad taste.

In sitting, ladies were admonished to avoid both stiffness and lounging and to sink into a chair with a grace and ease of manner. In walking, steps were to be short and gentle, not to exceed the length of the foot; the foot was not to be thrown out, since to do so would throw the body awry and give the person the appearance of being a professional dancer. The ideal was to walk with the head held high and the chest expanded. Though dancing was still admired as a way to develop grace of deportment, ideals of deportment were no longer set by the dancing master, but by the professional teachers of manners and movement.

The bow and the curtsy were still used for formal occasions; but on the street or indoors, the raising of the hat, the nodding of the head, or the shaking of hands was a quite acceptable salutation. The man's bow was now merely an informal bending from the waist, sometimes with the right arm across the waist. To curtsy, the female lowered her head and sank gently within her skirt and petticoats by placing one foot behind the other and bending the knee.

One should also not forget how important to the cultural texture of this period was sentimental family feeling among the conservative middle class. (The rules for manners and movement were reserved for the upper class.) This stress on the familial and the domestic was what finally changed Regency England to the Victorian Age and Empire France to the age of Louis Philippe. This new middle-class morality emphasized an unostentatious, moderate, simple, and direct approach to life and thus eschewed the loose-moraled, the ribald, and the exaggeratedly sensuous in favor of all the arts of comfortable domesticity.

The Theatre

The major aspects of romantic theatrical presentation during the early nineteenth century were a growing interest in historical fact, a fascination with superficial historical accuracy, a demand for ever more spectacle to please the instincts for variety and sensationalism in the expanding middle-class audience, and finally, an emphasis on faraway and long-ago settings for the escapist romantic-melodramatic tales spun out in front of audiences. To house these spectacular performances and accommodate the vast increase in audience size, the theatres themselves became larger and larger as the century progressed. By the 1830s and 1840s most major metropolitan houses seated three thousand spectators or more. As a result of the increasing urbanization and industrialization in western Europe and the United States, the cities became flooded with workers; the audiences gradually changed from a middle-class majority in the late eighteenth century to a truly mass audience by the middle of the nineteenth century. The total spectrum of theatrical experience had, therefore, to be greatly expanded, and theatrical performances ranged from all types of variety and circus entertainment to opera and the classics. In many ways, during those early years of the nineteenth century, the theatre became an entertainment medium for the masses in much the way that television is today. Productions often included a play, short song and dance acts, a light comedy, and possibly even a short light opera; and they lasted from seven in the evening until well past midnight.

In the beginning of the romantic period, the major method of organizing theatrical production was still the repertory method, in which a group of actors presented a rotating series of plays during a given theatrical season. The great companies on the Continent were government-supported national theatres like the Comédie Française and the Vienna Burgtheater; in England, the theatres with a royal patent, Covent Garden and Drury Lane, had to rely on the box office attraction of their acting talent. With the advent of the railroads, the older repertory system was gradually replaced by the "long run" and the tour, in which a play or a production was used as a vehicle for a star performer, often surrounded by a rather mediocre supporting company. This development gradually changed the theatre by the late years of the nineteenth century into a money-making investment rather than an art form.

The interiors of the theatres, with their large seating capacity, were usually arranged in a series of boxes on the sides, opening out into balconies or galleries at the rear. At first the old orchestra, or main floor area, was still flat with much standing room, but gradually the floor became sloped and contained expensive seats at the front and benches to the rear. These seats gave better audibility and sight lines than could be had from the old aristocratic side boxes. By the second half of the nineteenth century, these new orchestra seats had finally replaced the old box seats in cost and desirability (Figure 12–10).

The stage became more and more cluttered with attempts to suggest a full and detailed representation of past times and faraway places. Even when the work was unrealistically romantic—like that of Byron or Hugo—much attention was paid to specific historic or geographic details. In particular, the Shake-

Figure 12–10 Engraving of the interior of the Burgtheater, Vienna; early nineteenth century. Illustrates the change to permanent seating in the orchestra, although the floor was still flat. Photo courtesy of the Austrian National Library.

spearean revivals of the time became an excuse for the presentation of multitudinous historical facts and effects. This trend reached its height at the very close of this period. In his Shakespearean revivals of the early 1850s, Charles Kean required months of preparation by teams of art historians and archaeologists who gathered background material for the productions. The program notes were so extensive that they read like a small pamphlet or book; and the productions were intended to be an educational, rather than a theatrical, experience.

Scenery was still painted in perspective on backdrops and wings, but the latter were now frequently solid and three-dimensional, arranged in asymmetrical patterns to break up the monotonous equal balance of the stage scene. Though some of the wing pieces still moved on and off stage by being fastened in grooves or to masts attached to chariots on tracks below the stage floor, many large pieces were moved on and off stage manually. The favorite scenic method was to develop partially three-dimensional and asymmetrically placed wing pieces that could then frame the more distant backdrop in an illusionistically real scene. This illusion was assisted by the development of gas lighting, which allowed for the raising and dimming of stage lights. Throughout the early part of the century, the stage floor was usually sloped or raked to aid the illusion of distance; only in the 1840s, with the first experiments with a three-walled boxed-in set, were steps taken to shift to a flat floor playing area.

Costumes were also based more fully on documented historical fact with modifications for theatrical effect; unity, beauty, and overall theatricality were less admired than authenticity of detail. What resulted was a piling up of complex detail with little regard for artistic and mood-evoking effects.

The Plays

Though many plays of great historical pageantry were written during this period as vehicles for star performers and as an excuse for heavy production, few of them have retained a literary or theatrical reputation today. Victor Hugo's *Hernani* is not a great play and is viewed with a smile today, but it caused such a sensation when it was first presented at the Comédie Française in 1830 that its performance has since been used to mark the final triumph of romanticism in France. *Hernani* today is performed only in its operatic form entitled *Ernani*, with music by Giuseppe Verdi.

The play is not a romantic tragedy but essentially a melodrama with an unhappy ending. It tells the story of the noble outlaw Hernani and his attempt to wed Doña Sol over the opposition of the king and her guardian, both of whom also love her. After a number of very romantic adventures, many of which take place in the atmospheric shadows of the night, Hernani weds Doña Sol, and a happy future seems assured. But at the height of the wedding festivities, Doña Sol's old guardian, who had saved Hernani's life and to whom Hernani had pledged to give up his own life if his savior ever demanded it, sounds a horn signaling that the pledge must now be honored. In the climactic denouement of the play, Hernani chooses suicide rather than dishonoring his vow, and Doña Sol follows her husband in death.

The play is structured into five acts, each in a different setting. Each act develops the themes of honor versus passionate love and of duty versus personal feelings, not in the reasoned classical tradition of Racine but in a high-flown, excessive, overwritten poetic mode that roused the original audiences to high-pitched emotional responses. The play was originally condemned by the classicists for its total break with the accepted rules of theatrical decorum: Hernani is a bandit and not a prince, even though he is of noble background; he is first seen at night in the heroine's bedchamber; the king, who in Act IV becomes the Holy Roman Emperor, actually hides in a closet in the bedchamber; and the play employs a number of words that were considered an absolute breach of good theatrical manners. Though today such attacks seem petty, the play does suffer from a very

Figure 12–11 Engraving depicting a scene from the original production of Victor Hugo's *Hernani*, showing the King, Doña Sol, and Hernani. Illustrates an asymmetrical, painted, historically based setting, the romantic use of light and shade, and costumes that combine historical accuracy and touches of current fashion. From *Le Théâtre Romantique* by Paul Ginistry, 1922.

loose and disunified structure. Each act concerns a separate event or action; there is little continuity of development; and the ending does not develop from the characters or events. Like most romantic art, the play is an excuse for spectacle, high poetic passions, much theatrical posturing, and self-indulgence.

Characterization is secondary to feeling and an exaggerated devotion to the romantic ideals of honor and duty. Basically, the interest is centered on Doña Sol and Hernani; the other characters are used merely to illustrate a feeling or an idea or to support the love of the two central characters. Like much romantic drama, the message is that the world of men and affairs is ugly and corrupt and that individuals with high ideals and great passions are crushed by the evils of the establishment. The language of *Hernani* is colorful, high flown, and poetic, intended less to reveal character and relate story than to achieve a grouping of rich images and soaring rhythms that will evoke an immediate emotional response in the audience. The longer speeches are like arias in an opera and need supporting music to be effective.

It is little wonder that this play has remained in the modern theatre only as *Ernani*. The general rhythm of *Hernani* contains the sweeping crescendos, abrupt shifts, and contrasts characteristic of romantic opera. The range and variety of rhythmic effects are extensive all the way from quiet interior monologue to scenes of heavy exterior action and pageantry; it is this great variety of visual, vocal, and rhythmic effects that gives the action of the play such a sense of richness. Yet at no point in the play is the rhythm light-hearted or gay; throughout it remains heavy, sonorous, operatic, and grand.

The staging requirements for *Hernani* are varied. As specified by Hugo, much attention must be paid to historical detail in the design of the five sets. Varied textures in sets and costumes, sensuous use of color, and massive costume and scenic forms are necessary to support the overblown emotions of the script and its poetic dialogue (Figure 12–11).

Acting and Directing the Plays

Actors, actresses, and directors should prepare for a production of a high romantic drama by first studying the art of the period. As a painting like *The Death of Sardanapalus* indicates (Figure 12–1), movements must be larger than life, and gestures must be expansive, moving from the body outward. In addition, more than in most other styles of acting, the costumes must be matched to the player's role and to the richness and size of the play. Flowing open lines achieved by large hats, wide mantles, long trains, and hanging open sleeves, for example, are needed to make gestures and movements seem grander than they would if the actor depended solely on his own physical deportment. Directors should plan the blocking on great sweeping curves to enhance size and grandeur of movement. Actors and actresses must also train their voices to go up and down in volume and pitch until they can command a tremendous vocal range. Then they must practice reciting the high-flown poetic dialogue until they can achieve a thundering vocal climax without evidencing any vocal strain, shouting, or loss of word clarity. Much time must be spent in vocal exercises, sometimes with musical support, before acting romantically with voice and gesture can be mastered. It is not enough to feel great emotions and to express them naturally. Players must learn to project both their voices and movements so that they will carry the size of the play's subjective emotions. In addition, actors and actresses must always be aware that the full romantic effect, as in opera, can be obtained only with full visual support. In high romanticism, one must always create—as did Ludwig Devrient in acting King Lear—the illusion that the player is larger souled, more golden voiced, and more superhuman than any mortal ever could be (Figure 12–12).

Figure 12–12 Engraving of Ludwig Devrient as King Lear, c. 1832. Illustrates the exaggerated, melodramatic stance and gesture used by romantic actors during the nineteenth century to convince audiences of their superhuman histrionic and emotional abilities. Photo courtesy of the Austrian National Library.

Designing the Plays

The designer of a modern production of *Hernani* should probably take note of the contemporary productions of Verdi's *Ernani*, using many of the same costume and staging devices. To have any hope of success, the play must have a larger-than-life size, sweep, and emotional grandeur. Each of the five settings must be designed to make them seem larger than the stage space that they inhabit. This may mean using forced perspective, letting sets rise out of sight behind a proscenium, framing action in massive draped curtains that rise up into a dark void, and scaling furniture and properties until they are larger and richer than in real life. Also, to project a sense of an open composition not restricted to normal stage space, furniture placement and blocking patterns could be on diagonal lines that lead off into darkness or into areas beyond and behind the proscenium. The resulting asymmetry will also add to a sense of movement and instability supporting the excess emotional tone of the play.

Textures and colors in scenery and properties should be rich, lush, and tactile—appealing in a direct emotional way to an audience's sensuous values and again surrounding and supporting the emotional size of the drama. The lighting of the play should emphasize romantic colors in the gels and strong contrasts of light and shade. Great shafts of smoky light penetrating into velvety darkness should be the idea to be achieved.

In costume the ideal should be richness and depth with a use of heavy textures and patterned materials that will produce monumental silhouettes on stage. Large pleats and folds, heavy pieces of fur trim, and a few pieces of metallic or jeweled ornamentation will add to the sense of size projected by each of the major characters. Fabric must be used in much larger amounts than in costuming the usual play, with long trains in the women's skirts; great trailing folds in the men's cloaks; great, open, hanging sleeves; and larger and wider collars than would be thought possible in developing designs from the styles of Spain in the early sixteenth century (Figure 12–11).

Thus it should be quite obvious that one cannot do a small limited cast production of *Hernani* and capture the sweep and grandeur originally intended by Hugo for the play. A pictorial equivalent for many of the emotional high points in the production can be found in the paintings of Eugène Delacroix, whose art was often inspired by reading romantic tales, listening to romantic music, or watching romantic tragedy on the stage (Figure 12–1).

PROJECTS AND PROBLEMS

1. Why did the rationalism of the Enlightenment suffer a severe setback at the end of the eighteenth and the beginning of the nineteenth centuries?

2. What was the new view of the past that characterized romanticism?

3. Why was individualism so important a quality in romanticism?

4. What was the concept of the sublime that was worshipped by romantics in the same way that classicists had worshiped reason?

5. Why are technique and form less important in romantic art than in other styles of art?

6. What aspects of the staging in *The Death of Sardanapalus* by Delacroix (Figure 12–1) could be borrowed for the theatre? What is the blocking of the scene? What characterizes the acting? What kind of staging effects would be needed to make this scene work in the theatre?

7. What are the qualities in Turner's *The Slave Ship* (Figure 12–2) that might be useful in a romantic stage production? Without borrowing anything directly from the painting, what can a director or designer learn from his work?

8. Why is Friedrich's *Cloister Graveyard in the Snow* (Figure 12–3) like a staged scene from *Hamlet*? What is the relationship between the mannerism in *Hamlet* and the melancholy romanticism in this painting? How does this painting relate as a romantic work to the paintings of Delacroix and Turner?

9. Why does the Brighton Pavilion (Figure 12–4) remind us of Disneyland? Why is it almost impossible for us to take the structure seriously? How would you feel appearing in a production set in or in front of this structure? What kind of production would use this structure as a background?

10. Why is Berlioz's music like a painting by Delacroix or a poem by Byron? Why are so many of his works related to literature? Why did Berlioz feel that he had to have large halls and huge performing groups to project his works? How is the *idée fixe* related to characterization in later romantic and realistic playwriting?

11. Why are the arts of the nineteenth century so frequently eclectic? Characterize eclecticism. Why was the romantic artist a visionary seer? Why was the romantic artist so frequently cast in an anti-societal role? How did Schopenhauer change the nature of romanticism? Explain Hugo's Preface to *Cromwell.*

12. Look closely at Lami's illustration for *Summer in Paris* (Figure 12–5). What is the mood of the scene? How do the participants deport themselves? What does this illustration communicate about romantic society? How is the furniture used? How are the clothes worn?

13. Imagine dining in the banquet room at the Brighton Pavilion (Figure 12–6). How would you feel? What kind of play would contain such a scene? How would the decorative ornamentation affect you? What can a director and a designer learn from studying this room?

14. Borrow some costumes of the period with the appropriate padding and corseting and practice moving, sitting, standing, and walking in them. What happens to your movement? What is specifically romantic about the clothing? How are the men's and women's clothing alike?

15. What are the prime characteristics in the fashions for 1837 (Figure 12–7) that affect movement and one's sense of self? Compare these fashions with those of today.

16. Look at the costume illustration from *Le Petit Courrier des Dames* of 1829 (Figure 12–8). What is pleasing about the costume? What is ridiculous? What does it do to movement, gesture, and the way you would hold your head? How would you feel wearing the costume?

17. Look at the ladies in the fashion drawing from *Godey's Lady's Book* for 1842 (Figure 12–9). How do they differ from the lady of fashion of 1829 (Figure 12–8)? Why the change? What is the difference in the view of women? What is the difference, if any, in the movement and gestures affected by these new fashions?

18. Explain what constituted good manners in the romantic period. Try doing a series of standing, walking, sitting, and gesturing exercises based on the precepts set down in this chapter in the section on manners and movement. Perfect them and don a period costume and do them as if on the stage.

19. Explain smoking etiquette during this period. Why did women's manners and movement change from the very early romantic age to the late romantic period? How did one curtsy, bow, and tip one's hat? Why did the handshake symbolize the new order of society in this period?

20. Characterize the theatre in the romantic period. How large were the theatres? How long was the performance? Who attended the performances?

21. Look at the interior of the Burgtheater in the early nineteenth century (Figure 12–10). Describe the auditorium and the stage and the relationship between the two.

22. Why is *Hernani* difficult to produce today? Why is it still successful as *Ernani,* the opera? What are the structural, character, and mood qualities of the play that make it completely romantic? Characterize its language. Do a scene from the play in the costumes of the period and describe your response. What are the demands made on the leading actors?

23. Look at the drawing of the original production of *Hernani* (Figure 12–11). Characterize the scenery and costumes. Are the costumes absolutely accurate historically?

24. What can the director, actor, and designer learn about producing a romantic play from a study of Delacroix's *The Death of Sardanapalus* (Figure 12–1)? Summarize in abstract metaphorical terms the kind of fabrics and clothing lines needed to support a high romantic tragedy performance.

25. Characterize the performance of Ludwig Devrient as King Lear (Figure 12–12). Play the storm scene in *King Lear* as Devrient might have performed it. What does this romantic acting do to Shakespeare's plays?

BIBLIOGRAPHY

Arvin, Neil S. *Eugène Scribe and the French Theatre, 1815–1860.* Cambridge, Mass.: Harvard University Press, 1924. A very useful although rather dated study of the development of the well-made play from the earlier melodramatic form.

Barzun, Jacques. *Berlioz and His Century.* New York: Meridian Books, 1956. An excellent introduction to the romantic era in France through the life of Berlioz and his relationships with other literary and artistic leaders.

Berger, Klaus. *Géricault and His Work.* Lawrence: University of Kansas Press, 1955. An excellent study of Géricault and his relationship to the times that shaped him and his art.

Booth, Michael R. *English Melodrama.* London: Herbert Jenkins, 1965. A study of the rise of melodrama at the close of the eighteenth century, its spread during the first two decades of the nineteenth century, and its triumph as a dramatic form after the middle of the century.

Brion, Marcel. *Art of the Romantic Era: Romanticism, Classicism, Realism.* New York: Praeger, 1966. An excellent survey of art during the romantic age.

Canaday, John. *Mainstreams of Modern Art.* New York: Holt, Rinehart and Winston, 1959. Covers European and American art from the American Revolution to the middle of the twentieth century.

Carlson, Marvin A. *The French Stage in the Nineteenth Century.* Metuchen, N.J.: Scarecrow Press, 1972. A survey of nineteenth-century stage production in France with attention also given to playwriting style.

Clark, Kenneth. *The Gothic Revival.* New York: Charles Scribner's Sons, 1929. Study of the change from classical to medieval sources in architecture during the mid-eighteenth century to the end of the nineteenth century.

Clement, N. H. *Romanticism in France.* New York: Modern Language Association, 1939. A survey on romanticism as a style as it developed and then receded in France during the nineteenth century.

Courthion, Pierre. *Romanticism.* Translated by Stuart Gilbert. New York: Skira, 1961. Another excellent and well-illustrated volume on romanticism during the early to mid-nineteenth century.

Downer, Alan S. "Players and the Painted Stage: Nineteenth Century Acting," *PMLA* 61 (1946): 522–76. A fascinating article on nineteenth-century acting in relation to the theatre, architecture, and stage settings of the day.

Friedlander, Walter F. *From David to Delacroix.* Cambridge, Mass.: Harvard University Press, 1952. An excellent picture of the shift from the cold classicism of David to the tempestuous emotion of Delacroix.

Hoffmann, Werner. *The Earthly Paradise: Art in the Nineteenth Century.* Translated by Brian Battershaw. New York: Braziller, 1956. An interesting survey of some little-known works of art and architecture.

Honour, Henri. *Romanticism.* New York: Harper & Row, 1979. An excellent, finely illustrated, up-to-date survey of romanticism in art.

The Journal of Eugène Delacroix. Translated and edited by Walter Pach. New York: Crown Publishers, 1948. This book affords brilliant insights into the attitudes and ideas of the most famous artist of the romantic movement in France.

Lucas, F. L. *The Decline and Fall of the Romantic Ideal.* New York: Macmillan, 1936. An excellent study of the problems of romantic art, particularly those of technique and structure.

Lynton, Norbert. *The Modern World.* Landmarks of the World's Art Series. New York: McGraw-Hill, 1965. Beautifully illustrated with many color plates, this book discusses European art from the American Revolution to the present.

Melcher, Edith. *Stage Realism in France from Diderot to Antoine.* Bryn Mawr, Pa.: Bryn Mawr College, 1928. Study of the use of realism in French theatre.

Newton, Eric. *The Romantic Rebellion.* New York: St. Martin's Press, 1966. A very popular and readable look at the cultural, social, and artistic rebellion that we now label romanticism.

Nicoll, Allardyce. *History of the English Stage, 1660–1900.* 6 vols. London: Cambridge University Press, 1955–1959. The middle part of this study is useful in understanding romantic drama.

Novotny, Fritz. *Painting and Sculpture in Europe, 1780–1880.* Pelican History of Art Series, Baltimore: Penguin Books, 1960. Gives a clear picture of the arts in Europe during the rise of the Industrial Revolution.

Odell, George C. D. *Shakespeare from Betterton to Irving.* 2 vols. New York: Charles Scribner's Sons, 1920. An excellent picture of Shakespearean production on the romantic stage.

"The Romantic Movement: A Current Selective and Critical Bibliography," *English Literary History* (1937–1949), *Philological Quarterly* (1950–present). An excellent and very useful list of publications devoted to the development of the romantic movement in England.

Rowell, George. *The Victorian Theatre.* Oxford: Clarendon Press, 1956. A unique insight into the atmosphere and artistic outlook of the English stage during the nineteenth century.

Walzel, Oskar F. *German Romanticism.* New York:

G. P. Putnam's Sons, 1932. A solid survey of German romanticism, particularly in the theatre, during the late eighteenth and early nineteenth centuries.

Watson, Ernest Bradlee. *Sheridan to Robertson: A Study of the Nineteenth Century London Stage.* Cambridge, Mass.: Harvard University Press, 1926. A very useful summary of theatrical production in London from approximately 1790 to 1865.

Realistic Style

By the middle of the nineteenth century, the overblown, subjective idealism of romanticism began to seem meaningless in the face of modern industrialism with all its attendant social and economic problems. After the unsettling political and social reorganization at the time of the French Revolution and the years of the Napoleonic Empire, Europe after 1815 became once again a grouping of oppressive monarchies, with little attention paid to written constitutions and human rights. Though several other revolutions had occurred during the romantic period in an attempt to overthrow such oppressive regimes, there was no real reform. After the final defeat of liberal and radical ideas in the many revolutions that broke out throughout Europe in 1848, artists and intellectuals began to develop new modes of art with strong social themes. Dreams, escapism, and fantasy were gradually put aside in favor of a systematic search into the human personality and society. Observation, clinical analysis, and the scientific study of peoples and institutions began to replace the shopworn clichés of subjective romantic idealism.

As the factory system drew more and more workers into urban slums and the general misery of the masses increased with expanding industrialization and urbanization, philosophers began to question the whole escapist idealism on which mid-nineteenth-century European culture was based. A major contributor to questioning this outlook and to establishing new goals and concerns for society was Auguste Comte, often considered the father of sociology. His writings between 1830 and the early 1850s argued for studying society in a carefully controlled, scientific manner. Comte called his new philosophy positivism. He insisted that with the new scientific method, events in society could be predicted and determined in a cause-and-effect relationship. This concept was further reinforced by the theories of Charles Darwin, who developed the doctrine that all forms of life developed from a common ancestry and that

[handwritten margin notes: AUSTRIAN METTERNICH; TOO GENERAL]

267

the evolution of all living things was based on the concept of the survival of the fittest. Darwin's theories, coupled with those of positivism, made heredity and environment very important to both sociologist and artist. If human behavior became something beyond the control of the individual, then only improvements in society could better the human condition.

All these ideas, however, were considered radical and subversive by the middle-class society that dominated the cultural scene. Like the mannerist ideals that had twisted and repressed the more open and natural ideals of the Renaissance, middle-class mores in the nineteenth century hung on to worn-out, rigid, often distorted versions of the subjective romanticism of the early part of the century. The richness and expansiveness of romanticism gave way to an excessive, layered materialism usually disguised as escapist decoration borrowed from the historic past or the exotic faraway. This materialistic pastiche of exotic and historical sources was supported as art by the wealthy, capitalist nouveau riche who equated it with position, power, and good taste. There was a definite cultural separation between the mass eclectic taste, still based on debased forms of the old romanticism, and the *avant-garde* intellectual interest in realism and social change. Thus the style of realism did not belong to society in general but only to the avant-garde artists, intellectuals, practical craftsmen, and industrialists in their business procedures as opposed to the ideals of their private life.

There was a kind of realism in architecture during this period that might also be called functional, practical, or rational. While it was the result of practical problem-solving in the construction of warehouses, bridges, exhibition halls, and factories, "true" architecture was concerned with the various historical styles of architectural ornament applied to homes, public buildings, and monuments. The greatest late nineteenth-century monument to this opulent, excessive eclecticism is undoubtedly the Paris Opera House, planned by Emperor Napoleon III as a symbol of the

material wealth, grandeur, and power of the Second Empire (Figure 13–1). It stands for the two great repressed drives of all political leaders and industrialists in the late nineteenth century—the desperate attempts to make nouveau riche ideals aristocratic and to turn back time. It was not until the very last years of the century that the division between this *Beaux Arts* tradition and the new structural engineering was broken.

One of the earliest structures for a large-scale public purpose that was completely designed and built in the new "realistic" tradition was the great exhibition building, or Crystal Palace, designed by Joseph Paxton for the London Exhibition of 1851 (Figure 13–2). With little time to get ready for the great exhibition, Paxton, a distinguished gardener and horticulturist, designed and built a gigantic greenhouse of glass and iron, new materials that had been used in warehouses and factories since the early 1800s. The exhibition authorities marveled at the speed with which the structure arose in Hyde Park (within six months' time) and at its acres of unimpeded interior space, both achieved because of the standardized prefabricated materials used in construction. In fact, this structure and the exhibition itself really marked the beginning of the new practicality and realism of the late nineteenth century that slowly eroded over the next half-century the mass cultural ideals of a dying, second-hand romanticism.

The London Exhibition was followed by one in Paris in 1855. Here the banner bearer of realism in painting, Gustave Courbet, set up his own gallery, calling it the Pavilion of Realism, after two of his major works had been rejected by the jury as coarse and materialistic. Challenging the sentimentality, stock classicism, empty romanticism, and exaggerated escapist heroics that made up the usual Academy exhibitions, Courbet demanded that people look at what Baudelaire called the "heroism of modern life." One of his most controversial works in the Pavilion of Realism was *The Stone Breakers*, painted in 1849. It stirred violent protests because of its "socialistic" and "communistic" content and

Figure 13–1 Charles Garnier, the Paris Opera House, 1861–74. Probably the greatest monument to opulent, excessive, nineteenth-century eclecticism. Planned by Napoleon III as a symbol of the material wealth and grandeur of the Second French Empire. Photo courtesy of the French Cultural Services, New York.

Figure 13–2 Sir Joseph Paxton, the Crystal Palace, 1850–51. An example of the new structural engineering of iron and glass, based on greenhouse and factory architecture, that was constructed in six months to house the great London Exhibition, but was not considered architecture. Photo courtesy of the Crown Copyright, Victoria and Albert Museum.

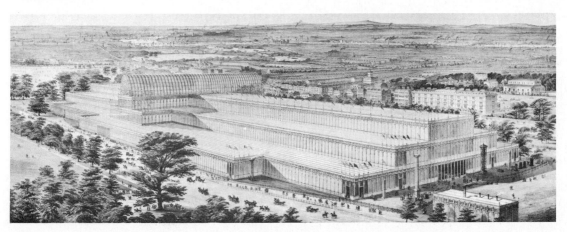

because it was painted directly and objectively without sentiment or idealism (Figure 13–3). Courbet said, "The art of painting can consist only in the representation of objects visible and tangible to the painter" and "Show me an angel and I'll paint one." We know from other statements that *The Stone Breakers* was inspired by his seeing an old man and a boy working on the road. Asking them to pose for him in his studio, Courbet then painted them life-size with great matter-of-factness and solidity. The result is in sharp contrast with the overblown, romantic rhetoric of Delacroix's *The Death of Sardanapalus* (Figure 12–1). Though Courbet employed many painting techniques from Caravaggio, Rembrandt, and Louis LeNain, the public saw no further than what was labeled "primitivism" and "crude brutality."

Now let us compare *The Stone Breakers* with *L'Eminence Grise* by Jean Léon Gérôme (Figures 13–3 and 13–4). Gérôme may be more accurate in his use of form, more technically exact, and more objectively observant in his contrived "academic exercise," but because Gérôme is uninvolved in his subject and interested primarily in a historical surface realism, his work has none of the subjectivity of Courbet's painting. A fear of the rawness of reality led the respectable bourgeois public

Figure 13–3 Gustave Courbet, *The Stone Breakers,* 1849. Illustrates the new realism in subject matter and painterly detail introduced by Courbet at the beginning of the second half of the nineteenth century. Formerly in the State Gallery, Dresden, that was destroyed during World War II. Photo courtesy of the State Picture Gallery, Dresden.

Figure 13–4 Jean Léon Gérôme, *L'Eminence Grise*, n.d. A contrived "academic exercise" in painting that was admired by the academic salons of the nineteenth century. Its realism lies in its meticulous detail, not in its artificial, contrived subject matter that merely allows the artist to demonstrate his virtuoso technical ability. Photo courtesy of the Museum of Fine Arts, Boston. Bequest of Susan Cornelia Warren.

to prefer the glossy surface wrapped in the atmosphere of the past and reflecting the world distantly, as if through a looking glass. They thought that art should be a refuge— an asylum from the wild pace of the industrial revolution, the pressures of labor unrest, and the noise of factories and trains.

Throughout the late nineteenth century, these two kinds of realism existed side by side in art and in the theatre. In fact, in the theatre the historical melodramas like the storytelling historical paintings frequently have as much, if not more, attention paid to exact surface detail than does a realistic drama by Ibsen.

Thomas Eakins, America's greatest real-

istic painter, added another realistic element to his work that was missing from Courbet's, namely, the portrayal of a subject at a moment of pause in life. This portrayal gives the viewer a deep psychological insight into the subject's personality. In *The Pathetic Song*, painted in 1881, Eakins (like Chekhov a decade and a half later) captures a quiet moment of pause and reflection after a song has concluded and before the sound of the music has faded from the air (Figure 13–5). In addition to the accurate rendering of every detail, the painting gives us a glimpse into the inner personality of the singer.

Edgar Degas was another master at cap-

turing character relationship and personality attributes through the compositional arrangements of his seemingly accidental scenes. In his painting *Interior: The Rape*, personality and situation are revealed by the placement of the subject within a particular furniture arrangement and lighting focus (Figure 13–6). A heavy, ominous atmosphere is evoked as we look at the woman seated, weeping at her dressing table. A traveling case lies open on the table; an iron bed lighted by a small lamp lies diagonally off to the right; and the ominous figure of a man lies almost hidden in shadows by the door. One immediately senses that the man is a threat to the girl, from whom he is separated by two important symbolic objects: the bed at its ominous upstage angle

Figure 13–5 Thomas Eakins, *The Pathetic Song*, 1881. Captures a quiet, thoughtful moment after action has ceased in order to gain psychological insight into character. Photo courtesy of the Corcoran Gallery of Art, Washington, D.C.

Figure 13–6 Edgar Degas, *Interior: The Rape*, 1874. A "slice of life" in Paris in the late nineteenth century. Every item—furniture, people, and light—is carefully selected and planned to create a subtle but strong dramatic effect. Photo courtesy of the H. P. McIlhenny Collection.

and the open case on the table. This painting with its camera angle, "snapshot" effect into the corner of a room, is very much like the climactic scene from a realistic play, such as Strindberg's *Miss Julie*.

Music

Richard Wagner was an outstanding realistic composer of the late nineteenth century. He took the ideas of romanticism and, through integration, structure, and technique, developed a music drama that, except for its subject matter, resembles the plays of Ibsen in its technical exactness. Corresponding to one's first view of the Paris Opera House, Wagner created rich, overwhelmingly opulent, large-scale musical effects. He did his utmost to overwhelm his audiences with the length, density, and power of his larger works. Like the painters of the great "academic machines" (Figure 13–4), Wagner was more careful in his method, form, and technique than were other more immediately popular late romantic composers. Since he wrote his own libretti, or books, as he preferred to call them, he was able to match their solid construction to the intricate, mosaiclike pattern of his music. Doing away with the old recitative, Wagner replaced it with a stream of accompanied declamation in which entire scenes or acts became musical units. His huge operatic orchestra became, in a sense, the main character, constantly carrying forward, illustrating, or commenting on the action. Old-style themes and melodies were replaced by an intricate web of *leitmotivs*—melodic snatches, rhythms, or single chords associated with specific characters, objects, ideas, or emotions. If Wagner had chosen to portray contemporary social relationships instead of stories of medieval gods and goddesses, he would have been the Ibsen of music, since he was a realist in his structural and technical method.

His greatest claim to fame is, of course, the monumental *Ring of the Nibelung,* and among the most powerful examples of his method in this group of music dramas is the conclusion to *Die Walküre.* Here he makes full use of the leitmotiv effects as, for example, when Wotan tells Brünnehilde that she must lie in magic sleep to be awakened by the first man who finds her—who is Siegfried, announced by the sound of four horns. Probably the most complex, innovative, and spectacular moment arrives at the very close of the drama with the *Magic Fire Music.* Low, shuddering strings first suggest some primordial force. Then, on stage and in the orchestra, flames shoot forth and spread with great delicacy. Soon the entire orchestra is shimmering and glowing to match the blaze on stage; the painting with music that Wagner accomplished here is both enchanting and awesome. He included music for six harps, a tingling glockenspiel, and a high, single shimmering piccolo—all to mirror in music the magic fire that he directed to be created on stage.

Life and Cultural Ideals

In the disillusionment that followed the failure of the liberal revolution of 1848, artists and intellectuals began to question all the high-flown ideals and suprahuman values that had inspired the romantics for over a half-century. This period has frequently been called the objectivist phase of romanticism; and it is well to remember that in the larger view of nineteenth-century stylistic developments, realism was only a phase in the decline of romanticism. In this phase artists, writers, and philosophers turned to the narrow limitations of the immediate phenomena surrounding their everyday existence for study and thought. Life and value for these intellectuals lay in no outside value system or ideal moral code but in the pure encounter of the artist or writer with the individual personality of a character viewed objectively within the context of everyday life. The self, and, therefore, personal self-worth, could be understood only by facing, unflinchingly, the true facts of life and by talking only about the phenomenal world. Today's exaltation of the objective scientist derives from this realistic phase in nineteenth-century romanticism. Certainly the bible during this period was *The Origin of Species*, published by Charles Darwin in 1859, just when it was needed by the cultural pioneers of realism or objectivism.

Undoubtedly, the greatest literary monument to this new outlook is Gustave Flaubert's *Madame Bovary*; there has never been a novel written with such perfect objectivity. Flaubert said: "I want my book to contain not a single agitated page." Although *Madame Bovary* is a faithful picture of all that Flaubert detested in rural bourgeois vulgarity, it contains no satire, personal comment, or personal emotion. Denounced by the critics on its publication, *Madame Bovary* was fully appreciated by the poet Charles Baudelaire, who commented to all authors after reading it: "We must employ a style that is terse, vivid, subtle, and exact on a subject that is banal. We shall imprison the most burning and passionate feelings within the most commonplace intrigue. The most solemn utterances will come from the most imbecile mouths."

Charles Darwin in his sequel to *The Origin of Species* of 1859 (entitled *The Descent of Man* and published in 1871) carefully and painfully developed the idea that Man had not developed as in idealized myths like that of the Adam and Eve story but from a branch of the primate world. His concluding page reads as follows:

> The main conclusion arrived at in this work, namely that man is descended from some lowly organized form, will, I regret to think, be highly distasteful to many. . . . For my own part I would as soon be descended from that heroic little monkey, who braved his dreaded enemy in order to save the life of his keeper . . . —as from a savage who delights to torture his enemies, offers up bloody sacrifices, practices infanticide without remorse, treats his wives like slaves, knows no decency, and is haunted by the grossest superstitions.
>
> Man may be excused for feeling some pride at having risen, though not through his own exertions, to the very summit of the organic scale; and the fact of his having thus risen, instead of having aboriginally been placed there, may give him hope for an even higher destiny in the distant future. But we are not here concerned with hopes and fears, only with the truth as far as our reason permits us to deliver it; and I have given the evidence to the best of my ability. We must, however, acknowledge, as it seems to me, that man with all his noble qualities, with sympathy which feels for the most debased, with benevolence which extends not only to other men but to the humblest living creature, with his god-like intellect which has penetrated into the movement and constitution of the solar system—with all these exalted powers—Man still bears in his bodily form the indelible stamp of his lowly origin.

Though Darwin and other intellectuals wished to sweep away romantic illusion in favor of reality and truth, the middle class maintained its romantic illusions and ideals. But in the process of clinging to the romantic past, the middle class gradually became hardened into a ritual of living, a ritual of thinking, and a ritual of relating to things that supposedly contained romantic feelings and associations. In everyday life, one sensed the change to a mannered, borrowed, heavy-handed, secondhand romanticism that was intended to obscure the brutal facts of the new industrial-capitalist age. Just as the natural and positive ideas of the Renaissance had become hardened, twisted, and distorted by late Renaissance mannerism, so the ideals of romanticism were distorted during the late nineteenth century. Romantic flamboyance and expansiveness in manners, clothing, furnishings, bric-a-brac, and personal memorabilia gave way to tightness, distortions, exaggeration, and excess.

These qualities give a slightly ominous and depressing touch to all the furnishings and interior in the engraving entitled *Grand Reception of the Notabilities of the Nation* from *Leslie's Magazine*, 1865 (Figure 13–7). The women's clothes cling to the expanded, rounded skirt lines of the romantic past, but they are now rigidly held out by hoops and loaded with excessively heavy and large dec-

Figure 13–7 *Grand Reception of the Notabilities of the Nation,* engraving in *Leslie's Magazine,* 1865. Illustrates the subdued, restricted sense of romanticism that prevailed in fashion and interior decoration in the second half of the nineteenth century. Note how the hoops worn by the women distort the human form. Photo courtesy of the Library of Congress.

orative trim. The grand draping of the doorway has become layered and heavy instead of emotionally appealing; and the same is true for the tight patterning in the carpet, the heavy tension in the ceiling decoration, and the size and detail of the chandeliers. To the modern eye, the late nineteenth-century attempt to pile romantic image upon image, rather than

To underline further the fact that late nineteenth-century surroundings were often a desperate and unsuccessful attempt to re-

to create a climax of emotional feeling, produced an oppressive, unnatural, hothouse atmosphere similar to the oppressiveness of the Baroque interiors, clothes, and furnishings at the close of the reign of Louis XIV. In every way, mass taste at this time attempted to turn back the clock and to keep alive a style that was emotionally dead and untrue to real life.

Interiors and Furniture

turn to the romantic preindustrial past, let us look at the library of the Leland Stanford family residence in San Francisco (Figure 13–8).

Figure 13–8 Library of the Leland Stanford family residence, San Francisco, 1876. Illustrates the oppressive, layered, cluttered interiors of the late nineteenth century with great emphasis placed on collected artifacts, memorabilia, and varied historical details. Photo courtesy of the Stanford Archives, Stanford University.

The room is oppressive; not a single space is left free of decoration, collected memorabilia, or architectural trim. It feels like an immense cavern encrusted with the leavings of several generations of inhabitants. The walls are treated like an immense family album on which are placed plates, souvenirs, books, statues, and "good buys" from travels abroad. It is the romantic idea of associationalism carried to a pathological level—a cocoon of collected personal memories to shut out the reality of the industrial world. Such a room insistently asserts the historical learning and cultural appreciation of the owner to state that he was a person of education, position, and material power. And to the modern viewer, it speaks volumes about the fears and repres-

sions of the late nineteenth-century Victorian Age.

To gain some idea of the composite *Beaux Arts* eclecticism of late nineteenth-century furniture, look at the furnishings of this library. There is a lack of interest in good, clean, structural lines; and the tightness, complexity, and placement of the decorative motifs create a pasted-together look, as if the pieces were put together from four or five pictures in a historical furniture book. All the lines and decoration are derivative; the pieces of furniture have no individual qualities. They symbolize the middle-class materialist fascination with decorative "things" with no thought given to function, structure, or tastefulness. From middle class through upper class, realism meant only an interest in collecting an assortment of very detailed objects that in some way stood as symbols or memories of one's past life and inheritance. Sitting in a room like the Stanford library, one would be overcome by the sheer oppressive weight of the decoration; one can easily understand why so many free spirits felt absolutely trapped inside such hothouse, nightmarish interiors. An actor or actress who can absorb fully the feeling of such surroundings will not find it difficult to empathize with Hedda Gabler's claustrophobia in Ibsen's great drama. Hedda is one of the famous theatrical victims of this late nineteenth-century Victorian repressed romanticism.

The costumes of the period, though not as decorative as the interiors, were also inhibiting and oppressive. Both the boned cagelike crinoline that held the skirts out into a bell shape, and the bustle, which distended the back of the skirt with pads during the following period, gave the female form an unnatural, almost grotesque appearance, similar to the unnatural distortions of the human body created by sixteenth-century mannerist costume. Even the trim on the women's gowns, particularly for evening, looked outsized, unnatural, and disproportionate to the human figure, similar to the outsized patterns on the gown of Eleanor of Toledo in the mid-sixteenth century (Figures 6–8 and 13–7).

Male costume after 1848 was a restrained version of the tight-fitting, slim-waisted silhouette of the romantic era. The top hat was still obligatory but was now made of silk, not of beaver, and lacked the flaring crown of the earlier period. The hair was full but not as curled as in the past, and beards became very prevalent. By 1860 a man's daily outfit tended to be sober and uniform in color and was considered a "suit of clothes." Trousers, though narrow, were no longer tight fitting or fastened under the shoe; frock coats and tails were no longer fitted snugly at the waist; and high straight collars that bent out from the chin over the cravat replaced pointed standing collars. In every way, flair and romantic excitement were replaced by boxy, sober, formal, rather repressive clothing. Clothing was specifically detailed for special occasions: the frock coat and top hat for formal afternoon wear; the bowler and short sack suit, including matching waistcoat, pants, and coat, for business wear; short hunting or fishing jackets with leggings for country wear; and a full black outfit of tails with a white vest and tie for formal evening wear. Overcoats superseded the cloak for outdoor wear; and laced shoes began to replace pull-on boots for everyday dress. The *Grand Reception of the Notabilities of the Nation*, depicting Lincoln's second inaugural ball, shows male evening dress (Figure 13–7).

From 1848 until about 1870, female dress concentrated on the rise and fall of the great hooped skirt. About mid-century, the weight of the many petticoats that had created the tea-cozy look brought about a graduated series of metal or boned hoops suspended from tapes to hold out the skirts. The width of the skirt now increased dramatically as the eye moved down the skirt from waist to floor. At their greatest width, about 1860 to 1865, these crinolines were almost grotesque—another symbol of what had happened to the original romantic curves of the 1830s. The hair was now either parted in the middle, waved over the forehead and caught in a twisted bun or bunch of curls over the ears, or drawn in soft waves from the center part of the back of the head and held in a chignon or soft roll. The former style was preferred by Queen Victoria; the latter by Empress Eugénie, wife of Napoleon III, who, with the help of her couturier, the founder of the House of Worth, was the leader of European fashion until 1869. Under her influence the poke bonnet was replaced by a small straw hat with a ribbon at the back or a tiny bonnet set on the back of the head. The hoop skirt, based in part, like the furniture, on Rococo design, usually consisted of several layers of varying lengths: a series of overlapping flounces at the hem;

Costume and Accessories

graduated panels edged with strong trim that expanded in size as they spread out over the skirt; or flowers, fringe, and garlanded ruching layered over it. The trim of the skirt was repeated in the bertha around the shoulders and on the triangular pagoda sleeve with its undersleeves of white tulle. For evening, short cap sleeves and low décolletage were the fashion, while daytime wear required long sleeves and a high neck except for some summer frocks. Fabrics ranged from silk taffetas, damasks, brocades, and velvets to light muslins, gauze, and *crepe de Chine*. Cloth boots were worn by day, slippers by night, and shawls and shaped mantles were worn outdoors. Again, examples of the style can be seen in *Grand Reception of the Notabilities of the Nation* (Figure 13–7).

During the 1870s and 1880s, imitation styles from the past continued to multiply in interiors, furniture, and decoration; it is little wonder that impressionist painters and sculptors like Rodin attempted to move outside of this dead, hothouse confusion of styles. Unfortunately, fashion for the most part continued to follow the mass taste of the times; the only major change was from the exaggerated hoop to the bustle. Even more than the expanded hoop, the bustle created an unnatural and even grotesque effect, which underlined once again the many similarities of this period to Renaissance mannerism.

Masculine dress continued to be very conservative, dictating a set uniform for each part of the day. Formal dress for morning now became as exact as that for afternoon and evening: it consisted of a stiff-bosomed shirt, wing collar, ascot or scarf-cravat, light gray vest, sloped, swallowtail coat, gray striped trousers, pearl gray gloves and spats, and a top hat—all items that are still worn for formal weddings. The formal afternoon garb remained as before, but for informal evening or dinner wear, the tuxedo was introduced. It consisted of a satin-lapeled black jacket of fingertip length, black trousers, a black vest, stiff shirt, wing collar, and black bow tie. Formal evening wear and the business suit continued

with little change; but for sporting events, there was a great variety of Norfolk jackets, knee-length knickerbockers, straw hats, fore-and-aft caps, and leggings. Overgarments were the Inverness caped coat and the Chesterfield overcoat.

In feminine wear, the fabric pieces put together to make a gown greatly increased in number, and the dressmaker's art rose to a truly high level. In skirts, as in interior decoration, folds were draped over pleats, pleats over draping, fringe over brocade, velvet over satin, and trim over trim. Everything seemed a complex juxtaposition of lines, fabrics, and colors. The first bustle, a horsehair pad or small metal-webbed cage, was worn low on the buttocks; the outer skirt was then draped loosely over this protrusion. The upper part of the figure was firmly encased in a corset that pushed up the bust and squeezed in the abdomen and waist; necks were high and sleeves full length except for the short sleeves and low neckline in evening wear.

By the late 1870s, the bustle began to disappear as the outer skirt was draped tighter and tighter about the lower part of the body. In this fish-tailed style that reached its peak about 1880, the hips, waist, and bust emerged with a magnificent flourish created by the careful line of the corseting and a little judicious padding. Evening gowns of this style can be seen in Béraud's *Evening Party Given by the Caillebottes*, painted in 1878 (Figure 13–9). In the early 1880s, the bustle returned; it was now worn higher on the waist, giving the female figure the look of a centaur. A skirt with a bustle was worn with tailored jackets, skating outfits, and topcoats; all were cut to fit the exaggerated protrusion of the back line of the figure. Hair was piled up toward the back of the head with tight curls falling down the back; small hats with flowers, ribbons, and feathers perched atop this hairdo were kept on by a ribbon or a hat pin. Ankle-high buttoned shoes were worn during the day, the heeled slipper in the evening. In general, this dress was an uneasy union of romantic ideals with distortion and repression.

Figure 13–9 Jean Béraud, *Evening Party Given by the Caillebottes,* 1878. A grand gathering of notables including generals, ambassadors, professors, and aristocrats in the salon of a man who supplied equipment to the armies of Napoleon III. Here female fashion has become more distorted through corseting and tighter "fish tail" draping from the knees down. Photo courtesy of Comte Balny d'Avricourt.

Manners and Movement

The precepts for ladylike and gentlemanly manners and movement did not really change from those of the earlier part of the century; they merely became more formalized, rigid, and unnatural during this almost "mannerist" age of upper-class etiquette. A wealthy American wife of an English duke wrote in her diary how she dreaded the heavy protocol of evening meals—the continuously changing table service, profusion of courses, discomfort of eating in tight corsets, only the most perfunctory polite conversation, and an absolutely rigid prescription for carrying out a toast to another guest. Not only the formal dinners but also the entire day was organized in the same rigidly unnatural fashion—from breakfast, through morning coffee, letter writing, promenading, luncheon, tea time, dinner, and an evening of gaming or dance. In its own middle-class-aristocratic way, daily routines must have been as unnaturally regimented as those at the court of Queen Elizabeth I.

As far as male manners and movement were concerned, simplicity and unobtrusive correctness still were in vogue but now without the expansive, outgoing ease of the romantic era. The sober conservatism of men's clothing with its repressive dark colors and exact lines gives us the best key to male manners and movement; that is, manners and movement had to be as unobtrusive as the clothing. Salutations were now limited to lifting the hat, nodding the head, and shaking hands; the bow was relegated to formal court ceremonies or dances.

Now that business was what made the world go round, the calling card was the absolute, essential property for gaining entrance to anyone's house. Cards on which were imprinted a person's title and position were kept in silver cases in the breast pocket of the coat and were left in a salver placed in the entry hall. A gentleman calling on a family asked for the lady of the house, not the master, unless it was merely a business call. If he learned from the servant that the lady of the house was not home but her daughter was, he merely left his card since it was not proper for him to see a young lady in private. If the lady of the house was at home, he was ushered upstairs to the drawing room. He took his hat, cane, and gloves with him but left his outer coat and umbrella downstairs to indicate that

Figure 13–10 William Frith, *The Railway Station* (detail), 1862. Illustrates romanticism within a Victorian framework. The reserve and restraint of the partings contrast with the romantic female clothing, certainly unrealistic wear for train travel. Photo courtesy of Royal Holloway College, University of London.

the call was to be brief, since to stay too long was considered very poor manners. During the visit, he held his hat gracefully in the hand, but if it were necessary to have his hands free, he placed his hat on the floor close to his chair. Mornings were considered a very poor time for such visits; afternoons were preferred.

Ladies, like the gentlemen, were supposed to be reticent and unobtrusive in manners and movement. In the early nineteenth century, movement was quite natural and had a certain gaiety and expansiveness. By the late Victorian period, however, a super-erect posture supported by the tight corseting under the bodice gave what has been called the "hollow backed" look to ladies of fashion when sitting or walking.

Since manners and movement were really a repressed version of those in the romantic period, let us concentrate on the visit as a symbol of the exactness with which things were carried out. First, the lady had to be dressed in a prescribed calling costume. No more than three days were to elapse between receiving and returning a call, and no call was to be longer than a quarter of an hour. This meant that the lady had to restrict the discussion to polite short sentences and to be always conscious of the time. Like the gentleman, the lady wore her hat and outer wrap up to the drawing room and carried her parasol. The lady visitor did not wait to be invited to sit but took a chair immediately, making certain that it was not one favored by the lady of the house.

The Railway Station, painted by William Frith in 1862, brilliantly summarizes the Victorian period with its depiction of the complex social scene that took place in Paddington Station just before the departure of the train, a symbol of one of the new ceremonies created by technology and industrialism (Figure 13–10). One is immediately struck by the contrast between the basically romantic line of the women's gowns and the enclosed repressed feeling of the way the layers of fabric cover and inhibit the natural lines and movement of the human body. One is also struck by the somber uniformity of the male frock coats and top hats and by the enclosed, inhibited rigidity of the dress, especially in collars and cuffs. No person in the entire station suggests an uninhibited, open, emotional response to the separations that the train's departure will bring. All emotion and personal relationships are sentimental and restrained. Finally, one is struck by the anachronism of the formal elegant dress in the dusty, steamy industrial railway station. In the reality of the dirt, noise, and pollution of the new industrial age, Victorian society clung desperately to the escapist ideals of the past.

The Theatre

The ideas of realism were slow to take hold in the theatre, and the mass audience generally continued to patronize romantic melodramas and variety entertainment. The major change came in the well-made boulevard plays, which now dealt much more frequently with current social problems, although these were treated sentimentally and melodramatically. The physical structure of the theatre changed only slightly during the latter part of the century. It was still usually very large, composed of an orchestra floor that now had a slight slope and permanent seats, a circle of balconies in either a horseshoe or U-shape, and extended galleries at several levels at the rear of the theatre.

There was an ever-increasing attempt to present plays, whatever their period, within a setting based on the careful study of historical reality. More pieces of scenery built in solid three dimensions were used to frame the illusionistically painted backdrops, and the entire set was illuminated by gas lighting to give as great an illusion of reality as possible. For plays that required one or more interiors, the trend was toward the three-walled box set with accompanying ceiling. Although the "New Drama" plays, like *La Dame aux Camellias* by Alexandre Dumas *(fils)*, were really romantic melodramas, everything was done to present them in realistic sets and costumes. But only in the plays of Ibsen, Zola, Hauptmann, and Brieux did the settings and costumes become an integral part of the drama and essential to the establishment of the play's psychological environment.

With the integration of background and action came the demand for integrating all aspects of a production and the resultant need for a trained stage director. George II, Duke of Saxe-Meiningen, is usually credited with developing an integrated approach to sets, costumes, acting, and lighting in his large-scale historical productions that toured Europe in the last quarter of the nineteenth century. The Duke worked out blocking and picturization in conjunction with his designs

for sets, costumes, and lighting, and with his stage director drilled his company through a long period of rehearsals.

It remained for independent, noncommercial groups in Paris, Berlin, and Moscow to introduce these new staging methods into the productions of the realistic dramas of Ibsen, Hauptmann, Becque, and Brieux. At the Théâtre Libre, founded in Paris in 1887, André Antoine stressed absolute naturalness in his scenes that incorporated items taken from real life, as can be seen in his setting for Ibsen's *The Wild Duck* (Figure 13–11).

In the preface to *Miss Julie*, the playwright, August Strindberg, insisted that the setting be not only real in its accoutrements but also like a Degas painting (Figure 13–6), asymmetrical, so that the viewer glimpses only a corner of a room: "The very fact that the room is not seen in its entirety (nor all of its furnishings) gives us the incentive to conjec-

Figure 13–11 Setting used for the original production of *The Wild Duck* at André Antoine's Théâtre Libre, 1891. Illustrates the new naturalism in settings pioneered by this leader in realistic production who took as many properties and set decorations as possible from real life. Photo courtesy of the Bibliothèque de l'Arsenal, Paris.

ture. . . . I have placed the rear wall and the table obliquely across the stage for the purpose of showing the actors full face and in half-profile while they face each other across the table."

In the last two decades of the nineteenth century and in the early years of the twentieth century, the Freie Bühne in Berlin, the Independent Theatre in London, and the Abbey Theatre in Dublin also focused on the new realism; but the most lasting influence, especially in the training of actors, came at the Moscow Art Theatre founded in 1898 by Stanislavsky and Danchenko.

Stanislavsky eventually published his theories on actor training in *My Life in Art* and *An Actor Prepares;* his basic precepts are as follows: The actor or actress should have perfect voice projection and body control and be able to identify with the role through the recall of personal experiences. He or she should be able to define and outline the role, particularly the key desires that motivate the character through the play; this ability can only be projected to an audience if the actor is able to fuse, through full concentration, all his onstage work into a single purpose. The actor's response to other actors, sense of the play's rhythmic development, and ability to work continuously toward refinement and perfection are all related to the ideal of onstage concentration.

The Plays

Of the many contributors to the drama of realism, probably the two most important were Ibsen and Chekhov. Though Ibsen borrowed his careful plotting from the well-made plays of Scribe and Sardou to achieve a suspense analogous to that in modern mystery melodramas, his primary aim was to portray a subtle analysis of character within themes of social import. Chekhov, on the other hand, developed the play of mood to project the hidden longings and frustrations of human nature. Like Wagner, Ibsen stressed the structure and craftsmanship of his playwriting, while Chekhov de-emphasized the mechanics of his works so that he could illumine the moods and rhythms of actual life.

Ibsen's *Ghosts* is a typical thesis play that includes the thrill and tricks of a Parisian boulevard melodrama at the same time that it presents a very true picture of the hollowness of a conventional nineteenth-century marriage. In one way, the play pretends to be life; in another, it is artfully crafted in the tradition of the well-made play. The play, therefore, can be viewed as a rational welding together of a clear-cut moral thesis with a subtle look into the human character, in particular into the soul of Mrs. Alving, who carries forward an "inner" story with the outer action. The play is actually a series of debates on conventional morality between Pastor Manders and Mrs. Alving, Pastor Manders and Oswald, and Oswald and Mrs. Alving. Each act concludes with an exciting moment that underlines the issues and promises intriguing new developments. Always behind the surface events of the story lies a vaguely suggested tragedy based on a deep and brooding view of the human condition (Figure 13–12).

Each of the principal characters suffers, searches for answers, and gains new psychological insights with each reversal of the action, much as is the case in *Oedipus Rex*. As in *Oedipus Rex*, we are shown only the end of the search, when the events of the past are illuminated by those of the present. Mrs. Alving finally realizes what the past and its dead ideas have done to her and her household when the "ghosts" from that past come to haunt the present. She thus becomes both a symbol of the play's theme and a very real, warm, and deeply understanding human being. Her son, Oswald, a pathetic human being, symbolizes the dissolution and decay that are a result of the past. Pastor Manders, who is a mere shell of a man, represents all the conventional clichés of a repressive bourgeois morality. All the major characters are

Figure 13–12 Scene from *Ghosts* by Ibsen, produced by the American Conservatory Theatre, San Francisco, 1980, directed by Allen Fletcher. Illustrates the absolute factual fidelity projected in this somber, realistic tragedy. Photo courtesy of Ron Scherl.

thus both believable human beings and stock characters of boulevard melodrama.

The dialogue is everyday speech interlaced with symbolic and mood-evoking expressions meant to suggest a hidden poetry that can be exploited only by the histrionic ability of the actor. There is, therefore, no verbal music in the play, only hidden poetry masked as realistic reporting that comes alive in an on-stage performance. As for the rhythm

of the play, it is on two levels: the rhythm of the everyday life and events within a bourgeois household and the rhythm developing from the mood, inner life, and suffering of the characters.

The detailed stage directions for the play testify to its employment of realistic techniques. The Victorian parlor setting is backed by a large window showing snowy Norwegian peaks that are included to create a sharp, symbolic contrast with the cramped and oppressive interior. The characters are obviously heavily influenced by their physical environment, and the sets and costumes are meant to exploit this sense of limitation and repression to the fullest. The movement and action of the play also stem from this physical environment, the demands of character, and the structural organization of the play. Furniture, in particular, is used to assist, block, or complicate this action. As has been pointed out in the discussion of Degas's painting, the furniture can be arranged to give great meaning to the personal relationships in the play (Figure 13–6).

To understand the full range of realism, it is important to contrast Ibsen's *Ghosts* with a play like Chekhov's *The Cherry Orchard*. By the time that Chekhov wrote *The Cherry Orchard*, the well-made play—with its ambitious mechanism for embedding information and action into a drama with a social message—had begun to lose its popularity. *The Cherry Orchard*, devoid of the mechanical plotting of the well-made play, is constructed around a series of seemingly casual incidents of a familial-ceremonial character. It is basically a theatrical poem that derives directly from the pathos and suffering accompanying individual and social change. The play has no theme in the accepted sense of that word; any theme must be read into the action. Because Chekhov, like many of the symbolist poets, believed that the perceptions preceding rational analysis are the most deeply felt and true, he selected those moments within a family when the characters are the most open and vulnerable—when personal relations are most directly felt and perceived. Each of the four acts is a ceremonial family moment: the arrival from Paris to take up the old life, the pause at sunset when all the characters fleetingly see themselves and their lives for what they really are, the slightly hysterical party when the announcement of the sale of the orchard is finally made, and the final departure.

There is a great difference between what we learn about the characters from hearing their conversations and from observing their actions and silences. Chekhov is, therefore, extremely dependent on the subtle interpretive abilities of his actors and on their completely orchestrated interplay. In a play with a strong social message Lopakhin would have been portrayed as a man of action symbolizing the future, but here he is shown in a pathetic way in his weak moments of reflection, indecision, and personal suffering. Madame Ranevsky, who in another play might be treated as a symbol of the passing aristocratic way of life, is seen here as a confused, impractical, emotionally immature woman trying unsuccessfully to face herself and her past. In fact, all the characters are portrayed as fragmented, insecure, groping, and confused human beings. Particularly in Act II, each character reveals himself or herself within a mood in which rational processes seem to have been abandoned in favor of subconscious longings.

The dialogue is difficult to define because it can be given full meaning only through active interpretation on stage. Pauses, breaks, half phrases, whispers, giggles, exclamations, tears, and laughter are as much a part of the dialogue as the words themselves. Chekhov knew that the poetry of modern realism could be found in those inarticulate moments when a human being is responding unknowingly but directly to his human situation.

Nothing illuminates more clearly the difference between the dramaturgy of Ibsen and Chekhov than the rhythms in the two plays. In *Ghosts* the rhythm is tightly developed from incipient conflict to crisis to denouement, while in *The Cherry Orchard* it is only loosely tied to three ceremonial family occasions. Yet the rhythm in the plays of Chekhov, subordinated to the moods of the characters and the subtle poetry of the setting, is one of the strongest values in the play—an inexorable flow of feeling like a waking dream seen occasionally with sharply focused, wide-awake eyes.

The Cherry Orchard requires three realistic

sets, two indoors and one outdoors. It should be quite obvious that what is needed more than realistic environmental settings is the portrayal of mood and suggestion. By Chekhov's day the symbolist movement in literature and the impressionist movement in art had reached full development, and many of the secondary effects in *The Cherry Orchard* are impressionistic (Figure 14–1). Only by understanding how an impressionistic painter would have perceived light filtered through cherry blossoms, the sunset hours of the day, and a chandelier-illuminated party can the director and the actor have an appropriate feeling for the settings, costumes, and atmosphere in this play.

The plays also differ in their use of furniture. Ibsen, like Degas, uses it to strengthen conflict, control action, and focus movement and climax. Chekhov uses it for mood and symbolic effect, as a reminder of the past and as a catalyst for feelings long forgotten. In addition, the furniture underlines the halting, broken rhythms of the play's development, as, for example, when Epihodov stumbles over a chair after his entrance.

The acting required by Ibsen and Chekhov, although related, is quite different. In Ibsen's plays, actors and actresses must organize their roles in such a way that the parts coincide with the structural climaxes in the play, while in Chekhov's work, the players must be more interested in the rhythm of the particular roles. Basically, this means that the actor or actress in Ibsen's plays must present his or her role in a clear and organized manner so that the great burden of past experience and fact comes across clearly. The player must present a fully developed, realistic three-dimensional personality within the confines of a carefully detailed directorial plan closely tied to the development of the story. In contrast, in Chekhov's work, this background experience and information is not released to an audience directly, but indirectly in pauses, phrasing, gestures, looks, or whispers. The fully three-dimensional personalities of the characters

Acting and Directing the Plays

must come to the audience inadvertently, as if they were discovering the depths of the characters without the knowledge of the playwright. The director is very important, since it is he or she who must establish the mood of a scene and its rhythm and then orchestrate all character action to develop and underline this mood.

The key to both styles of realism, however, is a very careful study of character within a social framework and a developed sense of emotional recall and concentration to make the character personal and truthful. It is only at this point that the works of the two playwrights divide: in Ibsen, into the carefully planned and orchestrated beats of unraveling character knowledge; in Chekhov, into the subterranean rhythm of character that allows character psychology and information to slip through to the audience within the development of the action.

Designing the Plays

In a contemporary production of *Ghosts*, a designer does not have many choices of staging. A direct use of stage realism demands a fourth-wall approach, in which the audience is shown a room interior with realistic furnishings and accessories, though in-the-round and cut-down set pieces and walls are also possible. In such a setting the designer must work with great subtlety and care in order that mood, space, texture, line, and color are subordinated to the environmental character reality of the scene. The single interior in *Ghosts* needs to give the impression of the intimacy of Mrs. Alving's parlor as well as to focus audience attention on the dense and concentrated nature of the play's construction. Each of the five characters must be related to the setting in such a way as to illuminate character and the events that have previously transpired in the room. The single most important mood to establish is that of the ghost of Captain Alving—a sense of what the past twenty years of Mrs. Alving's life have been like. Decorative detail should not clutter the walls and furnishings, obscuring the overall effect of the central mood image. Selective realism balances the fussy detail of a Victorian interior with a careful arrangement of space and furnishings to support character and action.

Couches, tables, and chairs are key items in the conflicts and debates that take place in the parlor, and they must be of appropriate size and shape to complement and support stage action. They can act as supports and barriers, as objects to be caressed or pushed around, or as symbols of persons and objects loved or hated. Furniture, more than any other design contribution, can make the blocking patterns effective in their evocation of the prisonlike atmosphere that has inhabited the house since Mrs. Alving's marriage to Captain Alving. Like the careful design that Degas thought out in a painting such as *Interior: The Rape* (Figure 13–6), single stage settings for realistic plays have to carry a great weight of mood and meaning. They often profit from having the asymmetrical "snapshot" angles demanded by Strindberg in his Preface to *Miss Julie* and brilliantly used by Degas in his interiors.

The costume designs for *Ghosts* should reflect a balance between realistic period clothing for character and a subtle evocation of the mood and atmosphere of the play. The Norwegian costume sources of the early 1880s should be both exaggerated and simplified, with the lines of the clothing following period sources but with those slight changes and exaggerations that will underline character. Complicated Victorian detail should be secondary to clarity of accent and focus and the demands of character. Finally, the stiff, heavy, oppressive textures and the muddied, grayed colors of the Victorian era go hand in hand with the mood of the play.

By the time that Chekhov wrote *The Cherry Orchard*, the mechanisms of the well-made play had begun to be replaced by human emotions presented not in the action of life but in its pauses. Thus in the design of the three settings for this play, photographic reality should be completely replaced by impressionistic suggestion. Lighting should be used indirectly and subtly, like that found in an impressionistic painting. Only in this way can the light filtering through cherry blossoms, the light of the setting sun, and the light of a hectic party illumined by chandeliers support the moods and emotions in the four acts of the play.

Chekhov also differs from Ibsen in his use of furniture. Ibsen uses it to strengthen conflict, control action, and focus movement and climaxes. Chekhov, with his indirect playwrighting method, uses it more as an emotional symbol of the past to call forth the mood of events and feelings long forgotten.

The textures and colors used in *The Cherry Orchard* should appeal to a sense of association—to nostalgia for a past that is drifting away. The soft quality of tears, which continually erupt in Act III, must be reflected in the colors of the upholstery and draperies and in the soft lines of the furniture, paneling, and set decorations. All textures should help to establish the poetry beneath the realistic plot, character, and dialogue of the play. The poplar trees, which are the key to the mood of Act II, should have the mournful "dying fall" supporting that nostalgic sense of the passage of time so important to this act, just as the chandelier-lit room in Act III should enclose in its sad grandeur a hectic happiness.

A look at the clothing in the paintings of Renoir and Monet will help the designer capture the vague impressionistic effects that are right for this play. Thus soft-textured woolens should be used for the men's clothing, while the women's gowns should be made of fabrics with undefined patterns or surfaces that change with movement and lighting. Particularly effective is the use of lace over solid silks to create the mottled and broken color and surface effects of impressionism. Muted colors, pastels, changeable colors, mottled colors, and broken color effects are needed to support the broken and shifting rhythms, dialogue, and characterizations in this play. Thus the strong plot lines and character delineation

in *Ghosts*, which demand strong, focused costume effects, are missing from *The Cherry Orchard*, whose costumes must suggest wispiness, a sense of the passage of time, and the loss of the past.

PROJECTS AND PROBLEMS

1. Why is the year 1848 usually cited as the beginning of the period of realism?

2. Why did realism gradually supersede high romanticism as a style and cultural outlook among artists and intellectuals after 1848?

3. What did Auguste Comte and Charles Darwin contribute to the concept of realism in the late nineteenth century?

4. Why is the mass, middle-class culture of the late nineteenth century called mannerist or repressed romanticism?

5. Is there such a thing as realism in architecture? Explain.

6. From the viewpoint of an actor, director, or designer, what are the attributes of the Paris Opera House (Figure 13–1)? What does it communicate about upper-class culture in the Second French Empire? Imagine yourself arriving by carriage in front of this structure for a gala performance. How would you feel, dress, and move? How would the whole affair differ from a similar affair before the French Revolution?

7. Why was the Crystal Palace not considered architecture when it was built in 1851 (Figure 13–2)? What would you have felt if you were among those viewing it for the first time at the Great Exposition of 1851? Why is it an example of realism in architecture?

8. What would have been your response to Courbet's *The Stone Breakers*, if you had been a nineteenth-century gallery goer at the time of its first exhibition (Figure 13–3)? Why was this painting disliked and accused of being communistic? Why are the subject and technique of execution labeled realistic?

9. Is there anything realistic about Gérôme's *L'Eminence Grise* (Figure 13–4)? Why is the painting, which is in some ways similar to Delacroix's

The Death of Sardanapalus (Figure 12–1), less interesting and dramatic as a staged scene? Why does the scene have the look of a historical melodrama?

10. What is interesting and useful to an actor or director of Chekhov in Eakins's *The Pathetic Song* (Figure 13–5)? Why do you feel sympathetic and close to this lady who has just finished the last note of her song? How has Eakins staged the scene and used lighting to enhance the effect of his staged moment?

11. In Degas's *Interior: The Rape* (Figure 13–6), why does one feel that he or she is looking through a peephole at an intimate personal scene? What directorial and stage techniques does Degas use to achieve his dramatic moment? How are furniture and spatial arrangements used to enhance the moment of drama and give information to the viewer? Imagining yourself as an actor or actress in this scene, give some information about the personal lives of each of the characters.

12. In what way is Wagner's music part of the realistic movement in art and literature? Why does Wagner's work superficially seem analogous to the artistic method used in the design of the Paris Opera House? How are *leitmotivs* used to aid and support characterization and dramatic action? Why is Wagner's work referred to as musical drama rather than opera?

13. What is objectivism? How does Gustave Flaubert's *Madame Bovary* differ from earlier novels about the provincial French scene? After reading *Madame Bovary*, discuss Darwin's statement from *The Descent of Man*. What is his major point?

14. How was the romanticism of the late nineteenth century analogous to the Renaissance ideals of the late sixteenth century? Why can the engraving *Grand Reception of the Notabilities of the Nation* (Figure 13–7) be labeled an example of repressed romanticism? Imagining yourself as a participant in this scene, describe the mood, atmosphere, and your movement and clothing.

15. What would it be like to sit in the library of the Stanford family residence (Figure 13–8)? What does the room communicate about the interest and attitudes of the time? Of the owners?

16. In what ways were female fashions of this period (Figures 13–7 and 13–9) similar to those of the sixteenth century (Figures 6–8 and 6–10)? What was the mood and character of male clothing between 1848 and 1890? How was it worn? How did it fit? How did it feel?

17. What did the hoop skirt do to the female silhouette of the romantic period? Why can it be classified an example of repressed romanticism? Imagine yourself in a full-hooped skirt of the 1860s (Figure 13–7). How does it feel? What happens to your movement? What kind of step must you take? Borrow a hoop skirt to validate your responses.

18. What did the bustle of the 1870s and 1880s do to the female body? Why is the bustle also a form of repressed romanticism? Imagine your movement and describe your personal feelings if you were one of the women in Béraud's *Evening Party Given by the Caillebottes* (Figure 13–9).

19. Describe the mood and character of Béraud's *Evening Party Given by the Caillebottes* (Figure 13–9). How do the men's clothes fit? How are they worn? How do the women's fit? How are they worn?

20. Why was entertaining in the late nineteenth century so difficult and exhausting? Characterize male manners during the late nineteenth century. Act out a little scene of paying a call on a lady. Why is playing this scene so difficult?

21. What was the role of women in the nineteenth century? Why was it impossible for these ladies to have a relaxed intimate relationship?

22. Describe the character of the scene in *The Railway Station* (Figure 13–10). Why does the clothing seem unsuited for train travel? What does this clothing communicate about the differing cultural impulses behind fashion and the expanding transportation industry? What personal relationships are portrayed in the scene? Develop a role for one of the persons in the scene.

23. Describe the physical theatre, lighting, and scenery in the late nineteenth century and the settings. Build a model setting for a play like *Ghosts, The Wild Duck,* or *The Cherry Orchard.*

24. Describe Antoine's setting for *The Wild Duck* (Figure 13–11). How would it affect the acting that would take place within it? How is it related to a realistic painting like *Interior: The Rape* (Figure 13–6)?

25. Develop a scene from *Ghosts* in which the furniture is an integral part of the action. Diagram the rhythm of the scene as you intend to play it. Design a ground plan and a sketch or model for the set needed in *Ghosts.*

26. Do a scene from *The Cherry Orchard.* How does the rhythm differ from that of *Ghosts?* How does the relationship of character to furniture differ? How would the setting differ in its spatial arrangements? Design a model or sketch for one of the sets required in the play. Summarize the difference in the way the dialogue works in the two plays.

27. What is the difference in the way an actress or actor would approach *Ghosts* and *The Cherry Orchard?* How does the mood differ in each play? How do the character rhythms differ in the forward progression of each play?

BIBLIOGRAPHY

Antoine, André. *Memories of the Théâtre Libre.* Translated by Marvin Carlson. Coral Gables, Fla.: University of Miami Press, 1964. An invaluable firsthand record by Antoine of what he accomplished and hoped to accomplish with his Théâtre Libre.

Baudelaire, Charles. *The Mirror of Art.* London: Phaidon, 1955. Excellent essays and criticism on the nature of art and artistic ideals in the new age of industrial reality.

Becker, George J. *Documents of Modern Literary Realism.* Princeton, N.J.: Princeton University Press, 1963. Essays and other documentation on realism in literature after the middle of the nineteenth century.

Boas, George, ed. *Courbet and the Naturalistic Move-*

ment. Baltimore: Johns Hopkins Press, 1938. A very solid study of the naturalistic movement espoused by Courbet and his small group of colleagues and supporters.

Bradbrook, Muriel C. *Ibsen the Norwegian.* London: Chatto & Windus, 1946. An excellent study of Ibsen and his method; also discusses the influence of Ibsen's Norwegian background on his work.

Brockett, Oscar G., and Findlay, Robert R. *Century of Innovation: A History of European and American Theatre and Drama since 1870.* Englewood Cliffs, N.J.: Prentice-Hall, 1973. A marvelous compendium in written and pictorial form on theatre in Europe and America since Ibsen made his mark on the European scene.

Burchell, S. C. *Age of Progress.* Great Ages of Man Series. New York: Time-Life Books, 1966. A beautifully illustrated book, with extensive color photographs, covering the major intellectual, artistic, and cultural developments in the late nineteenth century.

Carlson, Marvin A. *The French Stage in the Nineteenth Century.* Metuchen, N.J.: Scarecrow Press, 1972. Survey of stage production in France.

Gorelik, Mordecai. *New Theatres for Old.* New York: E.P. Dutton, 1962. A brilliant study of the stylistic changes in theatre from realism through Brechtian relativism.

Hamilton, George Heard. *Manet and His Critics.* New Haven, Conn.: Yale University Press, 1954. An excellent discussion of the various revolts against the art of the French Salon carried on under the reluctant leadership of Edouard Manet during the third quarter of the nineteenth century.

Hibbert, Christopher. *Daily Life in Victorian England.* A Horizon Book. New York: American Heritage, 1975. Gives particularly interesting insights into Victorian life and has excellent illustrations.

Hobson, Harold. *French Theatre Since 1830.* London: Calder, 1978. An easy-to-read survey by this eminent London critic with strong emphasis on the development of realism in the theatre.

Hunter, Sam. *Modern French Painting 1855–1956.* New York: Dell Publishing Co., 1956. An easy-to-read survey for the nonspecialist on the trends and developments in French painting in the century following the advent of realism in art.

Klingender, Francis D. *Art and the Industrial Revolution.* Rev. and enl. ed. London: Evelyn, Adams and Mackay, 1968. A very interesting study of the relationship between the arts and the industrial revolution.

Larkin, Oliver. *Art and Life in America.* New York: Rinehart, 1949. A study of art in America in the late nineteenth century and its relationship to the culture.

Lynton, Norbert. *The Modern World.* Landmarks of the World's Art Series. New York: McGraw-Hill, 1965. Discusses European art from the American Revolution to the present.

Matlaw, Myron. *Modern World Drama: An Encyclopedia.* New York: E. P. Dutton, 1972. An excellent reference book of plot summaries and factual details about drama since 1870.

Northam, John. *Ibsen's Dramatic Method: A Study of the Prose Dramas.* London: Faber & Faber, Ltd., 1953. A very illuminating study of how the dramas of Ibsen are constructed.

Reynolds, Graham. *Victorian Painting.* London: Studio Vista, 1966. A very useful look at the themes, techniques, and goals of the artists painting in and around London in the late nineteenth century.

Rowell, George. *The Victorian Theatre.* 2nd ed. London: Cambridge University Press, 1978. A unique insight into the English stage during the nineteenth century.

————.*Queen Victoria Goes to the Theatre.* London: Elek, 1978. An excellent scholarly and witty look at Queen Victoria's taste in theatre by an outstanding British authority on the Victorian theatre.

Sloane, Joseph C. *French Painting between the Past and the Present.* Princeton, N.J.: Princeton University Press, 1951. Another excellent survey of French painting since the middle of the nineteenth century.

Slonin, Marc. *Russian Theatre from the Empire to the Soviets.* Cleveland: World Publishing Co., 1961. An excellent survey of the development of modern Russian drama and theatre from just before the time of Stanislavsky until the death of innovative dramatic development after the Russian Revolution.

Stein, Jack M. *Richard Wagner and the Synthesis of the Arts.* Detroit: Wayne State University Press, 1960. A full picture of Wagner's innovations in the stage and musical arts.

Stone, Edward. *What Was Naturalism? Materials for an Answer.* New York: Appleton-Century-Crofts, 1959. An interesting study of naturalism in art.

Waxman, S. M. *Antoine and the Théâtre Libre.* Cambridge, Mass.: Harvard University Press, 1926. Still an excellent study of Antoine and his theatrical art.

Zucker, A. E. *Ibsen, the Master Builder*. New York: Holt, Rinehart and Winston, 1929. Another rather dated yet still very useful study of Ibsen's structural techniques.

Symbolist Style

After the first full flush of romanticism early in the nineteenth century, the development of theatrical style in relation to culture was a very complicated affair. While mass culture carried on the traditions of romanticism in an oppressive, tight, often unnatural form that we may label neomannerist, the artists and intellectuals were searching for individual personal styles. They hoped that these personal styles would become the spearhead of a new cultural synthesis, a new community of cultural and artistic understanding. Many artists and intellectuals disliked the new realism because it seemed to deny their special roles in society and to debase art into a mere reportage of the facts of life. Those who rejected realism as the answer to the challenges of modern industrial society were not merely late-blooming romantics; they were modernists who wished to probe below the surface of life to expose the subconscious source of human action and feeling. It is no accident that these artists and intellectuals were developing a literature and art based on the subconscious at the same time that Sigmund Freud was investigating the same area in medicine.

The new symbolists, following the suggestions of the poet Baudelaire, had an unremitting concern for structure and composition that would turn the intuitive, irrational, and subliminal into a carefully planned artistic product. Art was viewed as a movement, a self-conscious attempt to impose a personal style and form onto the intangible moods and feelings lying below the surface of life. The entire nineteenth century, with all cultural absolutes removed, had been a battleground between the alienated painters and intellectuals and the great academics and middle class who perpetuated the false prestige and historic superficialities found in mass literature, painting, and public architecture. Artists hoped to create a way of seeing and feeling that would reunite them with the discriminating public. Following the symbolist and impressionist experiments in literature and painting in the 1870s and 1880s, there did emerge in the 1890s a new artistic style based on mood, feeling, and abstract form. This *art nouveau* style, the precursor of modernism in all the arts, was the first all-European artistic movement since the Rococo style that pervaded furniture, interior decoration, painting, posters, architecture, and literature.

The new movement, which in literature and theatre is usually termed *symbolism*, had three separate lines of development: (1) artistic products that stressed the inner secrets of life through mood and suggestion without much concern for form *(impressionistic symbolism)*, (2) artistic products that stressed style and manner of presentation over content *(stylism)*, and (3) artistic products that depicted inner emotional states through violent, harsh, and distorted attacks on the senses *(expressionistic symbolism)*. All these lines of development were closely related: all turned their backs on objective reality, and all used symbols to stand for subliminal, intuitive feelings.

Impressionistic symbolism was an art of suggestion, in which the early poets and painters used vague symbols to suggest deeply buried inner feelings. Even impressionism in painting—originally intended to expand optical reality by concentrating on an isolated moment—gradually drifted into vague, moody, dreamlike effects in which the facts of the scene were obscured by the subjective response of the artist. In *Rouen Cathedral*, which Monet painted many times in order to capture its mood at different moments, the building's structural form is obscured by mist, light, haze, and atmosphere. Here the artist paints not what is actually seen but a memory of how he felt about the Cathedral at a specific moment in time (Figure 14–1). As in a stage setting by Adolphe Appia or Gordon Craig, the lighting and mood stimulate the viewer's imagination. Here a personal vision takes precedence over visual facts; and, following the philosophic concepts of Henry Bergson, reality is now made up of a series of deeply experienced intuitive moments. Later, Marcel Proust was to define reality in terms of memory in his great work *Remembrance of Things Past*.

Figure 14–1 Claude Monet, *Rouen Cathedral*, 1894. Illustrates the dissolution of reality and structural form through mist and light so that personal vision takes precedence over visual reality. Photo courtesy of the Metropolitan Museum of Art, bequest of Theodore M. Davis, 1915.

In literature, the symbolist poets were heavily influenced by Edgar Allan Poe, who though a romantic, wrote stories and poems that were remarkable for their portrayal of subliminal feelings. It was the deep sense of fear, not the story values, in *The Pit and the Pendulum* and *The Masque of the Red Death* that interested the symbolists. In *The Raven*, the image of a raven sitting on a bust of Pallas Athena intoning "Nevermore" speaks more directly of death than do the events described. The favorite artist colleague of the symbolist poets, Odilon Redon, used Poe's mixture of the fantastic, mysterious, and subliminal in many of his works. Like the famous descriptive phrase that had been used by Delacroix, he wished that his art were like "the memory of music" that had passed away. Of his painting *Reverie* and others with such cryptic titles as *Silence* and *The Dream*, Redon said that he was attempting to "put the logic of the visible at the service of the invisible." He used the resources of the inner mind and not the world of the senses to develop his images. In drama this method was fully developed by Maurice Maeterlinck, whose play *Pelléas and Mélisande* came to full realization only when Claude Debussy, the great exponent of the impressionist tradition in music, made this drama into an opera. In Debussy's vague, moody, shifting evocations of the forest, moon, and sea, we have in music what the painters and poets so longed for in their art.

As can be seen from the paintings just described, impressionistic symbolism tended to be formless. In contrast, the stylistic branch of symbolism emphasized mood and feeling married to a strong sense of form and design. These artists used many of the impressionists' images and symbols but made design and pattern equal to mood. A certain artificiality and sense of style was developed as an end in itself, much as it had been in sixteenth-century mannerism.

This same ornamental approach can be found in art nouveau design, which was based on organic forms suggesting movement and growth. Its typical motif is the undulating, sweeping, serpentine line that wraps around or rises from a structural base, figure, or compositional frame and ends in loops and scrolls. This style evokes a feeling of elegant fantasy that was adapted to furnishings, interiors, book designs, posters, and even the entrance to the Paris Metro (Figure 14–2). Probably the most famous purveyor of this art nouveau style was Aubrey Beardsley, whose illustrations for Oscar Wilde's deeply symbolist

Figure 14–2 Hector Guimard, the Monceau entrance to the Paris Metro, c. 1900. Illustrates the *art nouveau* style of design in which organic growth forms reach out in serpentine, undulating lines and wrap around a structural base in loops and scrolls. Projects a mood of elegant, sophisticated mystery in the symbolist tradition. Photo courtesy of the French Cultural Services, New York.

drama, *Salomé*, epitomize the elegant, ornamental, neomannerist decadence of the best designed products and illustrations. In *Salomé with the Head of John the Baptist*, a complete, imaginative world of sensuality and decadence is suggested through the strong contrasts of black and white, the sensuous and evil curve of the lines, and the overall patterned strength of the design (Figure 14–3). The illustration portrays a hidden world of the psyche without resorting to moody mist and vagueness of form—a very difficult accomplishment.

Still another aspect of symbolism developed in the 1890s in the work of artists who were neurotically at odds with society and who found art nouveau design techniques and the soft moods of impressionistic symbolism weak and diluted in their emotional effect. The paintings of Edvard Munch, James Ensor,

Figure 14–4 Edvard Munch, *The Scream*, 1893. Illustrates expressionism in painting with the use of swirling brush strokes and exaggerated shapes that carry the subjective and violent inner images of fear to the level of nightmare. Photo courtesy of the National Gallery, Oslo.

Figure 14–3 Aubrey Beardsley, *Salomé with the Head of John the Baptist,* pen drawing, 1892. A complete world of sensuality and decadence is suggested through strong contrasts of black and white, sensuous and evil curves of line, and an overall strength of design. Photo courtesy of the Princeton University Library.

and Vincent Van Gogh and the plays of August Strindberg, Georg Kaiser, and Ernst Toller reflect the tremendous psychic strain experienced by extremely sensitive and neurotic personalities in a modern, industrial, bour-

geois society. For example, Edvard Munch's *The Scream* presents a stark and terrifying image of fear and suffering that is meant to represent the fate of modern man (Figure 14–4). Dehumanized and alone, the figure emits a deep scream of pain that is silent and unheard by the world at large. The rhythm of the long wavy lines scrubbed into the background carries the echo of the scream into every corner of the picture, making earth and sky a great sounding board of fear and suffering. In all the variations of expressionistic symbolism, patterns and symbols present the outer world of reality in a distorted, violent, explosive, nightmarish manner that reflects the inner world of the artist. In its attacks on the suffering, horror, and injustice of modern life, expressionistic-symbolist art produced results that were distorted and shocking abstractions from real life.

Auguste Rodin and Antonio Gaudí were two brilliant and unique artists who united the three separate forms of symbolistic development and whose art, in many ways, represents the last theatrically violent attempt to say something new, modern, and exciting within the emotional context of dying romanticism. Their work is a testimony to the true symbolist belief that reality can be reached only through mood, feeling, distortion, and symbol and also seems to be a reaction against the rising interest in objectivity, form, function, and pure abstract design.

The work of Auguste Rodin, the greatest European sculptor since Bernini, represents both the softness, mood, and mystery of impressionistic symbolism and the violent, distorted, and pulsating surfaces of expressionistic symbolism. It also clearly gives evidence of the Bergsonian idea that reality is forever in flux—a process of dynamic growth and decay. For example, the famous *Burghers of Calais* is an intensely expressionistic work (Figure 14–5). It commemorates a heroic episode in the Hundred Years War, when seven leading citizens of Calais offered their lives to the conquering English in exchange for the lives of all their fellow citizens. Each of the

Figure 14–5 Auguste Rodin, *Burghers of Calais,* larger than life size, bronze, 1884–86. Illustrates a powerful image of human suffering and despair created through exaggeration and distortion of pose; intensified, pulsating texture; and lighting that breaks and shatters on the surfaces of the bronze statues. Photo courtesy of the Musée Rodin.

individual figures is a convincing study of despair, resignation, or quiet defiance; however, these psychic effects are underlined by the exaggeration and distortion of surfaces, poses, and movement. The work is very dependent on the way that lighting breaks up and reflects from the body surfaces of the individual figures. It is an expressionistic statement of deep feeling without the superficial distortions frequently found in many expressionist plays and paintings.

Antonio Gaudí in architecture also attempted to escape from the normal, academic tradition and to suggest the random nature and sublimation of feeling that were the essence of reality to the symbolists. In his still uncompleted Church of the Holy Family, the general silhouette is Gothic; the curves and ornament are art nouveau; and the mood and imagery are like symbolist poetry (Figure 14–6). There is no question that in this attempt to create a modern, spiritual equivalent for medieval spiritual fervor and mysticism, Gaudí was working in the same vein as the expressionists. All of Gaudí's structures contain a fascinating array of forms and architectural imagery very useful to theatrical designers and directors in achieving appropriate emotional backgrounds for expressionist dramas.

Figure 14–6 Antonio Gaudí, Church of the Holy Family, Barcelona, begun in 1888. Gothic in outline, the design is based on the curves and ornamentation of *art nouveau* style carried to the level of expressionistic nightmare. Photo courtesy of the Office of Spanish Tourism.

Music

The symbolist poets and painters had in Claude Debussy a musical counterpart. By developing a hypersensitive tonal palette, Debussy was able to create a multitude of musical images from subtle perfumes (*Sounds and Perfumes on the Evening Air*), submerged architecture (*Engulfed Cathedral*), moody seascapes (*La Mer*), exotic festivals (*Iberia, Fêtes*) to flashing fireworks (*Feux d'Artifice*).

Claude Debussy translated Maeterlinck's *Pelléas and Mélisande* into the perfect symbolist opera or dramatic tone poem. In this drama of dramatic pauses, Debussy filled in the silences with the necessary nebulous sounds that give voice to the "murmur of eternity" and that link one dreamlike scene with another. It is as if his music were specifically created to provide the tonal envelope for Maeterlinck's "ominous silence of the soul." The musical references to the sea, on which all the characters symbolically float to their unknown destiny, are especially subtle and appropriate. There is musical water imagery in almost every scene, from the spring in the forest, to the fountain in the park, to the well in the courtyard, to the fetid pools in the underground caverns. This ever-present water imagery symbolizes the flowing, fleeting nature of existence; it captures the mood and vague atmosphere that must be deeply felt for the opera to be effective.

In developing his tonal method for this musical masterpiece, Debussy followed Wagner in giving the orchestra the primary task of carrying the story. The singing is merely a dramatic commentary on the action. Like Wagner, Debussy believed that melody impeded dramatic progress because it could not suggest the constant changes of rhythm and emotion in life. He thus brought the vocalized dialogue closer to everyday speech, allowing the dramatic action to proceed without interruption, the rhythms to be free and without any regular accentuation, and the words to achieve a flow and elasticity never found before on the operatic stage.

The musical motifs in the opera parallel the literary symbols and are often mere fragments of melody. Rather than underline specific personality traits, they suggest, like Wagner's *leitmotivs*, a mood connected with a character. The harmonic method also supports the ambiguities of the literary and poetic symbols. Centers lose their boundaries; progressions move about freely in tonal space; tritone intervals accent indefiniteness and drift; and everything seems to be in a state of flux—never arriving at a definite conclusion.

The instrumentation is particularly uncanny, as, for example, when Mélisande's soft and silky voice is carried by the woodwinds that dominate the orchestral coloration with their peculiar, poignant, penetrating sound. It is very important that performers know how to project this intangible music. They must make the music live and breathe and have an appropriate elastic rhythm, filling the silences in the story with the correct sense of meaning and mood.

Richard Strauss and Alban Berg were two other outstanding expressionist composers during this period. Strauss's *Salomé*, created in 1905, is an excursion into abnormal psychology with sensuous sounds and rich orchestral colors building to the climactic amorous soliloquy of Salomé holding the severed head of John the Baptist. The combined attraction and repulsion of the piece produced a tremendous emotional excitement in the audience; when first presented, the opera was banned in many places. Strauss's *Elektra*, created in 1909, is a violent and near-psychotic rendering of the heroine of Sophocles's tragedy, filled with excessive emotional climaxes, blood-curdling screams, and lurid orchestral sounds. Berg's *Wozzeck*, written in 1912, telescopes the rise to musical climax through dissonances that jump from soft to loud, high to low, without any melodic progression.

Life and Cultural Ideals

Though the ideals of the symbolist movement were developed by Baudelaire in the 1860s, the designs of art nouveau were not incorporated into household art until the turn of the century. In addition, not until the years before World War I did the movement have a philosophic base, which was formulated by Henri Bergson. Bergson was convinced that the intellect was inadequate for dealing with the "fringe of intuition, the vague and evanescent that surround every clear idea." He believed that we all "change without ceasing" in the endless flow of psychic life and at the subconscious level, inaccessible to reason. The deep self, according to Bergson, was immersed in a movement of time that he called "duration," which cannot be measured by hours or days but only felt and remembered as a memory. Intuitions, therefore, have a mobility that permeates and envelops our deep experiences like an atmosphere, saturating the level of consciousness where perceptions melt one into another as in a dream. Thus true reality is lived, not thought. Though we may think in categories of time and place, we exist in an inner world of duration made up of the continual shift from one state of soul to another. In this way, Bergson created the philosophic basis for the artistic effects found in the plays of Maeterlinck and Yeats, the poems of Mallarmé and Verlaine, the paintings of Redon and the later ones of Monet, and the more superficial artistic forms of art nouveau.

In the poetry of Stephane Mallarmé, we have an excellent example of an emphasis on design, style, and mood at the expense of information and fact. Mallarmé creates an impermeable surface of beauty consisting of subtle metaphors that glide into one another to create a mood like that found in Debussy's music. It is impossible to ask what the metaphors are for or about —they are not about anything. The greatness of Mallarmé lies in his ability to keep the reader suspended over a void of nothingness. For example, take section III of *Hérodiade* published in 1887 (translated by C. F. Macintyre).

The sun that is exalted
by its supernatural halt
forthwith redescends
    incandescent

I feel how vertebrae
in the dark give way
all of them together
    in a shudder

and in lonely vigil
among flights triumphal
of this scythe's swings
    my head springs

as the downright rupture
represses or cuts rather
the primordial clash
    with the flesh

Drunken with abstinence
may it stubbornly advance

in some haggard flight
    its pure sight

up where the infinite
cold does not permit
that you be its surpasses
    O all glaciers

but, thanks to a baptism
shining from the chrism
of that consecration
my head bows salutation.

Finally, let us quote from Oscar Wilde, one of the most influential dandies and stylists of the late nineteenth century. His belief that any life that was worth living had to be designed, had to have a style, and had to have a mood and essence that artistically expressed the inner personality was an exaggerated symbolist or art nouveau ideal. In a very diluted form it permeated everyday culture in the succeeding Edwardian age. This quotation is from *The Decay of Living*, published in 1889:

Life imitates Art far more than Art imitates Life. This results not merely from Life's imitative instinct, but from the fact that the self-conscious aim of Life is to find expression, and that Art offers it certain beautiful forms through which it may realize that energy. It is a theory that has never been put forward before, but it is extremely fruitful, and throws an entirely new light upon the history of Art. . . .

The final revelation is that Lying, the telling of beautiful untrue things, is the proper aim of Art.

Interiors and Furniture

Though the move toward a unified style in furnishings and interiors had developed earlier in the Craftsman Movement led by William Morris—with its emphasis on good lines and carefully controlled patterns—the heavy, eclectic ugliness of Victorian interiors did not disappear until about 1895, when it was replaced by the freshness of the art nouveau style. In Vienna, Paris, Brussels, London, and New York, interiors and furnishings began to adopt the growth lines and sinuous curves of this new style. Let us look at the entry to the Hotel van Eetvelde in Brussels, designed in 1895 by one of the leading art nouveau architects and designers, Victor Horta (Figure 14–7). Obviously, the weapon used here against eclectic historicism is ornament that is no longer historical but is abstracted from the growth lines of nature into a dynamic and organic statement of style, projecting what Wilde said about nature imitating art. The key to the excitement in this new form is the ever-changing and dynamic adaptability of the organic growth lines and the ease with which they flow over and beyond normal structural boundaries. Floors, lighting fixtures, furniture, wall paneling, and ceilings create a linear unity of curved lines and surfaces, and the impression of organic growth replaces the traditional concept of architecture as rational construction. The room symbolizes a state of mind, a process, a "becomingness" that is related to what Mallarmé did in poetry, what Monet did in painting Rouen Cathedral, and what Bergson meant when he spoke of reality as a psychic process of "change without ceasing."

Figure 14–7 Victor Horta, entry to the Hotel van Eetvelde, Brussels, 1895. Here the weapon used against the eclectic historicism of the earlier nineteenth century is ornament that is not historical but is abstracted from the dynamic growth lines of nature to create a world of fantasy, artificiality, and style. Photo courtesy of the Museum of Modern Art.

In the fashions of this period, elegance and style dominated in men's clothing; and frothy, romantic impressionism in a grand manner marked female dress until the stylistic revolution of 1912. The Edwardian age, though only a decade in length, was completely devoted to a sense of elegance and style. Male fashions changed only slightly during this period, though casual clothing originally conceived for sports and outings now became more prevalent even for city wear. The fashionable ideal was the subtly tailored and elegantly fitted suit of clothes worn by the dandy or "dude." Hair was now frequently parted in the middle; clean-shaven faces reappeared, and many varieties of soft homburgs, fedoras, straws, and caps began to replace the rigid topper and bowler. Very high, stiff collars were still the rule whether they were winged or standing, though the softer, turndown collar was used for casual wear. The ascot and four-in-hand ties were now rivaled in popularity

Costume and Accessories

by the bow tie. Shirts, though stiff bosomed for formal occasions, were soft for informal wear and were often striped, with only the separate collar and cuffs remaining white. Though the formal morning coat, tails, tuxedo, and frock coat were still worn, they were now more frequently put aside in favor of blazers, Norfolk jackets, cardigans, and variations on the sack suit. There were also both single- and double-breasted vests and waistcoats, often contrasting in color and pattern with the coat and trousers. Trousers were slim, pressed into a crease, and frequently turned up into a cuff. Knee trousers or knickers were worn with long woolen stockings by young boys and by men for sporting occasions. Ankle-length button shoes were worn in winter; low oxfords in summer. Spats were very fashionable. Heavy or light overcoats, sometimes in a plaid pattern with shoulder cape, at other times with fur lining and trim, were worn for outer garments.

Figure 14–8 Jean Béraud, *Jardin de Paris, The Night Beauties,* 1906. An image of languid sophistication created by the setting, poses, and soft, feathery, layered, semitransparent fashions worn by the ladies. They express the male fantasy of the ideal female at this time—windblown birds of plumage or froths of meringue drifting among the black and white uniforms of male society. Musée Carnavalet, Paris. Photo courtesy of Giraudon, Paris.

In female dress, the first major change was the disappearance of the bustle. This allowed the female form a much softer silhouette, with only a certain amount of residual drapery at the rear of the skirt. By the mid-1890s, the skirt became a smooth, many-gored, flared affair with extra fullness at the back; and large leg-o'-mutton sleeves and a tiny waist brought back some of the expanding lines of early nineteenth-century romantic fashions. The dresses remained high-necked and long-sleeved for daytime, with décolleté and short-capped sleeves for evening. A feminine version of the male suit appeared in the 1890s, consisting of a tailored jacket and ankle-length skirt worn with a shirt-blouse and tie; but its severity did not markedly interfere with the frothy smother of lace, frills, and trimming that went into blouses and bodices for the daytime fashions of the woman of leisure.

In the first years of the twentieth century, a new corset line appeared that pushed the bust forward and the hips backward to create the famous sway-backed S-curved art nouveau line found in furniture and decoration of the time. Hair, which had been drawn fairly close to the head, now became fuller, softer, and surrounded the temples, ears, and forehead with a massive halo. Flowered and beribboned hats, which had small brims in the 1890s, expanded into great, broad-brimmed creations saturated with plumes, ribbons, and birds. By 1908, the silhouette was slimmer, the bust had become higher and more prominent, and the hips were tightly held in by the corset. Three years later the revolution in women's dress began. At first, there was a brief revival of pseudo-Empire styles; then the corset was completely thrown aside. The one-piece, kimonolike costume took over, with much tight draping about the legs to gain a diamond-shaped silhouette and the famed hobble-skirt effect. Large, floral, oriental, and art nouveau patterns became fashionable; hats became smaller; turbans became popular; and hair became much simpler, softer, and shorter.

To make the revolution in clothing fully apparent, look at a painting done in 1906 and a fashion illustration from 1912. In *Jardin de Paris, the Night Beauties* by Jean Béraud, the ideal woman is still a "princess" or a "queen," set off from active modern life, swathed in laces and layers of fabric that fall to the floor, her face framed by a great spreading hat brim (Figure 14–8). Both the painting technique and the lace and ruffles of the gowns reinforce the subjective mood of romantic illusion and impressionistic unreality. The painting represents the last attempt at nineteenth-century romanticism in women's dress before the women's suffrage movement brought about a totally different image. In short, this painting is impressionistic symbolism in terms of female dress.

Contrasting with this is the fashion illustration of a 1912 evening gown from *Journal des Dames et des Modes*, where both the costume and the rendering technique have been altered sharply (Figure 14–9). Gone is the fuzzy moodiness and escape into a romantic world of illusion. We now have a full-fledged art nouveau statement in illustrative technique as well as in dress design. The shimmering illusion of the queen or princess has given way to the *femme fatale* or "vamp." The costume is cut with few seams to allow free, sensuous movement of the body, and long hair and a large hat have been replaced by short hair and a tight turban. In every way, the figure has been transformed from a romantic illusion into a strong, clear, and decorative silhouette of pure pattern and movement.

Finally, a word must be said about the male image. It did not make a dramatic change

Figure 14–9 A fashion design from *Journal des Dames et des Modes*, 1912. Illustrates the revolution in women's dress that took place between 1910 and 1912. This is a full-fledged *art nouveau* statement with emphasis on tunic shapes, draping, and large flat patterns. Bertarelli Collection, Milan. Photo courtesy of the Archivio Fotográfico dei Civici Musei, Milan.

as did the female image. The elegance and sophistication of the Edwardian ideal is summed up in *Portrait of Count Robert de Montesquieu*, painted by Giovanni Boldini during the first decade of the new century (Figure 14–10). The image is one of absolute sophistication and impractical elegance, one that was to be swept away by World War I.

Manners and Movement

Manners did not change very much until after World War I. The upper classes still kept their links to the aristocratic past, and even in the United States, it was always English and French customs that were followed. "Traditional" behavior was still admired, beginning

Figure 14–10 Giovanni Boldini, *Portrait of Count Robert de Montesquieu,* c. 1906. Illustrates the perfect gentleman at the opening of the twentieth century in his absolute sophistication and subtle elegance. The Museum of Modern Art, Paris. Photo courtesy of the French Musées Nationaux.

with the rules inculcated by the "nanny" and continuing in private schools or under governesses and tutors. The dancing classes, physical drills, lessons in French, and exercises on how to stand, sit, rise, walk, greet people with a wave of the hand, and bow for formal occasions remained.

In particular, male behavior did not change much as life turned into a new century. The image of the male as the dominant sex in all matters, except control of children and management of the household, still held.

Men, in theory, were still complete masters of their households, dispensing justice and wisdom like oriental potentates. The Victorian image of the family attacked by Ibsen in his play *The Doll's House* had not changed forty years later. Men reserved for themselves all types of special privileges. Women were banned from voting booths, clubs, restaurants, saloons, and tobacco shops; and, as late as 1904, a woman was jailed in New York City for smoking in public. The male, whether an aristocrat, bank president, or head clerk, managed to fit himself out in a style that proclaimed him a member of the privileged sex. Take, for example, his impressive array of toiletries: ivory-handled straight razors, decoratively tooled leather razor straps, shaving brushes of soft badger hair, personally monogrammed china shaving mugs, colorful glass bottles of shaving lotion, ornamental jars of pomade for the hair, wax for the mustache, and hair dye to preserve a youthful look. In addition, there were the inevitable pipes and cigars, ornamental jars of tobacco, cigar cutters built like small guillotines, plug tobacco for chewing, shiny brass spittoons, fancy crystal decanters of whiskey often locked into a portable carved or tooled carrying case, handy breast-pocket flasks, poker chips, and counters for various card and dice games.

The males still retired with their cigars from the company of women after a dinner party, retreated to their all-male clubs or saloons after work, or gathered to exchange stories in their all-male barbershops. In summary, this almost obsessive demand for male dominance in both private and social domains helped to spark the development of the women's suffrage movement at the end of the first decade of the twentieth century.

The few slight changes in manners for men that did occur were as follows: Whereas in the past a gentleman took his hat and stick with him into the drawing room, holding them until he had seen the mistress of the house, he now followed the new fashion of leaving the hat and stick in the hall. When walking with a lady in the street, the gentleman still observed the old custom of walking on the outside, but he did not remove his hat in a public entrance or shop unless he expected to meet a lady friend or acquaintance. As far as shaking hands was concerned, much more discretion was now left to the individual as to when and how to practice this universal salutation. The many small rules and suggestions for manners were less important, however, than maintaining an image of dominance and, if the male held a high position, one of elegance as well (Figure 14–10).

Since the woman's place was still firmly in the home, her major concerns were keeping or supervising the house, caring for the children, and attending to various social engagements. She was expected to entertain her husband's business partners and friends, make visits to hospitals and the poor, and work with ladies' guilds or other charitable organizations. The most important function of all, however, was subtle control of the men. Women dressed, moved, and talked in order to dazzle their menfolk with feminine "wiles," a practice aided and abetted by the flood of women's romantic fiction promoting the ideal of the softly genteel but indomitable female. Articles preached decorum, cautioned against dangerous new ideas, and called the works of Ibsen, Zola, and Shaw "cancerous literature." Though women in increasing numbers were working in office jobs, factories, and shops, the feminist movement tried to sweep many more into political activity. But public life and outside work were adventures for only the daring minority; the average woman concerned herself with the traditional roles of obliging her husband, rearing her children, making her nest a cozy place, and easing her cares with light reading.

A firsthand account by Princess Marie Louise of England in her book *My Memories of Six Reigns* gives us an insight into the polite life of manners and movement at an Edwardian ball. At one end of the ballroom, the king and queen sat on a dais with other members of the royal family. When the procession of the royal party first entered the hall, the guests rose and remained standing during the dancing of the state quadrille. During this first

dance, the princesses danced with ambassadors and cabinet ministers. As Princess Marie Louise observed, some of the men were so out of practice that they had to be pushed through the steps of the dance. After the dance, the princesses returned to their elegant gold and white chairs, and everyone remained seated until the first waltz of the evening, which was the "Blue Danube." At midnight the dancing was interrupted for supper, and the royal procession was formed again, followed by the diplomatic corps, cabinet ministers, and peers of the realm. They proceeded into the state dining room, where the table was resplendent with fine gold plates and a lavish feast.

After supper the guests returned to the ballroom for more dancing, which ended with the *lancers* about two in the morning. As the royal party left, amid the singing of the national anthem, the farewells were as follows: "The Queen and the royal ladies made three profound curtsies, first to the left where the *Corps Diplomatique* were seated, then to the right where the peers and peeresses were seated, and finally *en face* to the general company. Meanwhile the King and Princes bowed, also three times and in the same order."

To summarize the mood, manners, and movement of this period, let us look again at J. Béraud's *Jardin de Paris, The Night Beauties* (Figure 14–8). The first thing that strikes one's attention is the overall atmosphere of languor and sophistication that typified the Edwardian era. Then one notices the layers of soft semitransparent material worn by the "ladies of the night," which convey the male fantasy of the female ideal rather than a realistically conceived human form. These costumes in movement epitomize the impressionistic symbolism that was the basis of art and philosophy during this period. The two ladies are like windblown birds of plumage or froths of meringue drifting among the black-and-white society uniforms of the males. Again we are looking at the last portrayal of romanticism in impressionistic-symbolist guise before the radical shift to the strong outlines, patterns, and abstractions of art nouveau.

The symbolist movement in the theatre had its origins in the theatrical and musical theories of Richard Wagner who dedicated himself to the fusion of music, dialogue, color, light, shape, and texture. In his theatre at Bayreuth, he used a double proscenium, a curtain of steam, and controlled lighting between auditorium and stage to create a mystic void between audience and stage. At the end of the century, artists of the symbolist theatre, like Paul Fort and Lugné-Poë, employed many of Wagner's techniques; in the 1892 première of Maeterlinck's *Pelléas and Mélisande* at the Théâtre l'Oeuvre, a transparent curtain was used in front of the action to create a realm of mood and mystery. About this same time, the stage designer and theorist, Adolphe Appia, began to experiment with stage lighting as the great unifying element in production. He defined the actor in space against simple, abstract, three-dimensional forms and sup-

ported the shifting moods of the action by using stage lighting as if it were music (Figure 14–11). At the beginning of the new century, a young English designer, Gordon Craig, further developed these same ideals and placed even more emphasis on blending action, words, space, color, and rhythm into a single, unified, artistic product.

By the end of World War I, the influence of these two theatre artists pervaded most artistically designed productions. The theatre artist who most fully transformed these impressionistic-symbolist techniques into a variety of exciting productions was Max Reinhardt, who took Craig's slogan "Not realism, but style" and gave new meaning to the term *regisseur*. Reinhardt paraded before the public theatrical styles of the past and from the Orient in productions that made brilliant use of visual and aural symbols to gain total unity of mood and effect. Although his eclec-

Figure 14–11 Adolphe Appia, design for *Parsifal,* 1896. Illustrates the "New Stagecraft" in which scenery and lighting were designed to express and heighten a playwright's theatrical intention from moment to moment without distraction from realistic historical detail. From George Altman, Ralph Freud, Kenneth Macgowan, and William Melnitz, *Theater Pictorial* (Berkeley: University of California Press, 1953). Photo courtesy of William Melnitz.

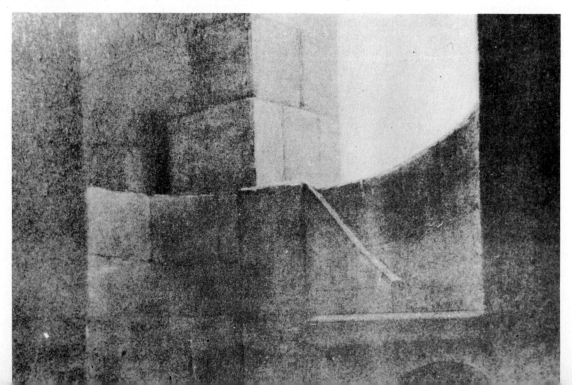

Figure 14–12 Robert Edmond Jones, sketch for Act III, scene 4, of *Macbeth* designed for a production at the Apollo Theatre, New York, 1921. Directed by Arthur Hopkins. Illustrates violent expressionism in the theatre using findings in abnormal psychology to underline and express the emotions of the protagonist. From Ralph Pendleton, ed., *The Theatre of Robert Edmond Jones* (Middletown, Conn.: Wesleyan University Press, 1958). Photo courtesy of Mr. Robert Thirkield.

ticism was criticized by the modernists, he returned the visual arts to a key position in the theatre.

Meanwhile, the beginnings of expressionistic symbolism in art and playwriting had begun to develop, and during World War I, experiments in expressionistic production began. Because of the particular moment when these innovations occurred, the physical attributes of the productions were heavily influenced by cubism. Most early experimental efforts used the sharp edges and angles of cubism to create interiors and exteriors that were distorted from their normal real-world relationships (Figure 14–12). When the New Stagecraft reached America after World War I in the work of Lee Simonson, Robert Edmond Jones, and Norman Bel Geddes, the ideals of Appia, Craig, Reinhardt, and the expressionists were all subjected to experiment and interpretation.

The Plays

The play that most strongly demonstrates the ideals of impressionistic symbolism is Maurice Maeterlinck's *Pelléas and Mélisande*. For this moody, legendary tale, crying out for music to support its mystery and unreality, the perfect wedding of playwright and composer occurred when the drama was finally made into an opera in 1902. The play, based on Dante's tale of Paolo and Francesca, consists of a series of loosely connected scenes depicting the fated love of the two protagonists. Each scene involves some mood-evoking symbol: in one, Mélisande's doves leave her forever; in another, she loses the ring that symbolizes her marriage vow; in another, Yniold tries to lift a stone that symbolizes the weight of sin that has fallen on the family. It is mood and theme that count, and the number of scenes can be expanded or contracted without much effect on the development of the story. Scenes are thus connected by atmosphere and symbol, not by a cause-and-effect chain of events.

The characters are also vague and mysterious. Moved by feelings and desires, not thought, they are destined to live and die without enlightenment at the mercy of some inexplicable fate. We know only their age, social class, and desires; their personalities are only vaguely suggested. Maeterlinck was not interested in creating flesh-and-blood individuals but rather walking states of mind at the mercy of an inscrutable fate.

Motifs are repeated to support the mysterious mood. Water symbolizes the mystery of life as in the forest pool near which Mélisande is first discovered, the fountain in which she loses her ring, the bottomless pits of water that lie under the castle, the water used to wash the blood from the steps, and the sea that beckons the soul with its sense of escape. A similar effect is created by the use of light versus dark. The forests are dark; the characters are described as being in darkness groping for light; lamps die out and cannot be relit; and love and happiness are portrayed as forces of light struggling with fate and the forces of darkness. In his own way, Maeterlinck was more pessimistically determinist in his outlook than were the realists, since he saw all life as a mysterious and impenetrable unknown.

The language of the play is extremely simple and repetitive so that words and phrases ring in the ear as symbols of inexplicable feeling. In his essay *The Treasure of the Humble*, Maeterlinck described a secondary language—the dialogue of the soul—in which apparently unnecessary words and phrases

speak to man's deepest sense of truth and beauty. The playwright expected his audience to search behind the words and the pauses between the words for the play's ultimate significance. The rhythm of the play, closely tied to this use of words, is gentle, shifting, vague, and without abrupt changes. It is like the moods and rhythms of soft, flowing music.

The visual demands are both insistent and elusive. The original production was performed behind a scrim; low-intensity overhead lighting was used; costumes were done in gray tones; and movements and gestures were trancelike and unreal as if the actors' bodies were motivated by unseen forces. The key to the successful production of this play is the subtle play of misty, moody lighting on the action.

Expressionistic symbolism, the counterpart of the impressionistic symbolism expressed in *Pelléas and Mélisande*, did not reach full development in the theatre until just after World War I. *From Morn to Midnight* by the German dramatist, Georg Kaiser, written before World War I and produced for the first time in 1917, is a clear-cut example of this style. While retaining the personal, subjective vision of the symbolist movement, the play assaults the audience's sensibilities in its depiction of a world of twisted, distorted, and inhuman values.

Written in scenes rather than acts, the drama follows the methods of a medieval morality play in its depiction of the fall of modern man in seven steps. The time from morn to midnight covers the journey of the Cashier, the play's leading character and a representative of modern man. Like Oedipus, Faust, and Mrs. Alving in *Ghosts*, the Cashier searches for answers and fulfillment—a quest that ends in the hopeless debasement of modern man. Unity in the play comes not from a logical organization of scenes or events but from the play's concentrated theme and the psychological deterioration of the Cashier as Everyman. As a fugitive from his bank and society, the Cashier thinks that money will give him freedom and the key to all life's possibilities. Then he meets Death for the first time, and in subsequent scenes, he explores the love of family, the power of politics, the pursuit of sensual pleasure, and the solace of religion without finding any answers. His final disillusionment comes when the Salvation Army girl—someone he has trusted—turns him over to the police for a reward. At the play's close, a tangle of flashing wires outlines the figure of Death as the Cashier runs onto the wires with arms outstretched like Christ upon the cross. As the crackling of electricity and the exploding of lamps fades, the policeman gives the final unfeeling comment: "There seems to be a short circuit in the wiring."

The characters in this play, as in most fully symbolist dramas, have labels rather than names, and each character is a symbolic robot projecting Kaiser's mechanistic view of modern life. Only the Lady from Italy, who represents an older way of life, and the Cashier, who symbolizes the search for a new mode of life, escape the mechanistic pattern to some extent. As the playwright's spokesman, the Cashier is the only one who understands that there must be an escape from the machine-dominated existence of modern life. Although he learns from his various experiences before his death, he never reaches understanding or a fully dimensional personal reality. He, too, remains merely a symbol of modern man.

The theme of the play—that the mechanistic quality of modern life must be changed—is obvious. Though the play is pessimistic, there is a slight suggestion that a new man may emerge from our mechanistic age. The language is also developed along mechanistic lines with short, staccato patterns reflecting the violent, direct, short-circuited effects found in telegraphy and radio communication. Kaiser uses language that is repetitious, heightened in volume, forced in pace, and harsh in effect to achieve a maximum aggressive attack on the audience's sensibility.

The third scene offers the best clue to the visual demands of the play in its transformation of a tree into a skeleton. Visual distortion is also required in a less striking degree in the other six scenes. In the original productions of many expressionist dramas after World War I, great use was made of distorted, cubist settings with many tilted angles and size variations. Color was unnatural and emotional; and great attention was given to exaggerated and violent effects in stage lighting.

Acting and Directing the Plays

Symbolist plays require at least three distinctly different levels of acting: the dreamy moodiness needed for the impressionistic *Pelléas and Mélisande*, the mixture of psychological realism and mood needed for the plays of Chekhov and Tennessee Williams, and the violent, exaggerated role portrayals needed for the more extreme expressionistic dramas. Impressionistic and expressionistic plays are easier to act than are the more realistic ones; in particular, expressionistic plays make little demands on the actor or actress since the effects to be created are usually broad and unsubtle, with much depending on the creative pattern and vision of the director.

In developing a role for a play like *Pelléas and Mélisande*, more attention must be paid to the players' vocal and physical projections than to their projections of psychological realism. The director acts much like a choreographer and a vocal coach in opera, developing patterns of sound and repetition of words and phrases, orchestrating voices and movement, and integrating them with the lighting of the action against the atmospheric settings. The action of the play must be orchestrated like a tone poem—a soft, flowing, subtle picture in which the player is mainly a choreographed instrument rather than a personality. Actors and actresses must listen to themselves on a tape recorder, look at their movement in front of a mirror, and try to let the mood of the play seep into their inner consciousness. Listening to Debussy music while one looks at impressionistic and symbolist paintings may also help in grasping the fleeting moods.

With expressionistic symbolism, much the same thing is true, but now the poetic mood is put aside in favor of choreographed violent, mechanistic actions done to discordant, dissonant music and vocal exercises that make use of staccato sounds, mechanistic expression, violent contrasts, and broken rhythms. Again the actor or actress is more the choreographed robot and team player within the creative plan of the director than an individual creating his or her own character or individual role. Acting to music, working with recorders, and performing in front of mirrors is good preparation.

Since both the impressionistic and expressionistic modes of acting are removed from the cultural life-style of everyday life, it helps only peripherally to know about the life and times of the period, although it is very useful to understand the art and music. However, in acting plays that combine symbolism and psychological realism, one should concentrate on the cultural background of the action as well as on the mood of the play and the sources on which it is based. Primarily, the character and his relation to the play and other characters must be analyzed with the same thoroughness and depth as one would use in a straight realistic play; all the precepts advocated by Stanislavsky and his followers must be put into practice. For example, *Mourning Becomes Electra* by Eugene O'Neill and *Camino Real* by Tennessee Williams are excellent examples of plays that combine realistic psychological acting with mood and symbolic meaning. Here considerable study must be given to the visual materials, the music, and the rhythmic mood flow that lies under the outward action of the plays. More than in any other style of drama, the actor or actress of symbolism must be able to absorb and see the mood and atmosphere of the play from the director's point of view.

Designing the Plays

The director of a contemporary production of *Pelléas and Mélisande* (though one is more likely to find the operatic version of the story produced today rather than the play) must concentrate on a strong sense of mood and atmosphere. The use of curtains to divide the scenes should be removed, and there should be a continuous flow of action from scene to scene supported and brought into focus by the lighting. The shifting of set pieces should be as simple as possible to avoid interrupting the play's rhythm and audience concentration. Simple shapes and forms, with a stress on sensuous textures, should be used to suggest the locations within the play, and the entire action should be orchestrated by light and developed as if part of a musical composition. Sharp, bleak rocks, jagged branches against a dying sky, heavy, shadowed castle stones lost in a veil of mist—each specific image must be simple without the clutter of atmospheric detail that marked symbolist production in the first years of the twentieth century. The pattern of movement within the setting should be choreographed to achieve a vague, floating, musical effect that is the essence of this play. Textures within the setting should be soft, vague and light-absorbing, without sharp, harsh details. Color, if it is used, should be soft and gray, not hard and brilliant, able to be transformed by subtle changes in the lighting. All lines and shapes within the setting should be developed to gain a maximum impact on the senses and the fullest use of the symbols of the play with a minimum of means (Figure 14–11).

The costumes must suggest rather than state their effect, and the audience should not respond to them as period clothing. Instead, costumes should recall a generalized, vague, unspecific time in the past, with concentration on the subtle, abstract, mood effects of color, texture, line, and movement rather than on period detail. Early medieval sources with their flowing, draped lines (rather than late Gothic sources with their richness of pattern and ornament) could provide inspiration. The costume fabrics should probably be changeable materials: chiffons, gauzes, Chinese silks, and soft woolens and piles. Layers of filmy fabrics can also be used over shimmering metallics to gain a sense of richness and depth.

In producing an expressionist drama such as *From Morn to Midnight*, it might be difficult to revive the play because of its naive simplicity, but if great stress were placed in production on the sensual, visual, and movement effects found in rock musicals, light shows, welded sculpture, and junk art, the play's message might seem as immediate as the themes in some popular songs.

The quality sought in designing for the play is a reflection either of the smooth, riveted, machine-tooled, colorless surfaces that we find in industrial machinery or of the corroded, broken, decaying forms found in junk yards or the wastebins of modern industry. The first approach would be most effective in the scenes at the race track and in the bank; the second, in the scene of Death appearing in a tree and in the final scene of the Cashier's running into the tangled wires that cause his death. Whatever the source for the colors, lines, and textures of the setting, the lighting must act as a major unifying and projecting element for the visual presentation of the play. Borrowing from "light show" effects, one could create explosions, spiraling effects, bursts of color—all used to underline the near-psychotic, emotional character of many scenes. Electronic music might also support the play's mood of mechanization.

This same quality should also appear in the costumes. If a smooth, polished approach is chosen, then costumes should reflect the metallic, plastic, manufactured look of space suits. If a decaying, corroded approach is used, then melted nylon, burnt sponge rubber, and acid-eaten plastics (painted to further the effect of decomposition) would be effective in indicating the final ending for mechanized man.

PROJECTS AND PROBLEMS

1. Why did so many late nineteenth-century artists find realism unacceptable as an artistic style?

2. How are Sigmund Freud and the symbolists related?

3. Why is *art nouveau* considered the first Europeanwide artistic movement since the Rococo style?

4. What are the differences between impressionistic symbolism and stylism? Between impressionistic symbolism and expressionistic symbolism?

5. Look closely at Monet's painting of *Rouen Cathedral* (Figure 14–1). How would an audience feel sitting in front of a stage setting of *Rouen Cathedral*? How would a director and a designer develop a stage production based on this painting? How would an actor or actress develop his or her role in this type of production?

6. Why was Edgar Allan Poe so much admired by the symbolists?

7. Describe the lines and forms in Guimard's entrance to the Paris Metro (Figure 14–2). What is the physical and psychological feeling underlying this design? Define and characterize this entrance in terms of a difficult and ambiguous character in a play.

8. Characterize Beardsley's illustration of *Salomé* (Figure 14–3). What is gained by the absence of color? How does the artist make the illustration seem sensuous and evil? Why is it so totally different from, and yet related to, Monet's *Rouen Cathedral* (Figure 14–1)?

9. Compare Beardsley's illustration of *Salomé* (Figure 14–3) with Munch's *The Scream* (Figure 14–4). Describe the physical feeling of pain in *The Scream*. What kind of production would you have if you staged all the qualities in *The Scream*? How would the audience react?

10. Why is Rodin's *Burghers of Calais* (Figure 14–5) both impressionistic and expressionistic? What can an actor, designer, and director gain from a study of these figures? What is the physical feeling that you get from the work? Plan a scene based on a study of this work.

11. Describe the Church of the Holy Family (Figure 14–6). How would you feel exploring the inside and outside of this structure? How is it related to Gothic cathedrals? In what way is the church a Freudian symbol or image?

12. Why was Debussy the perfect composer to transpose Maeterlinck's *Pelléas and Mélisande* into an opera? Why was water imagery so useful as a symbol to a composer and a playwright working within the symbolist movement? What similarities in their methods link Wagner and Debussy? Why do we say that the music of Debussy never comes to a definite conclusion?

13. What was Henri Bergson's contribution to the symbolist movement? Why was the study of time important to Bergson's philosophic concept of reality?

14. Characterize the way that Mallarmé writes poetry. After reading section III of *Hérodiade*, what can you say about the way Mallarmé uses words and ideas? How would you as an actor or actress read those lines?

15. Why did Oscar Wilde in *The Decay of Living* contradict what realists said about art? Why did Wilde think that life imitates art rather than vice versa?

16. Study the entry to the Hotel van Eetvelde (Figure 14–7). What kind of people would live here? What kinds of social scenes would take place here? Describe your feelings in this atmosphere. What plays might take place in such a setting? What would the characters and dialogue be like?

17. Why did clothing in the first decade of the twentieth century look rather "impressionistic," even though it still embodied many Victorian ideals? What fabric, in particular, makes this so?

18. Borrow a costume of this period and try posing and moving in it. What are the problems? What are the things that one would have to worry about in a production?

19. Compare the *Jardin de Paris, The Night Beauties* (Figure 14–8) with the fashion design from the *Journal des Dames et des Modes* (Figure 14–9). Why is the contrast so great? What effects from art are at work in this fashion design? What is the new image of woman that is projected? How will movement change in this gown?

20. Look closely at Boldini's *Portrait of Count Montesquieu* (Figure 14–10). As an actor how would you characterize the man? Getting inside the character of the painting and the Count's clothing, describe the feeling and movement.

21. What was the structure of the family at the opening of the twentieth century? What are some changes in manners that occurred at this time? Imagine yourself at the Edwardian ball described by Princess Marie Louise and re-create the event as a scene from a play. What is its general character?

22. Look at Béraud's *Jardin de Paris, The Night Beauties* (Figure 14–8). What is the character of the scene? Of the movement? Of the fashions? How is the image created here related to symbolism?

23. How does Appia in his design for *Parsifal* (Figure 14–11) differ in his approach from a realistic or even a romantic designer? Why would lighting be so important in creating the final character for the setting?

24. In Robert E. Jones's sketch for a production of *Macbeth* (Figure 14–12), what are the effects that would appeal to the director? The designer? The actor? Describe the directorial method at work here.

25. Prepare a scene between Pelléas and Mélisande from the play of the same name by Maeterlinck. How would you develop the roles? Why are the voice and body projection so important? How would you handle the dialogue, the costumes, and the sets? What do you hope will be the effect on the audience?

26. Prepare a scene between the Cashier and another character in *From Morn to Midnight*. How is your approach similar to what you did in *Pelléas and Mélisande*? How different? What about the movement and dialogue here? What about the sets and costumes? What do you hope will be the effect on the audience?

27. In a play more rooted in a period background or setting, yet still developed within a symbolist method, what methods or techniques would you advise for the development of a role?

BIBLIOGRAPHY

Appia, Adolphe. *The Work of Living Art: A Theory of the Theatre*. Coral Gables, Fla.: University of Miami Press, 1960. Discusses the theories of impressionistic symbolism (the "New Stagecraft") in staging with particular emphasis on the importance of lighting in capturing dramatic mood.

Bergson, Henri. *The Creative Mind*. Translated by Mabelle L. Andison. New York: Philosophical Library, 1946. An important philosophical work that explains the impressionistic-symbolist interest in changing moods and the passing moment.

Brockett, Oscar G., and Findlay, Robert R. *Century*

of Innovation: A History of European and American Theatre and Drama since 1870. Englewood Cliffs, N.J.: Prentice-Hall, 1973. Discusses history of the theatre in Europe and America since Ibsen.

Burchell, S. C. *Age of Progress.* The Great Ages of Man Series. New York: Time-Life Books, 1966. Covers the major intellectual, artistic, and cultural developments of the late nineteenth century.

Carter, Huntly. *The Theatre of Max Reinhardt.* New York: Benjamin Blom, 1964. A standard work that gives an excellent picture of the theatrical contributions of Max Reinhardt to the early twentieth-century theatre.

Chipp, Herschel B. *Theories of Modern Art.* Berkeley: University of California Press, 1968. A very interesting essay on the many competing theories of art that in combination constituted the early twentieth-century artistic outlook.

Cornell, Kenneth. *The Symbolist Movement.* New Haven, Conn.: Yale University Press, 1951. An excellent survey of the meaning of symbolism in all the arts, particularly the theatre.

Craig, Edward Gordon. *On the Art of the Theatre.* New York: Theatre Arts Books, 1957. The best book for understanding this designer-theorist's demand for a single, aesthetic, artistic control in the theatre and his emphasis on theatrical mood and simplicity.

Fowlie, Wallace. *Age of Surrealism.* Bloomington: Indiana University Press, 1960. A very good book for demonstrating the closeness of symbolism to the later development of surrealism, with particular emphasis on the importance of fantasy and the subconscious.

Gorelik, Mordecai. *New Theatres for Old.* New York: E. P. Dutton, 1962. Study of stylistic changes in theatre from realism through Brechtian relativism.

Jones, Robert Edmond. *The Dramatic Imagination.* New York: Theatre Arts Books, 1941. An inspiring and stimulating book on theatrical design by the leading symbolist designer in America in the early twentieth century.

Lehmann, Andrew G. *The Symbolist Aesthetic in France, 1885–1895.* 2nd ed. New York: Barnes and Noble, 1968. An excellent overview of the symbolist movement during its major period of impact.

Licht, Fred S. *Sculpture of the 19th and 20th Centuries.* Greenwich, Conn.: New York Graphic Society, 1967. A solid pictorial survey with accompanying text on Western sculpture from the early nineteenth century to the middle of the twentieth.

Madsen, Stephan T. *Art Nouveau.* New York: McGraw-Hill, 1967. One of many fine books that surveys that artistic phenomenon labeled art nouveau.

Rewald, John. *The History of Impressionism.* Rev. ed. New York: Museum of Modern Art, 1980. An updating of one of the definitive surveys of impressionism in art by one of the leading historians of the movement.

Rheims, Maurice. *The Flowering of Art Nouveau.* Translated by Patrick Evans. New York: Abrams, 1966. Still another very good survey on art nouveau during its period of major impact: 1890–1914.

Rookmaaker, H. R. *Synthetist Art Theories: Genesis and Nature of the Ideas on Art of Gauguin and His Circle.* Amsterdam: Swets and Zeitlinger, 1959. A useful but overly intellectual analysis of the ideas on art developed by Gauguin and those around him.

Sayler, Oliver M., ed. *Max Reinhardt and His Theatre.* New York: Brentano's, 1926. A great collection of essays in tribute to Reinhardt by those who intimately knew and worked with him.

Schmutzler, Robert. *Art Nouveau.* Translated by Edouard Roditi. New York: Abrams, 1962. An excellent survey of the art nouveau movement.

Selz, Peter, and Constantine, Mildred, eds. *Art Nouveau: Art and Design at the Turn of the Century.* New York: Museum of Modern Art and Doubleday, 1960. An excellent pictorial survey on art nouveau design.

Volbach, Walther. *Adolphe Appia: Prophet of the Modern Theatre.* Middletown, Conn.: Wesleyan University Press, 1968. Discusses the new ideas of theatrical design and production brought to the European theatre by an artist who wanted to paint with light.

Willet, John. *Expressionism.* New York: McGraw-Hill, 1970. An excellent summary of expressionism in the theatre with superior analyses of a number of scripts.

Relativism or Modern Style

Although symbolism as a movement continued well into the twentieth century, it reached a point of crisis by World War I because of its subjective view of art and culture. Throughout the nineteenth century, art had become alienated from science and technology. Artists from Turner and Delacroix to Munch and Van Gogh were unable or unwilling to use the methods of science in their work. At the height of the Enlightenment, artists had related their work to scientific concepts, but the romantics and symbolists, with all their interest in form and style, appealed only to the emotions and the imagination. Even the impressionists, who had begun painting with a scientific interest in optics and light, drifted into vague moodiness and subjective images. Similarly, realistic dramatists, like Ibsen and Chekhov, who began by probing the mores of contemporary society, became more and more interested in symbolism and mood images. What was needed was a concentrated emphasis on intellectual ideas and rationality of form rather than a preoccupation with mood and the psychology of the unconscious. The only nineteenth-century sciences that had awakened a strong response in nineteenth-century artists were Darwinian biology and the new Freudian psychology—disciplines concerned with animal instincts and subjective impulses. In addition, although industrial engineers had developed many new designs for commercial structures such as bridges, warehouses, exhibition halls, and train stations, their scientific and intellectual methods were not allowed in residential and public architecture. The old, decorative, historical architectural "frosting" of the Beaux Arts tradition continued into the twentieth century. In short, art in all media suffered from the lack of a firm intellectual base.

The first major nineteenth-century artist, who did attempt to probe the problems of pictorial structure beneath the visual world, was Paul Cézanne. Although he exhibited with the impressionists and sympathized with the immediacy and vitality of their methods, he opposed their vagueness and lack of structure. In his late experiments in Aix-en-Provence, Cézanne attempted to bring to impressionism the solidity and intellectual foundations of classical art. In the series of landscapes and still lifes on which he worked until his death in 1906, Cézanne attempted to underline the carefully built structure of a scene by piling up blocks and spots of unblended color and value to recast a momentary expression into a long analytical view of the inner and outer structure of the subject. The differences and similarities between his works and Monet's can be readily seen by comparing *Mont Sainte-Victoire* c. 1905 with *Rouen Cathedral* of 1894 (Figures 15–1 and 14–1).

Within a year or two after Cézanne's death, Pablo Picasso and George Braque began to take the concept a step further, and by 1908 cubism was born. In cubism, the artist dismembered the geometric relationships of the real world and reorganized them so that they would be viewed by the mind and analyzed by the intellect rather than just be seen by the eye. Unlike the symbolists who distorted life for emotional effect, the cubists and other abstractionists took things apart in a semi-scientific way to see how they worked and then put them back together to show both their inner and outer dynamics. This concept of the simultaneous perception of several separate views of reality evolved at a time when science itself was in the process of promulgating the theory of relativity. This theory implied that even the laws of science were mutable and changing and that reality was not fixed, as it had been in Newtonian physics, but was based on flux and change.

The new art differed sharply from

Figure 15–1 Paul Cézanne, *Mont Sainte Victoire,* c. 1905. Illustrates Cézanne's structuring and organizing of impressionism in order to give it the solidarity of classical art. Photo courtesy of the Philadelphia Museum of Art, the George W. Elkins Collection.

nineteenth-century art, in fact from all art since Giotto, because it stressed how the artist thought and not how he saw. It was intellectual, scientific, and organizational, projecting the inner and outer structure of life at the same moment. Popular theatre, such as the Commedia dell'Arte, had done much the same thing previously by making the audience aware of both an actor and his character at the same time, though this duality concept had never been consciously studied before.

The new style could still express deep emotion as in *Guernica*, painted as a monumental triptych in 1937 after Picasso had read of the terrible bombing of the ancient Basque capital in northeastern Spain (Figure 15–2). The painting does not depict the actual bombing but evokes horrible images of total war. Included are many symbols from past works of art and literature. The brilliance of the piece comes from the reorganization of reality through dislocation, fragmentation, and met-

amorphosis, with the added suggestion that many shapes have been cut from the newspaper that detailed the horrible event. This cutout effect, developed by Picasso and others earlier in the century, represents the new art of collage: shapes in various textures are cut out and juxtaposed with real objects and painted effects to underline the intersections of various levels of reality. The collage thus became a diagram of the shifting planes of reality. In *Guernica*, Picasso proved that this diagram, limited to black, white, and gray colors and without the support of highlight and shade, could project an overpowering emotional image and a brilliant intellectual idea.

The same ideas of multiple reality, or seeing several facets of reality at the same time, also carried over into architecture and sculpture in a less complicated manner. For example, Bernini in the early seventeenth century had exploited the concept of space as

Figure 15–2 Pablo Picasso, *Guernica,* 1937. The terrible bombing of the ancient Basque capital of Spain immortalized by organizing exaggerated and distorted symbols of war into a painted collage. Permission V.A.G.A. Photo courtesy of the Museum of Modern Art.

a force to be overcome by the dynamic unwinding stance of his *David* (Figure 7–2). In the twentieth century, however, sculptors began to show the impact of space on a figure or an object by showing changes in the object. In his *Internal and External Forms*, Henry Moore developed an interpenetration of space and form in order to suggest a number of levels of reality—particularly that interaction of realities created by a woman carrying an unborn child (Figure 15–3).

In architecture, the concept of relativism was known as modernism and developed into an expression of the space or reality of the outside world penetrating the solid walls and structure of a building or home, primarily through the use of many transparent glass walls. For example, in the Tremaine House—a typical California home designed by the Austrian architect Neutra—the inside is part of the outside, and the outside penetrates the interior until the normal divisions are erased, as anyone who has bumped his nose on such seemingly missing glass walls can testify (Figure 15–4). The most perfect examples of the penetration of space into a construction are the mobiles of Alexander Calder, whose forms change with the slightest movement of air or space.

The same concepts and ideas are also found in the literary works of Thomas Mann, Franz Kafka, Gertrude Stein, André Gide, and, most importantly, James Joyce. T. S. Eliot wrote that there should be many levels of reality in verse writing in an age of relativity and that a word can be understood as a word, a word among other words, a sound, a symbol, and a point in a structural development. The most important literary landmark to make a very complex, intellectual use of this method is James Joyce's *Ulysses*, in which each phrase has three or four different levels of meaning. There is always an ambiguity in this kind of work—an indeterminate quality, a crowding of multiple images, a cinema-inspired "montage" effect, a shifting backward and forward in time, and a compression and expansion of facts and details.

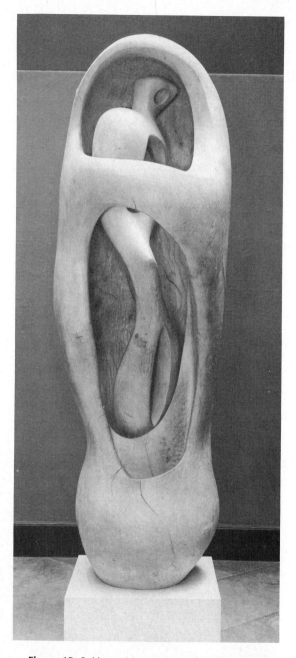

Figure 15–3 Henry Moore, *Internal and External Forms*, 1953–54. The interpenetration of space and form and form inside of form in order to create numerous levels of shifting reality. Photo courtesy of the Albright Knox Gallery, Buffalo.

As Marshall McLuhan and others have said, a culture seems to bring forth a new technique or medium of expression at that moment when it most needs a new mode of communication. The printing press came when the demand for books could no longer be met by illuminated manuscripts; opera was invented when the grand, sensuous, integrative forces of Baroque art needed a popular outlet; the box camera was invented when nineteenth-century culture became enamored with realism; and the cinema was invented when artists, scientists, and intellectuals came to view reality as a shifting, changing series of multiple relationships. The leading film makers realized that in this new form, reality was not an object or a causally connected sequence of events, but a graphic, pictorial conflict among different recurring images and points of view. The most obvious use of this idea was in the so-called "montage," in which many images were seen simultaneously. In the best cinematic technique, reality is always portrayed as a series of changing relationships rather than as a single sequence of events.

The logical result of all this experimentation in levels of reality, abstract forms, and probing of the structure beneath the surface of reality was the liberation of art from subject matter. Though this retreat from subject matter had begun even before World War I in the

Figure 15–4 Richard J. Neutra, the Tremaine House, Santa Barbara, California, c. 1952. Typical of much modern domestic architecture, particularly in the southwestern United States. The space surrounding the structure also seems to penetrate its interior. Photo courtesy of the Stanford University Art Department slide files.

work of Malevich, Kandinsky, and others, it did not reach its climax until the arrival of abstract expressionism after World War II.

This concern with pure relationships came to an end in the early 1960s. Though field relationships were still stressed, humorous comments and an occasional real object were included in abstract art. Shapes, figures, and textures gradually came back into art, not as objects, but as important accents in a field of relationships. In the "A-literature" of Robbe-Grillet and in the early experiments in op and pop art, interesting objects and facts from life are recorded, but there are no strong points of view, no individuals, and no characters— merely entities. Until the mid-1960s, the denial of the complexities and problems in our culture was so strong that most artists did not bother to interpret the scene but merely recorded facts and relationships as fascinating, humorous, or decorative effects.

Music

The musical counterpart of this movement in art was signaled by a breaking up of traditional tonality and a search for new forms of expression. As early as 1913, Igor Stravinsky in his *Rite of Spring* introduced angular melodies, polyrhythmic textures, and geometric organization similar to the components of early cubism. Then, in 1915, Arnold Schoenberg introduced the twelve-tone scale of musical composition that answered the demand for a new order and a stricter form after the amorphous flow of Debussy's impressionist pieces. Schoenberg "constructed" rather than composed his music. He began by setting forth a row of twelve different tones, which could be played in normal order, upside down by melodic inversion, and upside down again in a backward movement. Also, they could be played as a whole or in part, simultaneously in a chord or tone cluster or serially as with a melody. A given row could be taken as an entity or broken up into shorter themes or motifs.

This method has an infinite number of variations, just as cubism is found in painting, collage, and sculpture. The system provides the composer with a wealth of material and a sense of freedom within a tight framework. It produces analytical music that appeals to the mind rather than to the emotions. For example, in Arnold Schoenberg's piano piece *Opus 33b*, written just before he emigrated from Germany in 1933, the basic twelve-tone series is heard melodically as a jocular, widespaced theme divided between the right and left hand in the opening measures. The development of this melodic pattern through a series of variations then gives a vague and nebulous quality to the piece. The piece lacks any definable feeling; no rhythmic patterns are sustained long enough to serve as an organizing principle for clapping or tapping. It is music based on the interplay and interpenetration of its parts.

Life and Cultural Ideals

The fact that a typical anthology of twentieth-century philosophical writings is entitled *The Age of Analysis* suggests that modern philosophers are little concerned with moral philosophy; they are more interested in taking apart words and philosophic ideas and in analyzing what it means to be a philosopher rather than in setting down a coherent philosophy of life. Bertrand Russell, Rudolf Carnap, and Ludwig Wittgenstein are among this school of philosophers who dissect language, logic, and mathematics to see how they work in much the same way that the analytical cubists did in art and the serialists did in music.

In literature, André Gide was an early practitioner of this new method of analyzing reality from various angles. He made a very illuminating statement about his method when he said, "I arrange facts in such a way as to make them conform to truth more closely than they do in real life." In his *Journal des Faux-Monnayeurs*, which is about the writing of his novel *Les Faux-Monnayeurs* (1919–1926), he says, "What will attract me to a new book is not so much new characters as a new way of presenting them.'' In *Les Faux-Monnayeurs* he wrote a novel about an individual's attempt to write a novel and presented at least three or four levels, or views, of reality. As Edouard, the leading character, says about the novel he intends to write: It will be:

a rivalry between the real world and the representation of it which we make ourselves. The manner in which the world of appearances imposes itself upon us, and the manner in which we try to impose on the outside world our own interpretation—this is the drama of our lives.

Edouard also complains that previous novels have been like pools in a garden:

their contours are defined—perfect, perhaps, but the water they contain is captive and lifeless. I wish it now to run freely. . . . I choose not to foresee its windings. . . . I consider that life never presents us with anything which may not be looked upon as a fresh starting point, no less than as a termination.

Finally, Edouard says something that the cubists and Pirandello might also have said:

Everything hangs together and I always feel such a subtle interdependence between all the facts that life offers me, that it seems to me impossible to change a single one without modifying the whole.

This statement summarizes relativism as a style, namely, that it has no absolutes and that all things are relative—change one thing and everything else is also affected. It is also a brilliant summary of the twentieth-century outlook.

In addition, many twentieth-century authors wrote poetry and prose that borrowed from the montage concept in film making. As Wylie Sypher points out in *Rococo to Cubism in Art and Literature*, one can take many moments in the works of T. S. Eliot and James Joyce and view them as a form of montage. Take the lines that open the third section of Eliot's *The Waste Land*.

The river's tent is broken: the last fingers of leaf
Clutch and sink into the wet bank. The wind
Crosses the brown land, unheard. The nymphs are departed.
Sweet Thames run softly, till I end my song.
The river bears no empty bottles, sandwich papers,
Silk handkerchiefs, cardboard boxes, cigarette ends
Or other testimony of summer nights. . . .

What is created here is a multidimensional vision by placing together words, phrases, and statements that create a collage of poetically related yet divergent images, discords, and incongruities. James Joyce carried the same idea to a more abstract level in *Finnegans Wake*, which gives instantaneous cross-references between myth, linguistics, psychology, and music through its montagelike stream-of-consciousness method. Here is a paragraph from this complex work:

Can't hear with the waters of. The chittering waters of. Flittering bats, fieldmice bawk talk. Ho! Are you not gone a-home? What Tom Malone? Can't hear with bawk of bats, all thim liffeying waters of. Ho, talk save us! My foos won't moos. I feel as old as yonder elm. A tale told of Shaun or Shem? All Livia's daughter-sons. Dark hawks hear us. Night! Night! My ho head halls. I fell as heavy as yonder stone. Tell me of John or Shaun? Who were Shem and Shaun the living sons or daughters of? Night now! Tell me, tell me, tell me, elm! Night night! Telmetale of stem or stone. Beside the rivering waters of, hitherandthithering waters of. Night!

As for the common man during the period from World War I to the 1960s, his most overriding preoccupation was with business, the stock market, technological and industrial progress, and money making. Attendant upon this preoccupation, despite the varied outlets of travel, film, sports, and other weekend and vacation outlets was the dehumanizing and mass grouping of people by the organizational patterns of the Western business world. To illustrate this, let us look at a photograph of Fifth Avenue at 42nd Street in 1926 and place it against a photo of commuters arriving in Park Forest, Illinois, in 1958 (Figures 15–5 and 15–6). In each case, the massing of individuals, the uniformity of clothing and demeanor, and the overall loss of individuality project in daily life what the philosophers and artists dealt with at an intellectual and artistic level—namely, the dehumanization of the individual and the interest in organizational and structural patterns.

Interiors and Furniture

The same dehumanized approach also dominated furniture design and interior decoration between World War I and the 1960s. Architects and interior designers influenced by the teachers and theorists of the Bauhaus School in Dessau, Germany, developed a "machine aesthetic" that gave an interior beauty, not "frosting" decoration, through form and function alone. Look at the interior of the Tremaine House (Figure 15–4). The preoccupation is with simple, cool, abstract, geometric space blocks enhanced by fine materials like chrome, marble, onyx, and ebony. The organization of the room is intended to facilitate the normal functioning human movements inside the room to the point that the design can truly be called a machine for living. Even the furniture has a smooth, cold, geometric, abstract machinelike quality that may make it look comfortable and efficient, but not as if it were designed for the non-machine contours of the human body or for pleasing the human interest in warm textures and emotions. An individual in this type of interior has a tendency to suppress his emotions in favor of more abstract ideals of efficiency, organization, promptness, maximum output for energy expended, and other business and industrial considerations.

Both the actor and audience seeing such a setting in the theatre will respond quickly to these mechanized considerations; the actor will certainly find it very difficult to create a warm, individualistic, emotional performance in such a milieu. Though it is unfair to sum up almost forty years of cultural development in the Western world in terms of this one room, nevertheless, it does represent the major cultural outlook during the years from World War I to the early 1960s.

Costume and Accessories

In some ways it is more difficult to deal with fashion during this period than with anything else, since the fashion business has decreed that styles, at least for women in the twentieth century, must change every two or three years. Again, however, there are some constants. The male business suit, or uniform, that has represented the Western world's preoccupation with capitalism since the late nineteenth century changed only marginally between World War I and the 1960s. Look at the men lined up on Fifth Avenue in 1926 and compare them with the commuters that have just stepped off the train in 1958; the clothing images are remarkably the same (Figures 15–5 and 15–6). Except for the collars, the hat brims, and the very slight changes in cut, the uniform of the businessman and desk clerk changed little during more than thirty years.

Sports clothes certainly showed greater changes, but they do not represent the major cultural preoccupation of the twentieth century any more than they did in the eighteenth century.

The major change in male clothing after World War I was toward more comfort and greater informality. The frock coat finally disappeared altogether, leaving only morning coats and tails as the modern remnants of formal nineteenth-century dress. Collars became moderately soft turnovers, with the exception of the occasional formal, white, winged collar worn with tails. During the 1920s, the stiff, rounded-corner turnover was popular, however. The felt slouch hat or fedora came to dominate the derby, bowler, and top hat, although the latter was still worn on very formal occasions. During the thirties and

Figure 15–5 Photograph of Fifth Avenue at 42nd Street, 1926. Illustrates the modern massing of individuals, the uniformity in clothing, and the loss of identity and individuality that artists and writers of the early twentieth century described as the dehumanization of modern man in an urban, technological culture. Photo courtesy of Culver Pictures, Inc.

forties, the brim of this slouch hat became very wide, while in the fifties it became much narrower. By the mid-1960s, the felt fedora had almost disappeared, although there were all types of new sports caps and hats. After World War I, low oxford shoes took over almost completely from high shoes, and spats almost completely disappeared. In the 1920s, the male silhouette tended to have a slim and boyish look; in the 1930s, it became broad-shouldered with wide pleated trousers and cuffs; then in the 1940s and 1950s, it had narrow shoulders and lapels and looked tight and constricted. Sportswear had greater va-

Figure 15—6 Photograph of commuters, Park Forest, Illinois, 1958. Symbolizes the organizational patterns of the dehumanized corporate business world. Photo courtesy of Sandra Weiner, New York.

and in the 1940s and 1950s, the duffle coat. By the late 1940s and early 1950s, wash-and-wear fabrics, creaseless and stainless materials, and longer wearing synthetics made men's clothes more efficient and practical.

The year 1914 was the watershed in women's fashions, when functionalism finally began to triumph over the previous complexity of line and excess decoration. Following the introduction of the draped-kimono line, dresses and coats fell loosely about the body, and the skirt became shorter to increase efficiency in movement and to decrease the cleaning problem for skirt hems. Following the introduction of women's suffrage, there was a change toward efficiency and masculinity in women's dress throughout the Western world. After World War I, straight lines, short hair, and boyish shape became the feminine ideal; by 1923, feminine fashions had developed a short, absolutely straight dress (usually sleeveless), hanging from the shoulders and with the waist around the hips. The curves of the body were ignored, and the female form was presented as a tube without bust, hips, or waist. At the same time, the Eton crop, bobbed short hair, and a *cloche* hat that fitted tightly over the ears and almost covered the eyebrows were the rage. The *Portrait of Madame Jasmy Alvin*, painted in 1925 by Kees Van Dongen, says a great deal about the culture of the time (Figure 15–7). The image combines sophistication and decadence in a boyish androgyny.

About 1930, evening gowns became much longer again, first at the back and then all the way around; they were now frequently backless and cut on the bias so that they would shape themselves over the bust, hips, and thighs and cling to the body. For a time, feminine curves reappeared in evening wear. In day wear, the waist was again normal, but, as in men's wear, the shoulders broadened; and long, straight lines predominated in coats and dresses. Toward the end of the 1930s, skirts rose to knee length; hats were either felts with tiny brims, pillboxes, or turbans; and hair was generally parted in the middle

riety. The 1920s had baggy plus-fours or oxford bags for golfing; in the early 1930s, colorful, open-necked shirts, shorts, slacks, and swimming trunks made their appearance, along with special costumes for skiing. The most unique garment in the 1920s was the raccoon coat; in the 1930s, the trench coat;

Figure 15–8 Coco Chanel and a model, 1955. Illustrates the simple, practical, efficient suits with boxy jackets and skirts introduced by this famed Parisian fashion designer. They symbolize the unemotional efficiency of women's clothing in the 1950s. Photo courtesy of *Paris Match*.

Figure 15–7 Kees Van Dongen, *Portrait of Madame Jasmy Alvin*, 1925. This portrait has a hard, decadent, masculine quality that subordinates the beaded ornamentation to the straight, functional lines of the gown. The image created seems to combine the unnatural, abstract effects found in the famous Egyptian bust of Nefertiti with a dehumanized, functional androgyny. The Museum of Modern Art, Paris. Photo courtesy of the French Musées Nationaux.

and waved and rolled up and to the back. There was also great experimentation with wide slacks, playsuits, tennis dresses, bathing suits, sandals, and shirtwaist frocks.

During World War II, military wear influenced women's fashions. But in 1947, a great change came in the short-skirted, tubular, broad-shouldered look that had been in vogue since the end of the 1930s. The "new look," established by Christian Dior in Paris, stressed narrow shoulders, a smooth bust, a normal waistline, and a long skirt with a wide hem. Then in the early 1950s, the House of Balenciaga entered the field with the chemise or sack dress; and by 1956, Dior had produced his H-line and A-line dresses, while Coco Chanel had popularized the simple suit with boxy jacket and skirt (Figure 15–8). These simple, geometrically shaped basics for women dramatized the unemotional efficiency in everyday women's clothing prevalent toward the end of the period of relativism. Though there have been variations—like the miniskirts of the early sixties, jumpsuits for leisure wear, and experiments with all types of synthetic and plastic materials—the basic move in women's clothing from World War I to the mid-1960s was toward comfort, efficiency, and geometric design, like that in architecture, interiors, furniture, and paintings of artists like Piet Mondrian.

The wrenching dislocations in society brought about by World War I halted the publication of books on manners and etiquette; not until the early 1920s was an attempt made to reestablish the rules of good manners that had predominated before the war. By the end of the 1920s, there were new ideas about how to behave in good society. The strict rules of the past were gone; books of etiquette stressed that manners now depended on the person, the occasion, and the circumstances of the moment, not on set rules. Almost every suggestion for good manners was noted as optional and dependent on personality and circumstance, as if to underline the relativism in art, music, and literature.

In the 1920s, it was still considered a part of good upbringing for a man to know how to enter a room, how to greet a lady, and how to dress. In addition, the gentleman was expected to precede a lady when entering a crowded public place, to walk on the outside of the street, and to remove his hat on entering a private residence, a shop, or hotel. As time passed, however, these rules seemed more and more rigid and archaic to the new international set; particularly after World War II, manners and customs for men seemed to change with the moment and the person involved. The age of the common man had arrived, in which courtesies were dictated almost completely by personal reaction to the occasion. For the uncommon men who dominated the news of the upper-class social scene, it was also personality rather than rules that governed behavior.

The greatest changes in manners and movement for women came with the changes in their clothing after World War I. Physical activity, strenuous recreational pursuits, and comfort were now emphasized. No longer were girls and women regarded as rather frail beings moving through their daily occupations with a certain gentility. Women now

Manners and Movement

played tennis and ball, swam, and skied with as much physical output as men did; as a result, they actually grew in size and strength. This difference in size and strength can be observed by comparing a prim, bustled woman of 1880 playing croquet with a short-skirted girl of the 1920s or 1950s swinging into a tennis volley. The ideal female figure also became thinner to match the lithe, active, feminine form; the rounded hourglass forms of the nineteenth and early twentieth centuries disappeared. The female pose became long, languid, and uninhibited; relaxed, uncorseted female film stars were often photographed draped over furniture or leaning sinuously against a door or mantelpiece.

In addition, as women began to enter such vocations as teaching, law, business, medicine, and politics, there was less emphasis on training them in the home occupations and social niceties. Moreover, as women began to compete with men in the job market, long-established courtesies, such as a gentleman's giving up his seat on a crowded, rush-hour train, were gradually set aside. Men and women thus began to share in the fatigues and problems of daily work and travel.

The one courtesy that did not change greatly was the salutation of shaking hands, although it was now practiced according to individual temperament. A lady still shook hands with everyone presented to her in her own home. In high society such introductions were still acknowledged with a slight bow, and it was the privilege of an elderly lady or one of rank to offer her hand after an introduction as a mark of friendliness. A number of etiquette books in the 1920s and 1930s acknowledged that when to shake hands and when not to was an open question and that it was better not to do so if one were in doubt. When one introduced persons of lower rank, their names were usually given first, as were those of unmarried ladies and children. A gentleman, whether of higher rank or not, was always introduced to the lady rather than vice versa, and it was customary for the gentleman to ask a lady's permission before introducing her to someone else. The upper-class gentleman still lifted his hat and inclined his head and shoulders in a slight bow when meeting a lady; the lady, in turn, made a slight suggestion of a curtsy. Then they might also shake hands. But in the often hatless hurry and bustle of the modern city, such sensitive old customs were mostly a fading memory. As far as paying calls on friends during the day was concerned, the custom of leaving a card was dead by the years following World War II because servants were mostly a thing of the past; the lady of the house usually answered the door herself.

In the period between the wars, dancing involved very varied and active steps that demanded equal participation by the partners; it was common to spend the evening with the same partner, often improvising variations on the basic steps of the dance. After World War II, there was even more improvisation; steps were angular, broken, and very physical; and partners often danced apart facing each other and touching only intermittently. The Charleston of the 1920s, the jitterbug of pre-World War II, and rock and roll of the late 1950s and early 1960s—all stressed angular movements. To see this physical-mechanical angularity, let us examine the cover of *Life* magazine for February 18, 1926 (Figure 15–

Figure 15–9 Cover of *Life* magazine, February 18, 1926. This cartoon effectively underlines the physical-mechanical angularity of dance rhythms and movement during the age of relativism. Photo courtesy of Culver Pictures, Inc.

9). This cartoon beautifully exaggerates the mechanical angularity of dance movements and rhythms during the age of relativism.

The Theatre

The impulse to experiment with multiple reality in staging came slowly; it was not until Pirandello wrote and produced *Six Characters in Search of an Author* in 1923 that the new ideas were fully absorbed into dramatic art. However, there were earlier movements in the theatre, which made subtle, often unconscious use of the new concept of multiple reality. One of the first breaks from realistic stage illusion and the picture-frame view of a performance came with the attempts of William Poel to return to the Elizabethan platform stage for Shakespearean performances. The Elizabethan Stage Society, founded by Poel, insisted on using Elizabethan staging for plays written in that period in order to gain a sense of immediacy, a swift flow of action, and a direct storytelling without the distraction of illusionistic accessories. Without knowing it, Poel and his associates were taking a first step in reestablishing the stage as a stage—a permanent reality quite separate from the allusions to locale found in a play's story. Theirs was the first move toward Brechtian staging.

Just prior to World War I, Jacques Co-peau, at the Vieux Colombier in Paris, further developed the idea of a permanent formal stage by transforming a warehouse into a combined stage and auditorium without a formal break between the two areas. A permanent architectural setting thus remained for all plays, and only the essential properties and set dressings were changed from production to production. There were no footlights or curtains; only an architectural step made the break between actors and audience. The architectural background to the stage consisted of an arch with a stairway at one side leading to a walkway above the arch. Lighting came either from the side or from openly displayed sources in the auditorium. The concept that the stage always should remain a stage brought about the death of illusionism and the acceptance of the idea that a member of the audience should be aware of himself, the audience, the theatre, and the actor as interacting realities during a theatrical performance.

At the same time in Germany, experiments carried out by Max Reinhardt at the Circus Schumann and the Grosses Schauspielhaus led to a return of the Greek orchestra, which was placed in the midst of the audience; thus the audience was now included in the play's action. In his 1920 production of Romain Rolland's *Danton* at the Grosses Schauspielhaus in Berlin, Reinhardt staged Danton's harangue of the tribunal from a stage thrust out over the orchestra so that the audience felt as if they were members of the revolutionary convention condemning him to the guillotine (Figure 15–10). There were also other experiments involving a return to the simultaneous staging of the medieval theatre in which an audience could participate in a number of realities grouped together on the same stage.

But these experiments were conservative in comparison with the wild experiments in constructivist theatre carried out in Russia after the 1918 revolution. This form of theatre, in which plays were rewritten to have strong social messages, used a severely limited script that served as a type of libretto for physical action aimed at expressing the rhythm, tempo, and emotional structure of the play. Actors were trained in a system of biomechanics to become instruments of emotional-mechanical movement by master directors, like the difficult but imaginative Vsevelod Meyerhold. Emphasis was placed on ballet, acrobatics, gymnastics, and group movement rather than on the psychological interpretation of character. The setting became an abstract machine for such action—a construction in space upon which the actors operated like rhythmic pieces of moving machinery. Here was one of the sharpest intellectual statements to date about the distinctly different realities surrounding an actor as a character in a play. In many ways, it was one of the first applications of the theories of cubism to physical production in the theatre—the first use of the intellectual concepts of relativity and abstraction.

The most influential use of the new relativism came with the epic theatre productions of Bertolt Brecht and Erwin Piscator. In their productions, plays were presented as great, unrolling narratives using songs, slides, films, movies, signs, and special properties to support actors whose purpose was to demonstrate or present a character rather than to become one with the personality of a particular role. The audience was meant to respond intellectually, not emotionally, critically, or sentimentally. By using the production devices mentioned and by placing his stories in faraway times and places, Brecht hoped to remove his audience from any direct emotional involvement in the action. His avowed intention was to lead his audience into thinking about social problems rather than losing themselves in emotional identification with the characters. Thus reality was again portrayed on multiple levels.

Finally, in the 1950s, there was the development of absurdism, which was originally a philosophy of playwriting but soon became a method of production. In an attempt to portray the meaninglessness of

Figure 15–10 Sketch for a scene from Max Reinhardt's production of *Danton* by Romain Rolland, the Grosses Schauspielhaus, Berlin, 1920. Illustrates how this famous German director included the audience in the drama by thrusting the stage and the tribunal from which Danton harangues the revolutionary convention directly into the spatial world of the audience. From George Altman, Ralph Freud, Kenneth Macgowan, and William Melnitz, *Theater Pictorial* (Berkeley: University of California Press, 1953). Photo courtesy of William Melnitz.

everyday life in the modern age, productions presented an amalgam of expressionist exaggerations, pieces of bourgeois life, and symbolic bits of everyday living. These formed a collage of words and ideas presented by characters who seemed to have no single core of reality. The plays were intellectual games played with fragments from modern life, and, under a surface of humor, fantasy, evil, or mystery, they usually carried the pessimistic message of the meaninglessness of all life.

The Plays

Pirandello's *Six Characters in Search of an Author* sharply marks the emergence of twentieth-century playwriting from the feeling and emotionalism of late nineteenth-century realism and symbolism (Figure 15–11). It is the first avowed relativist drama—the first play in which the stage is a plane for the inter- penetration of art and life and for the collision of illusions and reality. A plot in the usual sense is missing, since the audience is supposed to move from a concentration on a seemingly real stage rehearsal to events in the lives of characters only partially completed by an unknown author. By refusing to use the

Figure 15–11 Scene from *Six Characters in Search of an Author* by Pirandello, produced by the American Conservatory Theatre for the Stanford Summer Festival, 1966. Creates a multiple reality effect by constructing the scene from backstage properties and set pieces. Photo courtesy of the American Conservatory Theatre, San Francisco; photograph by Hank Kranzler.

usual progressions of a normal plot, Pirandello, like Gide with *Journal des Faux-Monnayeurs*, was able to write about the artistic problem of writing a drama about the writing of drama. In tackling this problem, he used a technique similar to the visual collage developed by the early cubists. In fact, the clearest way to see what Pirandello is doing and the best way to present the play on the stage is to think of the drama as a collage. Pirandello pieced together a number of theatrical clichés to form his collage of interpenetrating, intermingling realities: the attitudes of the stage director and his actors, the values prized in the commercial theatre, relationships between stagehands and actors, the concept of a playwright who could not finish his play, and, finally, the brilliant idea of presenting as part of everyday reality six uncompleted characters from an unknown play. In a way, these characters are unreal; and yet in another way, they are far more real than the actors who play them on the stage. The play, or film of their lives, stops at a crucial moment that must be replayed forever, while the actors, director, and audience argue over the nature of reality.

Every moment of the play confirms Pirandello's thesis that reality is a shifting and changing thing and that the reality of art may be greater than the reality of life. As the director and actors argue with the "characters" about the nature of reality, the dialogue shifts without transition or warning from everyday conversation to intellectual discussion and theatrical clichés in order to demonstrate the multiple levels of reality. The rhythm of the play is like that found in experimental film, where the camera makes a story go backward, forward, dissolve into multiple images, or undergo a complete change of reality. In the same way, Pirandello makes his play stop, start, shift abruptly, and change levels without warning in a brilliant attempt to frustrate an easy acceptance of sequence and forward movement.

The visual demands for production consciously make use of the collage; bits and pieces of scenery and costume are collected to create Madame Pace's "establishment," and the backstage realities of bare walls, scattered props, stacked set pieces, and marshaled costume racks are used as needed to "present" the play. The result is an intersection of theatrical reality, life's reality, and the characters' reality.

If Pirandello was the first major playwright in the twentieth century to experiment with multiple reality and to call into question the very nature of reality, Bertolt Brecht was the most important and influential twentieth-century playwright to use the multiple realities of platform, story, and auditorium to comment on modern society. Though his visual statements were more varied, sensory, and complex than Pirandello's, Brecht's fundamental purpose was still to encourage intellectual, critical analysis and comment rather than an emotional response from his public.

In *The Goodwoman of Setzuan*, first produced during World War II in Switzerland, Brecht used the parable form to project his tale and removed the events to China to give his European audience a sense of distance from the action (Figure 15–12). The narrative, or epic character of the play, is established by a prologue that mingles dialogue and narration. The play's structure is composed of al-

ternating long and short scenes; the longer ones carry the action forward; the shorter ones break up the story with comment and discussion. This narrative is assisted by the inclusion of songs, speeches to the audience, signs, and filmed sequences, all of which are meant to play down the audience interest in individual character psychology and to underscore the social comment being made. Brecht felt that he had succeeded only when he could sum up each scene in a single declarative sentence. For an audience looking for clear, logical transitions and obvious character motivations, the play may be confusing; yet if accepted as a parable or a fable, it is clear and successful.

Characters are deliberately oversimplified to project social and economic relationships; many do not have names but social labels like gods, Wife, Carpenter, Old Man, and Policeman. Social behavior, not personal motivations, is the key to characterization. Only Shen Te, the heroine, makes a personal and moral decision, but even this is forced on her by the economic system described in the fable. In addition, by having Shen Te disguise herself as the ruthless and evil Shui Ta to preserve herself and her man, Yang Sung, Brecht, like Pirandello, makes brilliant use of the multiple reality idea.

The choice of good and evil confronting the heroine represents the moral dilemma facing everyone who lives within the economic conditions of Western capitalism. Brecht implies that not only capitalism but also working-class callousness and indifference support human suffering. The play is thus lifted above the social tract level by its suggestion that, regardless of the economic system, human nature will probably remain selfish and exploitative. This leaves the audience with feelings of ambiguity: optimism about the benefits of a possible social change and pessimism about the human condition.

The play's language combines direct character dialogue, narrative-descriptive speeches, critical comment, and symbolic verse and song. For example, "The Water

Figure 15–12 Scene from *The Goodwoman of Setzuan* by Brecht, produced by the Stanford University Theatre, Stanford University, 1983. A collage of costumes and settings taken from backstage storage, junk yards, and other sources of castoff materials. Photo courtesy of the author.

Seller in the Rain,'' sung by Wong, is used to break the narrative, to make a humorous comment on Wong's profession, and to symbolize our materialistic society by contrasting rain that is free with water that is sold. The rhythm of the play follows the dialogue and structure; it resembles the broken rhythmic effects of a cabaret evening of song, dance, dramatization, and political commentary on a single theme rather than the smooth flow of a realistic, sequential play.

The visual requirements are based on the collage concept; platforms, set pieces, properties, and costumes are organized and rearranged throughout the evening to meet the symbolic or narrative needs of the moment. The pseudo-Chinese setting and costumes consist of crates, corrugated metal, screens, burlap curtains, coolie hats, Mandarin tunics, and other interesting items chosen from stage storerooms or junk stores. All are used in a make-believe way to support and comment on the play without establishing a single, unified reality.

Acting and Directing the Plays

The actor or actress in relativist plays must be very highly trained technically. He or she needs the abilities that used to be required by the Commedia dell'Arte—that is, complete control of the body in all manner of acrobatic and gymnastic situations and a technical mastery of the voice that allows him or her to slip easily from song to narration to character acting (Figure 15–12).

The philosophy behind this kind of acting was well summed up by Brecht in his essay *The Street Scene*. Brecht wanted to break with the introspective Stanislavsky approach that actors utilized in realistic dramas by Strindberg, Hauptmann, and Chekhov. He did not want actors in his plays to impersonate a role but to present or demonstrate the behavior of a character in a specific situation. Actors were not to "live a part" but to analyze the social qualities of the role and then present it to the audience as a demonstration commenting on the social implications in the character's actions. In *The Street Scene*, Brecht likened his method to that used by an eyewitness to an auto accident in communicating to several bystanders what took place. It was not important for the eyewitness to reenact the whole accident with absolute fidelity; all that was required was to act out those parts and details important to a clear understanding of what happened. Thus some situations might demand imitation of voice, others a careful reenactment of posture, gesture, or facial expression—it all depended on the purpose of the demonstration. (In fact, actors in Brecht's company often said they did not approach their roles differently from those in other plays.)

This analogy works better on paper than on the stage; nevertheless, the idea behind it is correct for the actor or actress working within a relativist framework. The players must be able to slip in and out of character, to move easily from one reality to another, and to affirm continually to an audience that they are actors and actresses on a very solid, real, and immediate stage platform. One moment the actor or actress must make a ladder seem like a staircase, a mere hat an entire costume, a stool a small hillock. The next moment he or she must be able to talk or sing directly to the audience. It is a virtuoso type of acting that demands the skills of a realistic actor, of a singer and dancer, of a cabaret performer, and of a lecturer-narrator.

Designing the Plays

Since Pirandello's playwriting method was intellectually rich but visually spare, the visual choices for a contemporary production must be carefully selected to project the intellectual shifts in the argument without creating emotionally or sensuously distracting effects (Figure 15–11). The ritual of the actors' arrival for rehearsal can be made into a visually interesting charade; the arrival of the "characters" can be theatricalized with eerie lighting playing upon their pale faces; and the readying of the white parlor can be made into a dramatic moment by using floral decoration as a backing for the "characters'" story. The strongest visual moment in the play is the appearance of Madame Pace, who should move, as if by transmigration from another world, into a collage erected to represent her establishment. Lighting is important in all these episodes, as is a strong contrast in the use of makeup, costumes, properties, and scenery—a contrast of one reality placed within the frame of another. Any visual effects will be meaningless unless the philosophical framework within which the play operates is kept in sharp focus for the audience at all times. In all matters of sets and costume, the problem is one of selection rather than of design. For a collage or assemblage, the visual elements must be carefully chosen, placed exactly within the action, and used at a prescribed moment in a specified way.

While Pirandello used the stage and his theatrical "characters" as a means of calling into question the nature of reality, Bertolt Brecht used the effects of the multiple reality of actor, character, and audience—of platform, place, and auditorium—to comment on modern society. Although he used a more sensory and more complicated visual statement to arouse the interest and attention of the audience, he encouraged intellectual, critical comment rather than emotional response from his public.

In *The Goodwoman of Setzuan*, Brecht wanted the visual elements to be free from pictorial illusionism and to project a childlike näiveté—a simple make-believe created with fragmentary sets, properties, costumes, bright circus lights, and musicians on stage. This play, which is set in ten different places, can be staged with a very few scenic elements. A mobile arrangement of flats and wagons can be pushed and pulled and turned around by the actors to suggest different locations. Properties, set pieces, signs, posters, projections, and films can be added and subtracted during the course of the action. Such a setting may seem inartistic, a mere piling up of findings from storerooms and secondhand stores, but it is the arrangement of these findings to support the action and intellectual comment of the play that challenges the designer's skill. When Kurt Schwitter's *Merz* constructions first appeared in Germany after World War I, they too were frequently seen as nonart; but later they became the forerunners of so-called junk art, a legitimate part of the modern scene. A Brechtian set may look like junk art, but if it works effectively to project and comment on the play, it is a success.

The pseudo-Chinese setting for *The Goodwoman of Setzuan* might use the shapes and textures of shipping crates, Chinese lanterns, corrugated metal sheets, bamboo poles, paper screens, burlap, and choice items from the junk shop and Chinatown novelty shop—all used in a childlike, make-believe way to comment on and support the action (Figure 15–12).

The costumes should look like clothing selected from a wardrobe or secondhand store with items put together that do not seem related but in conjunction make a comment on the action. For example, the gods in the play might combine the diplomat's formal wear from the Western world with the mandarin robes of the Orient and wear bowlers topped with Chinese lanterns—in short, a collage of oriental and Western elements that comment on their role in the play. While the costumes should communicate the reality or information required at a given moment, the audience must always perceive them as theatrical "dress-ups" for the stage.

PROJECTS AND PROBLEMS

1. Why did symbolism reach a point of crisis just before World War I?

2. Why were science and art so separated throughout the nineteenth century?

3. Why was Darwinian biology the only science that appealed to artists and intellectuals in the late nineteenth century?

4. Compare Cézanne's *Mont Sainte Victoire* (Figure 15–1) with Monet's *Rouen Cathedral* (Figure 14–1). Why does the Cézanne painting appeal to the mind as much if not more than to the instincts and emotions?

5. What is meant by *simultaneity*?

6. Why is *Guernica* (Figure 15–2) able to express profound emotion as well as intellectual abstraction? How is the real world brought symbolically into the painting? What is collage, and how is the painting related to this art form?

7. How does Henry Moore include the space surrounding his sculptures in the sculptures themselves (Figure 15–3)? What does he gain by this? What does the result say to the viewer?

8. How does this idea of space inclusion work in architecture (Figure 15–4)? What happens to our sense of reality when we are not certain whether an area of architecture is indoors or not? What use does this concept have in the theatre?

9. Why is the mobile the perfect invention for demonstrating the reality of space and its effect on a sculptural construction?

10. Why was the invention of the motion picture the perfect new medium for expressing relativity and simultaneity? Give some examples of how the cinema does this. Explain James Joyce's use of the montage effect found in cinema?

11. Why is Stravinsky's *Rite of Spring* sometimes compared to Picasso's cubism? How is Schoenberg's twelve-tone scale method analogous to cubistic painting or collage art?

12. Why is the period of the early twentieth century from World War I to the beginning of the 1960s sometimes called the Age of Analysis? Why is much of André Gide's literary method described as relativist? How are sections of T. S. Eliot's *The Waste Land* and Joyce's *Finnegans Wake* analogous to the collage?

13. How are the photos of people on Fifth Avenue at 42nd Street in 1926 (Figure 15–5) and of commuters arriving in Park Forest, Illinois, in 1958 (Figure 15–6) related to abstract art? Why do both photos express a sense of dehumanization? What do they tell us about individuals and human emotions during this period?

14. Describe the men in the photo of Fifth Avenue (Figure 15–5) and in the commuter picture (Figure 15–6). What are the characteristics of their clothing? Why do they seem dull to us?

15. Why did female fashion make such a major change in 1913? What was the feminine ideal during the 1920s? Describe how you would feel dressed like Madame Jasmy Alvin (Figure 15–7). What different image of womanhood and different sense of movement are conveyed by *Jardin de Paris, The Night Beauties* (Figure 14–8)?

16. Look at the photo of Coco Chanel with a model (Figure 15–8). What does it say about the function of this kind of suit or dress in the 1950s?

17. How was the concept of relativism reflected in books on etiquette, manners, and customs after World War I? After gathering pictures of the "new woman" of the 1920s and borrowing costumes of the period, try to capture the poses and movement in the pictures while wearing the clothes. How do you feel? What are the problems an actress would face in a production laid in this period?

18. Why is the young heroine in a tennis dress so typical of the characters in comedies of manners during this period? Why should a twentieth-century woman be so interested in sports and physical activity? Why was the rounded image of woman abandoned after World War I?

19. Look at the cover of *Life* magazine for February 18, 1926 (Figure 15–9). Why does it symbolize dance movement since World War I? What does it say about modern dance movement in general? In the appropriate costumes, do the Charleston, the jitterbug, and modern rock and roll dancing. What does each do to your body and movement?

20. Why was the Elizabethan theatre movement a first step in modern relativist theatre staging? What qualities are basic to relativist staging? How did Reinhardt's staging of *Danton* (Figure 15–10) involve the audience in the play?

21. Why was constructivism and its acting technique, known as biomechanics, the ultimate stage statement of twentieth-century dehumanization and relativism? How is a setting for a constructivist production like a relativist sculpture or mobile?

22. Why was Brecht a relativist playwright? Why is reality in Brecht always multiple? Why were the absurdists of the late 1950s relativists?

23. Why is Pirandello's *Six Characters in Search of an Author* called a cubist play? How is it organized like a collage?

24. How did Brecht's method differ from that of Pirandello? How did Brecht bring into his productions even more levels of reality than Pirandello did? How are Brecht's plays like medieval cycle dramas? Why are the settings and costumes needed for a Brecht production like a collage?

25. After reading *The Street Scene*, prepare a scene from a Brecht play in which you demonstrate rather than totally re-create one of the characters. What are the differences? What are the demands made on the actor and his training?

26. Read *Mother Courage* or *Galileo*. Why can one not completely follow the precepts set down in *The Street Scene* in acting these plays? If you were to direct one of these plays, what would you tell your actors? How would you organize the staging? What aspects of psychological realism and full relativism would you stress?

BIBLIOGRAPHY

Arnason, H. H. *History of Modern Art*. New York: Abrams, 1968. One of the better surveys of modern art, with particular attention paid to the developments between the wars.

Balakian, Anna E. *Surrealism*. New York: Farrar, Straus and Giroux, 1959. A useful study of surrealism in art and theatre, with clear examples of how the style is used and developed by a playwright.

Battcock, Gregory, ed. *The New Art: A Critical Anthology*. New York: E. P. Dutton, 1968. A very useful compilation of writings about art and culture by the artists and intellectuals of the first half of the twentieth century.

Brecht, Bertolt. *Brecht on Theatre*. Translated by John Willet. New York: Hill and Wang, 1965. An excellent collection of all the best essays that the German playwright wrote on theatrical production.

Clark, Barrett H., and Freedley, George. *A History of Modern Drama*. New York: Appleton-Century-Crofts, 1947. A very useful survey of drama during the twentieth century up to 1945.

Colton, Joel. *Twentieth Century*. The Great Ages of Man Series. New York: Time-Life Books, 1968. Beautifully illustrated with extensive color, this concise and easy-to-read text covers the major intellectual, artistic, and cultural developments up to the early 1960s.

Elsom, James. *Post-War British Theatre*, Rev. ed. London: Routledge, 1979. An excellent survey of the developments in the British theatre after the end of World War II and up until the close of the 1970s.

Esslin, Martin. *The Theatre of the Absurd*. Garden City, N.Y.: Doubleday, 1969. Characterizes the playwrights of the absurd and defines their views of reality.

Fuerst, Walter R., and Hume, Samuel J. *Twentieth Century Stage Decoration*. 2 vols. New York: Alfred A. Knopf, 1928. An excellent pictorial survey, with commentary, on the great breakthroughs in theatrical staging and design from 1910 to 1928.

Greenberg, Clement. *Art and Culture: Critical Essays*. Gloucester, Mass.: Peter Smith, n.d. An interesting collection of essays relating artistic and cultural developments in the early twentieth century.

Hainaux, René, ed. *Stage Design throughout the World since 1935*. New York: Theatre Arts Books, 1956. An impressive visual coverage of costume and stage design in all the leading theatrical centers of the world in the late period of relativism.

Hamilton, George Heard. *Painting and Sculpture in Europe, 1880–1940*. The Pelican History of Art Series. Baltimore: Penguin Books, 1967. An excellent survey of sculpture and painting that documents the arrival of relativism in the arts.

Knowles, Dorothy. *French Drama of the Inter-War Years, 1918–1939*. New York: Barnes and Noble, 1967. A clearly written summary of the changes in French drama taking place in this twenty-year span.

Ley-Piscator, Maria. *The Piscator Experiment: The Political Theatre*. New York: James H. Heineman, 1967. A very useful study of the methods used by Piscator in the development of epic theatre.

Moussinac, Leon. *The New Movement in Theatre: A Survey of Recent Developments in Europe and America*. London: Batsford, 1931. A standard work documenting the arrival of new production methods and playwriting techniques in the first three decades of the twentieth century.

New Art around the World. New York: Abrams, 1966. An excellent pictorial look at the new art of the twentieth century up to the early 1960s.

Rickey, George. *Constructivism: Origins and Evolution*. New York: Braziller, 1967. A very fine study of cubism and its relationship to the other arts in the twentieth century.

Roters, Eberhard. *Painters of the Bauhaus*. New York: Praeger, 1967. A study of the painters who carried the functional ideals of the Bauhaus into easel painting and collage.

Sandler, I. *The New York School: The Painters and Sculptors of the Fifties*. New York: Harper & Row, 1979. An excellent look at the abstract art experiments in the international school based in New York at the close of the relativist movement.

Southern, Richard. *The Open Stage*. New York: Theatre Arts Books, 1959. A helpful study of the redevelopment in the twentieth century of the thrust and open stages in which the audience surrounds much of the acting area.

Symons, James. *Meyerhold's Theatre of the Grotesque: The Post Revolutionary Productions, 1920–1932.* Coral Gables, Fla.: University of Miami Press, 1969. A very solid analysis of the theatrical techniques of Meyerhold.

Contemporary or Post Modern Style

The tired and complacent culture of the Eisenhower fifties in this country, with its images of the man in the gray flannel suit, suburban tract living, and the superiority and narrowness of "cold war" thinking, began to change in the early sixties under the energetic idealism of John F. Kennedy. A new feeling of commitment suddenly spread across the land, evident in such diverse locations as college campuses and executive board rooms and reflected in the new Peace Corps, the civil rights movement, and the call for freedom throughout the world. Once again, humanistic values were more important than analytical, organizational, and structural values. There was also the new belief that the world was becoming a totally interdependent global village, as popularized by the Canadian academic Marshall McLuhan. With the arrival of the space age, philosophers and intellectuals saw the earth as a small planet with finite resources that must be conserved if future generations were to flourish. Even economists like John Galbraith commented on this growing interdependence—exemplified by the rise of multinational corporations—which gradually brought about the erosion of national capitalism, national thinking, and strictly national business laws. Since the mid-1960s, the Western world has moved in the direction of international thinking and planning.

Even after the assassination of President Kennedy and the escalation of the war in Vietnam, both of which the idealists blamed on supporters of the "old order," the youth of the nation refused to retreat into an apathetic acceptance of the old evils. The Berkeley free speech movement, the volatile escalation of the civil rights movement, and the angry opposition to the rising tide of American participation in Vietnam exemplified this unwillingness to accept the old way of life. From this variety of causes grew a movement dedicated to change and the overthrow of the old order. Lapel buttons of the sixties carried such phrases as "We shall overcome"; "Legalize spiritual discovery"; "Turn on, tune in, drop out"; "Suppose they gave a war and nobody came"; and "I am a human being: do not fold, spindle or mutilate." All these slogans proselytized the message that a mechanized, corporate, organization-man approach to life had deadened feelings, moral values, and the basic humanity of the individual.

The answer for the naïve and idealistic young seemed to be in a renewal of love; this word plus the marijuana euphoria that supported its mood dominated the great gatherings of the so-called hippies in the Haight-Ashbury section of San Francisco in the summer of 1967, in New York's East Village, on Boston Common, in the hills outside Los Angeles, in the Pennsylvania farmlands, and in the New England woods. The climax of the movement came in 1969 at the gigantic rock festival love-in near the town of Woodstock, New York. The hippie movement was the outward symbol of a new philosophy that questioned the Protestant ethic of hard work, respectability, and competition for material success. An entire generation of youth—plus millions who copied its clothing, hair styles, sexual freedom, rock music, and general outlook—seemed to have found the plastic society of the establishment lacking. Particularly in popular music from Elvis Presley, through Bob Dylan, to the current punk rock groups, emphasis has been on freedom from the world of the establishment, freedom to leap into life as experience.

Gentle love, however, gave way to political violence in activist circles as the United States became more deeply enmeshed in the Vietnam War and as the black ghettos began to erupt in violent frustration. By this time, the phenomenon was not just American but worldwide, with supporters from Rome to Amsterdam, from London to Tokyo. In 1968 in Chicago, pitched battles between demonstrators and police disrupted the Democratic Convention; in Paris, the violence of political upheaval almost toppled the de Gaulle government; and in Tokyo, there were vicious explosions of antigovernment feeling. In the next few years, demonstrations and violence

dominated college campuses throughout the world. Only with the financial recession, energy shortage, and gradual disengagement from Vietnam in the early 1970s did the movement of confrontation and revolt recede. Although the ideals of the sixties also seemed to recede into a concern for self in the 1970s, and gaining wealth and power with the growth of the "yuppie" generation of the 1980s, there still remained a basic spirit of concern for human values and for openness over duplicity. This concern carried into the furor over Watergate and Irangate, support for Amnesty International, mass contributions for Ethiopian famine relief, and irritation over continuing cold war policies in Central America.

Still another phenomenon of the past twenty years has been the growth of the occult in Western society as an alternative or an addition to the scientic method. Today bookstores and the media are filled with stories of ancient astronauts, exploits of psychokinetic key benders, advertisements for biorhythm calculators, reports of post-death experiences, conversations with plants, tales of Bigfoot the abominable snowman and the Loch Ness monster, and articles on every aspect of extrasensory perception.

Like the explosive revolution of 1830 in which the nineteenth-century romantic movement reached an early climax and then continued in a quieter and more distilled manner, so the cultural aftermath of the sixties seems to be continuing in subdued fashion. The cool-hip chic of the sixties, with its scorn for sentiment and its do-your-own-thing code, has gradually given way to a new nostalgic romanticism. Films like the heart-grabbing *Rocky*, the moralistic parable *Star Wars*, and the freedom and adventure of *Out of Africa* have been runaway successes. Dinners and tea dances have returned; full-dress Viennese balls are in vogue; and the nostalgia craze is everywhere.

Thus the romantic primitivism and back-to-nature movement of the sixties and early seventies has gradually aged into the more middle-aged romanticism of nostalgia and release, and corporate yuppies and their lawyer wives escape to Austrian ski lodges, medieval castle hotels, and vine-covered bed-and-breakfast hideaways on weekends and for vacations. It is all reminiscent of what happened in style and fashion when the early romanticism that led to the French Revolution and the Empire period finally matured into the conservative, nostalgic romanticism of 1840.

In art, the movement that heralded a change from the hard-edged abstraction and expressionist probings of the action painters was in many ways as much theatre as it was art. In 1959, Alan Kaprow published an outline for an artistic event that he labeled a *happening*, and he later gave a public showing of this event. The term *happening* soon became the name given to an artistic "event," in which improvisation and chance played a major role. The idea was that participants through sensuous, physical involvement, rather than through intellectual criticism and appreciation, would awaken a whole new dimension of nonintellectual, nonverbal communication in a society lacking these human values. By the mid-1960s, many groups within our culture became interested in body awareness, massage, mind expansion, group interaction, and other related subjects.

Also, in the early 1960s, all the arts began to return to an interest in human subjects and realistic images. In gradual defiance of the modernist dogma that humanity in painting had been killed by abstract art and photography, realism returned in as many forms as there were painters. Even the abstract painters who remained were now released from the severity of their intellectual mission and were not embarrassed to paint interesting patterns and pure decoration.

This image hunger first exploded in the early sixties in the pop art movement, in which artists seized upon popular photography, advertising, magazine illustrations, and comic strips as the part of our daily environment that cried out for examination. Though Marcel Duchamp and a few fellow Dadaists after World War I had experimented with this realm of modern culture in their collages and painting, this time the experiments reconnected art with life and culture.

One of the most irreverent and inventive new artists of the 1960s was Robert Rauschenberg. As early as the late fifties, he established the basic cultural assumption that a work of art can exist for any length of time, in any material, for any purpose, and in any place whether that be the museum or the trash heap. Rauschenberg emphasized that a work of art can be made from anything from a stuffed goat to a live human body; can be placed under water, on the face of the moon, or on the television screen; can be used to amuse, threaten, or invoke contemplation; and can exist for a moment or forever. Art historian Robert Rosenblum said that Rauschenberg is "a protean genius" and that "every artist after 1960 who challenged the restrictions of painting and sculpture and believed that all of life was open to art is indebted to Rauschenberg—forever."

What Rauschenberg did was to free the collage from its relativist interest in form, arrangement, and structure and to make it an actual, physical, instinctive, and free commentary on modern life. Since the early 1960s, he and other artists have moved art from the realm of thought, analysis, and structure into the full range of living experience. Building on the post-World War I work of the Dadaists, especially the work of Kurt Schwitters, Rauschenberg exploded the limited philosophy of that movement and gave to his "combines" a loose, free, ironic, almost lecherous imagery. His early work *Odalisk* parodies the harem nudes of Ingres and Matisse with its box on a pillow plastered with pinups and reproductions of classical nudes, while the chicken on top reminds us that one of the French terms for an expensive courtesan is a *poule de luxe* (Figure 16–1). A dramatic example of this combination of found objects, photographs, painted detail, and collage arrangement can be seen in the *History of the Russian Revolution* by Larry Rivers (Figure 16–2). Like a great three-dimensional newsreel or television montage, the gigantic work dominates the viewer and the space surrounding it.

This concept that art is now free from the boundaries of the studio and the separate categories of sculpture, painting, and architecture has even led to mammoth undertakings in nature referred to as ecological art and often ephemeral in character. For example, in 1976, the artist Christo erected a cloth, sail-like fence that covered over twenty miles of the Sonoma County (California) landscape before dipping into the sea (Figure 16–3). It was in place for less than a month; yet it drew crowds of tourists and photographers and created a great stir in the media. *Running Fence* was intended to make a gallery out of nature, to force a new look at the land in relation to this fence, and then to make the public aware of the land

Figure 16–1 Robert Rauschenberg, *Odalisk,* 1958. Illustrates the free use of nonart materials to create works in which questions of meaning dominate over aesthetic content and in which witty satire governs the choice of motifs rather than considerations of form. Photo courtesy of Wallraf-Richartz Museum, Cologne; photograph by the Rheinisches Bildarchiv.

Figure 16–2 Larry Rivers, *History of the Russian Revolution,* 1965. A combination of found objects, photographs, and painted detail that resembles a giant, three-dimensional television montage. Photo courtesy of the Hirshhorn Museum.

Figure 16–3 Christo, *Running Fence*, Sonoma County, California, 1976. An example of ecological art. Photo courtesy of the *San Francisco Chronicle*, © Chronicle Publishing Co., 1976.

again after the fence was removed. Implicit in this project was an emphasis on size and on art as part of natural growth and decay. Also related to this ecological art are folk art manifestations like barn, fence, and billboard paintings by groups and individuals.

In this new form of physical, unlimited art, it is difficult to talk about sculpture as separate from painting or architecture. However, the so-called tableaux created by artists

from the 1960s to the 1980s are close to the standard concepts of sculpture, although they combine stagecraft, collage, and painting. Here the artist creates life-size environments from furniture, discarded objects, and plaster of Paris castings of human form in order to take us physically into the meaning and commentary of the work. For example, in Edward Kienholz's *The State Hospital*, we see a ward for senile patients with a naked old man strapped to the lower bunk (Figure 16–4). His skin is leathery and discolored; his head is a fish bowl with live goldfish inside; and when the work was originally exhibited, a sickly, hospital smell came from it. *The State Hospital* is vividly realistic and physically direct; yet the abstract device of the fish bowl also gives it an unrealistic quality. The brilliant metaphor of the live fish inside the goldfish bowl that replaces the patient's head makes the viewer aware of the patient's actual experience of himself.

What about architecture? Has it gradually changed in the last decade and a half from the consistent concentration on glass, chrome, and rectangular form to something more alive, more human, and more expressive than the standard city skyscraper or apartment buildings of today? Ricardo Bofill, a Spanish architect of the Taller de Architectura of Barcelona, has designed a fascinating con-

Figure 16–4 Edward Kienholz, *The State Hospital,* 1966. A realistic tableau showing two senile patients strapped to their beds with faces of goldfish bowls, within which real goldfish swim to dramatize the patient's experience of himself. Photo courtesy of the Nationalmuseum, Stockholm.

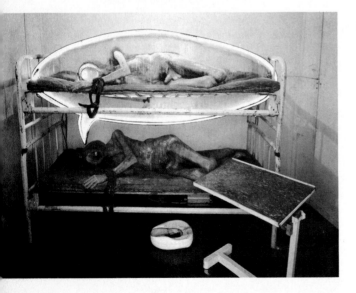

dominium complex named La Muralla Roja, which does reflect a more humanistic feeling (Figure 16–5). Laid out along pop-fantasy lines in a series of bold red color tonalities, it is a vacation residence for professional people, who call it the Crusader's Castle. The building does not fit any structural preconceptions but follows a natural pattern of human growth. Although it looks a bit like a beehive or a Chinese puzzle, La Muralla Roja lacks the rigid intellectualized structure and formality of the standard apartment complex. Its openness, variety of perspectives, and warm colors signal the new tradition in art and culture that has taken hold in the last decade or two. It is usually labeled as Post Modern architecture and is characterized by a judicious reintroduction of decoration, color, and abstracted ornamental quotations from the past. Still using the technical and structural methods of Modernism (the glass and steel box), it adds touches of nostalgia for the past and aims to please not through mere function and efficiency but through discrete ornament and decoration.

In nonurban settings, housing has returned to less geometric structure with more the look of Romanesque additive architecture—as if the house or group of houses grew gradually with need and expanding imagination. Natural materials, like wood, brick, and stone, have also returned. The house is no longer viewed as a machine for living but as an extension of an ecological setting and its mood.

Recently, in the early 1980s, there has been a movement known as Bad Painting or the Transavantgarde, which believes in a certain crudity in painting besides suggesting that the old Modernist ideal of the "avant-garde" has been outstripped and left behind. In the United States the group's leading figure has been Julian Schnabel, who is famous for huge canvases in which paint is applied to broken pieces of crockery glued to the surface. Once again, it is a tactile-physical assault on the viewer, a mechanism for freeing the creative subconscious.

Figure 16–5 Ricardo Bofill, La Muralla Roja, an apartment complex in Barcelona, Spain, 1975. Laid out along pop-fantasy lines, this complex done in bold red tonalities is often referred to as the Crusader's Castle and was designed to answer basic human psychological and physical needs. Photo courtesy of Glen Allison, Santa Monica.

Music

The major changes in music, as in art, come from the tremendous expansion in musical sources. Instead of traditional instruments, all types of electronically generated sounds have been added and frequently coupled with complicated light shows, as in the first performance of John Cage's *HPSCHD*, a computer printout for harpsichord, in which sixty-four projectors were synchronized with the performance, which lasted over four hours.

The so-called *concrete music* is the most like the free-form assemblages of Rauschenberg and is the most opposed to the rigid mathematical structure of the earlier twelve-tone serialism. Like the artist who collects coke bottles, birdcages, bedsprings, and newspapers to create a three-dimensional collage, the composer of *concrete music* takes sounds from the environment—the clanking of trash cans, the whine of jet engines, the roar of traffic, and the scream of sirens—and records them on a sound track. These environmental sounds are then edited; sequences are controlled; and the tape is run at varying speeds, spliced, and played backward. The possibilities are immense, as the composer adds and subtracts, isolates certain sounds, fragments certain sections, and breaks down parts into separate components. Sometimes this electronic material is coupled with live musical situations;

it is even possible to write a symphony in which electronic sound becomes one of the sections of the orchestra.

John Cage, who worked with Robert Rauschenberg when they were both experimenting early in their careers, is one of those composers of electronic music who has revolted strongly against the rigid ordering and excessive control of twelve-tone serialism. His work attempts to create conditions in which nothing is foreseen and in which sounds are freed from formal continuity. He espouses a healthy lawlessness, a collage of noises that gives homogenized chaos, carrying no program, plot, or personal statement. According to Cage, music should involve its listeners, that is, give them the feeling that they are doing something rather than having something done to them.

HPSCHD is scored for one to seven harpsichords to play simultaneously and consists of random fragments from the music of Bach, Mozart, and Beethoven and from jazz and blues. The entire composition is played against a background of one to fifty-one computer sound tapes superimposed on one another in a random way. The result is a sequence of melodic goals without beginning, middle, or end. At any given point, one hears sounds, which then cease as others begin. There is no organic structure, just chance happenings and ramblings in sound. When this happening in sound is coupled with the complex projections of a light show, the result is a direct participation in sound and light without any involvement with story, sequence, or rational thinking.

Recently, composers like George Rochberg have created a neo-romantic style of music that is largely tonal, often lyrical, and with haunting moods. It is a modern romanticism filtered through a contemporary mind, using old forms manipulated freshly through the unique vision of the composer.

Life and Cultural Ideals

Certainly the change in outlook among the artistic and intellectual leaders in the industrial world during the 1960s was quite remarkable. From an age of analysis, structure, and abstraction came a renewed emphasis on human values; an interest in parapsychology, astrology, and the occult; and the realization that human beings have an interlocking relationship with the plants and animals of the earth. Today most educated people are aware that the earth's resources are finite and cannot be replaced and that humankind must change its ways as a violator and excessive consumer of nature and its resources.

Arnold Toynbee, in an article entitled "The Genesis of Pollution," published in *Horizon* magazine in summer 1973, argued that many of today's pollution problems can be traced back to a religious beginning in the rise of monotheism. He saw the biblical doctrine about man's relation to God and nature as the problem:

> This doctrine is enunciated in one sentence in the Bible: "And God blessed them, and God said unto them, Be fruitful, and multiply, and replenish the earth, and subdue it: and have dominion over the fish of the sea, and over the fowl of the air, and over every living thing that moveth upon the earth". . . . According to the Bible, God had created the world; the world was his to do what he liked with; he had chosen to license Adam and Eve to do what *they* liked with it; and their license was not canceled by the Fall. The tenant who had parked in the Garden, rent free, was now rack-rented: "In the sweat of thy face shalt thou eat bread . . ." But as an effort, the disgraced human tenant, expelled from the Garden of Eden and let loose on the wide world, was not prohibited from easing the payment of his punitive rent to God by harnessing natural forces to do his work for him. . . .
>
> "Where your treasure is, there will your heart be also." Westerners have put their treasure in the increase of material affluence; they have set their hearts on this; and "verily . . . they have their reward."

Reiterating what many leaders of the counterculture had said during the late 1960s,

Toynbee suggested that man must reintegrate himself with nature by taking ideas from Eastern faiths like Hinduism, Buddhism, Taoism, and Shintoism. He related the intellectual, philosophic, and artistic direction of the immediate future to the ideal of harmonous cooperation between man and nature rather than to the immoral directive to "subdue."

The new counterculture of the 1960s was the utopian "commune," in which several dozen people lived a nomadic, disorganized, "natural" existence. It was a primitive romanticism. In the late 1970s and 1980s, the new romanticism is sentimental and nostalgic. In a *Time* essay for January 30, 1978, Frank Tippet described this new phenomenon as follows:

> The pronounced American yen for romanticism and sentiment has surfaced intermittently in one place or another for several years now, but it is finally blooming in virtually every zone of the social spectrum, in folkways and cultivated appetites, among middle-brows and high-brows alike. Take America's dance floors—often a useful symbol of how people view themselves. Partners are touching each other again, and dancing to music that is meant to have them do just that, such as the marvelously variable hustle. Extraordinarily, the old-fashioned, dress-up tea dance has returned from oblivion to become a popular mixer all over the country—a departure, to say the least, from the meat-market atmosphere of the singles bars. The disco scene has grown generally less barbarous, and is now in retreat from the narcissistic solo gyrations that became fashionable in the early '60s. . . .
>
> In fact the relationship between the sexes, so buffeted by the feminist movement, seems once again to be taking on subtlety and civility. Men are sending women flowers in greater numbers, the florists say, than at any time in the past decade and are regaining some of the manners that they felt superfluous when faced with militant wives or sweethearts. Women today are less apt to dress like sodbusters on a holiday, and frilly dresses, flouncy skirts, ruffled underskirts, lace, gauze blouses—all as feminine as possible—have returned to everyday fashion. Advertisements heralding coming spring fashions ooze lyricism, and sentimental trinkets

and totems are booming. "Everyone is into hearts" says a Chicago shopkeeper, "the same way they were into peace symbols a few years ago."

Actually a reversal of roles has occurred, much as it did after the romantic revolution of 1830. Many elements and ideals of the counterculture have been incorporated into the establishment; at the same time, many establishment ideals have been adopted by the revolutionaries. For an example of this absorption of counterculture ideals into the mainstream of American life, one need only look at an art fair held at a shopping mall, fairground, or school yard (Figure 16–6). At such a gathering, there are all types of handmade items, based on primitive and folk crafts from around the world, representing a great unspoken celebration of the physical and emotional involvement of the human body and spirit in natural non-machinemade products. At a typical arts fair, one can find dancing, jewelry making, pottery making, musical improvisations, ballet exhibitions, clowns, poetry readings, and blue-jean embroidery lessons. In this modern version of the Eastern bazaar, there is an implied renunciation of the technological social structuring of our culture and a determined drive to experience, feel, touch, and work with the hands and to respond strongly to the natural, emotional, and physical in life.

Still another way in which to feel the pulse of cultural ideals and interests in the late 1970s and 1980s is to look at a sample of short course offerings in a typical urban or suburban community college. One finds courses entitled The Holistic Health Happening, Belly Dancing, Fiesta Mexicana, Mediterranean Cooking, Yoga for Weight Reduction, Lymphatic Energy Balancing, Special Biorhythms for Special People, Self-Hypnosis, What Parapsychology Is All About, Biofeedback, Problems of Meditation, Backpacking Fundamentals, and many more. All the offerings come under the label of personal expression or physical improvement. None are strictly academic and intellectual.

Figure 16–6 Arts fair; Inverness, California; 1977. A bazaarlike atmosphere in which dancing, jewelry making, pottery crafting, ballet exhibitions, poetry readings, blue jean embroidery lessons, and various crafts stalls mix and vie with one another to create an open, nonstructured, tactile, emotional experience. Photograph by the author.

Interiors and Furniture

The major trend in the last decade and a half has been toward rooms that reflect human values. Rich and varied natural textures have returned; there is a renewed interest in antiques; and a Third World eclecticism, underlining an emotional interest in handicrafts from exotic places around the world, now dominates many upper-middle-class homes. The collection of fascinating craft items from around the world began in the middle 1960s and reached a hysterical peak in the much-photographed hippie "pads" of the last years of that decade. These interiors were literally encrusted with collected memorabilia, craft items, interesting castoffs from society, and personally made items created from bits and pieces collected in the pursuit of daily existence. Like the antiheroes in many literary

works of this era, these pads or rooms represented a new romanticism. They became the cluttered, personalized, womblike refuge of the romantic individual and were similar in feeling to those more respectable interiors common during the age of repressed romanticism in the late nineteenth century. Though these new romantic rooms had the same clutter and sentiment-evoking qualities as those in the late nineteenth century, the artifacts were now antisocietal and anticultural.

When the militant revolution of the late 1960s ended, the establishment gradually began to adopt the more acceptable aspects of counterculture interior fashion. Middle-class rooms began to put aside the cold, structured, machinelike furnishings that had been prescribed by architects and interior decorators in favor of personally chosen antiques or furnishings that had much more appeal to the senses. Rich woods; soft, thick upholsteries; heavy padding; decorative floral patterns; and interestingly textured walls, rugs, and draperies returned to give interior decoration great variety that emphasized humanity and sensuality rather than intellect and structure. Look at the room designed by Michael Rose (Figure 16–7). Heavy, rich, wooden furniture, some of it antique, is placed in an area that has two walls deliberately paneled in worm-eaten wood to give an interesting texture to the room. The fireplace is made of stone; the floor has an interesting texture; and the entire effect is one that appeals deliberately and insistently to the tactile, textural, sensuous interests of the human inhabitants. Just as the conservative and tradition-oriented Victorianism that began to blossom in the 1840s replaced the more flamboyant romanticism of the 1830s, while still incorporating many of its basic premises in a more repressed and conservative way, so the past decade has done much the same with the ideals of the 1960s and early 1970s.

Figure 16–7 Michael Rose, house interior, Chevy Chase, Maryland, 1976. Illustrates the new interest in wooden furniture, antiques, worm-eaten paneling, stone fireplaces, and textured floors that appeal to the tactile, textural, sensuous interests of the inhabitants. Photo courtesy of Michael Rose, photograph by J. Alexander.

The youthful rebellion of the 1960s showed itself very prominently in dress. Clothes became an important weapon in the struggle against the establishment with its uniform of black sheath dresses and gray flannel suits that had been standard since the late 1950s. One day the rebels would be barefoot, ragged, and primitive; the next day romantically decked out in gypsylike attire of colorful boots, leathers, blouses, and scarves. Both sexes let their hair grow natural and full. For the first time, the style setters were not a few exclusive designers or the elegant women who wore their clothes. Fashions now came from the street; and designers like Rudi Gernreich and Mary Quant watched closely what the young people of the 1960s were putting together before coming out with their own adaptations.

The key to male fashions of the past twenty or so years has been the gradual loosening of the century-and-a-half-old image of gentility. An increasing number of young men and some older ones no longer think it necessary to wear the traditional capitalist uniform of coat, vest, and trousers; they present instead a silhouette composed of a close-fitting, waist-length jacket, often in leather, and tight trousers reminiscent of those worn by the young man of 1490 (Figure 5–7). Although in the past decade men's fashions have once again become more conservative, they are still tremendously eclectic, especially those worn at less formal functions. Leather and denim jackets may be seen at the theatre and cocktail parties along with three-piece suits. Male fashion is derived almost as much from the old so-called outdoor "lower class" pastimes like motorcycling, riding, hiking, mountain climbing, and skiing as from the latest sketches of Savile Row tailors. In fact, the art of tailoring has become less important in men's clothes today; the new male boutiques do not stress subtleties of cut and drape but rather texture, sexiness, variety, and a kind of romantic exoticism. Today the erotic principle long absent from male attire is balanced against the return of the dark, pin-striped business uniform as a symbol of position.

There is a pervasive feeling that the male should dress to please himself when away from business.

One of the most interesting fashion stories of the 1960s and 1970s was the triumph of blue jeans. First made by Levi-Strauss of San Francisco for miners and then for cowboys in the middle of the nineteenth century, jeans remained a specific, lower-class uniform throughout the first half of the twentieth century, although they conveyed a faint aura of romanticism because of their association with the open prairies and the nonurban freedom of the past. Then came the youthful revolt of the 1960s, when boys and girls began wearing faded and torn blue jeans and jackets to symbolize their romantic objection to urban, establishment regimentation. Jeans were the perfect uniform for rebellious youth because they were associated with the lower class; they faded to make the wearer look as if he or she had weathered them in the world of nature; and they shrank to show off the physical contours of the body. To gain a more undressed and primitive look, sleeves and legs were often raggedly cut off the denims. In addition, the faded denims were embroidered, patched, and inset with brightly colored yarns and fabrics (Figure 16–8).

By the early 1970s, entire books and articles were devoted to the craft ornamentation of blue jeans, and fashion designers and boutique operators were packaging sophisticated prefaded denim jackets and trousers with flared bottoms. "Flares" were the clothing industry's answer to the homemade effect created by the rebels of the 1960s who had inserted colored fabric in the bottom side seams of blue jeans to give them a floppy, colorful look. Still other artificial and mannered effects introduced into the industry's packaging of blue denims included the machine-stitched compartments that were created all over jackets and trousers to give surface interest and the mechanized photographic reproduction of patches on jackets and pants.

Then came designer jeans, with famous

prestige labels on the back pocket to give status and position to the wearer. Recently jeans and denim jackets have begun to appear in dark faded magentas, indigo blues, and blacks, while the cut and shaping, particularly in jackets, has included off-the-shoulder, bulky, pleated, buckled, and removable sleeve effects.

There has been even more variety in feminine dress in the past two decades. The social and political movement behind much of the change in women's clothing in recent times has been the renewed demand for women's rights and equal opportunities in all walks of life. In the 1960s, in order to remind everyone of the change in the woman's place that had come about in the 1920s, the miniskirt appeared. There was also a new movement to narrow the difference between male and female attire, similar to that of the 1920s, when women's clothes became simpler and more efficient. Young men and women began to wear the same pants, the same long hair, and the same colorful, shabby clothing. It was difficult to tell male from female unless the male wore a beard.

By the opening of the 1970s, pants suits, slacks, and tight jeans with flared legs had become as important, if not more important, to a woman's wardrobe than dresses and skirts; prominent women secretaries and executives, as well as fashionable women about town, wore pants suits in one form or another. Skirts and dresses were reserved primarily for balls and parties in which a woman could indulge her taste for romantic and exotic past times and faraway places. In fact, the predominant fashion force of the past two decades, beside the interest in slacks and male-inspired attire, has been the emphasis on rich, natural textures and exotic and romantic images from other cultures. Russian, Indian, African, gypsy and oriental borrowings have jostled one another in the same season and in the same costume to create a sharp contrast with the efficient black sheath dress accented with a string of pearls—the standard cocktail dress of the 1950s. Furs, leathers, rough knits, colorfully woven woolens, and exotic silks in

Figure 16–8 Embroidered blue denims, late 1960s and early 1970s. Illustrates the mystique attached to blue denim clothes. The jackets and jeans mold to the contours of the body, have a weathered, lower-class look, and are exotically embroidered to give a primitive, handcrafted, personalized look to the whole. Photo courtesy of Levi-Strauss of San Francisco; photograph by Baron Wolman.

blouses, ponchos, shawls, scarves, and jackets have created a rich textural display (Figure 16–9).

Nostalgia for various decades of the past half-century has influenced feminine style since the late 1970s, particularly the use of padded shoulders and shoulders dropped or

(a) (b)

Figure 16–9 Male and female fashions of the 1970s. (a) A grouping of separates in a soft Dacron knit that has a natural look. The idea here is to mix casual and practical garments that reflect women's new place in society with a romantic feminism. (b) Business suit and casual wear that include a leather jacket and boots on one model and a youthful three-piece business suit topped off with a short raincoat and scarf on the other. Photos courtesy of the Emporium, San Francisco, and the Sabina and Grimmé model agencies. Permission also granted by male models Jack Mice and Eddie Donlin and female models Karen Mirner and Beverly Leftwich.

widened to the upper-arm level. There also has been a great fad for bulky looseness and layered effects among the young, popularized, in particular, by the dynamic fashion company for the young known as Esprit de Corps. At the same time the business suit, not the pants suit, has returned in full force for the corporate woman, and little deviation or originality has been allowed in this uniform for the female office corps. Yet, despite this new conservatism, fashions in the Western world over the past two decades have been physical and tactile, basically carrying a personal romantic tone. This physical, tactile look has been most obvious in the continuance throughout this period of stylish leather boots and coats (and sometimes pants) for women in all levels of society (Figure 16–10). Black leather has also been a major aspect of punk styles, with its antinatural hair styles, hair colors, chains, safety-pin jewelry, and images of deformity and violence. Punk styles have marked a symbolic, contemporary revival of mannerist ideals from the sixteenth century (Figures 6–6 and 6–8).

Figure 16–10 An advertisement in the fall-winter catalog of Tannery West. Note that even in the sophisticated and conservative 1980s the wonderfully tactile and physical combination of fur and leather is considered stylish. Courtesy Tannery West and the Agency, stars.

Manners and Movement

The major social change since the early 1960s has been the abandonment of the old idea of gentility as the standard of deportment in Western society. Though there has been no major change in the mercantile-industrial-capitalist routine that shapes the work of most people in society, manners, clothing, and movement are based more on instinct and personal feeling today than at any time in the past. The most decorous and restrained people within our society used to be bank personnel; now one finds lower-level bank personnel wearing all types of clothing from pants on the women to occasionally colorful dress on the men. Although this clothing is never sloppy or excessive, it is a long way from the gray uniform look of a generation past.

In movement, this change means that what is correct is what one feels is correct in a particular situation. There are no longer strictures about crossing one's legs, balancing on the arm of a chair, sitting on the floor, or moving with a prescribed grace on a dance floor or at a reception. Superimposed on the regimented routine of our industrial society is a romanticism of personal instinct and feel-

ing that guides all manners and movement. An indulgent, hang-loose casualness is the key to living within the routine and dullness of daily employment in the capitalist world.

For an example of the manners and movement of the times, let us look at a photo of a Friday night beer party in an apartment

Figure 16–11 Beer party in an apartment complex, Torrance, California, 1967. The whole scene is excessively casual in clothing, groupings, and stance with individuals leaning against railings, drinking from beer cans, drooping with hands in pockets and in every way making a full attempt to "hang loose." Photo courtesy of *Life magazine*, © Time, Inc.; photograph by Arthur Schatz.

complex in Torrance, California (Figure 16–11). The whole thing is excessively casual in clothing, groupings, and stance. Individuals lean against railings, drink beer from cans, droop with hands in pockets, lean into a con-versation, and in every way hang loose, without a thought as to how they stand or look except for a vaguely self-conscious sense that they must appear relaxed and casual.

The Theatre

More than anyone else, Antonin Artaud has been responsible for the direction of theatre in the past twenty years, although he lived and worked in the period between the two wars and died in 1948. He created a theatre of cruelty that worked like a plague—by intoxication, infection, and magic. Artaud thought theatre had been devoted too long to psychological, social storytelling in which the text was paramount. He advocated a theatre in which the theatrical event itself stands in place of the text as the foremost concern of actors, directors, and designers, since he was convinced that audiences could not be reached through the use of language and concepts of the rational mind. Artaud worked on the audiences' collective subconscious by stressing the sensory and the physical, the ritualistic and the supernatural. He wanted to make the invisible in life visible through the immediacy and physical presence of the actor. These ideas were completely unheeded until the opening of the 1960s when the theatre and society began to turn its back on the intellectual games played by the relativists and absurdists.

The most influential high priest of this form of theatre in the English-speaking world is the famous English director Peter Brook, who has been a brilliant "enfant terrible" in the theatre since his teens and who has presented exciting visual productions of Shakespeare since his direction of *Love's Labour's Lost* at the Stratford Memorial Theatre in 1948. By the early 1960s, Brook was experimenting with the ideas of Artaud and borrowing from the physical immediacy of "happenings." After his famous production of *Marat/Sade* for the Royal Shakespeare Company in 1964, in which he used many of Artaud's ideas, he continued to work in this same direction. In 1968, he published a book, *The Empty Space*, in which he divided theatre into the "deadly," the "holy," the "rough," and the "immediate." By the first, he referred to the usual offerings of the commercial theatre; by the second, to the ritualistic-ceremonial theatre of Artaud; by the third, to the street theatre that is closest to the people; and by the last, to any theatre that speaks to the immediate problems of society. He was most concerned, however, with the holy theatre; it was this path that he followed in his memorable productions of *A Midsummer Night's Dream*, *The Tempest*, Seneca's *Oedipus*, *Timon of Athens*, the documentaries *USA* and *The Ik*, and more recently his version of *Carmen*.

His methods, now famous throughout the world, were brilliantly presented in his production of *A Midsummer Night's Dream*. The stage was enclosed on all three sides by white, unadorned walls, with the empty space broken by an almost invisible door at the back. The forest was suggested by loosely coiled metal springs attached to fishing rods, and the flying immortals were raised and lowered into the setting on trapezes. The basic costumes were very simple light-colored circus-like jumpsuits or robes with occasional splashes of dazzling color. Everything was done to divest the production of its romantic aura of enchanted fairies and haunted woods and to make it a direct, simple, physical attack on the sensibilities of the audience (Figure 16–12).

Another theatrical innovator and experimenter, who also influenced Peter Brook and scores of other leading directors and theatrical troupes throughout the world in the 1960s, was the Polish director Jerzy Grotowski. He also believed in direct physical immediacy in performance and was particularly opposed to technological aids in production. His was a "poor theatre," in which the only elements were actor and audience. Brook in *The Empty*

Space described Grotowski's method as facilitation, the "auto penetration" of a role; that is, removing every psychological and physical barrier for the actor until he released his own personal secrets, his own body magic into a role. An American actor, Steven Weinstein, who participated in the Grotowski training methods, described the strenuous sensuous-physical exercises that Grotowski used for his actors in an issue of *Alternative Theatre*:

> People found a big barrel of water and splashed each other. Soon you'd get water on you, and wheat rubbed on you in different ways. It was like an initiation. . . . They'd dug a big mud-hole. People jumped in and out. Boy, did resistance come up in me. I felt like a kid. Pressure. You'd be a baby if you didn't. . . . Everyone finally did. Stripped to underwear. Slid down a mudslide into a river. Cold but fun. . . . There were little fires on the earthen floor, to run or dance through. A barrel of wet mud in the next room. Drums. Haze. We got dumped in the barrels. I was keyed up, tired of not letting go. There were buckets of water around. We splashed each other. We splashed each other, wet already, stripped to bloomers, underwear, no one naked, danced, stepped through the fire. Something extraordinary happened to me. I was getting closer to people. Lots of joy, love. Lots of life.

Grotowski worked on his actors through body and mind-expanding exercises, popular in the United States and western Europe in the late 1960s, in order to remove the veneer of rationalism and civilization and to gain a theatre of tribal ceremony and archetypal patterns independent of time and space. Like Artaud, he developed a performance for the sole purpose of making the actors and audience confront each other at the most basic levels.

Another shorter-lived experimental group that gained great publicity in the late 1960s was the Living Theatre, founded and directed by Julian Beck and Judith Malina and dedicated to revolutionary political statement and to a direct confrontation with the audience through the use of nudity, obscenity, and violent action.

Other theatre groups, like the famed

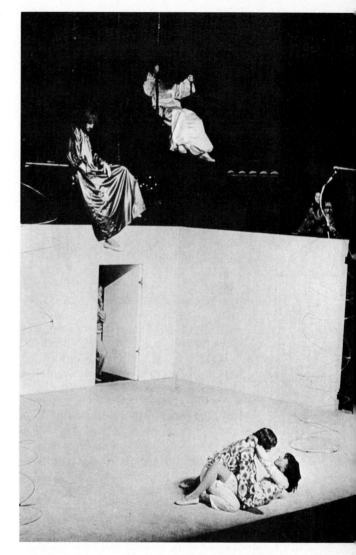

Figure 16–12 Scene from *A Midsummer Night's Dream*, produced by the Royal Shakespeare Company, 1970. Directed by Peter Brook, designed by Sally Jacobs. Illustrates the simple, white, empty box setting espoused by Peter Brook in which the players in comfortable, colored jumpsuits and robes display great physical-lyrical action. Photo courtesy of the Royal Shakespeare Company.

Open Theatre of New York, concentrated on evolving scripts through improvisation and game playing, with a few actors taking on and discarding identities as required by the actions improvised. Once again in these theatre groups, the emphasis was on the physical and emotional realities that lie below the superficial sophistication of our culture. One of the more challenging applications of theatrical space to support this kind of environmental theatre was accomplished by the Performance Group founded in 1968 by Richard Schechner. Its performances, of which the most famous were *Dionysus in 69* and *Commune*, lay somewhere between the happening and a traditional performance. Because the audience occupied the same physical space as the actors and participated fully in the performance, the group seldom worked in a regular theatre unless it had been totally rebuilt as environmental space.

The Roger Planchon Company of France is another theatre group whose presentations, though similar to those of the Performance Group, are more in depth and sophisticated. This company was officially known as the Théâtre de la Cité centered in Villeurbanne until the French government made it the second theatre of France, the Théâtre National Populaire.

Planchon synthesized the work and ideas of Grotowski, Brecht, Artaud, Brook, and the Living Theatre into plays or collage performances that distill historical and contemporary material into the dimensions of a dream. His characters are figures in a historical landscape that can only be conjured up, but never reconstituted. They act as vehicles for the subterranean thoughts and feelings that permeate the organized and anarchical levels of the times. In his *Arthur Adamov*, he created a nightmarish, dreamlike existence that jostled the life facts of the absurdist playwright Arthur Adamov amid recurring images of persecution, impotency, death, and the need for a political belief in socialism. In this production, Planchon made brilliant use of such recurring images as Adamov's being stoned in his crib by his father and friends, the floating past him of his mother as an image of cold, unreachable beauty, his inability to move through piles of blue sand to reach a prostitute, and the waving of a revolutionary red flag by troops passing by on a flat car. It was a brilliant, physical-visual collage of images that told the life of the playwright from a subconscious, personal, dreamlike point of view.

Recently, tours of the plays of the Polish playwright-director, Tadeusz Kantor have been much talked about. In productions like *Dead Class* and *Wielepole*, Kantor is both horrified and fascinated (as is the audience) by his "still-life" picture groupings of the dead. During a family wedding photograph in *Wielepole*, the old-fashioned camera turns into a machine gun that kills everyone; the mother is raped by conscripts; corpses are resurrected to die again to the tune of a war march. Objects are removed from their everyday context and deprived of their regular function to serve as a theatrical prop in Kantor's theatre, which terrifies with images that in their graphic cruelty remind one of the pain and death in Goya's *Caprichos*.

On a more traditional level, productions of Shakespeare in the late 1970s and early 1980s have been labeled as "post modern" as directors like Ariane Mnouchkine and others have put aside the metaphysical dimensions of the plays in favor of sheer physical theatricality. Mnouchkine's *Richard II* and *Twelfth Night* were triumphs of pure theatre when they toured to the Los Angeles Olympics of 1984—*Richard II* for its marvelous mixture of oriental and Western pageantry; *Twelfth Night* because of its feminist study of gender identity through having the girls' roles played by boys (as in Shakespeare's time) (Figure 16–13).

Even in the work of America's most famous current playwright, Sam Shepard, who seems to write a kind of symbolist realism, the plays are really collages, jazz improvisations with abrupt changes and shifts. Everything in his plays germinates from a central idea and then erupts like a geyser from the core of the play, scattering bits and pieces of a fractured whole.

Another striking development in mass theatrical entertainment during the past twenty years has been the rock concerts that developed from the sound and light shows of the 1960s. They are now a multimillion dollar business in which the senses are dominated by an overwhelming amalgam of sonic crescendo, violent physical excitement, and overpoweringly complex lighting effects. In its outrageousness, personified by performers like Mick Jagger, Prince, and Michael Jackson, this rock theatre is an appealing mass answer to the theatrical demands of Antonin Artaud.

In addition, costumes and settings have changed markedly over the past twenty years. In settings, the direction has been toward creating spaces for action—settings waiting to be completed by actors—great Saharas of open acting space. For example, Victor Garcia used a vast tilted trampoline for an entire production of *Yerma;* Peter Brook tore out the inside of a Paris theatre for a production of *Timon of Athens,* in order to seat the audience around the vacant space that was left; Robin Wagner used a dozen mirrors as a background for *Chorus Line;* and Erik Vos placed a production of *Medea* on a tilted triangle of sand-colored carpet highlighted with mystical circles of colored sand. Always there is a tactile-physical as well as a subliminal-symbolic relationship between the actors and their surroundings. Costumes, too, are simple, physical, and tactile, often mixing rehearsal clothing with period or street dress overlaid with symbolic accessories of rich texture and color.

Figure 16–13 Scene from Shakespeare's *Twelfth Night;* produced by the Théâtre de Soleil under the direction of Ariane Mnouchkine at the Olympic Arts Festival of Los Angeles, 1984. The production is a brilliant theatrical collage in which oriental and Renaissance theatrical techniques are merged with contemporary physicality to overwhelm an audience with visual metaphor. Photo by Andrew Innerarity. Courtesy of the Los Angeles Times © 1984.

The Plays

One of the most influential plays of the 1960s, that stands on the border between relativist reality and the play as a physical-theatrical event, is Peter Weiss's 1964 *Marat/Sade (The Persecution and Assassination of Jean Paul Marat as Performed by the Inmates of the Asylum of Charenton under the Direction of the Marquis de Sade).* Weiss's play is pure relativist theatre, since it contains a play within a play. The play is set in the year 1808 in the asylum of Charenton, where the Marquis de Sade is confined and passes the time writing and directing playlets that are performed by the patients for the amusement of the fashionable audience from nearby Paris. For an evening's entertainment,

de Sade presents a play about the assassination of Jean Paul Marat by Charlotte Corday during the height of the French Revolution in 1793. The Marquis de Sade participates in this play within a play as a philosophical antagonist to the patient who plays Marat. Both this play within a play and the scene introducing it are based on historical fact, since the Marquis de Sade did direct plays while confined in an asylum, and Marat was assassinated by Corday.

Peter Weiss prepares the audience for an intellectual debate between Marat and Sade by using the distancing effects of Brecht while commenting on contemporary events. He also puts the contemporary audience in a Pirandellolike situation as they become members of the fashionable Parisian audience of 1808, sitting with Coulmier, the director of the asylum, and his wife and daughter. In addition, he borrows from Artaud in his use of a chorus of patients to create a horrifying and very immediate physical, spectacular background action. Four patients comment musically and physically on each major forward step in the argument, while others in the background create a physical-vocal atmosphere of distraught, oppressed humanity. The patients are kept in order by male nurses who have the "appearance of butchers" and by nuns "played by athletic looking men." This second level brings the drama into the contemporary theatrical scene and makes it a major example of the "theatre of cruelty." Popularized by Peter Brook's famous productions in London and New York and on film and by the many amateur and semiprofessional pro-

ductions of the past dozen years, the play has become a symbol of the transition from the theatre of ideas and relativist reality to the "new theatre" (Figure 16–14).

The major argument of the play is the continuing debate between those who espouse the private, selfish interests of humankind versus those who espouse communal, revolutionary ideals. The Marquis de Sade argues that the strong always beat down the weak, that human beings are essentially selfish, and that it is useless to try to improve the human condition. Marat argues that, through revolution and change, human beings can invent a new meaning for life and can develop a mutual respect for one another that will better their condition. The structure supporting this argument is Brechtian in the shortness of the scenes, each with its separate title. The Herald, acting as a moderator-prompter and commentator, establishes a Brechtian sense of historification and alien-

Figure 16–14 Scene from *Marat/Sade* by Peter Weiss, produced by the Stanford Players, Stanford University, 1976. Directed by Robert Egan, costumes designed by the author. In this play, the playwright fuses the ideas of Brecht and Artaud to create an environment that combines multiple reality and intellectual debate with a violent physical-vocal theatre of cruelty. Photo by the author.

ation. Only the ideas and the Artaudian chorus of patients unify the play and lift it above the intellectual relativism of Brecht. The characters are largely one-dimensional (except for de Sade and Marat) since their primary function is to project the aberrations of mental patients. The play's rhythm is a broken one, based both on the interruptions of the songs and commentary of the chorus and on the background distractions of the patients' distorted physical action. As far as spectacle is concerned, the play plunges the audience into the total atmosphere of the asylum and forces them to participate in the physical and mental suffering of the patients.

Another example of the "new theatre" is the work of Roger Planchon for the Théâtre National Populaire. Because Planchon develops his own scripts, or historical collages, as he works with his company on a specific project, his theatrical event becomes more important than the historical material on which the production is based. In one of his projects, he presented in collage form the life of the medieval figure Gilles de Rais, who was an orgiast, blasphemer, and child killer. Gilles de Rais was also a wealthy and powerful baron, a Marshal of France, a man who kept a private retinue of priests, a dabbler in black magic and alchemy, and a theatrical angel who financed the performance of a mystery play at Orléans in 1434. He also fought beside Joan of Arc and later became a key figure in the struggle for the mastery of France between the King and the Dauphin.

This historical material acts as the substratum of the play *Gilles de Rais*. The characters figure in a historical landscape that can be conjured up only as a type of nightmare or dream. They speak and act, not as embodiments of thoughts or ideas, but as vehicles for the subterranean thoughts and feelings of this medieval period.

The action of the play recounts the known events in the last six months of Gilles's life in 1440, including his exploits as the head of a gang of sadists, whores, bullies, procurers, and fallen priests; his capture and torment of adolescent boys; his attempts to preserve his chateau and lands from rival barons; his sei-zure of a high-ranking priest and his subsequent arrest by the Duke of Brittany and the regional inquisitor; and his trial and incineration at the stake.

What is strikingly different in this play is the manner in which the story of Gilles de Rais is presented. The first image seen signals the complexity and ambiguity of Planchon's vision: A large rectangular box surrounded by a coarse, unpainted white tarpaulin appears on stage; in it are rocks of the type painted by Giotto and the Italian primitives. Thrown across these rocks and reaching into the auditorium like gangways to the present are three massive planks, on which is what appears to be a cluster of bushes. These bushes turn out to be little boys holding foliage to hide themselves. They jump up and run off as Gilles's gang begins to hunt them. The strangeness and the dislocation of this design stresses the turbulence of the medieval world as well as its ambiguous and fragmentary nature. Images of the uncertain political and spiritual reality of the times are everywhere: Gilles, played by Planchon himself, hangs on the opinions of his Florentine alchemist as if seeking in black magic some buttress for his violent and scandalous actions; a wandering soldier comes upon the scene and turns out to be a girl in disguise, thus echoing the Joan of Arc story; Gilles's arraignment and trial become a medieval mystery play; and the female consort of the Duke of Brittany delivers an ecstatic speech about boar hunting that brings to the surface the discontinuities and strangeness of medieval life.

In choosing the horrific cruelties of Gilles de Rais, Planchon adheres to the true Artaud tradition of creating a theatre of cruelty. He sees in this nightmare of excess one of the roots of drama itself. When interviewed about the play during its performance in 1976 and asked if the play might not be seen as an apology for a criminal killer, Planchon had this to say:

> Personally I have two children about the same age as the children Gilles de Rais killed. I do not know what my attitude would be if a sadist killed my children. It would certainly be the

most ghastly catastrophe that could happen to me. I have no intention at all of justifying Gilles de Rais. But a character that I couldn't begin to understand in life—in the theatre I try to fit my feet into his footprints, to see how far I can go along with him. It's in the theatre if anywhere that one should go along with criminals. It's one of the powers of a theatrical story—and not just a means of purging dark thoughts—that it allows you to reflect on crime by seeing just how far you can go along with it. It's no coincidence that playwrights have been interested in great madmen, great criminals. That's a special role for the theatre, one in which it speaks clearly, works on all cylinders. When Shakespeare writes *Macbeth*, it's the work of a generous-spirited poet trying to understand, and withholding judgment.

The most striking quality of this play-collage is the transition taking place at the close of the first act, with the appearance of an unknown figure who is obviously an archetype of the medieval character of Vice or the Devil. The story of Gilles's arrest and trial then becomes a haunting and ironic evocation of a mystery play. The stage is transformed into a fifteenth-century medieval theatre: a backcloth with signs of the zodiac comes on,

followed by medieval mansions—a tower of paradise, a house of despair, and a Hellmouth gaping in the plank flooring. The characters are also transformed: the adolescent victims become a host of winged angels clamorously ringing bells, the Wandering Soldier becomes the Virgin Mary; the Inquisitor becomes Abel; and the Unknown Man in an ironic inversion becomes God the Father. The script becomes a collage of lines from medieval drama and actual speeches made by Gilles at his trial.

Planchon's deeply serious point in this rather surrealist spectacle is that society, when confronted with a violently heretical and defiant personality like Gilles de Rais, must somehow find a place for his opposition and antagonism before putting him to death. This theme is not just stated but is embodied before the audience in a bewildering mixture of realities. Planchon demonstrates his supreme confidence that the powers of theatrical imagination can weld the disparate parts together. This form of multidimensional theatre written, acted, and directed by a supreme artist like Planchon opens many new theatrical vistas and takes the concepts of Brechtian relativism and Artaudian theatre of cruelty to new experimental heights in modern drama.

Acting and Directing the Plays

It should be obvious from the improvisation and physical training given to actors by Grotowski and the expectations of acting demanded by Brook and Planchon that the new theatre of the past twenty years is very involved in getting inside a character muscularly, physically, kinesthetically, emotionally, intellectually, and psychologically. When Peter Brook was interviewed in London in 1976 about the acting preparations for his latest documentary theatre production, *The Ik*, based on the death of an African tribal society, he had this to say:

We've been working on this piece for a year and a half. . . . The method used in making a piece of theatre is exactly the same as a sculpture: you chip a little here, a little there. You work around a piece. If you've been working on the intellectual side of a play, that's good for so long. Then

you go into the physical side. And that is good for so long. . . . Here, we worked improvisationally at first from photographs to the last crook of the Ik's finger. Copying that. Having copied the photograph so that the actor was in the exact pose of the photographs, we then tried to make an improvisation of what preceded the photographs three seconds before and three seconds after. It was the opposite of loose improvisation. Here it began with this tiny thing out of which we studied the difference in every aspect of our posture between ourselves and the Ik. Besides working our way inside the Ik this way, we did straight improvisation from Colin Turnbull's [anthropological historian of the Ik] book. We made a script which gave us a broad outline. Then we discarded the script and improvised page after page for weeks. The actors improvised and played an enormous amount of material. . . . It was very much like making a film. Thousands and thousands of feet on the cutting room floor with the actors' time spent doing all manner of characters, events, and unplayable things from the book.

Brook's statement sums up the new acting style. More attention is placed on the physical immediacy of performance than was the case with relativist theatre, in which the player's primary function was to speak to the intellect of the audience and to comment on the character performed, although he or she also needed to display singing, dancing and acrobatic abilities. As Brook said in his book *The Empty Space:* "The invisible must be made visible through the physical presence of the performer."

Designing the Plays

It should be apparent by now that the new, post modern theatre does not demand a pictorial illustration of place and time in its settings, but rather a box, a space, an arena for actor action that will respond to and support the characters' interaction, moving and changing if needed, presenting physical-tactile symbolic pieces when required, and always presenting a look that is subliminally strange and yet very much in tune with the action taking place on and in front of it. Often this setting is a neutral white, beige, or gray, to remove the spectator and the actor from normal reality to the inner screen or blank page of the creative imagination. The texture of the setting is often its most important attribute in suggesting the inner life or subtext of the drama. Often, earthy elements such as real fire, sand, dirt, sawdust, or water are incorporated into the setting to further underscore the tactile-physical aspects of the play.

As for costumes, a collage mixture is the designer's ideal—not the collage of intersecting realities that was so important in the plays of Brecht and Genet, but physical-tactile collages that mix rehearsal clothing, actor street dress, and symbolic or concept-oriented period pieces and character accessories. For example, many post modern Shakespeare productions will intermingle warlike street clothing of today (leather, studs, chains, and boots) with military pieces from the past in order to present a barbaric video-rock military presence instead of the more conventional and colorful period army of the past. The idea is to reach the audience on a subliminal level of response to the idea of "military" rather than to present a distant pictorial image. Costumes are thus a physical-tactile assault on the audience's subliminal psychic sensitivity.

Epilogue

How long this new style in art and the theatre will continue within the loose and broad outlines described is difficult to say. Western theatre has always reflected the changing views about man and his world; and, as morals, politics, and the social-cultural scene change, so will the theatre. Many new exciting innovations will be buried, while other trends now barely apparent may triumph. Only time will tell what will appeal to man's theatrical sensibility as personal, moral, social, and political ideals change and develop. One thing is certain, however: A period's style will always determine the theatrical style of an era.

PROJECTS AND PROBLEMS

1. What are some reasons for the rather abrupt changes in cultural outlook during the 1960s?

2. How are the 1970s and 1980s related to the more dynamic, outgoing, and radical 1960s? Explain.

3. Review Chapter 12 on romanticism. Why is it possible to compare the 1970s and early 1980s with the late 1830s and the 1840s? What was happening to culture at that time that seems to be happening once again?

4. Why did objects from the real world begin to filter back into art and replace nonobjective abstraction in the early 1960s? How did even the very abstract painters change their methods during this time?

5. Why is Robert Rauschenberg now consid-

ered one of the major contributors to our contemporary culture? What was his purpose in creating *Odalisk* (Figure 16–1)? Why did this kind of work appeal to the hippie, or counterculture, taste of the 1960s? How does it appeal to the mind? To the senses?

6. Why is Rivers's *History of the Russian Revolution* (Figure 16–2) representative of the art work of the 1960s? What, if anything, does it have to say about modern culture?

7. Why is Christo's *Running Fence* (Figure 16–3) considered a work of art in our contemporary culture? Why does it appeal to our values and ideas? Why does it appeal to our sense of theatre?

8. What is so striking about Kienholz's *The State Hospital* (Figure 16–4)? How does it differ from the conventional idea of sculpture? Why is the work so vivid? How is the work related to the theatre?

9. What makes the huge and supposedly impersonal grouping of living units in La Muralla Roja (Figure 16–5) seem more human, individualized, and personal than the standard oversized apartment complex?

10. What is concrete music? Why is it like the collages or assemblages of Rauschenberg? How has this kind of music expanded the concept of musical sound? In what ways does *HPSCHD* resemble a happening?

11. Why have we become so aware of the finite nature of our planet in the past decade and a half? Why does Toynbee think that the Judeo-Christian tradition is responsible for pollution and excessive use of energy in the modern world? Why have Westerners become so interested in Eastern religious faiths in the past decade and a half?

12. Describe the typical street fair of the past decade. Why is this phenomenon a product of contemporary society? Describe the photo of a street fair (Figure 16–6) and how you would feel participating in such a fair as a vendor or a viewer-participant.

13. What aspects of an upper-middle-class interior have changed gradually in the past decade and a half? How does the interior from the house in Maryland (Figure 16–7) differ from the ultra modern look in the Tremaine House of the early 1950s (Figure 15–4)? How would you feel in both rooms? What does the living room in the Maryland house communicate about contemporary taste?

14. Explain why, in the past decade and a half, fashion and clothing have come as much from the street as from the famous houses of fashion. What is appealing about the new fashions? Why are they often unacceptable to conservative, tradition-oriented people?

15. Why was the male fashion silhouette of the late 1960s rather analogous to that found in the last decade of the fifteenth century (Figure 5–7)? What new fabrics and textures have been introduced in male fashions?

16. Why have the new styles been based on work clothes and lower-class wear? Explain why this has not been true in the past. Why has the importance of men's tailoring declined since World War II?

17. Discuss the history of Levi's. Why did faded blue denim become the most popular fabric for youthful male and female clothing after the mid-1960s? What has been done to give variety and richness to such fabric? Why does tight, faded, blue denim (Figure 16–8) appeal so strongly to the senses?

18. What impact have foreign cultures and the cult of primitivism had upon fashion? What mannered, tense, artificial effects have crept into blue denim clothes in recent years?

19. Why did long hair and beards make such a striking comeback in the 1960s? Why have male and female clothes come to look so much alike? Why has ethnic ornamentation had such an impact on the fashion world in the past decade and a half?

20. Wear some of your most fashionable tight clothing. How does it feel on your body? Why is it sexy? Why are tight jeans sexier than tights? Define what you mean when you use the term "funky."

21. Summarize manners and movements in the past decade and a half. What is meant by the admonition to "hang loose," and why does this term sum up the cultural outlook of the past decade and a half? Characterize the beer party (Figure 16–11) as a social occasion.

22. What were Grotowski, Artaud, and Brook looking for in theatre and its relation to an audience (Figures 16–12 and 16–14)? Why have ceremony, improvisations, the communal aspects of living, and the environment become important in theatre in recent years? What is your opinion of the actor exercises devised by Grotowski?

23. What were the aims of the Living Theatre?

Of the Performance Group in its use of environmental theatre? Of Roger Planchon in his work with the Théâtre National Populaire? How is all this theatre related to the excessively popular rock theatre of the past two decades?

24. Which parts of *Marat/Sade* are reminiscent of Brecht and Artaud (Figure 16–14)? Why did Weiss go beyond the Brechtian approach in this play? Why did Peter Brook in his early production of the script stress the Artaud aspects of the play?

25. What was Roger Planchon attempting to do by dramatizing the story of Gilles de Rais? Why did he make the trial of the antihero a reenactment of a medieval mystery play? What kind of acting is required for this play?

26. Describe the training method Peter Brook used in preparation for his production of *The Ik*. How does it differ from psychological realism? From Brechtian acting? What are its major demands on you, the actor or actress?

BIBLIOGRAPHY

Arnason, H. H. *History of Modern Art.* New York: Abrams, 1968. One of the better surveys on modern art with particular attention to the developments in art between the wars.

Battcock, George, ed. *The New Art: A Critical Anthology.* New York: E. P. Dutton, 1968. A very useful compilation of writings about art and culture by the artists and intellectuals of the first half of the twentieth century.

Biber, Pierre. *The Living Theatre.* 2nd ed. New York: Horizon Press, 1972. A very readable survey of the methods and philosophy of the Living Theatre.

Brockett, Oscar G. *Perspectives on Contemporary Theatre.* Baton Rouge: Louisiana State University Press, 1971. An excellent commentary on the contemporary dramatic and theatrical scene.

Brook, Peter. *The Empty Space.* New York: Athenaeum, 1968. A seminal work by one of the great directors of the contemporary theatre scene in which he explains his ideas on deadly, holy, rough, and immediate theatre.

Clark, Brian. *Group Theatre.* New York: Theatre Arts Books, 1971. A very useful study of the methods and approach used in the development of group theatre and drama.

Clements, Marcel. *The Dog Is Us.* New York: Viking Books, 1985. An interesting series of essays on contemporary life and style in the United States.

Finch, Christopher. *Pop Art: The Object and the Image.* New York: E. P. Dutton, 1968. An excellent study of the art world's return in the 1960s to the depiction of images and social commentary.

Giedion, Siegfried. *Space, Time and Architecture.* 5th rev. enl. ed. Cambridge, Mass.: Harvard University Press, 1967. Covers the key ideas behind architectural design in the past twenty-five years.

Goodman, Ellen. *Keeping in Touch.* New York: Summit Books, 1985. Another collection of essays about the decline of interpersonal relationships in contemporary America.

Greenberg, Clement. *Art and Culture: Critical Essays.* Gloucester, Mass.: Peter Smith, n.d. An interesting collection of essays on artistic and cultural developments in the early twentieth century.

Grotowski, Jerzy. *Toward a Poor Theatre.* New York: Simon and Schuster, 1968. Presents the philosophy of one of the key experimental directors in the theatre in the past decade and a half.

Hainaux, René, ed. *Stage Design throughout the World, 1960–1970.* New York: Theatre Arts Books, 1972. Discusses stage and costume design throughout the world.

Kirby, Michael. *Happenings.* New York: E. P. Dutton, 1965. A very good introduction to the happenings, containing scenarios and photographs of many of these artistic "events."

Kostelanetz, Richard. *The Theatre of Mixed Means.* New York: Dial Press, 1968. A good parallel study to those on mixed media methods in the arts, showing how the same ideals are carried out in the contemporary theatre.

Kott, Jan. *The Theatre of Essence.* Introduction by Martin Esslin. Evanston, Ill.: Northwestern University Press, 1984. A number of interesting essays on the theatrical innovators of the past twenty years.

Lesnick, Henry. *Guerilla Street Theatre.* New York: Avon Books, 1973. An excellent survey of the development of the kind of theatre labeled "rough" theatre by Brook; that is, aimed specifically at the ghetto dweller and farm worker.

Lippard, Lucy R. *Pop Art.* New York: Praeger, 1966. Another excellent study of that artistic phenomenon during the 1960s, which was a compendium of advertising art and mass media techniques.

Lucie-Smith, Edward. *Movements in Art Since 1945.* London: Thames and Hudson, 1984. An excellent guide to artistic development since World War II with particular emphasis on the past two decades.

Matlaw, Myron. *Modern World Drama: An Encyclopedia.* New York: E. P. Dutton, 1972. An excellent reference book on plot summaries and factual details about drama since 1870.

McDowell, Colin, ed. *McDowell's Directory of Twentieth Century Fashion.* Englewood Cliffs, N.J.: Spectrum Books, 1985. An excellent survey that brings the reader up to the mid-eighties.

New Art Around the World. New York: Abrams, 1966. An excellent pictorial look at the new art of the twentieth century up to the early 1960s.

Parkinson, Norman. *Fifty Years of Style and Fashion.* New York: Vendome Press, 1983. An exciting visual walk through the past half-century of changes in female fashion.

Pasolli, Robert. *A Book on the Open Theatre.* Indianapolis, Ind.: Bobbs-Merrill, 1970. A study of open theatre as it developed in the early to mid-1960s with examples of the plays and how they were developed.

Popper, Frank. *Origins and Development of Kinetic Art.* Translated by S. Bann. Greenwich, Conn.: New York Graphic Society, 1968. An incisive look at the development of kinetic art, which brings together artistic ideals from sculpture, industry, optics, mathematics, advertising, and illumination.

Schechner, Richard. *Public Domain: Essays on the Theatre.* Indianapolis, Ind.: Bobbs-Merrill, 1969. Essays on the environmental theatre productions of the late 1960s and early 1970s.

Schevill, James. *Breakout! In Search of New Theatrical Environments.* Chicago: University of Chicago Press, 1972. Another useful study of environmental theatre.

Seitz, William C. *The Responsive Eye.* New York: Museum of Modern Art, 1965. A very rewarding essay on how to view and respond to contemporary art.

Taylor, John R. *The Angry Theatre.* Rev. ed. New York: Hill and Wang, 1969. An excellent look at the political and social anger that lies behind the making of theatre for the ghetto dweller and the farm worker.

Temkine, Raymond. *Grotowski.* New York: Avon Books, 1972. Another useful study on Grotowski and his method as he developed it in his Polish Lab Theatre in the 1960s.

Trewin, J. C. *Peter Brook.* London: Macdonald and Co., 1971. An excellent study of the contributions of Peter Brook to contemporary theatrical production.

White, Emily, ed. *Fashion 85.* New York: St. Martin's Press, 1984. A look at the nether side of fashion and the punk scene moving into the midyears of the eighties.

General Bibliography

Altman, George, et al. *Theatre Pictorial: A History of World Theatre as Recorded in Drawings, Paintings, Engravings and Photographs.* Berkeley and Los Angeles: University of California Press, 1953. A very useful pictorial reference showing the development of theatre from the earliest times to the middle of the twentieth century.

Bazin, Germain. *The History of World Sculpture.* Greenwich, Conn.: New York Graphic Society, 1968. A magnificently illustrated volume of the finest works of sculpture ever created.

Boucher, François. *20,000 Years of Fashion.* New York: Harry N. Abrams, 1967. A beautifully illustrated book, containing hundreds of color plates, showing the development of clothing, accessories, and period backgrounds in the Western world from primitive times to the present.

Brockett, Oscar. *The Theatre: An Introduction.* 4th ed. New York: Holt, Rinehart and Winston, 1982. An excellent introduction to all aspects of the theatre. The sections devoted to theatre history and to the outstanding plays in each period are particularly good.

———. *History of the Theatre.* 4th ed. Boston: Allyn and Bacon, 1983. A well-organized and quite complete general history of the theatre, probably the best present text in the field.

Clark, Kenneth M. *Civilization: A Personal View.* New York: Harper & Row, 1969. Discusses the development of art and thought in the Western world since the Dark Ages. Moderately illustrated.

Contini, Mila. *Fashion: From Ancient Egypt to the Present Day.* New York: Odyssey Press, 1965. A useful pictorial survey on fashion with many color plates; all illustrative material is taken from original sources.

De la Croix, Horst, and Tansey, Richard G., eds. *Gardner's Art through the Ages.* 6th ed. New York: Harcourt, Brace and World, 1975. An excellent and quite complete history of world art; very useful in reinforcing a sense of stylistic progression in art and culture.

Fergusson, Francis. *The Idea of a Theatre: A Study of Ten Plays.* Princeton, N.J.: Princeton University Press, 1949. An excellent series of essays on the development of drama with special emphasis on how each play's structural composition reflects the cultural ideals of the period in which it is written.

Fleming, William. *Arts and Ideas.* New York: Holt, Rinehart and Winston, 1974. An excellent survey of the arts, including music and its relationship to, and influence on, the intellectual thought of Western man from primitive times to the present.

Gascoigne, Bamber. *World Theatre: An Illustrated History.* Boston: Little, Brown, 1968. An excellent history of the theatre, containing pictorial selections not found in most other general histories of the theatre.

Gassner, John, and Allen, Ralph. *Theatre and Drama in the Making.* Boston: Houghton Mifflin, 1964. An excellent compendium of original source material on the history of the theatre, plays, actors, critics, and performances.

Glenn, Stanley L. *The Complete Actor.* Boston: Allyn and Bacon, 1977. A very complete text on acting with an excellent section devoted to the actor and style in Greek and Elizabethan tragedies and comedies of manners.

Hartnoll, Phyllis. *Oxford Companion to the Theatre.* 4th ed. London: Oxford University Press, 1983. The best single reference volume available to the student of the theatre.

Hauser, Arnold. *The Social History of Art.* 4 vols. New York: Random House, 1959. An excellent history of the artistic and cultural development of Western man.

Janson, H. S. *History of Art.* Englewood Cliffs, N.J.: Prentice-Hall, 1969. An excellent history of art that is very simply and clearly written to introduce the student to the mainstream of artistic development in the Western world.

Laver, James. *Costumes in the Theatre.* New York: Hill and Wang, 1964. An excellent short survey of the development of stage dress in the Western theatre from Greek times to the present, with special emphasis on Shakespeare and Baroque opera.

———. *The Concise History of Costume and Fashion.* New York: Charles Scribner's Sons, 1969. A useful and easy-to-read survey of the history of dress in the Western world from primitive times to the present with a small but select group of illustrations.

————. *Style in Costume*. New York: Oxford University Press, 1949. An excellent book for helping the student of costume trace changes in fashion.

Molinari, Cesare. *Theatre through the Ages*. New York: McGraw-Hill, 1975. An authoritative and beautifully illustrated history of the theatre containing some of the finest color plates illustrating the development of theatre in the Western world.

Nagler, Alois. *Sources of Theatrical History*. New York: Theatre Annual, 1952. An excellent selection of original source materials documenting the development of the theatre from Greek times to the close of the nineteenth century.

Norwich, John Julius, general ed. *Greek Architecture of the World*. New York: American Heritage Publishing Co., 1975. An excellent and very informative survey of world architecture. Many of the plates are in color.

Oenslager, Donald. *Scenery Then and Now*. New York: W. W. Norton, 1936. A charming book that introduces the student to the great periods of Western culture and demonstrates how a designer-director incorporates the cultural aspects of a period in staging plays.

————. *Stage Design: Four Centuries of Scenic Innovation*. New York: Viking Press, 1975. A beautifully designed book with pictorial material never before published on theatrical scenery since the beginning of the Renaissance.

Oxenford, Lyn. *Playing Period Plays*. Chicago: Coach House Press, 1959. A useful small volume, with a few line drawings, devoted to acting, costume, movement, manners, dance, and music in the medieval, Elizabethan, Restoration-Georgian, and Victorian periods.

Praz, Mario. *An Illustrated History of Furnishing from the Renaissance to the Twentieth Century*. New York: Braziller, 1964. A very useful survey on interiors and furniture since the Renaissance. It is particularly helpful because many of the illustrations include people in costume.

Roos, Frank J. *An Illustrated Handbook of Art History*. New York: Macmillan, 1937. A dated but still useful collection of over fifteen hundred pictures depicting all the major art works of Western man.

Rothschild, Lincoln. *Style in Art: The Dynamics of Art as Cultural Expression*. New York: Thomas Yoseloff, Publisher, 1960. A very useful book for understanding the origins of style.

St. Denis, Michel. *The Rediscovery of Style*. New York: Theatre Arts Books, 1960. One of the best analyses of style in the theatre.

Speltz, Alexander. *Styles of Ornaments*. New York: Grosset & Dunlap, n.d. Careful drawings of ornament and decoration from the earliest times to the middle of the nineteenth century.

Squire, Geoffrey, *Dress and Society, 1560–1970*. New York: Viking Press, 1974. An excellent study of the relationship between the visual arts and the cultural ideals of a period and its involvement in the development of fashion.

Tilke, Max. *A Pictorial History of Costume*. London: A. Zwemmer, 1955. A very useful series of watercolor plates depicting costume from the earliest times to the present. It is particularly useful in making comparisons between the costumes of western Europe and those of Africa and the Orient.

Wickham, Glynne. *A History of the Theatre*. New York: Cambridge University Press, 1985. The best new short history of the theatre in recent years.

Wildeblood, Joan. *The Polite World*. London: Davis-Poynter, 1973. A very useful survey of manners, movement, and deportment in England from medieval times to the years following World War I.